Rebellion and Democracy
in Meiji Japan

History has to be rewritten in every generation, because although the past does not change the present does; each generation asks new questions of the past, and finds new areas of sympathy as it re-lives different aspects of the experiences of its predecessors. . . . Each generation, to put it another way, rescues a new idea from what its predecessors arrogantly and snobbishly dismissed as the "lunatic fringe."

Christopher Hill,
The World Turned Upside Down

ROGER W. BOWEN

Rebellion and Democracy in Meiji Japan

A Study of Commoners in the Popular Rights Movement

UNIVERSITY OF
CALIFORNIA PRESS

Berkeley • Los Angeles • London

University of California Press
Berkeley and Los Angeles, California
University of California Press, Ltd.
London, England
© 1980 by
The Regents of the University of California
First Paperback Printing 1984
ISBN 0-520-05230-7
Printed in the United States of America

1 2 3 4 5 6 7 8 9

Library of Congress Cataloging in Publication Data
Bowen, Roger W. 1947-
Rebellion and Democracy in Meiji Japan.
Bibliography: p.
Includes index.
1. Japan—Politics and government—1868-1912.
2. Civil rights—Japan—History. 3. Peasant up-
risings—Japan. I. Title.
DS882.5.B68   320.9′52′031   78-51755

To my parents

Contents

Maps and Figure

Tables

Preface

In the same work from which the epigraph to this book is taken, Christopher Hill writes, "It is no longer necessary to apologize too profusely for taking the common people of the past on their own terms and trying to understand them." This book is an attempt to understand the politics of the common people of the Meiji period, and I make no apologies for trying. In going about this very difficult task, I have not so much tried to rewrite the history of the Meiji period as I have tried to complement it, by re-viewing the period and its common people from their perspective, from the bottom up.

Though I will not apologize for my approach, I do wish to point out one aspect of the book which the reader might find troubling. The manuscript is probably overburdened with Japanese words and names, but I must argue now that it was unavoidable. Lesser-known names and notions deserve, nay, demand a place in any popular history.

As a political scientist who sees in the present-day protest movements and citizen movements in Japan the quintessence of the democratic spirit in the participants' attempts to make government policy responsive to popular interests, past explanations of the democratic movement in Japanese history as provided by Western historians of Japan are far from being satisfactory. We must wonder whether, in Professor John Hall's words, present-day protest is in some way the "unconscious heritage of cultural behavior," or whether it might not reflect, again in his words, "the conscious effort of the society to 're-member' its past" and, I would add, to live up to what is best in it. In any case, I do believe with Professor Hall that "History as inheritance and history as remembrance are both significant dimensions of Japanese [political] culture today."[1] It is not surprising in this sense to learn that the farmers of Sanrizuka, who have for twelve years sought to prevent first the building of the Narita Airport on their land and then its opening, have invoked in the course of their battle against the modern gargantuan Japanese State the memory of the Chichibu rebels

1. John W. Hall, "The Historical Dimension," in John W. Hall and Richard Beardsley, *Twelve Doors to Japan* (New York, 1965), p. 129.

of 1884 and the Ashio Copper Mine antipollution protesters of a decade later.

Just as today's rebels recall the past and pay tribute to their predecessors for the lessons they taught, so too does the author wish to do the same here. I feel obliged first to acknowledge my intellectual debt to the writings of that great Canadian Japanologist, E. H. Norman. Though I criticize his work in the pages that follow, here I would like to credit his forever stimulating and provocative research into a Japanese past that had its democratic though lesser-known heroes. Of those living, there are several political scientists, historians, and sociologists who have in one way or another given generously of their time and ideas to my work. Good friend and mentor Professor Frank C. Langdon of the Department of Political Science at the University of British Columbia lent his keen critical faculties and wise judgments to this work since its inception. My debt to him can be acknowledged, but never repaid. Among those historians who graciously forgave the blunderings of a political scientist intent upon trespassing onto their rightful domain, and who guided my research at various stages, are Professors John F. Howes and W. Donald Burton; their encouragement was crucial to the completion of this book. My sincere gratitude to Philip Resnick of the Political Science Department at UBC is likewise extended. I must thank the University as well for the financial support it gave me over the years.

On the other side of the Pacific, Professor Inoue Kōji stands foremost in my list of debts. He gave my work the focus and direction it needed during the stages of formulation. Others in Japan who contributed assistance are Professors Kage Tatsuo and Haga Noboru, and at the National Diet Library, Messrs. Katō Rokuzō and Mitani Hiroshi. And though I have not had the pleasure of working personally with these men, I would like to credit the influence that the work of Irokawa Daikichi, Kano Masanao, and Hirano Yoshitarō had upon my study. Finally, it is necessary to recognize the support given by the Japanese Ministry of Education, enabling me to work at the Centre for Area Studies of the University of Tsukuba during my postdoctoral year there in 1977.

There are several old debts which I would also like to acknowledge. Professor Robert Ward, formerly of the University of Michigan, helped to keep alive my interest in Japanese politics at a time when I was losing it, and Dr. Roger Hackett was always kind enough never to censor the faulty products of an impatient neophyte in search of definitive answers to many problems in modern Japanese history. Both these gentlemen helped make my stay at Michigan a worthwhile one, but I should add that neither was in any way connected with the writing of this book. One who indirectly was and who made several helpful comments on some related work of mine during the final stages of preparing this manuscript for publication is Professor Charles Tilly; he, more than anyone else, led me to appreciate the importance of studying incidents of collective violence.

I am also pleased to be able to thank three friends who, though having different academic interests, unfailingly lent their time and ears to self-directed questions about the value of my research during moments when I would indulge in self-flagellating bouts of Maoist self-criticism; being there counted for a lot: warm thanks to Drs. Gerri Sinclair and James O. Hancey, and to Mrs. Agnes Lambe of Galiano Island. Mrs. Lambe's sharp mind, our afternoon brandy-drinking sessions, our evening discussions of Aldous Huxley, and her incredibly youthful septuagenarian typing abilities provided the author with just the right admixture necessary for transforming scattered ideas into what I hope is a defensible thesis.

Finally, during the penultimate stages of completing the manuscript, the assistance of a number of individuals and institutions was deeply appreciated. The Japan Foundation and Saint Mary's University in Halifax provided me with the time and financial support necessary to make several extensive amendments to the manuscript. A very critical anonymous reader for the Press prompted me to make those amendments: I thank her now, even though I know she will think that I did not go far enough. I thank Professor Mary Sun of Saint Mary's for liking my amendments enough to keep me from going too far. And the University Press, for employing Mr. Paul Weisser to edit the manuscript. To Barbara Bowen, who has been waiting several years for me to finish this book so that we could get on with the problems of real life, and who, to expedite matters, agreed to prepare the Index, thanks for looking after the children.

Though it may not be necessary, I will say nonetheless that I hold no one else responsible for the errors in fact, in translation, or in interpretation that may appear in this book—I alone am responsible.

RWB

Waterville, Maine
December 1978

Introduction

An alliance for freedom,
taken with the idea of freedom:
it all becomes clear
in the small mirror of sincerity.
Yet while we lament, asking
why our insignificant selves
were oppressed,
the rain still falls
heavily on the people.[1]

The poem quoted above was written by Ōhashi Genzaburō in October 1892, shortly before he died in his prison cell. He was a commoner (*heimin*) and a farmer, and by his own admittance "barely literate." He was also a member of the old Jiyūtō party (Freedom, or Liberal, party) that dissolved itself in late October 1884, barely a month after an attempt to overthrow the government had taken place. This attempt is known to later historians as the Kabasan Incident (*Kabasan jiken*), and Ōhashi Genzaburō had participated in that attempt at revolution.

This study is concerned with men such as Ōhashi and with the political party and movements in which they were involved. It is a study concerned not with Japan's great statesmen or the institutions they built, but instead is concerned with the common people who were compelled to suffer those great statesmen and their institutions. It is a study of the popular opposition known as the *jiyū minken undō* (Movement for Freedom and Popular Rights), a movement that began shortly after the Meiji Restoration (1868), coalesced in 1881 to form the Jiyūtō, and nearly collapsed in 1884 when the Jiyūtō dissolved. Our special concern is with the movement as it manifested itself in rural-based popular rights' societies of the late seventies and early eighties and how the members of these societies and similar political groups rose in rebellion to challenge the authority of the Meiji government.

Only those rural folk who were involved in the so-called *gekka jiken*, or "incidents of intensified [violence]," are the subjects of our study.

1. Quoted in Endō Shizuo, *Kabasan jiken* (Tokyo, 1971), p. 264.

Between 1881 and 1886, about a dozen of these incidents occurred in different parts of the nation—Akita, Fukushima, Niigata, Gifu, Gumma, Kanagawa, Ibaraki, Saitama, Nagano, Aichi, and Shizuoka prefectures. Although there were differences between them in terms of goals, class composition, number of participants, and the tactics employed, they all shared in common at least two elements: a strong connection with the popular rights movement, and the use of violence in an attempt to effect political reform. In general, the reforms they sought were democratic—for example, greater powers for local government, a popularly elected national assembly, and a constitution which would guarantee the basic rights of free expression, free association, and other civil liberties then being denied most of Japan's population.

Because the *gekka jiken* were violent and had a political coloring, they captured the attention of not only the authorities, but also the newspapers, the village historians, and the intellectuals of the period. All of these observed and wrote about the participants and the incidents of which they were a part, leaving us valuable records and observations on how the popular rights movement affected the lives and ideas of members of the lower classes.

The question may then arise, how representative are the rebels of the social classes from which they came? Is it fair to assume that the farmers involved in the *gekka jiken* accurately reflected the opinion of the farming class as a whole toward the political reforms being advocated by popular rights advocates? For as we know, "More often, historians have been inclined to treat the rebellious or revolutionary crowd as a militant minority to be sharply marked off from the far larger number of citizens of similar class and occupation who . . . played no active part in the event."[2] To test the truth of this statement, one need only consult any of the several volumes dealing with Japan of this period. Robert Scalapino's *Democracy and the Party Movement in Prewar Japan* devotes a bare four pages out of nearly five hundred to the *gekka jiken*; Nobutaka Ike allows nine pages; and E. H. Norman, whose sympathies for the lower classes were clearly strong, discusses these incidents in less than four pages.[3] Obviously,

2. George Rudé, *The Crowd in History: A Study of Popular Disturbances in France and England, 1730–1848* (New York, 1964), p. 211.

3. Robert A. Scalapino, *Democracy and the Party Movement in Prewar Japan: The Failure of the First Attempt* (Berkeley, 1967; originally published in 1953), pp. 104–7; Nobutaka Ike, *The Beginnings of Political Democracy in Japan* (New York, 1969; originally published in 1950), pp. 160–68; E. H. Norman, *Japan's Emergence as a Modern State: Political and Economic Problems of the Meiji Period* (New York, 1940), pp. 180–84.

none of these scholars believed that the rebellions of the eighties were anything more than short-lived and exceptional eruptions of peasant discontent, and the rebels themselves, by logical extension, extraordinary for their activism. Their lack of interest in Meiji rebellion is explained in part by the nature of their studies and the time period when they were written: All three of these works were sweeping in scope, covering decades of political development in Japan; and when they were written, there existed very little work in English that could be regarded as general histories of this period. There clearly existed a need for the types of work produced by Scalapino, Ike, and Norman.

Yet there appears to have been another reason for their having ignored the *gekka jiken*, one which has to do more with the focus of their analyses than with the absence of suitable material or with the period in which they were writing, although, contradictorily, all three reasons are related. What I mean is simply this: All were aware of the two attempts to establish a democratic form of government in modern Japanese history—the popular rights movement in the eighties and the so-called Taisho democracy of the 1920s. But at the time they were writing, Japan was entering a stage of ultranationalistic political development, or was just leaving it, having lost the Second World War and having been occupied by Western military forces whose purpose was to *impose* a democratic form of government on Japan. Each believed that democracy had failed in Japan, and Scalapino even went so far as to say that its failure was predetermined by the logic of Japan's past political development. The absence of a liberal tradition, the predominance of Confucian notions of hierarchy, the antidemocratic bias of the elite power structure, the close ties between "free enterprise" and the government, the imperialistic power structure of the world at the time Japan began her modernization, the tradition of glorifying the military and of despising the agricultural population—all these past elements of Japan's politics determined that the democratic experiment in Japan would fail. Likewise, these authors were less than sanguine about the future of democracy once the Allied Occupation had left Japan.

The "failure thesis" is, then, a convincing one. It is attractive because of its ability to weave together all the various threads of Japanese history, society, and politics into one neat explanatory piece of political fabric. However, the fabric is not without its loose threads and its gaps in the stitching. Probably the most unsightly of these gaps is the failure of the "failure thesis" to explain satisfactorily the success of democracy in those two periods when it was a political fact. Although the authors weakly acknowledge the fact, they attribute its origins primarily to exogenous factors or necessary external preconditions, and therefore they fail to consider seriously the possibility of indigenous political developments that may have prepared the way for the rise of democracy. What they have not seen is that a listing of necessary preconditions for the rise of democracy does not explain why or how democracy could burgeon when it did. For example, to discuss the expansion of industry after the First World War, the spread of international labor standards, the influence of the Russian Revolution on socialist movements in Japan, and so on, does not in itself tell us how or why industrial laborers and tenants organized themselves into unions, apparently democratic in both principle and practice, and made them effective means for getting demands met. Nor, for another example, does a mere recitation of the democratic programs imposed by the Occupation after the Second World War explain why the Japanese (not to mention the Germans and Italians)[4] were able to embrace democratic ideas and practices so warmly after a period of fascist rule.

I believe that the main weakness of the "failure thesis" lies in its neglect of the practice of politics at different levels of society. The level at which most specialists on Japan have aimed their historical analyses is the elite and national level of politics, the level occupied by national party leaders, the chieftains of big business, and high-ranking government officials. There has been a reason for this: Japan's modern history is replete with examples of great leaders in all areas of social life. The imagery is one of a squadron of captains, each ruling and directing the course of his own particular ship, yet in coordination with one another, toward a "rich country and a strong military" (*fukoku kyōhei*). But in focusing upon the "captains" of the ship of state, the lives and work of the many individual seamen, upon whose labor Japanese leaders greatly depended, have been ignored. More often than not, they have been treated as an unthinking body of men whose identity is a mere extension of the captains', and their duty whatever the captains order. In short, the lower classes of Japan, especially the farmers, have been treated as members of a "subject political culture."

---

4. "Fascism is inconceivable without democracy or what is sometimes more turgidly called the entrance of the masses onto the historical stage." (Barrington Moore, Jr., *Social Origins of Dictatorship and Democracy: Lord and Peasant in the Making of the Modern World* [Boston, 1966], p. 447).

This same attitude has prevailed in Western scholarship on the popular rights movement. The ideas and activities of such national leaders as Itagaki Taisuke, President of the Jiyūtō, have been given copious attention and have incontestably been shown to be less than liberal. On the basis of this, it has been assumed that the as yet obtusely identified followers of the liberal movement—conservative landlords, rapacious merchants, and illiterate peasants—were mirror images of the leadership. One aim of this work is to show that the logic behind this assumption is insubstantial and incorrect. But even at the most general level of analysis, the whole notion of a "subject political culture" or a passive peasantry makes it nearly impossible to provide a convincing explanation of rebellion. All that can be done and all that has been done in the past is to de-emphasize the historical significance of rebellion, arguing that it was temporary, short-lived, unusual, and inconsequential in comparison with Japan's overall success at modernization.

Unfortunately, this view ignores several crucial facts about the nature of rebellion: Rebellion signifies much more than simple violence or "peasant discontent"; rebellion represents a perhaps fatal questioning of the legitimacy of the established order; it means that the rebels are claiming that something is wrong with conditions as they presently exist; it means (though not always) that the traditional grounds of obedience upon which the state rests are being challenged. Rebellion, in other words, says something very definite about the nature of the order against which rebels take up arms; or as the Tillys have argued, rebellion serves as a "tracer" of a "much wider, but more elusive, set of politically significant encounters."[5]

Hannah Arendt has said that "the end of rebellion is liberation, while the end of revolution is the foundation of freedom. . . ."[6] The *gekka jiken* we will be studying were rebellions, not only in the sense that their goal was "liberation" from certain economic and political injustices, but also in the sense that they were less than revolutionary in *effect* (as opposed to intent), or, from another perspective, they were revolutions which failed in the attempt to establish a "foundation of freedom."

This study will focus on rural rebels as individuals and as members of political groups, and will do so by examining in detail three "incidents of intense violence": the Fukushima Incident of 1882 and the

---

5. Charles Tilly, Louise Tilly, and Richard Tilly, *The Rebellious Century, 1830–1930* (Cambridge, Mass., 1975), p. 248.
6. Hannah Arendt, *On Revolution* (New York, 1963), p. 140.

Kabasan and Chichibu incidents of 1884. We examine them for all the reasons social scientists study "mutinies": to learn why they happened; what they tell about general social, economic, and political conditions; and what consequences they had for society and politics as a whole. We also wish to discover whether the democratic ideals the participants espoused were shared by others within their class, and whether they had some impact upon later political developments in Japan. A word of caution: As there was no Gallup poll at the time these incidents occurred, in the final analysis it will not be possible to demonstrate with any degree of precision to what extent these early liberals and democrats represented others within their class; we can only present the best case possible, and then suggest the likelihood of representativeness.

The book begins with case studies of each of the incidents. The second chapter tries to pinpoint the conditions—historical, social, economic, and political—that helped to produce the three incidents. In the third chapter, we perform an in-depth analysis of the participants of the three incidents. Many of the rebels we will be examining may be regarded as local elites—that is, as the political, economic, and social leaders of local society. In terms of the earlier-used metaphor, these local elites might be thought of as "chief petty officers." Although in some respects their "rank" sets them apart from the many non-elites whom they led in the local popular rights movement and the related rebellions, in other respects they differed very little. But despite whatever differences that may have separated local leaders from followers, in the pages that follow it should become clear that both groups shared similar political goals, and that these shared goals set them far apart from the national liberal leaders and governmental rulers.

The nature of these goals is set forth in the fourth chapter, where we further identify the participants by examining their political beliefs and the political societies and parties to which they belonged. In the final chapter, we discuss the consequences that the individual participants suffered because of their involvement in the popular rights movement and the effects their rebellion had upon the Jiyūtō. We conclude by making some suggestions about the democratic experience in modern Japanese history.

One final word of introduction: The ultimate purpose of this study is to address itself to three types of critics, those whom Sir Isaiah Berlin cited in his introduction to Franco Venturi's *Roots of*

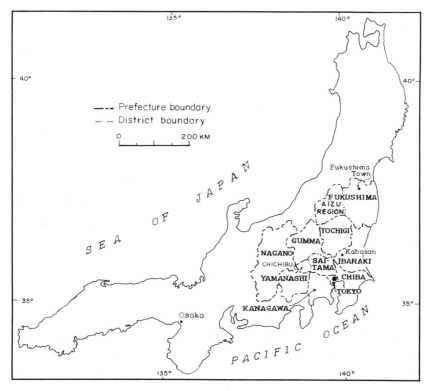

Map 1. The Kantō Region, and Fukushima and Nagano Prefectures

Revolution, deleting where necessary the reference to Russia and inserting a reference to Japan:

> Those who look on all history through the eyes of the victors, and for whom accounts of movements that failed, of martyrs and minorities, seem without interest as such; those who think that ideas play little or no part in determining historical events; and finally those who are convinced that [democracy in Japan] was simply the result of the [Allied Occupation], and possessed no significant roots in the [Japanese] past.[7]

7. Franco Venturi, *Roots of Revolution: A History of the Populist and Socialist Movements in Nineteenth-Century Russia,* trans. Francis Haskell, Introduction by Isaiah Berlin (New York, 1960; originally published in Italy in 1952), p. vii.

1. Incidents

I hold it that a little rebellion now and then is
a good thing and as necessary in the political world
as storms in the physical. Unsuccessful rebellions indeed generally establish the encroachments on the
rights of the people which have produced them. . . .
It is a medicine necessary for the sound health of
government.

Thomas Jefferson to James Madison
30 January 1787

The purpose of this chapter is a simple one: to provide a detailed
sketch of the Fukushima, Kabasan, and Chichibu incidents. Care will
be taken to introduce the main characters involved in each of the
jiken, to explain how and when they got involved, and what part they
played in the development of the incidents. The question of why they
involved themselves will be discussed in Chapters 3 and 4, where we
will look at the background of the participants in the first instance,
and their ideas as translated into action and organization in the second.

The Fukushima Incident

The Fukushima Incident was a lengthy affair, lasting nearly the entire year of 1882. Its beginning and end were clearly marked as Shimoyama Saburō tells us: "The incident began with the appointment of
Mishima [Michitsune or Tsūyō] as Governor [of Fukushima prefec-
ture] in early 1882, and ended with the mass arrests of Jiyūtō members in late November and early December."[1] The high points of the
conflict were centered alternately around two axes of popular| rights
opposition to the prefectural government. One was centered in the
Aizu region in western Fukushima. There the opposition movement
was widespread, well organized at the popular level, and carried out
for the most part within the bounds of law, although extralegal tactics

1. Shimoyama Saburō, "Fukushima jiken shōron," ed. Sakane Yoshihisa, *Jiyu minken*
10, *Nihon rekishi series* (Tokyo, 1973):162.

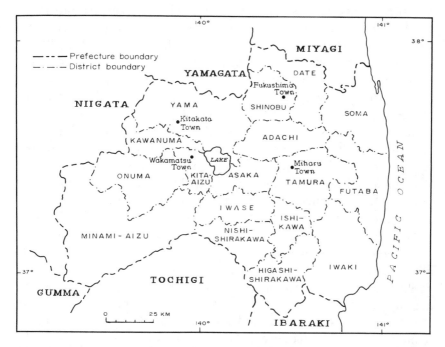

Map 2.   Fukushima Prefecture

were oftentimes advocated and occasionally employed. The other axis of opposition was in the eastern part of the prefecture and revolved especially around the activities of the Jiyūtō-controlled prefectural assembly. In many ways an institutional conflict, it was expressed as a struggle between the executive power of Governor Mishima and the powerless but power-seeking legislature. For most of 1882 the two conflicts, the western and eastern, remained separate affairs. Even though the two opposition groups eventually and belatedly merged in the form of a loose alliance against Mishima's government, the twain really only "met" at the end of the year in a state of shared persecution—the Governor's mass arrest campaign did not differentiate between eastern and western popular rights advocates.

Governor Mishima and the Aizu Jiyūtō

The appointment of Mishima Michitsune (1835–88), an ex-samurai from Satsuma who began his government service in 1871 with the Tokyo municipal government, was the catalyst that set into motion the subsequent clash between prefectural authorities, on the one side, and the prefectural assembly and especially its Jiyūtō membership, on the other.[2] Already serving as governor of Yamagata prefecture, a post he continued to hold until July, in February 1882 the "Devil Governor" (oni kenrei) was assigned the Fukushima governorship.[3] Upon this occasion Mishima reportedly confided to Satō Jirō (Head of Yama district) what his orders were from the central government: "I was given three secret orders along with my appointment. The first is to destroy the Jiyūtō, the second is to build up the Teiseitō [the government's "political party"], and the third is to construct several important roads."[4] Events subsequent to his appointment prove that Mishima acted faithfully to obey these three orders, even though, in terms of the sequence of events, the execution of the orders was reversed, and for good reason.

The destruction of the Fukushima Jiyūtō was not an easy task. Two branches, one in Aizu and the other in the east, had been established in December 1881, just two months after the founding of the national party. Of all the party branches later established across the nation, the Fukushima branches were popularly regarded as among the strongest.[5] At the time of Mishima's appointment, prefectural assembly members affiliated with the Jiyūtō outnumbered those of the other parties. The breakdown in the sixty-two-member assembly (with one seat vacant) was: Jiyūtō, twenty-four; Teiseitō, fifteen; Kaishintō, twelve; unattached, ten.[6] Besides holding a numerical superiority, the Fukushima Jiyūtō assembly members also shared a history of political activity in the popular rights movement that began in the mid-seventies (see Chapter 4). More than the members of the other parties, they were a readily identifiable and cohesive group. Moreover, outside the prefectural assembly, both in the Aizu and eastern Fukushima regions, Jiyūtō members held many positions of authority at the local level of government, e.g., village head (kochō), subdistrict head (kuchō), or as elected members of the village or subdistrict assemblies.[7] A number of Jiyūtō members had also held positions of re-

2. For a short biographical treatment of Mishima, see Takahashi Tetsuo, Fukushima jiken (Tokyo, 1970), p. 68.

3. Ibid.; the appointment was made on 25 January, but Mishima did not take up the post until 17 February.

4. Quoted in ibid., p. 70; and Shimoyama, "Shōron," p. 162.

5. Shimoyama, "Shōron," p. 162.

6. Takahashi, Fukushima jiken, p. 67. The breakdown by status was nine shizoku and fifty-two heimin. Economically, however, it was a fairly homogeneous group, as most were wealthy farmers, merchants, or village headmen.

7. A ku was an intermediate level of local government, located between the village or town and the district (gun). This level of government was eliminated in the late 1880s.

sponsibility during the tenure of the previous administration, but once Mishima took office they were summarily dismissed and replaced by officials personally loyal to him. In all, more than ninety known Jiyūtō officials or school teachers (who were employees of the government at this time) were said to have been sacked by Mishima.[8] These dismissals can be regarded as the first instance of Mishima acting upon his objective to "destroy the Jiyūtō." This instance, however, is of minor importance compared with subsequent attacks upon the Jiyūtō during the development of the Fukushima Incident. Mishima's opportunities to destroy the Aizu Jiyūtō were bettered, moreover, by the opposition that his third goal, building new roads, engendered among local popular rights activists.

The governor had been ordered by the central government to begin construction of several new roads in the Aizu region, which consists of the six districts located in the western part of the prefecture: Yama, Kawanuma, Ōnuma, Minami-Aizu, Kita-Aizu, and Higashi-Kabahara.[9] The project, one he had already begun during his tenure as governor of the Yamagata prefecture, was known as the "Three Roads" (sampō dōro) project, so called because it was to link Wakamatsu, the former castle town of Aizu han, with Yamagata prefecture to the north, Tokyo to the south via Tochigi and Ibaraki prefectures, and Niigata prefecture to the west. The total cost of construction in Aizu, 620,000 yen, was to be shared by the central government and the six districts of Aizu. The Aizu share, however, at 360,000 yen was substantially larger than the central government's and further represented a considerable extra economic burden for the 129,000 residents of the region.[10]

Mishima realized that this extra, unsought financial burden, announced within weeks of his taking office succeeding a popular governor, would not be enthusiastically received by Aizu residents, yet he also knew he would somehow have to gain the cooperation of the area's residents. To this end, on 28 February, Mishima sent from the capital (Fukushima Town) his construction chief Nakayama and his personal deputy Ebina, a former samurai of Aizu han, to Aizu for the purpose of assembling the six district chiefs (gunchō). They were ordered by Mishima's deputies to hold an election among village and town councilmen, with only councilmen serving as electors, to choose

8. Takahashi, Fukushima jiken, pp. 70–71.
9. In 1886, Higashi-Kabahara became part of Niigata prefecture. The other five districts still comprise the Aizu region today.
10. Shōji Kichinosuke, ed., Nihon seisha seitō hattatsu shi (Tokyo, 1959), p. 305.

one man from each district to serve as members of a committee which would then be responsible for establishing the rules to govern the election of residents who in turn would compose a standing committee called the *Aizu rokugun rengōkai* ("Six Aizu Districts' Joint Committee," hereafter cited as Rengōkai). The Rengōkai, representing the "people," was intended to serve to legitimize and rubber-stamp Mishima's policy, as yet unannounced, of carrying out the road construction. Mishima's own notion of the composition of the Rengōkai was a thirty-man committee, consisting of five people from each district and elected by village and town councilmen. Moreover, as communicated to Ebina, Mishima made it clear that all this business—the election of the rule-making committee, the determination of the rules for electing the Rengōkai members, and the election itself—should be concluded in several days time![11]

The election of the rules committee went as quickly as Mishima had wanted, and the six members first met on 5 March.[12]   In one day the rules for electing Rengōkai members were settled. But despite the alacrity, and because four of the six were Jiyūtō members, the rules finally settled upon for the Rengōkai election were much more democratic than Mishima had wanted. Instead of an indirect election by village and town councilmen serving as electors, the rules committee endorsed proportional representation, i.e., the number of Rengōkai members from each district would depend upon the district's population and would be directly elected by all male taxpayers twenty years of age or older. This scheme was accepted by Mishima for the sake of expediency, and two days later, on 7 and 8 March, the election of thirty-four Rengōkai members was held. (This number was later increased to forty-six once Ōnuma and Minami-Aizu districts, whose chiefs favored indirect elections initially, complied with the rules committee election criteria.)[13]

Although the procedure, the speed of selection, and even the idea of the existence of such a committee as the Rengōkai was questioned, or rather, protested against by Jiyūtō members of the prefectural assembly who regarded this as a violation of their right to advise the administration on important issues, their protests were muted by the aggressiveness and quick initiative that Mishima had taken on this

---

11. Takahashi, *Fukushima jiken*, p. 108.

12. The names of the six members (and their home districts) were: Nakajima Yūhachi (Kawanuma), Maeda Sōsaku (Yama), Chiba Uhachi (Ōnuma), Watanabe Matahachi (Minami-Aizu), Tatsuno Shūji (Kita-Aizu), and Yamaguchi Uramatsu (Higashi-Kabahara).   Ibid., p. 109.

13. Shimoyama, "Shōron," p. 163.

matter. The only really serious protest was lodged by the administrative head of Yama district, Igarashi Chikarasuke, a leftover from the previous administration, whom Mishima quickly replaced with his own appointee, Satō Jirō, who, in disposition and attitude toward the Jiyūtō, resembled the Governor.

From 14 to 16 March, just two weeks after Mishima initiated this entire process, the Rengōkai met for the first time in Wakamatsu to "deliberate" on the government's road construction plans. Most present were "large landlords or local notables (meibōka),"[14] and several were members of the prefectural assembly, such as Jiyūtō members Nakajima Yūhachi and Watanabe Ichirō. Nakajima, thirty-one-year old small landlord of Kawanuma prefecture, was elected chairman of the Rengōkai.

Their deliberations essentially revolved around a proposal earlier outlined by the six district heads in collaboration with Mishima's deputies. Pressured to "deliberate" quickly, debate over the government's proposals was sharply curtailed, and on 16 March the Rengōkai approved two resolutions. The first required (a) one day of corvée labor each month for a period of two years from all Aizu residents between the ages of fifteen and sixty, excluding the disabled and widowed; and (b) a substitute labor tax to be paid by those disinclined to work, at the rate of fifteen sen per day for male labor, and ten sen per day for female labor. The second resolution provided for village and town councils to take appropriate measures to ensure participation in the collection of taxes for substitute labor, and in the collection of road taxes which were based upon land value and the population of the village. The acceptance of both resolutions, however, was conditional on (1) the grant of supplementary funding from the central government and on (2) all work done by corvée laborers being restricted to level ground, only professionals doing the mountain and bridge construction.[15] It is important to note that nothing was mentioned about what course the road should take, who would oversee the workers, the precise amount of supplementary funds to come from the central government, or about the details of tax assessment. In this regard, almost all students of the incident agree that these mistakes or oversights by the Rengōkai were important factors in the growth of the incident.[16]

14. Takahashi, Fukushima jiken, p. 110.
15. The resolution is quoted in ibid., p. 163, and in Shōji Kichinosuke's collection of documents, Nihon seisha, pp. 305–6.
16. Shōji Kichinosuke, Nihon seisha, p. 306; Takahashi, Fukushima jiken, p. 110; Shimoyama, "Shōron," p. 163.

Since actual construction work on the roads was not due to begin until August, during the intervening months Aizu residents in general and Rengōkai members in particular had time to consider the details of the Rengōkai resolutions and to discover the oversights or omissions not covered by them. By June, in fact, several events had transpired that caused many Aizu residents to question the road plan seriously. First, in June it was learned that instead of the 260,000 yen in government funds initially promised, only 98,000 yen were granted.[17] This, of course, meant a correspondingly heavier financial burden for Aizu residents. Second, Mishima effectively suspended the Rengōkai, taking complete charge of the planning and supervision of road construction. As Takahashi Tetsuo evaluated this development, "The Rengōkai was nothing but a tool whose resolutions merely served to round up people to work on the roads. Its actual work was three days of debate, and then it had to close up shop. Or rather, from the standpoint of the governor and the district head, it had outlived its usefulness."[18] And thirdly, the governor ordered corvée labor dues to be made retroactive to March, when the resolutions were passed, and further ordered through the six district heads the speedy collection of these dues.[19]

In reaction to these developments, a good number of Aizu residents adopted defensive measures. Some, such as Rengōkai member Igarashi Takehiko of Yama district, began calling on other members to fight the government, specifically by demanding that a special session of the Rengōkai be called in order to oppose these recent developments. By 28 July, the efforts of Igarashi and other Jiyūtō-Rengōkai members had succeeded in gaining a majority (by one) of Rengōkai members to sign a petition calling for the special session. But on 14 August the petition was rejected, as were two other such petitions presented to the government before the end of the month.[20] Other local Jiyūtō members were preaching civil disobedience against the levies, saying,

17. Shimoyama, "Shōron," p. 165. In 1880, the central government began scaling down its grants to the prefectures for regional construction projects; thereafter, funds for such projects came from local taxes for the most part.

18. Takahashi, Fukushima jiken, p. 125.

19. Theoretically, the rate of assessment was left to the villages to determine in accordance with that part of the Rengōkai resolution that read, "ought to be suitable for each village." In fact, the Ōnuma gunchō initially assembled all village heads and instructed them to levy taxes at the rate of 60 percent by population and 40 percent by land value. Rich peasants in many villages protested against this scheme, and in many cases were able to alter the tax rate to 10 to 20 percent land value and 80 to 90 percent by population, thereby shifting the tax burden onto the poorer peasants. Some villages, moreover, rejected at the outset any levy at all. See Takahashi, Fukushima jiken, pp. 115–17.

20. Ibid., pp. 123, 125.

as Saji Kōbei of Takada village in Ōnuma district did, "It is not the duty of our citizens to obey this resolution" because of "the illegal and unfair election of the [Rengōkai] members."[21] (He was referring to his district's already mentioned failure to comply early on with the rules committee election criteria.)

Such attempts at initiating civil disobedience spread throughout the region, although they were mainly concentrated in Yama, Kawanuma, and Ōnuma districts. Reports sent to Mishima by Yama district head Satō further attest to such activity. "The Jiyūtō is agitating," wrote Satō, "by lecturing at village assemblies, involving often more than a hundred people, throughout the entire region."[22] Activist Uda Seiichi, for example, told the farmers of Atsushio village in Yama, "We ought to expand this [movement] into an extraordinary incident."[23] Proof that their "agitating" had some effect is seen in the growing numbers of village councilmen who were refusing to levy road construction taxes on their fellow villagers. Further evidence is the government's initiation of intimidation and bribery as means to dissuade Rengōkai members from organizing an opposition movement. The most blatant example of intimidation occurred on 18 August, the day after the government surreptitiously held a ceremony to mark the official beginning of road construction, when Jiyūtō members Uda Seiichi, Kōjima Chūhachi, and Tamano Hideaki were brutally attacked while sleeping at the Shimizu *ryokan* (hotel) in Kitakata by seven or eight Teiseitō party members. Kōjima was able to flee and escape injury, but the other two suffered a bad beating.[24]

This attack, known to later historians as the "Shimizuya jiken," is politically significant not only for showing the extent to which the government would go in order to suppress the Jiyūtō, but also for demonstrating how successful Mishima had been in accomplishing the second of his secret goals as governor, that of building a loyal and unquestioning Teiseitō. In going about this, Mishima had concentrated his efforts in Wakamatsu, the center of *han* (feudal domain) resistance during the Tōhoku region's primarily samurai-led counter-Restoration movement of 1868 and 1869 (known as the Boshin War). After their defeat by the new government, and the loss of their status as samurai and the stipends that went with that status, many ex-samurai of this region suffered unemployment and poverty. Many depended upon the goodwill of the new government in finding them employment, such as in the Asaka land reclamation project or in the local constab-

21. Ibid., p. 116.   22. Shimoyama, "Shōron," p. 170.   23. Ibid.
24. See Takahashi, *Fukushima jiken*, pp. 133–37, for details of this incident.

ulary. But in any event, there existed a free-floating population of ex-samurai in the Aizu region ready and able to be mobilized for one cause or another. Some joined the Jiyūtō, and others joined the Teiseitō.

On 30 June 1882, the Fukushima branch of the Teiseitō was organized, and under Mishima's direction founded itself on the principles of "love of Emperor and country, the defense of the righteous road of the fatherland, and the measured reform of society based upon the above two ideas."[25] In September it received through Mishima an interest-free loan of 196,000 yen from the central government, which served to finance the expenses of the party and its largely ex-samurai (*shizoku*) membership, and to establish a party headquarters and academy at Wakamatsu, called the *Nisshinkan* ("Hall of Daily Renewal").[26] Shortly after its founding, it claimed the support of more than 4,500 members, although the real figure was probably only half that number.[27] It received additional support from local businessmen and merchants who were eager for a new road that would facilitate commerce. The chief, self-defined duty of the Fukushima Teiseitō, and that which had the greatest impact on the Jiyūtō, was "to protect and enforce the Law Regulating Public Meetings (*shūkai jōrei*)."[28]

During the day of the evening when the "Shimizuya *jiken*" took place, Jiyūtō members of the Rengōkai secretly gathered in Wakamatsu, where they resolved that henceforth the Aizu Jiyūtō would take full responsibility for organizing a more wide-scale and structured protest against the government. Lawsuits and a tax boycott (of the substitute corvée labor fee), they decided, would constitute the core of their protest movement.

For the residents of the Aizu region, this Jiyūtō meeting, and the Teiseitō attack of the same day, marks the end of one phase in the *jiken* and the beginning of the next.

Governor Mishima and the Fukushima Jiyūtō

While these events were happening in Aizu, in the east, around Fukushima *machi* (town) equally significant developments had also been taking place. For different but nonetheless related reasons, the

25. Quoted in ibid., p. 132.
26. Shimoyama, "Shōron," p. 179.
27. See Takahashi, *Fukushima jiken*, p. 133, for an evaluation of the different estimates made by historians on Teiseitō membership.
28. Ibid., p. 132.

Fukushima branch of the Jiyūtō was assuming a posture of opposition to Mishima. During April when the prefectural assembly was in session, Governor Mishima, contrary to custom, failed to attend even one sitting, even though the assembly had requested his attendance on three separate occasions. On 1 May, the assembly chairman, Kōno Hironaka, an early popular rights leader, sent a personal messenger to ask the governor one last time to appear before the assembly, but again Mishima did not respond. Infuriated at Mishima's open contempt, on 4 May, during a debate on a bill relating to annual government expenditures, Kōno accepted a motion from the floor, made by Jiyūtō member and vice-chairman of the assembly Yamaguchi Chiyosaku, to suspend all business until the governor consented to appear. The motion was not approved, but the idea behind the motion began to gain currency nevertheless. From 5 to 7 May, the Jiyūtō caucus met and put together nineteen articles accusing Mishima of misgovernment, and further resolved to try again to garner sufficient support to suspend business in the assembly. The author of this measure was Uda Seiichi of Aizu's Yama district.[29] Uda's resolution was subsequently presented in the assembly three different times, on 7, 8, and 10 May. Each time it was approved by a bare majority, and the final vote was twenty-three to twenty-one (eighteen members were absent, and in mid-May, fearing Mishima's temper, they resigned).[30] Supporting Uda were nineteen other Jiyūtō members and three Kaishintō members. The final resolution, dated 12 May 1882, read in part:

> For acting contrary to public opinion, for not responding to the wishes of the public of this jurisdiction in regard to deliberating on policy, and in setting the matter of this year's taxes, this assembly withholds the disbursements of those funds. Also, we will vote down all such bills in the future.[31]

This action was without precedent in the few years since the July 1878 law permitting the establishment of prefectural assemblies had come into effect throughout Japan.[32] But because that law really accorded very little power to the assemblies—they had the "right to deliberate on bills" (*gian shingi ken*)—vis-à-vis the governor, who had the exclusive right to initiate legislation, the power to request the Home Minister to dissolve the assembly, and the further right to ig-

29. Shimoyama, "Shōron," p. 163.
30. Takahashi, *Fukushima jiken*, p. 72.
31. Quoted in ibid., p. 73. Also see Kurt Steiner, *Local Government in Japan* (Stanford, Calif., 1965), pp. 30–37, especially p. 31.
32. Shōji, *Nihon seisha*, pp. 254–75; also Steiner, *Local Government*, p. 31.

nore the assembly's deliberation, the Fukushima prefectural assembly's action to refuse to accept all future bills from the administration in effect merely amounted to a strong vote of censure against Mishima. It also provided Mishima with sufficient reason, under the law, to seek the aid of the Home Ministry, i.e., to involve the central government directly in prefectural affairs, which is exactly what he did on 22 May. Upon doing this, he received permission from the Home and Finance ministries to enforce the annual appropriations bill and to invoke Article 34 of the *Fū-ken-kai kisoku* (Rules governing Prefectural Assemblies), empowering him to suspend the right of election for a fixed period of time and to dissolve the assembly.[33]

Although this was not the least significant of Mishima's responses to the contentious assembly, it still represented only his *pro forma* reaction.[34] Equally significant was his campaign to suppress the Jiyūtō, which, as the following excerpt from a letter written by Uda to Miura Shinroku on 13 May shows, was intensive even before the vote of censure:

> Since this assembly convened, daily the risk of speaking freely in the assembly hall grows greater. . . . Ever since the present governor assumed office, the policy of government toward free speech in the assembly has changed for the worse. His actions are manifestly authoritarian, restraining the freedoms of the people . . . and he shows no regard for the opinions of the assembly.[35]

Earlier still, on 4 May, during the morning session, assembly chairman Kōno Hironaka took the floor and addressed its members:

> This assembly is founded on the premise that we ought to represent public opinion, and we ought to consider this and then enact public policy. . . . Since his arrival, Governor Mishima has removed himself many *ri* and has neglected the assembly and has acted without regard to public opinion. . . . Without regard for the wishes of the people of today for freedom of speech, he has for one thing employed the police against assemblymen involved in politics, and for another, against those who publicly gather, using the Law Governing Assembly (*shūkai jōrei*) with the utmost severity.[36]

---

33. Takahashi, *Fukushima jiken*, pp. 80–81; Shōji, *Nihon seisha*, p. 275; Shimoyama, "Shōron," p. 164.

34. Barely a week in office, on 6 March 1882, Mishima signed Order No. 43; it required prior approval from the police before groups were allowed to "discuss political matters" or to assemble. Quoted in Takahashi, *Fukushima jiken*, p. 94.

35. This letter appears in Shōji, *Nihon seisha*, pp. 409–10.

36. Quoted in Takahashi, *Fukushima jiken*, pp. 76–77; a *ri* is a measurement of distance equaling 2.44 miles.

Further proof of the pudding, moreover, that Mishima reacted oppressively against the assemblymen who voted to censure him came later with the arrest of all twenty-three men for the crime of "slandering a public official" (*kanri bujoku zai*); conviction of this crime carried a prison term of seven months to a year, and a fine of ten to twenty yen.[37] Later still, in December, Mishima ordered the arrest of most of the twenty-three assemblymen for the crime of treason.

After the motion of censure was passed, Mishima enjoyed no respite from the Jiyūtō attack. During the next several months, Jiyūtō members in eastern Fukushima relentlessly continued to contest the legality of Mishima's administration. Shortly after Mishima dissolved the assembly, Jiyūtō members sent memorial after memorial to the central government accusing Mishima of misgovernment. These memorials cited his summary dismissal of former officials, his contempt for the assembly, his handling of the Aizu road project, his suppression of freedom of speech, and so on.[38] On 5 July, another such memorial was sent, this time concerning alleged illegal practices in his taxation policy.[39]

The effects of their failure to elicit a satisfactory response from the central government to these memorials, and the more general problem of the repression they were suffering, are reflected in the growing tribute paid to more radical ideas by Jiyūtō leaders attached to the *Mumeikan* ("Hall of No Name"), the meeting place of the Fukushima branch of the Jiyūtō in the eastern part of the prefecture. Within this branch a faction calling itself the *Kyūshintō* or "Radical Party" under Hanaka, and later associated with Kōno Hironaka as well, was daily gaining influence among the party members.[40] Hanaka, its chief promoter, characterized it in this way: "Our ideology concerns how to obtain freedom quickly and to give vent to a radical philosophy, under the aegis of the Jiyūtō. . . ."[41] (See Chapter 4 for a fuller treatment.) After his arrest in late November, Hanaka made clear in his courtroom testimony why a more radical orientation was necessary for the Jiyūtō:

> The governor took on the dual job of firing [former] officials and crushing the Jiyūtō. On the one hand, he replaced [the former officials] with his own; on the other, he worked to organize the Teiseitō in order to suppress the Jiyūtō. . . .[42]

37. Ibid., p. 81.
38. Shimoyama, "Shōron," p. 164.   39. Ibid., p. 169.   40. Ibid., p. 171.
41. Ibid.   42. Quoted in ibid., pp. 171–72.

Clearly, Hanaka at least believed that radicalism was necessary at this juncture in order to preserve the life of the Jiyūtō. Moreover, this development coincides with the emergence within the national party of others holding similar radical beliefs, such as Ōi Kentarō and Miyabe Noboru who were elected to leadership positions in June 1882.

In Fukushima this growing tendency toward radicalism did not go unobserved by the authorities. The police chief of Miharu reported as early as late May: "People in the area are saying that by July of this year a new Jiyūtō government will be established and will rule the entire country."[43]

Having observed the developments in eastern Fukushima that took place before September, the narrative now returns to examine what was happening in Aizu after the important 18 August meeting of Jiyūtō members there, in preparation for showing how these two different anti-Mishima movements coalesced.

Mobilizing the People of Aizu

During late August and early September, a number of secret meetings between Aizu Jiyūtō leaders were held concerning the problem of how to involve large numbers of Aizu residents in the anti-road campaign. Up to this point, the local Jiyūtō leaders realized that the movement was what present-day scholars would call *jōryū minken* or an "upper-class people's rights movement," consisting mainly of landlords, ex-samurai (*shizoku*), intellectuals, and village officials. Though locally powerful, such men alone, they reasoned, would not be able to carry out a tax boycott or litigation campaign. To be effective, such action required mass participation in the first instance, and in the second instance, at least the written endorsement (power of attorney) of a substantial number of citizens in order to receive recognition by the courts. But in either case, their intent was to involve as many people as possible in a campaign of popular protest, and thereby to create a climate for the government that some of them termed "cloudy and foggy" (*unmu*), which they alone, upon government capitulation to their demands, would have the power to dissolve. As one of the Aizu Jiyūtō leaders, Nakajima, put it, "Through litigation on the road affair, we believe that we can realize our [immediate] objective of causing the government to be upset."[44] Pressure politics, employed through legal means on the one hand, coupled with a mas-

43. Quoted in ibid., p. 165.
44. Shōji, *Nihon seisha*, pp. 310–11.

sive civil disobedience campaign on the other (i.e., the tax boycott), could drive the government to recognize the right of Aizu residents to hold greater authority over local affairs.

Of the two-pronged attack against Mishima's actions concerning the road construction project, however, at this point litigation was more heavily relied upon. Since none of the Aizu Jiyūtō leaders were lawyers by profession, they naturally looked outside for aid. Interestingly enough, instead of turning to the Fukushima branch in the east, which was staffed by many competent lawyers, they sought aid from the Tokyo headquarters of the Party, mainly because even by this time the Fukushima branch had shown only nominal interest in, and concern for, the road issue.

Some time in September, Hara Heizō, a moderately wealthy farmer and *minken* activist since 1880 when he was twenty-one, and "the biggest hope of the Aizu Jiyūtō,"[45] went to Tokyo to seek the legal counsel of two of the national party's more radical lawyers, Ōi Kentarō and Hoshi Tōru. While Hara was in Tokyo, Jiyūtō activists in Aizu had begun organizing an effective litigation movement. Five men—Uda Seiichi, Akagi Heiroku, Igarashi Takehiko, Yamaguchi, and Nakajima—were present at the first such meeting in early September. A second organizational meeting was held soon after in Yamaguchi's village of Onomoto, but this time thirty Jiyūtō members were in attendance, including the important additions of Miura Bunji, Saji Kōbei, and Kaneko Tsunejirō. At the third organizational meeting, held at Komeoka village in Yama district on 28 September, over seventy were present, collectively holding the power of attorney of 3,400 to 4,000 supporters.[46] At this meeting the "Declaration of the Restoration of Rights" was formulated and approved (see Appendix A), and the movement was given added structure by selecting a three-man litigation committee (Uda, Nakajima, and Yamaguchi), a President (Akagi), and a Vice-President (Miura Bunji). Also at this gathering, Hara Heizō, back from Tokyo, reported on the legal advice given by Ōi and Hoshi. Briefly, they advised that success in the litigation movement could only be assured by acquiring the formal support of at least half of the region's 40,000 voting citizens.[47] The activists

45. Takahashi, *Fukushima jiken*, p. 125.
46. Shōji, *Nihon seisha*, p. 312. The organizers themselves claimed the figure was 4,083. Takahashi says it was about 3,400 (*Fukushima jiken*, p. 126).
47. Shōji, *Nihon seisha*, p. 306. Takahashi, *Fukushima jiken*, p. 126; Takahashi Tetsuo, *Fukushima jiyū minken undō shi* (Tokyo, 1954), pp. 108–9.

in attendance resolved to try to get the extra support of the 16,000 needed.

By the fourth organizational meeting, held on 8 October, again at Onomoto village in Kawanuma district, over 100 leaders were present, representing and holding the power of attorney of 5,792 Aizu voting residents, a gain of almost 1,800 in a little more than a week's time. Again it was resolved to continue the drive to recruit others to the movement, but in the meantime they decided that immediate action was necessary. First, Miura Bunji and Yamaguchi were to leave on 12 October for Tokyo to get further legal advice from Ōi Kentarō. Secondly, using what support they had already mustered, they would initiate a special type of lawsuit, a *kankai*, which would request of the Wakamatsu magistrate a ruling of arbitration on four points: (1) that the rule-making body for the Rengōkai and the election of its members were unfair; (2) that the course of the road was arbitrarily surveyed in disregard of centers of population; (3) that Mishima's refusal to reconvene the Rengōkai was improper; and (4) that action thus far taken by the authorities contravened the original resolutions adopted by the Rengōkai.[48]

This suit, soon after rejected on the grounds that the court was not competent to rule on the matter, was prompted by the increasingly repressive action taken by the authorities to break up the opposition movement—threats of expropriation of homes and property, public auctions of the protesters' household artifacts, summonses to appear before the local authorities for questioning, etc.[49]—and was therefore intended to serve as a "stopgap" measure against the government, and to demonstrate to the movement's supporters that action was being taken on their behalf. It was also hoped that this suit would serve to lessen the chances of capitulation by harassed farmers while the litigation committee continued to try to recruit the necessary number of signatures.

While this was the purpose of the suit for arbitration, the substance of the suit consisted of the central points made earlier in the third organizational meeting and incorporated in the Aizu activists' "Declaration of the Restoration of Rights." Besides the above-mentioned four points, the suit called for investing the Rengōkai with the necessary

---

48. Takahashi, *Fukushima jiken*, p. 127; Shimoyama, "Shōron," p. 180; Shōji, *Nihon seisha*, p. 311.

49. Takahashi, *Fukushima jiken*, p. 126. Nakajima's village, for instance, which was until then among the most active in opposing the road construction, capitulated to government threats and broke from the boycott.

authority to oversee the road construction. It was therefore not against the road as such but only opposed to "outside" control over it—that is, the suit was against the prefectural government's handling of the road. For this reason the Fukushima Incident is commonly regarded as one of the more dramatic episodes of the early rural peoples' fight for "the right of self-government" (*jichi kenri*).[50] Seen in this way, the "restoration of rights movement that developed in this region was connected with the fight for an autonomous governing body led by the Aizu branch of the Jiyūtō."[51] Local autonomy versus central control—it was a battle classic to most developing nations. The import of the conflict as regards the Japanese experience is neatly summarized by Kurt Steiner:

> A local government system that has grown up from below may emphasize the idea that the citizens of a community should be given the opportunity to realize their own interests within that community and that the state would exercise self-restraint for this purpose. A local government system imposed from above will put the interests of the state first, and will stress the duties, not the rights, of citizenship.[52]

This, certainly, is the fundamental issue raised by the "Declaration of the Restoration of Rights," seen equally clearly in the preface to the rules governing the litigation movement: "We who say we want to guarantee happiness and to regain rights for our members seek to achieve these goals through legal action aimed at reforming the government by simply putting a stop to the road construction."[53] On a more practical level, in order to achieve their goals they implemented resolutions that would fund the movement. Members were asked to contribute ten *sen* apiece (Resolution 5) to cover the costs of travel expenses for the litigation committee members (Resolution

---

50. The strongest proponent of this view is Shōji; see his commentary in *Nihon seisha*, pp. 306–9. Kano Masanao, *Nihon kindaika no shisō* (Tokyo, 1972), p. 116, also lends support to this view, saying, "The Fukushima Incident typically demonstrates the conflict between the local residents who favour self-government and the central government in the early Meiji period." He quotes Kōno Hironaka on self-government: "The decisions of town and village councils should reflect the views of their residents. If they express significant views in favour of local self-government, then whether they are different from those of the governor's or the central government's or not, the rights of local self-government must prevail" (pp. 117–18). Kano further argues that the fight for self-government in the Fukushima Incident is a continuation of the same fight that was begun in the Aizu *yonaoshi ikki* of 1868 (p. 113). Kōno Hironaka's speech notes on "decentralization" (*chihō bunken*) can be found in Shōji, *Nihon seisha*, pp. 206–8.

51. Shōji, *Nihon seisha*, p. 309.

52. Steiner, *Local Government*, p. 35.

53. Quoted in Shōji, *Nihon seisha*, p. 310.

6), and their lodging expenses (Resolution 6a). The organizational structure was also enlarged and made more efficient. Local village organs composed of one person per household and apportioned into ten-to-twenty-man units, who in turn selected a leader, were established as more efficient means to communicate information, to assign responsibilities, and to pressure collectively the local official in charge of road construction.[54] Through such organs they were also able to organize their tax boycott, which until then was largely limited to those villages where the more active of the regional Jiyūtō leaders resided.

Those villages where strong Jiyūtō leaders resided and often served as village heads (*kimoiri* or *kochō*), e.g., Shinai and Atsushio, were the same villages which sustained the tax boycott, despite threats and intimidation by the authorities, until the very end of the affair—until, that is, the mass arrests of late November and early December. Most such villages, it is important to add, were located in Yama district, which by October had become the center of opposition within the six districts of Aizu. By 20 October, in Yama district alone forty-two villages and 2,662 of their residents had handed over their power of attorney to the litigation movement. One week later, an additional 1,287 people of sixteen other villages in Yama had also signed up.[55] By mid-November, when many Yama residents were losing their property to government-enforced public auctions, only 132 of the several thousand involved had given in to governmental oppression.[56] In some villages, such as Miura Bunji's Atsushio, where 273 people were summoned to appear at government offices for "questioning," and where numerous others were losing their property to forced sales, none at all capitulated.[57]

Many others did, however. In mid-November, when property confiscation and police repression against boycotters was stepped up, many broke from the movement and promised either to comply with the corvée labor duty or to pay the substitute labor tax.[58] Among those who quit the movement were local Jiyūtō leaders Endō Naoyuki, Miura Shinroku, and Endō Shōzō, but only after they unsuc-

---

54. See Appendix B.
55. Kobayashi Seiji and Yamada Akira, *Fukushima-ken no rekishi* (Tokyo, 1973), p. 202.
56. Takahashi, *Fukushima jiken*, p. 142.
57. Ibid.
58. Takahashi, *Fukushima jiyū minken*, p. 109; and his *Fukushima jiken*, pp. 143–45. The first instance of the confiscation of a boycotter's property was recorded on 12 November. Akagi Heiroku of Shinai village (Yama district) had his household belongings seized and sold at public auction. Ninety-five others from the same village suffered a similar fate. The total number of households so affected was 578 in Yama district alone. Moreover, the

cessfully tried to reach a compromise with Mishima. Moreover, since many of the defectors were local village heads and therefore local men of influence, they were able to withdraw entire villages from the movement.

Such defections did not dampen the spirit of most activists. Several lawsuits against Mishima, and even against the Home Ministry, were carried on, meetings were called and speeches given in many villages, and most activists, as a result, remained loyal to the Restoration of Rights movement. Also, an outside force entered the fight to give added staying power to the movement: Belatedly, Jiyūtō members from the Fukushima branch of the Jiyūtō were coming to the rescue of Aizu people.

East-West Alliance

Despite the common party tie between the east and west branches, it is not surprising that the Fukushima branch stayed out of the Aizu conflict for so long. In the mid-to-late seventies, the predominant eastern popular rights societies served as patrons to the slower-organizing western society (the *Aishinsha*; see Chapter 4), but when in late 1881 the subject of consolidating into one prefectural branch party came up, Aizu residents opted to remain separate from their eastern brethren. Thereafter, each branch was regional in scope and in interest. This is easily seen in the fact that for the eastern branch the Aizu road struggle was only one among several of the charges cited against Mishima for misgovernment during the censure vote in May. In fact, that it was cited at all was largely due to the influence and insistence of Westerners in the largely eastern-dominated prefectural assembly, and to their friendship with Kōno Hironaka, rather than to the interest Easterners had in the affairs and problems of the Aizu party and the residents of the area. Most western assemblymen were not Jiyūtō members; only Uda, Nakajima, and Yamaguchi, and a few others stood as the proverbial lone voices of protest to represent their region's interest in a political wilderness dominated by eastern and prefecture-wide interests.

---

prices these household effects brought at public auctions was abysmally low. For example, a *tatami* mat sold for only three or four *sen*; a rain shutter for the same; a cupboard for five to six *sen*. The total sale price of all goods sold for all ninety-five households of Shinai was 799 *sen*, less than eight yen! In some cases, however, rich sympathizers were known to have purchased these confiscated goods and to have returned them to their former owners at sale price.

The estrangement of the west from the east stemmed in part from the earlier administrative division of the two regions. Less than a decade before, Aizu had been a separate prefecture with separate interests, and fought against amalgamation. Moreover, the Aizu Jiyūtō branch was organizationally autonomous from the Fukushima one, and its members differed substantially from the eastern members in terms of socioeconomic background. (See Chapter 3.)

In any event, with regard to the separate nature of the two branches vis-à-vis one another, the important points to make are these: First, "the disobedience campaign in Aizu was organized under the aegis of the Aizu Jiyūtō itself."[59] Secondly, the Fukushima branch did not lend a hand until less than a month before the Aizu movement was suppressed, and even during that last month, very few party men from Fukushima actually set foot in Aizu to lend aid. Thirdly, the separate quality of the relationship between the two branches is further attested by the earlier-mentioned instance of Aizu members going to Tokyo, and not to Fukushima, for legal counsel. Finally, of all the well-known eastern Jiyūtō leaders, only one, Tamano Hideaki, involved himself in the Aizu struggle before November, and then only by happenstance.[60] Prior to November, the eastern branch mainly directed its energies and attention toward Tokyo: It was too embroiled in the controversy surrounding Jiyūtō President Itagaki Taisuke's planned trip abroad to give the Aizu road problem much attention. In large part, this stemmed from the fact that Kōno Hironaka *qua* national party leader involved his branch in the Itagaki junket controversy, and himself spent most of October in Tokyo at the national party headquarters. When the Aizu problem was broached, Kōno was quoted as having responded on more than one occasion that it "ought not to be the main business of our party."[61] He gave as further reason not to involve himself, or his branch, the 1874 precedent of how Etō Shimpei, an early nationalist activist, and his followers in Saga were manipulated by similar circumstances into leading the ill-fated Saga Rebellion. Not until late October did Kōno and the *Mumeikan* of eastern Fukushima succumb to chance involvement.

On 17 October, Yamaguchi and Miura, who had been sent to Tokyo to seek additional legal advice from Ōi Kentarō, met there

59. Takahashi, *Fukushima jiken*, pp. 171–72.

60. Tamano had gone to Aizu in August in order to solicit funds for the recently established *Fukushima Jiyū Shimbun*, the prefectural party organ (Ibid., p. 172). In his 1954 work, *Fukushima jiyū minken*, Takahashi cites a slightly different reason (p. 101).

61. Takahashi, *Fukushima jiken*, p. 173.

with Kōno.[62] The two Aizu men requested of Kōno that he send eastern party activists to Aizu to lend a hand in the anti-road campaign. On 23 October, Kōno dispatched two of the more radical *Mumeikan* members, Satō Sumasu and Kamada Naozō, not because of the earlier request for help, but instead to investigate a rumor of Jiyūtō-provoked violence that supposedly took place on the twenty-first in Kitakata.[63] Kōno's two envoys reported back: "At this time, the people [of Aizu] have not yet reached the boiling point."[64] It was this seemingly insignificant non-event that served to open the doors for future involvement by the Fukushima branch into the Aizu conflict, for from this moment until the Kitakata incident on 28 November, the eastern branch became increasingly committed and receptive to pleas made by Aizu Jiyūtō leaders to assist them in the fight against the hastened tempo of governmental repression against the party. Moreover, the eastern commitment was strengthened once its own members fell prey to repression.

On 25 October, a meeting in Aizu between eastern and western Jiyūtō members was violently broken up by fifty or so Teiseitō members. On the evening of the same day, in Shinai village, Akagi's village, and the headquarters of the Restoration of Rights Movement, several tens of policemen under Ebina's command threatened eastern members Satō and Monna Shigejirō, who were acting as representatives for the villagers in a petition campaign. The same sort of incident occurred the next day as well, this time with another eastern Jiyūtō member, Kamada, also present. These confrontations, says Shimoyama Saburō, mark "the first time *Mumeikan* leaders directly participated in the litigation movement."[65] In terms of consequences, Kamada was arrested, and Satō barely escaped, only to return to the *Mumeikan* to report what had happened and to request that aid be given, prophetically remarking, "For our party, victory or defeat [in Aizu] will have great consequences."[66] Kōno's response to Satō's recommendation, however, cabled from Tokyo where he remained until 11 November, said the Aizu affair was not the business of the Fukushima branch, adding, "It might destroy our party."[67] In contrast, the *Fukushima Jiyū Shimbun* editorialized on 5 November,

62. Kobayashi and Yamada, *Fukushima rekishi*, p. 202.
63. Ibid.; Shimoyama, "Shōron," pp. 181–82.
64. Shimoyama, "Shōron," pp. 181–82.
65. Ibid., p. 183; Monna was from Wakamatsu.
66. Ibid.
67. Ibid., p. 184.

"The troubles in the Aizu region are not unimportant with regard to our Party's future growth."[68]

The Kitakata Incident

In Kōno's absence, opinion among *Mumeikan* members seemed to be siding with the "help Aizu" proponents.[69] On 9 November, Sugiyama Masagi, lawyer and later a Waseda University professor, and radical Sawada Kiyonosuke, signatory to a manifesto calling for the overthrow of the government,[70] were dispatched by *Mumeikan* leaders to Aizu. They were present when during the next few weeks the police began confiscating the property of the tax boycotters. They were also there when Jiyūtō activists Hara Heizō and Miura Bunji were arrested for "slander" on 19 November for having denounced the Yama district chief as a "criminal" for ordering the confiscation ("robbery") of the protesters' property. Reportedly, Sugiyama and Sawada were at least partly responsible for inciting a crowd of two thousand farmers, coming from villages recently raided by the police, to assemble on 23 November at the police station in Kitakata where Miura and Hara were being held. The reason for this illegal assembly was a rumor that the two Jiyūtō captives were going to be sent outside the district to Wakamatsu to be tried; only after the crowd received assurances from the Kitakata police that Miura and Hara would be tried in local court did it disperse.[71]

The arrest of these two men, and especially of Hara, became a *cause celèbre* among local activists and supporters. Leaders of the movement since the beginning and "defenders of the faith," their arrest aroused the anger of thousands of Aizu residents. It became even more intense the next day when it was learned that yet another Aizu Jiyūtō leader, Uda Seiichi, had been arrested. One of the early organizers of the anti-road movement, Uda was seized by policemen while on a recruitment drive in nearby Toyama prefecture.[72]

Uda's recruitment drive was not limited merely to Toyama. Before arriving there, Uda had toured much of the nation, giving speeches and meeting with Jiyūtō leaders in an effort to secure outside aid. It

68. Ibid.

69. Kobayashi and Yamada, *Fukushima rekishi*, p. 205.

70. See Chapter 4.

71. Kobayashi and Yamada, *Fukushima rekishi*, pp. 204–6; Takahashi, *Fukushima jiyū minken*, p. 112; Takahashi, *Fukushima jiken*, pp. 164–65; Shimoyama, "Shōron," p. 184.

72. Uda was accused of "fraud and extortion" (*sagi shuzai*), supposedly committed in the process of collecting contributions from supporters of the Restoration of Rights movement. He was later tried for sedition (Takahashi, *Fukushima jiken*, pp. 164–65, 197–98).

appears that his efforts were fruitful. In Gumma and Sendai, he received assurances that Jiyūtō organizations from those areas would send delegations to Aizu (several of whom were arrested; see Appendix B: Fukushima Activists). Around 18 November, after Kōno had returned to Fukushima from Tokyo, he and Uda engaged in several days of conversation, and as a result, Uda received a promise from Kōno that the eastern branch would commit itself to the Aizu struggle.[73]

Before any of these outside Jiyūtō groups could mobilize, however, certain events overtook them, as well as the Aizu protesters. The police took pre-emptory action, believing a rebellion of sorts was in the offing, and began arresting other Jiyūtō leaders. Between Uda's arrest and the Kitakata Incident on 28 November, another eleven Aizu Jiyūtō "ringleaders" were arrested for "assembling crowds for the purpose of rioting" (kyōto shūshūkyōsa),[74] presumably for their alleged participation in the 23 November disturbance in Kitakata. Ten other local Jiyūtō leaders, fearing arrest, fled. The situation, for both sides, was one of confusion and fear.

Against this backdrop of a largely leaderless Jiyūtō and a very apprehensive government, the Kitakata Incident occurred. The incident began to take shape on 26 November, two days before the event itself, at a meeting of Jiyūtō leaders and supporters held at the famous Chūzenji temple,[75] which is located in Tanaka hamlet of Shibage village, residence of Uda Seiichi. The purpose of the meeting was to consider what action should be taken in response to the arrest of Uda and the other Jiyūtō leaders. The principal speakers at the meeting were, besides Uda's father, Sugiyama Masagi and Satō Sumasu of eastern Fukushima, and Uryū Naoshi, a twenty-two-year-old Jiyūtō speechmaker and son of a headman of a Yama district village. The upshot of the opinion expressed by these men was that Uda was unjustly victimized for his efforts to contest the road project legally and was arrested on trumped-up charges. As most present shared this opinion, it was enthusiastically decided to gather as many supporters as possible and to march to the Kitakata police station where Uda was being held. According to an eyewitness account of the Chūzenji meeting, nothing was said or proposed about making the march a violent one; the purpose was reportedly to inquire about Uda's condition, to

73. Ibid., pp. 164–65; Kobayashi and Yamada, Fukushima rekishi, p. 206.
74. Fukushima-ken shi, 11, Kindai shiryō (Fukushima, 1964):482–83; Takahashi, Fukushima jiken, p. 165.
75. Chūzenji is a designated national treasure dating from the Kamakura period of the thirteenth century and visited by the author in 1971.

make sure that he would not be transferred to another jail outside the district, and, if possible, to demonstrate peacefully for his immediate release and that of Hara and Miura, who were also being held there.[76]

Independently, another group, this one from Ōnuma district, had arrived at a similar plan, and on 28 November, the two bodies of farmers met on the fields of Danjōgahara, located about five kilometers south of Kitakata. Estimates of the crowd's size vary from just over a thousand to 10,000, but the actual figure, the experts maintain, was probably closer to the former than to the latter.[77]

By the time all were assembled at Danjōgahara, it had been learned that Uda had already been transferred to Wakamatsu; the knowledge of this undoubtedly served to kindle the anger of the crowd. Sugiyama and Uryū addressed the crowd and, according to a police report, used inflammatory language: "Mishima's despotism is trampling over the rights of man."[78] The police also reported that Uryū urged the crowd to attack the police station in Kitakata and to free the Jiyūtō leaders being held.

From all accounts (other than police reports, although even these differ), it is unlikely that even if Uryū said such things, he really intended that the crowd attack the police station. For one thing, the crowd was not armed with weaponry of any sort; it was unlikely that they could or would risk their lives against well-armed policemen.[79] For another, even when the crowd did assemble in front of the police station, no one made any move to incite the crowd to storm the station. Even though they were unarmed, however, they probably could have overcome the fifteen or so police occupying and defending the station, but as mentioned, only at the risk of suffering many casualties. The most offensive action the crowd took during the twenty or so minutes they were assembled there was to shout words of abuse at the police, until, that is, someone threw several stones and broke several station-house windows, although even here it has been alleged by several historians that a police spy (agent provocateur) was responsible.[80] When this happened, three sword-swinging policemen charged the crowd, killing one, seriously injuring three, and arresting four. No police were injured. The crowd then immediately dispersed in flight,

76. Takahashi, *Fukushima jiken*, pp. 166–70, 177.

77. The official Party history says "a thousand several hundred"; police figures varied from a thousand to 10,000. See Takahashi, *Fukushima jiken*, p. 177.

78. Quoted in ibid., p. 178.

79. Ibid., pp. 179–83.   80. Ibid., p. 180.

and the "revolutionary riot and attack" (*kakumeiteki na kyōto shū-geki*), as the Kitakata incident was later termed by the police, came abruptly to an end.

If the Kitakata Incident can properly be regarded as the denouement of the movement, then the wholesale arrests which followed in its wake can be regarded as the climax of the Fukushima Incident. Until late December, the police embarked upon a massive arrest campaign against Jiyūtō members, supporters, and leaders, and many innocent farmers whose only crime was to have given support to the litigation movement. Throughout the entire prefecture, close to two thousand were arrested; some were later victims of torture while awaiting trial; and fifty-seven were sent to Tokyo to stand trial for the crime of sedition.

Since these post-Kitakata events were clearly an instance of government using a minor disturbance as a pretext for major repression, they will be discussed in detail in the last chapter, where the consequences of the *gekka jiken* and the government's reactions to them are treated.

The Kabasan Incident

Around eleven o'clock on the rainy Tuesday morning of 23 September 1884, a solitary mountain priest of Mount Kaba, Makabe district, Ibaraki prefecture, discovered that his mountaintop retreat had been occupied by an armed force. He sent this message to the police substation at Machiya, a small village at the base of Mount Kaba:

> Fifteen or sixteen men calling themselves Jiyūtō members, armed with various weapons, and bombs too, I believe, have assembled atop Mount Kaba, near Nagoaka village, Makabe district.[81]

Of all reports, newspaper and government, subsequently issued about the Kabasan rebels, this one by the priest, despite its brevity, was most accurate. The rebels in fact numbered sixteen; they were heavily armed with swords, a few guns, and about 150 homemade bombs; and if the several banners they raised atop Mount Kaba were a fair indication, then indeed they were Jiyūtō members. The banners read: "Charge Ahead for Freedom," "Overthrow the Oppressive Government," "Die for Patriotism," and "Friends of Freedom and Liber-

81. Quoted in Endō Shizuo, *Kabasan jiken* (Tokyo, 1971), p. 200. Another account has the priest sending this message at 5:00 P.M. See *Kabasan jiken kankei shiryō shū*, comp. Inaba Seitarō, with an introduction by Tōyama Shigeki and an afterword by Endō Shizuo (Tokyo, 1970), p. 766. (Hereafter cited as *KJKS.*)

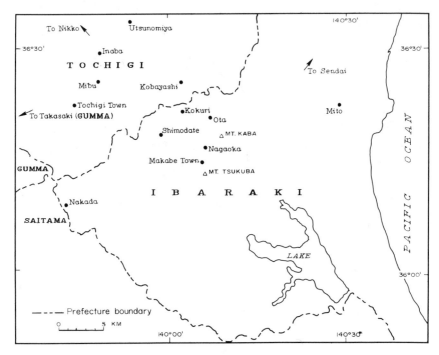

Map 3.   The Kabasan Area of Ibaraki and Tochigi Prefectures

alism."[82] The next day, as if to make their intentions and the identity of their group clearly known, the rebels hoisted yet another banner, reading "Headquarters of the Kabasan Revolutionary Party." They could also be heard singing the "Song of American Independence" (*Beikoku dokuritsu no uta*).[83]

The rebels were at Mount Kaba awaiting news about the scheduling of a ceremony to mark the opening of new government buildings at nearby Utsunomiya (Tochigi prefecture). On the day of the ceremony, they intended to assassinate the many highly-placed Ministers of State who were scheduled to be in attendance, to attack the prison there and release its inmates, and to lead these men and other local residents on a march against the central government in Tokyo. However, when they learned that the authorities were already aware of

82. Taoka Reiun (pseud.), *Meiji hanshin den* (Tokyo, 1953; originally published in 1909), p. 72; Wagatsuma Sakae et al., comps., *Nihon seiji saiban shi roku* 2 (Tokyo, 1969):48; Endō, *Kabasan jiken*, p. 201.

83. Itagaki Taisuke, *Jiyūtō shi* (Tokyo, 1973; originally published in 1913), III:54.

their existence and possibly of their plans as well, they decided to alter their original plans and take the immediate action of raising an army from the residents in the area. To this end, on 23 September, they raised their several banners calling for the revolution, wrote and distributed revolutionary manifestoes to Kabasan area residents, and launched an attack upon the nearby Machiya police substation, all done in order to demonstrate to the local populace the seriousness of their intentions. The rebels also attacked and robbed the wealthier residents of the area (to whom "receipts" were given for the money and merchandise taken) in order to secure arms, food, and money to meet their own needs and the needs of the embryo army of locals they expected to attract.

In reaction to these raids, several scores of policemen were sent to Kabasan. Their appearance forced the rebels to retreat back to the mountaintop, and also prevented some 100 to 200 local residents from joining the rebels. Isolated atop the mountain, troubled by a diminishing water supply, and frustrated by plans gone awry, on 24 September the rebels decided to fight their way through the police lines and head toward Utsunomiya, though to what purpose it is unclear, for they knew they would not find any of their assassination targets there. En route to Utsunomiya, by nightfall they had reached the rice fields of Nagaoka village. There they were forced to engage in a battle with about twenty police. Using their bombs, they killed one, injured four, and lost one of their own men. Also, during the confusion of the fight they had to abandon almost 100 bombs. Confronted with death and the loss of much of their weaponry, and fearing more police ahead, they backtracked towards Kabasan.

On 25 September, as they headed northwest from Kabasan toward Ōta village, they were being pursued not only by the combined police units from four villages in the Makabe district, but also by a squad of Imperial troops and ten metropolitan police earlier sent from Tokyo. Despite their fear of being overtaken by the authorities, on the twenty-sixth, around 1:00 A.M., they attacked two homes of wealthy citizens of Kokuri village (Makabe district). From there the rebels crossed into the mountainous district of Haga in Tochigi, where after dividing their money and weapons equally, they made camp at Kobayashi village and discussed their uncertain future. Finally, after protestations by several, and suggestions of mass suicide by others, they agreed to disband and to regroup in one month's time in Tokyo. However, before the month was over, all but two of them had been captured and placed under arrest. By February 1885, the other two had also been caught.

Thus ended the Kabasan Incident, the first instance in the Meiji period in which bombs had been used, and for revolutionary purposes.[84]

Interpretations

Several specialists on the Fukushima Incident believe that the Kabasan Incident of September 1884 marks the true ending of the Fukushima Incident. Their reasons for adopting such a view are not difficult to understand. First, of the principal Kabasan rebels (including several who did not climb the mountain, but who joined in the planning), eight of the twenty or so had been arrested for their participation in the Fukushima Incident, and another four Kabasan rebels were residents of Fukushima. Secondly, one of their principal targets of assassination was none other than the "Devil Governor" himself, Mishima Michitsune, who since 30 October 1883 had been serving simultaneously as Governor of Fukushima and of Tochigi, and therefore was to serve as host to the gathering of Tokyo officials at Utsunomiya.[85] As several have pointed out, "had there been no Mishima, there probably would never have been a Kabasan Incident."[86] In other words, for the Fukushima participants in the Kabasan Incident at least, the attack on Utsunomiya was a means to avenge the earlier repression they and the Fukushima Jiyūtō had suffered under Mishima during 1882. In this view, Mishima was a catalytic agent personified. Finally, during their trials several of the Kabasan rebels coming from Fukushima state unequivocally that their involvement stemmed from a hatred of Mishima.

Although there is good reason to accord credence to this view, at the same time there also exists reason enough not to accept this interpretation of revenge in its entirety. This view by itself does not, for instance, explain why those rebels coming from Ibaraki, Ishikawa,

---

84. For example, see Takahashi, *Fukushima jiken*. Also see *KJKS*, p. 773, for a review by Endō on how various specialists treat the dates for the beginning and end of the incident.

85. His dual appointment was intended to ensure that the Three Roads project, begun earlier in Fukushima and Yamagata, would be successfully extended into Tochigi perfecture. For the adverse reaction of the Tochigi prefectural assembly to Mishima's high-handed tactics in that prefecture, see Kenneth Strong, "Tanaka Shōzō: Meiji Hero and Pioneer Against Pollution," *Japan Society of London Bulletin* 2:14 (June 1972):6–11, especially page 8; and a more detailed report, Akagi Etsuko, "Tochigi ken no jiyū minken undo: chihō jichi no yōso wo megutte," *Tochigi Shiron*, 2 (1970):1–15.

86. For example, see Endō, *Kabasan jiken*, p. 15.

Aichi, and perhaps even Tochigi decided to join. Nor does it explain why several of the Fukushima participants during their court trials failed to cite revenge against Mishima as an important reason for participating. The revenge thesis also fails to take into account ideological beliefs as motivating forces which, as we shall see in Chapter 4, were much too strongly felt to be ignored. Finally, the single-factor interpretation of revenge does not even begin to explain the substantially different nature of the Kabasan rebellion in terms of the tactics, targets, and goals of participants. The Fukushima Incident may, then, be regarded as a starting point in the development of the Kabasan, perhaps even as one cause, but the fact remains that the Kabasan Incident was historically an event in itself. One final observation: Revenge against Mishima might have very well provoked the Kabasan rebels to act initially, but in the process of planning the assassination of Mishima they broadened their objective to include high-ranking government officials of the central government. Planning lasted over a year, and in the process the initial reason for involvement came to be less important to the conspirators than their ultimate goal, revolution. In the process, the Kabasan rebels appear to have experienced some change in political consciousness; this generalization applies to those coming from Fukushima prefecture as well as other areas.

Before looking at the development of the incident, it is necessary to first explain what is meant by development. In a small-scale conspiratorial plot such as the Kabasan Incident, development refers to recruitment, the process by which individuals and small groups come to know one another sufficiently to exchange confidences about ideas and plans that would conventionally be regarded as treasonable. As we shall see, from early 1883 until 23 September 1884, almost all of the twenty or so rebels lived alienating lives of intrigue, plotting, and conspiracy. Although each, it seems, determined for himself that revolution was essential, each of them also knew that alone he was unable to effect revolution. Hence, each realized the importance of finding others who shared this belief, and more importantly, who were willing to act upon it. This process whereby each found "like-minded" men (dōshi) constitutes the development of the incident. More than in either of the other two incidents, men rather than events form the core of the Kabasan Incident. The Kabasan rebels sought to make events, rather than to react to them.

Recruitment was of a particular kind. First, since most of the rebels were committed to assassination, recruitment was necessarily highly exclusive, as this type of adventure appealed only to very few. Status or social standing was not a criterion in choosing comrades. As one of the rebels phrased it, "From the outset, we did not place any importance on recruiting important personages (*meibōka*) to join our illegal rebellion."[87] Secondly, the nature of recruitment was very informal and secretive. A constant fear of police spies infiltrating their group, which as we shall see probably did happen, caused the rebels to exercise extreme caution in discussing their plans. Only those people known to hold strong anti-government views, and who attended illegal party meetings, were privy to the conspiracy. Monna Shigejirō, for example, testified on 10 November to the question:

Q: What methods were used to bring the comrades together?
A: Mine and others' were to speak only with those [interested in] this topic, and also to keep our ears open to bits and pieces [of information] coming from a wide variety of people at meetings of comrades. But as far as special methods, I say there were none.[88]

Finally, if we can believe the rebels' testimony in court and police interrogations, then for each rebel there is a somewhat different version of how they became involved. In reconstructing the chain of events, the few secondary sources—contemporary to the incident as well as present-day—are of little help in sorting things out. In these works, too much emphasis is placed on personalities, ideology, or "terrorist" tactics,[89] and too little on the intricacies of involvement. However, from a careful reading of the rebels' stories as told to the police and prosecutors, the process of recruitment can be pieced together. The stories told by all of the participants, except for one,[90] are characterized by forthrightness and apparent honesty, even to the extent that they earned seven of them the death penalty. This will be discussed further in the last chapter.

This said, we now move on to look at the development of the incident.

87. Testimony given on 8 November 1884; *KJKS*, p. 25. (Hereafter, unless stated otherwise in the text or in the footnote, all references to *KJKS* should be understood as official police interrogation, court testimony, or official documents of one sort or the other.)
88. *KJKS*, p. 19.
89. Endō is one who has attached the terms *terrorist* and *terrorism* to the rebels and their activities. For an ideological treatment of the rebels' ideology, see Hayashi Motoi, "Kabasan jiken nanajū shūnen," *Rekishi Hyōron* 59 (January 1955):54–61.
90. At the end of each defendant's testimony, he was given a chance to amend earlier statements. Most took advantage of this, possibly to avoid perjury; Tomimatsu rarely did. But besides this, he lied about knowing several close acquaintances.

Strategy and Recruitment

It will be remembered that during October 1882, as the leaders of the Fukushima Incident were turning greater attention to litigation as a means to fight Mishima, Monna Shigejirō, ex-policeman, Wakamatsu *shizoku*, and member of the litigation committee, was sent to Tokyo to seek further legal counsel from Ōi Kentarō. After the Kitakata incident of 28 November, Monna was arrested and in April 1883 was sent to Tokyo to stand trial for the crime of sedition. Acquitted of this crime, he sought to make Mishima pay for his arrest and imprisonment (and probably torture; see Chapter 5). Hence, in July, along with Jiyūtō activists Hara Heizō and Saji Kyomatsu, Monna went to Sendai, obtained a lawyer named Maezawa, and "called on a member of the appeals court (*Kōso Saibanjo*) in order to bring legal action against the unfair treatment suffered because of the Fukushima governor."[91] Unsuccessful there, he and his companions went to the Wakamatsu courts for the same purpose; but this time not only did he not have a chance to pursue his lawsuit, but as a result of trying was sought for the crime of "slandering a public official" (namely, Mishima). To escape arrest, Monna fled to Tokyo and went into hiding for three months. While there he met a number of Jiyūtō radicals, two of whom, Kōno Hiroshi (or Hiromi), nephew of Kōno Hironaka and also recently acquitted of treason, and Yokoyama Nobuyuki, ex-policeman and son of a low-ranking samurai of old Aizu *han*, were to join him later in the Kabasan Incident.

The content of the discussions held in Tokyo between Monna, Kōno, and Yokoyama during the winter of 1883–84 are of some importance in understanding subsequent events. By this time all three of these young Fukushima men, aged twenty-three, nineteen, and twenty-one respectively, had abandoned any notion of bringing about political reform by peaceful means and had concluded that only violence offered any hope of effecting democratic changes in the Japanese government. This common understanding gave them, and the others who were to join them later, the necessary basis to arrive at a plan for revolution. But at the same time, they disagreed on what type of violent strategy to employ. This disagreement proved to be an ongoing one, lasting until shortly before the rebellion itself, and determined to some extent exactly who would be among the sixteen men who climbed Mount Kaba on 23 September.

91. *KJKS*, p. 15.

The disagreement revolved around the distinction made by the rebels between *shō-undō* or "small movement" and *dai-undō* or "large movement." The strategy of "small movement," otherwise called "assassinationism" (*ansatsushugi*) by the rebels, and supported by Kōno and Yokoyama, held that "five men, perhaps ten men, having the same beliefs and aiding one another, could carry out assassination; in other words, a small movement." By "large movement," again quoting Kōno Hiroshi's courtroom testimony, its advocate Monna meant "getting a large number of like-thinking men from all over the country to meet in Tokyo and overthrow the government; in other words, a large movement."[92] To the rebels, this was also known as "raising-an-army-ism" (*kyoheishugi*). How many men were needed to comprise a large movement was suggested by one of the early plotters who withdrew from the rebellion because of disagreement over this issue of strategy. Ōhashi Genzaburō said during police questioning:

> To carry out the revolution (*kakumei*), 300 comrades would be sufficient to go to Tokyo and effect the overthrow. Using dynamite, probably 100 men would be enough to assassinate officials. *But the proper time to carry this out has not yet arrived* (emphasis added).[93]

According to Kōno, those advocating a "large movement" wanted "to wait three years to start the revolution."[94] Kōno, Yokoyama, and most of the others argued that it was not necessary to wait for the "proper time," that it was in their power to create the "proper time" by large-scale assassination of high-ranking government officials:

> To discuss [this issue of tactics] is senseless. To establish a constitutional system based on the rights of the people, it is necessary to overthrow the despotic government. To overthrow a despotic government, we cannot count on the remote possibility of such things as raising a prefecture-wide army. It is a far-fetched idea because we lack sufficient funds. Hence, instead we strike one blow aimed at the *genrō* ["senior statesmen"] of the government. This done, having lost its leaders ["head"], the government ["body"] will naturally fall.[95]

This problem of the best strategy to employ to overthrow the government resurfaced continually, even up until the day of the rebellion itself. Although more about the implications of this debate will be discussed in Chapter 4, for the present let it suffice to make three points: (1) a strong majority of the Kabasan rebels favored "assassina-

---

92. Ibid., p. 244.   93. Ibid., p. 120.   94. Ibid., 345.
95. Quoted in Taoka, *Hanshin den*, p. 59. The last sentence of this quote also appears in Hirano Yoshitarō, *Ōi Kentarō* (Tokyo, 1960), p. 84.

tionism" more or less consistently; (2) "more than half of the assassination faction had been connected with the Fukushima Incident";[96] and (3) even those against a "small movement" usually believed that once the assassinations were accomplished, either by design or by chance, an anti-government army would rise up. In any event, it is important to emphasize that regardless of which strategy a Kabasan conspirator advocated, he shared with the others the goal of overthrowing the government, and it was this that allowed him to cooperate with the others.

Through Yokoyama, Kōno and Monna became better acquainted with Yokoyama's patron, Koinuma Kuhachirō, the "fatherly master of the assassination faction,"[97] or as another contemporary called him, "friend to the commoners (heimin)."[98] Although less famous politically than the man whom the government mistakenly assumed was the real leader of the Kabasan rebels, Tomimatsu Masayasu, Koinuma was in fact the prime mover and organizer of the rebels until less than two weeks before the incident, when an accidental explosion of a bomb he was making cost him his left arm. Koinuma was thirty-two years old in 1884, was himself a commoner from Tochigi prefecture, and was the unsuccessful third son of a wealthy merchant/ farmer family. It is recorded that from the time he was a child, he was attracted to new types of mechanical devices,[99] a fact which might explain his ability to make bombs. This art, which he later taught to several of the other rebels, made him the likely leader of those who had opted for assassination.

Koinuma's radical tendencies are first known to have been expressed in January 1883, during a meeting of around 300 Kantō Jiyūtō members held in Tochigi Town. During the meeting, the purpose of which was to discuss what consequences the Fukushima Incident had on the growth and solidarity of the Party, Koinuma met privately with five other members who were well known for their radical ideas: Arai Shōgo, village head, secretary of the Tochigi Jiyūtō branch, magazine publisher, and intellectual;[100] Shiota Okuzō, a Jiyūtō prefectural assemblyman; Sakagihara Keibu, lawyer and brother-

96. Taoka, hanshin den, p. 60.

97. Endō, Kabasan jiken, p. 29, referring to Taoka's characterization.

98. Nojima Kitarō, Kabasan jiken (Tokyo, 1900), p. 23.

99. Nojima, Kabasan jiken, pp. 33-36.

100. Arai's wife was the daughter of Etō Shimpei, the leader of the Saga Rebellion of February 1874 who was beheaded for his crime. See Wayne C. McWilliams, "Etō Shimpei and the Saga Rebellion, 1874," paper delivered at the Association for Asian Studies Conference, Toronto, 21 March 1976.

in-law to Monna; Koinuma's "client" (*kobun*), Yokoyama; and Fukao Shigeki, a party member who was later accused of being a police spy.[101] All except Fukao were subsequently arrested for complicity in the Kabasan Incident.

What these men discussed with Koinuma still remains unknown to-day; but at another such secret meeting, held this time in Tokyo on 23 November 1883 at an Asuka-yama *ryokan* (hotel), it is known that about 100 young Jiyūtō members met "to discuss what *shishi* ['patri-ots'] should be doing."[102] One source claims that it was here that Koinuma met Ibaraki Jiyūtō leader Tomimatsu Masayasu, Kōno Hiro-shi, and others later involved in the incident.[103] Another source claims that at this meeting Koinuma first discussed with these men his intention to assassinate high government officials.[104] Koinuma him-self said that at this meeting he met Kōno and Miura Bunji through Kotoda Iwamatsu, another Kabasan rebel, and that they then began plotting the assassination.[105] But whatever the specific content of the discussion, it is likely that some talk of assassination did take place, for immediately after this meeting Koinuma began making bombs at his home in Inaba village.

Also at this meeting in Tokyo, Koinuma probably was introduced to Amano Ichitarō, nineteen-year-old *shizoku* who participated in the Fukushima Incident, and Yamaguchi Moritarō, eighteen years old and also a *shizoku* from Fukushima. Less than a month after the To-kyo meeting, these two youths went with Koinuma to Tochigi Town to spy upon, and to investigate the routine of, the newly-appointed governor Mishima Michitsune, whom they had chosen as a target for assassination. One source states that their journey was more than a mere scouting patrol, that they actually intended to assassinate Mishima then, but that they deferred because of respect for the Em-peror, who was visiting Tochigi at the time.[106]

Probably independently of this attempt, around January 1884, Kōno and Fukushima allies Kotoda Iwamatsu and Kusano Sakuma pledged to kill Mishima.[107] Kōno himself claimed during his court-

101. Endō, *Kabasan jiken*, p. 36; Nojima, *Kabasan jiken*, pp. 42–46, for a discussion about the contents of this meeting.
102. Endō, *Kabasan jiken*, p. 54.
103. Wagatsuma et al., *Seiji saiban shi* II:45.
104. *KJKS*, p. 764 (Afterword by Endō Shizuo).
105. *KJKS*, p. 102.
106. Taoka, *Hanshin den*, p. 45.
107. Itagaki, *Jiyūtō shi* III:44.

room testimony that "it was late last year [1883] or early this year that we first discussed [using bombs to assassinate government officials]."[108] But the "we" in Kōno's testimony refers not to Kusano and Kotoda, as the authors of the *Jiyūtō-shi* claim, but to "Yokoyama, Sugiura, and Saeki." Quite possibly both sources are correct to the extent that each refers to a different episode involving Kōno, for clearly several plots were in the making by this time. For instance, Kusano had already been recruited by fellow Fukushima activist Miura Bunji in mid-1883 for involvement in a plan to assassinate Mishima,[109] along with Amano, Yamaguchi, and Kokugi. And, as we have already seen, Yamaguchi and Amano by this time were assisting Koinuma in his own plot to kill Mishima. Hence, besides Kōno's scheming, at least two separate plots to assassinate Mishima, one by Koinuma and another by Miura, with overlapping membership, had been hatched in late 1883. The similarities in timing and in membership of the two plots lead us to believe that the two groups were probably in contact with each other by then. Moreover, Tomimatsu Masayasu, who was to assume leadership of the incident after Koinuma's accident, had by 23 November 1883 been alerted at least to Koinuma's plot, and probably was therefore not at all surprised when he was approached in mid-September for assistance.

The intricacies of recruitment thus far mentioned can be simplified. On the one hand, there was Koinuma's group: Amano, Yamaguchi, Kōno, and Yokoyama by late 1883; by late 1884, Saeki Masakado, Sugiura Kippuku, Kobayashi Tokutarō, and Isokawa Motoyoshi had learned through Kusano of Koinuma's intentions and had joined him.[110] All nine of these men, like their leader, Koinuma, were committed to "assassinationism."

More or less simultaneously to Koinuma's recruitment of this group, Miura Bunji, one of the principal activists in the Fukushima Incident, was assembling his own group, also committed to "assassinationism." Kokugi, Kusano, and Hara Rihachi, farmer and commoner from Fukushima, were its main "members"; Yamaguchi and

108. *KJKS*, p. 235.

109. Miura's testimony, *KJKS*, p. 29. Miura, you will recall, was a leader of the Restoration of Rights movement in Fukushima; he was later tried for treason.

110. *KJKS*, p. 46. After May 1884, Koinuma also entered into discussions with a number of radical Jiyūtō members who favored the "large movement" strategy. Among them were Ōhashi Genzaburō, Iwamoto Shinkichi, Tateno Yoshinosuke, Arai Shōgo, Shida Okuzō, and Sakagihara Keibu. Though several were later implicated and even imprisoned, none of them joined the actual rebellion.

Amano, whom Miura shared with Koinuma, made up the rest of Miura's group.

Besides the twelve thus far mentioned, four others eventually climbed Mount Kaba on 23 September.[111] From Ibaraki came Tomimatsu, former school teacher and head of an Academy for young Jiyūtō radicals located in Shimodate; his bodyguard and fencing instructor at the academy, Tamamatsu Kaichi; and one of the academy's students, Hotta Komakichi. The fourth was Koinuma's fellow Tochigi resident and Jiyūtō ideologue, Hirao Yasokichi, the only one of all sixteen to be killed in battle. The involvement of these men stemmed from either their personal contact with Tomimatsu, or from the contact they made with members of Koinuma's or Miura's group at a Tokyo Jiyūtō youth academy. (See Chapter 4.) As we shall soon see, the beginnings of their participation in the planning of the incident are dated around mid- to late-August.

Planning the Revolution

Not until about that time did the Kabasan rebels settle upon a concrete plan of action. It could hardly have been otherwise. Until then "recruitment" consisted mainly of individuals and small groups discovering the identity of others who shared a more-or-less vaguely expressed *intent* to reform the government and a more-or-less precisely expressed belief in eliminating the more obtrusive of the government's leaders as the most efficient means to effect reform. But as Koinuma became the hub of this underground movement, the focus of the rebel's enmity became, contradictorily, both sharper and duller. From the initial plans to assassinate only Mishima, they changed to include all high government officials. And since it was in the capital that all the important officials resided, the rebels moved from Koinuma's home in Tochigi, where most of the bomb-making and discussions between his group and Miura's had taken place since January, to Tokyo. From early summer until shortly before the *jiken* itself, most of the action takes place in Tokyo.

The center of activity in Tokyo was Kōno Hiroshi's apartment located on the third floor of a boardinghouse (*geshuku*) in the Nihonbashi district, and owned by Jiyūtō sympathizer Iizuka Denjirō.[112]

111. Actually, thirteen names have been mentioned, but Saeki, who was involved from the beginning, withdrew several days before the incident.

112. *KJKS*, p. 102; during a later testimony, Koinuma stressed that Iizuka was not involved in the planning sessions (*KJKS*, p. 108). Also see the 2 October 1884 interrogation of Sugiura (*KJKS*, p. 191), where he implicates Iizuka as "an intimate friend of Koinuma."

According to Koinuma, at Kōno's apartment in early July, he, Kōno, Yokoyama, Saeki, and Sugiura began planning to assassinate government officials.[113] The occasion was to be the 19 July ceremony welcoming the new nobility into the Peers (*Kazoku*), to be held at the Enryōkan, and to be attended, according to a newspaper report from which the five rebels took their information, by over 100 high government officials, including such notables as Itō Hirobumi and the recently appointed (12 December 1883) Home Minister, Yamagata Aritomo.[114] As Koinuma lectured his co-conspirators, this was their chance to emulate the Russian nihilists, to "bring about the revolution by assassinating ministers of state."[115] But as in the September incident, bad planning and bad luck prevented them from carrying out their plan. In the matter of bad planning, although Koinuma had been making bombs at least since January, he had not yet tested any, nor perhaps had he yet obtained all the necessary ingredients to make them effective. This is indicated by a number of large purchases made just before the day the ceremony was scheduled—2,500 pieces of iron shot bought in Tokyo on 19 July, and 120 tin tea containers (*chazutsu*) on 18 July, also in Tokyo—and by the bomb-testing sessions carried out by Koinuma and Kōno in Ishikawa district (Fukushima) on 29 July, and in Kamitsuga district (Tochigi) as late as 21 August. In the second instance, "bad luck" apparently hurt their plans, since the government postponed indefinitely (as it did with the Utsunomiya ceremony in September) the Enryōkan ceremony.[116]

The decision to carry out the Enryōkan assassination attempt was not made until 13 July, a bare three days after a meeting of Jiyūtō radicals—including Koinuma, Sugiura, Kōno, and a number of Tomimatsu followers as well—was held at an inn on Mount Tsukuba, Ibaraki prefecture, from 9 to 11 July. The meeting was supposed to be attended by radicals from Ibaraki, Tochigi, Fukushima, Saitama, and Gumma in order to, according to one account contemporary to this period, "together select the vanguard of the revolution."[117] How many attended is not known, but it is known that the Saitama and

113. *KJKS*, p. 112.

114. The peerage system had just been settled by law on 7 July 1884. See Nojima, *Kabasan jiken*, p. 158.

115. *KJKS*, p. 112 (Koinuma); p. 191 (Sugiura); pp. 235–36, 243 (Kōno); p. 22 (Yokoyama); and p. 258 (Saeki).

116. Further details can be found in Endō, *Kabasan jiken*, pp. 153–56; Taoka, *Hanshin den*, p. 61; Wagatsuma et al., *Seiji saiban shi* II:47; Nojima, *Kabasan jiken*, pp. 156–59; and Itagaki, *Jiyūtō shi* III:45.

117. Sekido Kakuzō, *Tōsui minken shi* (Shimodate, 1907), quoted in Wagatsuma et al., *Seiji saiban shi* II:46.

Gumma Jiyūtō branches failed to send delegates.[118] The meeting discussed the implications that the Gumma Incident (May 1884) had for the possibility of starting the revolution. Koinuma and his supporters argued that the failure of the Gumma Jiyūtō radicals to transform the incident's participants into an "army" proved the practical emptiness of the "large movement" strategy, and that accordingly "assassinationism" must be tried. The other faction,[119] however, primarily followers of Ōi Kentarō (who was lecturing in the Kansai region at the time), proposed organizing an advance guard composed of Tōhoku (Northeastern) patriots so that "when the moment of imminence comes, we will be ready to rally groups of Tōhoku shishi, who will come [to Kantō] as the pioneers of the revolutionary army (kakumei gun no semben)."[120] This faction also argued that their immediate concern, as a preparatory step to raising the army, should be party reform, centered around the creation of a new radical leadership. They maintained, "Reform of the Jiyūtō headquarters [leadership] and political revolution are complementary."[121] This group's position, though hurt because of Ōi's absence, appears to have carried the meeting, because Koinuma and his followers left it complaining that the meeting had failed to arrive at any concrete plan of action.[122] Given this, it seems fair to assume that Koinuma's plans to assassinate government officials at the 19 July Enryōkan meeting stemmed from the frustration and impatience he suffered because of the Tsukuba meeting.

Despite the Enryōkan disappointment, Koinuma's hopes rose momentarily when in mid-August he learned of a wide-scale disturbance at Hachiōji, beginning on 10 August and organized by local Jiyūtō and Komminto (Poor Peoples' Party) leaders. Perhaps this indicates that Koinuma was coming around to the "large movement" strategy, or perhaps he was just looking to recruit other comrades for a "small movement"; but in any event he sent Hirao, Isokawa, and Kobayashi to speak with leaders of the Hachiōji rising. Several days later, Koinuma's emissaries returned to report: "They were unable to understand our purposes at all. They are lacking in principles, in spirit, and in will, and were unwilling to discuss the matter seriously."[123] Again disappointed, he bided his time by testing his bombs.

118. Endō, Kabasan jiken, p. 149.
119. This faction has been called the "cautious faction" (shinchōba) as opposed to Koinuma's "decisive action faction" (kekkōba); Wagatsuma et al., Seiji saiban shi, pp. 46–47.
120. Quoted in Endō, Kabasan jiken, p. 151.   121. Ibid.
122. Nojima, Kabasan jiken, p. 153.
123. Endō, Kabasan jiken, p. 157–58.

Finally, good news arrived. On 20 August, the newspapers reported that on 15 September, a ceremony to inaugurate the relocation of the Tochigi capital to Utsunomiya would be attended by many high-ranking government officials from Tokyo; the host of the event, the papers also noted, would be Mishima Michitsune. The Kabasan rebels regarded this as "one chance in a thousand."[124]

Beginning of the End

Koinuma immediately arranged for all the bomb materials they had been buying, collecting, and hiding in Tokyo to be sent to his home in Tochigi. He also sent Sugiura, traveling under a false identity, to Utsunomiya to verify whether the newspaper reports were accurate, and he further called for his comrades to meet at Kōno's Tokyo apartment on 1 September. Assembling there to plan the attack on Utsunomiya were Koinuma, Kōno, Sugiura, Kotoda, Yamaguchi, Amano, Hirao, and Isokawa. As the official Party history has it, "There they united in a revolutionary alliance (*kakumei dōmei*)."[125] But, as it will be noticed, only half of the sixteen men who ascended Mount Kaba were at this time part of the "revolutionary alliance." In fact, as Kobayashi later points out in his court testimony, "The assembling of all seventeen [*sic*] and the mutual decision on our plan by all seventeen [*sic*] was not completed until 21 or 22 September. Before then the plan had only been discussed in small groups of five or ten."[126] At any rate, after the eight men vowed in Tokyo to begin preparing for the 15 September assassination plot, Koinuma left for his home in Tochigi to begin his own planning.

Now confronted with what almost certainly was the perfect opportunity to overthrow the government, Koinuma began to come around to the idea of raising an army. When he returned to Tochigi, he entered into discussions with a number of Jiyūtō radicals known for their support of the "large movement" strategy. In his own words, on 3 or 4 September he spoke with Ōhashi Genzaburō about "how the Jiyūtō could aid the ordinary people (*ippan jimmin*), . . . and together concluded that we must summon our energies to effect a revolution or die in the process (*kesshi kakumei*). . . . I told him of the plot to assassinate government Ministers. . . . We subsequently made a compact: Revolution or Death."[127] As a result of this compact,

124. Taoka, *Hanshin den*, p. 62.
125. Itagaki, *Jiyūtō shi* III:45; the *Seiji saiban shi* claims that they met at Koinuma's home in Tochigi on 1 September; the compilers of the *KJKS* say Tokyo.
126. *KJKS*, p. 455.   127. Ibid., p. 103.

Ōhashi opened his home to bomb-makers Kusano and Isokawa. Secondly, Koinuma approached the local "strong man" (*kyōkaku* or "Robin Hood"), Kumakutsu Torashi, about gaining help from him and his many followers who were miners at the Ashio copper mine, hoping to raise an army once the assassination was carried out.[128] Finally, Koinuma chose four men—Kōno, Yokoyama, Sugiura, and Miura—to draw up a plan of attack that included freeing the inmates from Tochigi prisons and jails as a prelude to inducting them into the revolutionary army.[129] Similarly, he also hoped to recruit the local poor into the army.[130] Koinuma's plan, then, was "if the attack on Utsunomiya is successful, then we will raise an army" that would in turn march on Tokyo, where an appeal would be made to the Emperor to change the government.[131] Like Oliver Cromwell, for whom Koinuma expressed admiration, this Japanese revolutionary had no difficulty in pinpointing the locus of sovereignty.[132]

Around the same time, and most probably with Koinuma's approval, Kōno, Yokoyama, and Kobayashi, who had remained in Tokyo after Koinuma and the others departed for Tochigi, met with Monna Shigejirō at the Jiyūtō youth center, where they unsuccessfully tried to solicit party funds for the revolution.[133] They needed the money in order to buy additional bomb materials, e.g., fifty pounds of potassium chlorate and 200 pounds of red phosphorous. In lieu of a party contribution, they proposed to Monna that the four of them should rob a Kanda area pawnshop, whose owner was known not only to have 300 to 400 yen on hand usually,[134] but also to be a generous moneylender to the nobility (*Kazoku*). As a pure "raise-an-army-ism" proponent, Monna was reluctant to join these three "assassination-

---

128. Endō, *Kabasan jiken*, pp. 164–65. The Jiyūtō leaders of the Gumma Incident (May 1884) had done the same, recruiting local *kyōkaku* and gambler chief Yamada Bunnosuke. Yamada, however, withheld support of his some 2,000 followers at the time of the incident. See Fukuda Kaoru, *Sanmin sōjō roku: Meiji jūshichinen Gumma jiken* (Tokyo, 1974), pp. 11, 17, 95.

129. Endō, *Kabasan jiken*, p. 172; also see Aoki Keiichirō, *Nihon nōmin undō shi* 2 (Tokyo, 1958):359.

130. Endō, *Kabasan jiken*, p. 173.

131. Ibid., pp. 173–74.

132. *KJKS*, p. 107. It is not surprising that Koinuma should be acquainted with the English Revolution and Cromwell. See a reference to this experience in English history in a *Jiyū-Shimbun* editorial of 19 October 1884 that also includes a reference to the Kabasan rebels. Besides the newspaper itself, the article can be found in Shimoyama Saburō, ed., *Jiyū min-ken shisō* 2 (Tokyo, 1961):181–84, especially p. 182.

133. Taoka, *Hanshin den*, p. 62.

134. The amount is mentioned by Kōno in his testimony of 29 September 1884 (*KJKS*, p. 234).

ism" advocates, but did so on the understanding that his portion of the money stolen would be used "to raise funds for the army."[135]

Thus it came about that around 7:30 P.M. on 10 September, these four men, each armed with a bomb, broke into the Kanda pawnshop, surprising its owner whose screams brought a nearby policeman running to the scene while simultaneously whistling for other policemen to respond. Kōno alone, said Yokoyama later,[136] threw his bomb, causing serious injury to one passerby and slight injury to another passerby as well as to one policeman. Monna too was slightly injured by the blast, and was captured. The other three—although the pawnshop owner said he saw only two others—escaped and hid that night in Tokyo. The next morning they left for Koinuma's.

The "costs" of the robbery far exceeded the "benefits" the rebels derived. First, they managed to steal only four yen. Secondly, although Monna managed to conceal his identity from the police for several days after the robbery, once it was discovered they further learned who his comrades were that night (except for Kobayashi) and began a Kantō-wide manhunt. Thirdly, as the "Ogawa jiken" (Ogawa is a section of the Kanda district) was the first time in Japan's history that anyone had been injured by a bomb, the authorities were all the more persevering in their attempt to capture the rebels. Finally, it is likely that the apprehension the robbery provoked in the authorities was responsible for the postponement of the Utsunomiya ceremony, scheduled for a mere five days after the robbery.

The rebels did not hear of the postponement until four days later, on 14 September. By that time they had suffered yet another, perhaps more serious reverse to their cause. On 12 September, with eight other rebels present, Koinuma seriously injured himself at his home in Inaba when a bomb he was making exploded. Koinuma lost his left arm, suffered a serious concussion, and had to be hospitalized at Mibu Town. The next day he was visited by the local police. Despite his serious condition, Koinuma did not break under police questioning and refused to say anything. Not until October did Koinuma confess his role in the incident.[137]

135. KJKS, p. 15.
136. See Itagaki, Jiyūtō shi III:46–47; also Endō, Kabasan jiken, pp. 167–70; and 6 November 1884 testimony of Yokoyama (KJKS, p. 21).
137. Almost simultaneous to this accident, Tateno Yoshinosuke, Jiyūtō member and friend of Koinuma, lost his right arm when a bomb he was making for Koinuma exploded accidentally (Endō, Kabasan jiken, p. 176).

For the rebels, the immediate consequence of the loss of their leader was, of course, fear of being discovered and arrested. They therefore fled to Ibaraki, to the Literary and Martial Arts Hall (*Bunbukan*) of Nakada village, where they stayed one night. The next day (the fourteenth) they went to Tomimatsu Masayasu's *Yūikan* in Shimodate. There they remained until the Kabasan *jiken* on 23 September. By 18 September, Kōno, Yokoyama, and Kobayashi had arrived there as well, after first stopping at Koinuma's on 13 September, only to hear of his accident. (Incredibly, though not yet known to the police as an "Ogawa *jiken*" participant, Kōno visited Koinuma in the hospital on the thirteenth.) By 18 September, then, all sixteen rebels who were to climb Mount Kaba were assembled for the first time since the 1883 beginning of the recruitment process.

Having lost their former leader, by going to Tomimatsu they gained, albeit reluctantly, a new one. I say "reluctantly" because Tomimatsu was dedicated to Ōi Kentarō's faction of Jiyūtō radicals who believed in waiting and quietly preparing for some future revolution. How Tomimatsu got involved in what he called "this risky revolutionary undertaking,"[138] he explained during his trial on 19 January 1885:

> On September 14, 1884, Hirao Yasokichi and Kotoda Iwamatsu came to see me. They expressed their approval of my work [at the *Yūikan*] and said that they agreed with it. . . . They then informed me repeatedly that they were making bombs and that they planned to use them against important people at the Utsunomiya ceremony in the hope of reforming the government. After that they asked if five or six others could come and talk with me, to which I said, "certainly." That afternoon I spoke with Hara and four or five other Jiyūtō members who had come and who agreed with the plot. . . . On September 18, Kōno and several others arrived, bringing our company to sixteen.[139]

On the same day that Tomimatsu invited the rebels to his school, the rebels learned that the Utsunomiya ceremony had been postponed. This in part explains why Tomimatsu, who in the past had consistently opposed the "small movement" strategy of revolution, agreed to involve himself—that is, since there was no immediate danger that the rebels would take any action, he may have seen this as an opportunity to convert fifteen very dedicated and politicized men to his way of thinking. Certainly, it was not simply because he was flattered by their praise of his work that he joined them, since he realized that

138. Quoted in ibid., p. 186.
139. *KJKS*, p. 447.

"I was made their leader (*shukai*) . . . because I am well known in this region and could therefore persuade people to give us men and provisions."[140] But perhaps the best explanation for Tomimatsu's participation was, as the author of the 1907 work *Tōsui minken shi* argued, that Tomimatsu had come to believe that "assassinationism" could serve as the first step to raising an army of revolution.[141] His own words support this contention. On 22 September, Tomimatsu told his fellow conspirators: "Our aim is defined: to go to Kabasan until the ceremony at Utsunomiya is held; then to go there and raise an army; then [to overthrow the government] and effect reform (*kairyō*) of the central government."[142]

The events that forced the sixteen rebels to leave the *Yūikan* and go to Kabasan were several. First, on 21 September, several of the rebels attracted the attention of neighbors by stupidly testing some bombs near the *Yūikan*. Secondly, a warrant had been issued for the arrest of Kōno and Yokoyama on the eighteenth; they learned of the warrant on the twenty-first. Thirdly, Hotta had been sent to Utsunomiya to learn when the ceremony would be scheduled; he found out that it had been moved from the twenty-fourth (the second scheduling) to the twenty-seventh. (It finally took place on 22 October.) Finally, on the evening of the twenty-second, a "friend," or a police spy according to one contemporary source,[143] visited the *Yūikan* to report and warn that, "Tonight policemen are coming here. I tell you this for your past kindnesses."[144] Supposedly surprised at this news, Tomimatsu ordered the fifteen to collect their bombs, gather provisions, and head for Mount Kaba.

What happened there, as we saw at the beginning of this narrative, constitutes the climax of the Kabasan Incident. If the rebels ever had a chance to realize their plan, it was lost the next day when the governor of Ibaraki cabled the Home Ministry: "3,000 rioters on Mt. Kaba. Send aid immediately."[145]

The Chichibu Incident

At 5:00 P.M. on 1 November 1884, as the last of the government troops were arriving in Tokyo from Ibaraki, where they had been sent

140. Ibid., p. 448.
141. Quoted in Endō, *Kabasan jiken*, p. 188.
142. *KJKS*, p. 448.
143. Quoted in Endō, *Kabasan jiken*, p. 192; Itagaki, *Jiyūtō shi* III:50.
144. Quoted in Endō, *Kabasan jiken*, p. 191; also Taoka, *Hanshin den*, p. 69.
145. Quoted in Ishikawa Naoki, *Tonegawa minken kikō* (Tokyo, 1972), p. 53.

Map 4.   Chichibu District and Surrounding Areas

five weeks earlier to suppress the Kabasan rebels,[146] about 3,000 farmers, hunters, small tradesmen, Jiyūtō party members, and local school teachers were meeting at the Muku temple, situated on a high tree-covered hill in the village of Shimo-yoshida, Chichibu District, Saitama Prefecture. The people present were armed with rifles, swords, and bamboo spears. Most were wearing white headbands (*shiro-hachi-maki*), straw sandals (*waraji*), short coats (*hanten*) with their sleeves girded up and held by white cords, and tight-fitting trousers that were pulled up at the groin. Before them stood Tashiro Eisuke, sericulturist, once-convicted gambler, self-proclaimed lawyer (*daigennin*), the son of a low-ranking samurai, and a man of patronage who was able to count several hundred people as "clients" (*kobun*). But at this mo-

146. *Japan Weekly Mail*, 1 November 1884. Other primary sources of aid in relating the details of this first day include Tanaka Senya's 1884 eyewitness account entitled "Chichibu bōdō zatsuroku," found in Vol. II of *Chichibu jiken shiryō*, comp., Saitama Shimbun Sha (Urawa, 1970):555–77 (hereafter abbreviated *CJSR* I and II); an account written by a shop owner of Ōmiya at the time of the rebellion, entitled "Chichibu bōdō jiken gairyaku," *CJSR* II:589–607; and contemporary newspaper accounts by the *Tokyo Nichi Nichi Shimbun*, *Yomiuri Shimbun*, *Chōya Shimbun*, *Yūbin Hōchi Shimbun*, *Jiyū Shimbun*, *Jiji Shimpō*, and the *Japan Weekly Mail* and its translations of articles appearing in the vernacular newspapers. All dates were checked against the details of the incidents as related by Ebukuro Fumio, *Chichibu sōdō* (Chichibu City, 1950); and Inoue Kōji, *Chichibu jiken* (Tokyo, 1968).

ment, he faced the crowd that was assembled within the outer compound of the temple as their "supreme commander" (sōshireikan), as leader of the Poor People's Army (Kommintō).

To one side of Tashiro stood his "Chief of Staff" (sambōchō), Kikuchi Kanbei, another "lawyer," who had come from Saku district of neighboring Nagano prefecture to join the Kommintō only four days earlier. The other officers of the Kommintō, standing on the temple steps with Tashiro and Kikuchi, were individually introduced. "Vice-Commander" of the Army was Katō Orihei, a gambler and philanthropic pawnshop owner of Isama village. The two "treasurers" were Shinto priest and longtime friend of Tashiro, Miyakawa Tsumori, and Jiyūtō member and farmer of Shimo-yoshida village, Inoue Denzō. Those introduced as "battalion commanders" were Shibaoka Kumakichi, Arai Shuzaburō, and Iizuka Morizō, also residents of the Chichibu region. Under them were several assistant commanders of the three battalions; below them squadron leaders, provisions officers, and so on. In all, over sixty men were introduced to the crowd as officers of their army.

When the crowd was silent, Kikuchi read the "army code," or "articles of war," that would henceforth serve to guide the behavior of the army. It prohibited drinking, the violation of women, arson without permission, and the withholding of appropriated goods and money from the army command.[147] When this was done, one of the leaders, perhaps Kikuchi again, read the "Goals for Action" (kōdō mokuhyō) that would serve to give definition to the aims of the army. The first rule was to "aid the poor people"; the others served to pinpoint the targets of the rebels: creditors' homes, police stations, government buildings, and the official documents found in these places.[148]

With these formalities disposed of, the last order of business was to assign all those present who were not already members of one of the village squads to units of their own. By 8:00 P.M., this work was done and two battalions were assembled. The "First Battalion" (kō-tai), numbering 2,000 men, was led by Katō Orihei, Arai Shuzaburō, and Ōno Naekichi. It began marching southwest toward the market town of Ogano. The "Second Battalion" (otsu-tai), under the leadership of Tashiro, Iizuka, and Ochiai Toraichi, took a different route to

147. Testimony of Tashiro Eisuke, 16 November 1884; CJSR I:106–7. (Hereafter, all references made to official documents appearing in either volume of CJSR will simply be cited with volume and page numbers unless the date of the testimony or document is relevant to the text.)

148. Tanaka Senya papers, CJSR II:555.

Ogano, enabling the Kommintō army to surround the town eventually. Earlier, before the two battalions began marching, Takagishi Zenkichi had taken a squad of men to Shimo-ogano in order to scout ahead of the main force. By eleven o'clock that evening, the Kommintō army had begun invading Ogano; and before the day was over, it had placed the town under Kommintō rule.

These events of 1 November mark the formal beginning of the Chichibu Incident. The "formal" end of the rebellion came ten days later, when the government announced that the last remnants of the Kommintō army had been routed. In fact, however, these dates represent only the beginning and end of open large-scale hostilities between government and the rebels. Here we will examine the actual origins of the conflict, and in Chapter 5 we will show that the incident produced effects that manifested themselves politically well after 10 November.

Towards Rebellion

The first known instance in which individuals, who later were instrumental in organizing the Kommintō and the rebellion, took concerted action to aid the poor people of Chichibu was in December 1883. At that time, Takagishi Zenkichi, Sakamoto Sōsaku, and Ochiai Toraichi presented a "petition admonishing usurers" (*korigashi setsuya seigan*) to the administrative head of Chichibu district (*gunchō*), requesting that the government intervene on behalf of the indebted, order creditors to permit interest payments on loans to be deferred, and also to initiate a scheme whereby repayment of all outstanding debts could be made annually over a forty-year period. The district head, however, argued that he did not have the authority to accept such a petition and sent the three men away.[149]

The next instance of importance with regard to the later rebellion took place in the spring of 1884. In March, following a February speaking tour throughout Chichibu by the well-known Jiyūtō radical, Ōi Kentarō, the same three men who in December had petitioned the government now joined the Jiyūtō and then attended its national conference in Tokyo. With Ōi Kentarō, who by then was Jiyūtō director of the Kantō region (*Kantō chihō jōbi-in*), they secretly pledged to overthrow the government. They also agreed to serve as the Chichibu

---

149. Inoue, *Chichibu jiken*, p. 38; Wagatsuma et al., *Seiji saiban shi*, p. 72; Ebukuro, *Sōdō*, p. 49; and *Saitama-ken shi*, ed. Tayama Soka, vol. 2 (Tokyo, 1921):584. According to the verdict passed on Katō Orihei, he too was supposed to have taken part (*CJSR* I:359).

representatives for the Jiyūtō headquarters.[150] Also during March, and on into April, these same three, along with other later Komminto leaders, Inoue Denzō (Jiyūtō member), Inoue Zensaku, Tomita Seitarō, and Arai Shigejirō, again petitioned the district head with the same demands that were made in December. Again they were refused, this time on the grounds that a recent edict governing the presentation of petitions did not allow the petitioning of district or prefectural officers without first receiving formal permission from the village heads (*kochō*) of the petitioners concerned. Ignoring this, they subsequently once again petitioned, but failed.[151]

For most of these early activists, who were farmers, the next two months were the "busy season" (*nōhanki*) when sericulturists were forced to give the utmost care and attention to their spring silkworms. Not until July did organizational activity resume in Chichibu. To the north, however, in Gumma prefecture, which borders Chichibu, several thousand impoverished farmers followed local Jiyūtō members and others into a rebellion that May; this was known as the Gumma Incident and was one of the several *gekka jiken* of 1884.[152] It is noteworthy because, in October and November, several prominent Jiyūtō members from the region in Gumma where the incident took place came to Chichibu to offer their services to the Chichibu rebels.

In July, according the Meiji government officials, organizational activity that later led to the building of the Komminto began anew. When the government tried Arai Shigejirō, a forty-four-year-old impoverished sericulturist from Isama village in Chichibu, for his participation in the rebellion, he was accused and found guilty of "helping to organize the Komminto between July 12 and September 1, 1884, along with Ochiai Toraichi and Takagishi Zenkichi. . . ."[153] The government's contention that organizational activity was taking place since July is supported not only by Arai's testimony itself, but also by records that show farmers gathering during July to protest against high in-

---

150. Ide Magoroku, *Chichibu Komminto gunzo* (Tokyo, 1973), p. 43; Inoue, *Chichibu jiken*, pp. 30–31; Gakushūin Hojinkai Shigakubu, comp., *Chichibu jiken no ikkōsatsu* (Tokyo, 1968), p. 43.

151. Ebukuro, *Sōdō*, p. 50; Inoue, *Chichibu jiken*, p. 38.

152. For a short sketch of the Gumma jiken, see Maeda Renzan, *Jiyū minken jidai* (Tokyo, 1961), p. 270. The only book-length treatment of the disturbance is Fukuda Kaoru, *Sammin sōjō roku: Meiji jūshichinen Gumma jiken* (Tokyo, 1974). Discussion of how the Gumma jiken connects with the Chichibu can be found in Ide, *Komminto*, pp. 160–67; Inoue, *Chichibu jiken*, pp. 34–36, 43–44; also see *Gumma ken hyakunen shi* 1 (Maebashi, 1971):582–96.

153. *CJSR* II:202; also Ide, *Komminto*, p. 17; and Inoue, *Chichibu jiken*, p. 86.

terest loans. On 16 July, for example, farmers from the villages of Min-ano, Shimo-yoshida, and Ogano met near Ogano for this purpose.[154]

Although some organizational activity occurred during July, it is the month of August that really marks the beginnings of serious and consequential organizational activity by the farmers of Chichibu. The mechanism that brought farmers together in August and that allowed them the opportunity to begin organizing was the silk market. In early August, sericulturalists took their worms, cocoons, and silk to market for sale. And the market, as Inoue observes, "was where local farmers communicated to one another their thoughts about local conditions."[155] In early August, their thoughts centered around the fact that the value of their products was only about half their 1882 value.[156]

Such was the case on 10 August, when at least a dozen farmers who were doing business at the Ogano market decided, on whose suggestion it is not known, to meet secretly in the forests of nearby Mount Azawada in order to organize some kind of response to the deteriorating economic conditions. On that day the Poor People's Party was born. According to the later courtroom testimony of Takagishi, the nucleus of the Kommintō was formed and the origins of a platform were established:

> Iizuka Morizō, Ochiai Toraichi, Inoue Zensaku and eleven or twelve others, including myself, discussed how we ought to obtain an eight-year, annual debt repayment scheme.[157]

Although no explicit reference is made to the term "Kommintō" in this passage, there is nonetheless reason to think that by this time (10 August) the term was being used frequently by Chichibu farmers.

For one reason, since April the Kommintō of Hachiōji, located about forty kilometers southeast of Ōmiya, had been actively—sometimes peacefully, sometimes violently—engaged in a fight against the usurers of their region for the reduction of interest on loans. In fact, on 10 August itself, the very day the Chichibu organizers were meeting on Mount Azawada, the Hachiōji Kommintō led a rebellion of several thousand farmers from several villages against local loan companies and government officials.[158] It is also important to note that

154. Ebukuro, *Sōdō*, p. 51.
155. Inoue, *Chichibu jiken*, p. 39.
156. Wagatsuma et al., *Seiji saiban shi* II:68; Ebukuro, *Sōdō*, p. 51; and Inoue, *Chichibu jiken*, p. 39.
157. *CJSR* I:47; Inoue, *Chichibu jiken*, p. 39.
158. Irokawa Daikichi, *Shimpen Meiji seishin shi* (Tokyo, 1973), pp. 298–99.

their rebellion met with partial success, especially in regard to the re-scheduling of loan repayments.[159]

Elsewhere in the country, organizations of indebted farmers, bear-ing different names but making the same type of demands, had been springing up since 1882. In August of that year, farmers of Shimane prefecture had formed the *Yohaka Shakuchitō*, or "Yohaka Leased Land Party." "Debtors' Party," or *Shakkintō*, was another title that indebted farmers took for their organizations in Shiga and Fukuoka prefectures during 1883, and in Shizuoka and Iwaki prefectures in early 1884.[160]

In Chichibu itself, there is evidence that the title "Kommintō" was already gaining currency by early August. A farmer from Akuma vil-lage, from which many later joined the November rebellion, was quoted as saying, "In mid-August I went to a meeting of the Kom-mintō." In another instance, a young carpenter of Tochiya village (near Ōmiya) said, "On August 18, we gathered at a temple in our mountain village. It was said that a large crowd from Ogano was com-ing to attack (*uchikowashi*) a local usurer. We decided that we ought to join them."[161] "We" here meant the village Kommintō organ.

While this was going on, the initial organizers of Mount Azawada were also busy. Several of the Jiyūtō members among them, such as Ochiai and Takagishi, had begun making lists of the names of indebted farmers, then approached their creditors requesting relief, and trav-eled throughout the many mountain communities giving lectures, holding meetings, and organizing local Kommintō organs.[162] Arai Eitarō of Isama village and Takeuchi Kishigorō of Kami-hinozawa were two such village leaders who were prompted by the early Kom-mintō organizers to build village parties.[163] In some cases, it appears that joining the local Kommintō was a preliminary move to joining the Jiyūtō itself.[164] Moreover, during August and early September, organizational activities by Kommintō leaders reached beyond the

159. Irokawa Daikichi, "Kommintō to Jiyūtō," *Rekishigaku Kenkyū* 247:8 (August 1961):1–30. Also see *CJSR* II:284, for the testimony of one farmer from the Ofusuma dis-trict in Saitama who joined the Kommintō. He explains in his testimony that when he first attended a Kommintō organization meeting he was told there was reason to hope debt can-cellation would work in Chichibu because it had in the Hachiōji region.

160. Hayashi, "Kabasan jiken," pp. 58–59; also see Ide, *Kommintō*, and Irokawa, "Kom-mintō," for a development of the debtors' and poor people's parties of the 1880s.

161. Quoted in Inoue, *Chichibu jiken*, p. 40.

162. Wagatsuma et al., *Seiji saiban shi* II:73; Ebukuro, *Sōdō*, p. 51.

163. Inoue, *Chichibu jiken*, p. 40.

164. Ebukuro, *Sōdō*, p. 52.

boundaries of Chichibu district and spread into neighboring Kodama, Hanzawa, and Ofusuma districts. Even the neighboring prefectures of Gumma and Nagano were not immune to the organizational activities of the early Kommintō organizers.[165] Hence, "Around this time the name 'Kommintō' came to be widely used."[166]

Kommintō leaders reached beyond the boundaries of Chichibu district and spread into neighboring Kodama, Hanzawa, and Ofusuma districts. Even the neighboring prefectures of Gumma and Nagano were not immune to the organizational activities of the early Kommintō organizers.[165] Hence, "Around this time the name 'Kommintō' came to be widely used."[166]

By late August and early September, the organizational process was proceeding well in the eyes of its initiators, but they also had reached the conclusion that the leadership of the Kommintō was as yet diffuse, that it needed a well-known and strong figure to unite and cement the bonds of membership. The one whom they were able to agree upon, the person who was later to become "Supreme Commander of the Army of the Poor People's Party," was Tashiro Eisuke. According to the posthumous letters of Ochiai, it was Katō Orihei who first suggested Tashiro Eisuke as the ideal candidate.[167] Tashiro was known to be sympathetic to the Jiyūtō, if not actually a member himself; in addition he was a local *meibōka* ("famous personage"); a patron (*oyabun*) who had several hundred clients (*kobun*) under obligation to him; a known gambler, once convicted, who was obviously not averse to opposing authority; and finally, he was a self-declared *kyōkaku*, or "Robin Hood," who believed he should "help the weak and crush the strong." In all, Tashiro seemed to be the ideal person to head the Kommintō. Thus, beginning 21 August, Tashiro was approached at least three times by the early Kommintō organizers (Inoue Denzō; Horiguchi Kōsuke of Gumma and one of Tashiro's *kobun*; Iizuka Morizō; Jiyūtō member Kokashiwa Tsunejirō, also of Gumma; and Takagishi Zenkichi). Not until 8 September, however, did Tashiro consent to serve as leader. It appears that Tashiro's reluctance to join was due to a fear that the Kommintō would ultimately

165. Ibid., pp. 53–54; Inoue, *Chichibu jiken*, pp. 40–41; and Wakasa Kuranosuke, "Chichibu jiken ni okeru Jiyūtō Kommintō no soshiki katei," *Rekishi Hyōron* 260:3 (March 1972):30–50. The latter article stresses how important family ties that crossed prefectural boundaries (i.e., between Chichibu and Gumma) were in aiding the organization of the Kommintō.

166. Ebukuro, *Sōdō*, p. 53.

167. *CJSR* II; also see the 14 November 1884 editorial in the *Yomiuri Shimbun* entitled "The Origins of the Riot."

resort to rebellion and that in the process lives would be lost.[168] However, with the addition of Tashiro, the settling of the leadership problem was accomplished, and the Kommintō leaders henceforth proceeded to devote all their energies to further organizational efforts.

For the next month, organizational activities took the form of Kommintō aid to indebted farmers who were having difficulty with creditors. Kommintō members would either confront creditors directly on the question of deferring repayment of loans, or they would encourage local farmers to organize themselves into local Kommintō branches for the same purpose. They were aided in their attempts to capture new Kommintō members by both the recalcitrance of creditors to comply with such demands, and by the effects that suppression of village meetings by the police had in alienating the poor farmers from the authorities. Nearly all the efforts by the Kommintō during this month met without success in reducing or deferring debt repayment. This fact prompted the Kommintō leadership to call a meeting at the home of Inoue Denzō on 12 October, to discuss how the Kommintō was going to respond to its lack of success in helping the indebted farmers.

According to the *Nichi Nichi Shimbun* account, nine leaders were present at this meeting: Tashiro, Katō, Inoue Denzō, Arai Shūzaburō (a school teacher), Takagishi, Sakamoto Sōsaku, Kokashiwa of Gumma, and Kikuchi Kanbei of Nagano![169] They discussed the failures thus far of Kommintō members to make any gains with creditors over the terms of loans, and the district government's refusal to intervene on behalf of Chichibu's poor farmers.[170] To date, they noted, the Kommintō had worked within the confines of the law, relying upon the means of organization, persuasion, and negotiation to try to get demands met. This, they decided, had proved ineffective. Unanimously, they decided that rebellion was the only alternative.

Having reached this conclusion on 12 October, they closed the meeting until the next day, when they met at the home of Katō Orihei. There they tackled the problem of how to implement the decision to rebel. Two immediate problems arose: first, the problem of how to communicate their decision to Kommintō supporters through-

168. Inoue, *Chichibu jiken*, pp. 51–52; Ebukuro, *Sōdō*, p. 53. Ebukuro claims that Tashiro joined a day earlier, on 7 September, after meeting with Shibaoka Kumakichi.

169. November 24, 1884. It is doubtful if Kikuchi was present, since he was not supposed to have arrived in Chichibu until 28 October. Ide, *Kommintō*, p. 21, claims that Inoue Zensaku and Kadodaira Sōhei were also present.

170. Other attempts were made during August and September. See ibid., pp. 20–21.

out Chichibu and, likewise, how to convince them of the wisdom of the decision; and secondly, the problem of how a group of indebted farmers could acquire sufficient money and provisions to effect a rebellion successfully.

The solution to the latter problem, it was decided, perhaps on Tashiro's suggestion,[171] was to "liberate" funds from the wealthy residents of the region. On 14 October, the next day, Miyakawa, Sakamoto, Horiguchi, and several others broke into the home of a wealthy merchant of Yokose village and stole four swords, a spear, and 100 yen. Arai Shuzaburo followed suit on the fifteenth, but was only able to steal fifty *sen* from a reputedly wealthy farmer.[172] But once the actual fighting began in November, the Kommintō increasingly turned, with greater success, to robbery, to confiscation of goods, weapons, and food, and to impressment in order to meet their needs of money, supplies, and men for the rebellion.

In response to the first problem of how to mobilize their sympathizers throughout the district, the Kommintō leaders apportioned Chichibu district into a number of ten-village units and assigned to each of themselves the responsibility for mobilizing one of these units. Tashiro, for instance, who was responsible for the villages encircling his own home town of Ōmiya, began on 15 October to visit each of these villages on a *rekihō* ("round of calls"), advocating to the villagers that they should be prepared to join in "smashings" (*uchikowashi*) against their creditors.[173] (Ultimately, once the rebellion began, only three of his villages responded.) Not all of the Kommintō leaders, however, employed this method of "round of calls" to mobilize followers, usually because it was not necessary. Since many villages had begun organizing themselves since late August, mobilization in these cases amounted merely to the conveyance of a message from Tashiro, or one of the other leaders, to a village Kommintō leader. Such, for instance, was the case with Fuppu village. But whatever the means employed to mobilize the villagers, police reports on the condition of the region clearly show that Chichibu residents were busily engaged in organizing after mid-October. Yet even though the police were aware of this, they maintained as late as 21 October that "the situation is not such that [we expect] a rebellion soon." They argued this on the basis of knowledge of traditional agricultural patterns, saying

171. Inoue, *Chichibu jiken*, p. 54.
172. Ibid.; Ebukuro, *Sōdō*, pp. 66–67.
173. Inoue, *Chichibu jiken*, p. 71; Ebukuro, *Sōdō*, pp. 63–64; also see Tashiro's testimony of 15 November 1884 in *CJSR* II:101.

that early November was an unlikely time for rebellion because this was when the Chichibu farmers began planting wheat (*mugimaki*).[174]

Just five days later, however, on 25 October, at Shimo-yoshida's Mount Ano, near where the Yoshida and Isama rivers converge and where 160 Komminto members had met for an organizational meeting on 6 September, the Komminto leadership gathered to decide upon the date to begin the rebellion.[175] Kokashiwa, who two months earlier had come from his native Gumma to help the Chichibu farmers organize the Komminto, argued on this occasion for a 28 October rising. Tashiro, supported by Inoue Denzo, recommended a late November beginning, mainly on the grounds that it would take at least a month to mobilize and coordinate other groups and areas in the Kanto region. Only by involving the poor people of Gumma, Nagano, Yamanashi, and Kanagawa prefectures, Tashiro maintained, would the Chichibu rebellion have a chance of success. Kokashiwa, like most of the others present at this 26 October meeting, believed that the peoples of these other prefectures would rise spontaneously once the Chichibu Komminto led the way. Kokashiwa's views won the day; and as the meeting ended, all present agreed upon 1 November as the date the rebellion was to begin.

"Headquarters of the Revolution"

Kokashiwa and his supporters at the Mount Ano meeting were not the only ones in Chichibu impatient to begin fighting. On 31 October, while most Komminto leaders were meeting at Kami-hinozawa in the morning, and at Kato's home in Isama in the afternoon, in order to make final preparations for the rebellion, the Komminto branch of Fuppu village located in the far northeast of Chichibu district, numbering 130 to 140 men, began marching southeasterly in order to meet up with the main body of the Komminto then beginning to collect at Shimo-yoshida. En route, the advance squad of the Fuppu organ met and fought with forty-five policemen who had been sent from Yorii (Hanzawa district) to investigate rumors of rebellion. According to newspaper reports, which told of a "poor people's rebellion in Fuppu,"[176] twelve of the rebels were captured before they managed to rout the police and continue their march, attacking the homes of usurers along the way.

174. Quoted in Inoue, *Chichibu jiken*, p. 60.
175. Ebukuro, *Sōdō*, p. 68.
176. *Tokyo Nichi Nichi Shimbun*, 3 November 1884; also see its editorial of 12 November 1884: "Chichibu bōtō shimatsu."

The same evening, before the rebellion was scheduled to begin, Arai Shūzaburō, Shibaoka Kumakichi, and Kadodaira Sōhei led forty men against a loan company in Kami-hinozawa and destroyed 10,000 yen worth of mortgaged land deeds.[177] They also reportedly set fire to the homes of the president of the loan company, of the village head (kochō), and of a local pawnbroker, and took the latter's brother as hostage.

The next day, prior to the large gathering of the Komminto army (mentioned at the beginning of this section), yet another battle took place, this time at Shimo-yoshida. Though reinforced by police sent from Ogano, local police were nonetheless outnumbered by the rebels and were forced to flee after two of their members and one Komminto member were killed, the first of the very few recorded deaths in the Chichibu rebellion. While this fighting was going on, other Komminto men were storming the office of the kochō. After capturing it, they proceeded to burn all official records stored there—land registries, tax assessments, family registries, etc. This practice of the destruction of official records was repeated throughout the remaining days of the rebellion.

Another instance of this practice, again occurring on 1 November, is exemplified by the activities of Sakamoto Sōsaku and his "guerrilla" unit of 150 men, one of three such units active during the rebellion.[178] On the first day of open rebellion, his unit was active in and around Shimo-yoshida. They entered the different hamlets, attacked the homes of usurers and the offices of officials, burned documents, stole weapons and money, and invited or enjoined villagers to serve in their unit. In some villages the people willingly joined, but in others where the population was generally apathetic or unsympathetic to the rebellion, men were impressed into service. One person per household was the customary demand made by the rebels. In this way, by 2 November, Sōsaku had increased his force to 300, doubling its original number. This practice of recruiting or of impressing Chichibu residents also occurred throughout the remainder of the rebellion.

By the end of 1 November, as seen earlier, the Komminto army had captured the market town of Ogano. There the local government office was set afire, destroying all public documents; the police station was attacked and its defenders sent running; the homes of six

177. *Tokyo Nichi Nichi Shimbun*, 3 November 1884.
178. "Guerrilla" (*gerira-tai*) is Inoue Kōji's term (*Chichibu jiken*, pp. 103–7).

usurers were destroyed; and food and arms were appropriated from the residents of the town. From Ōmiya, the district capital (present-day Chichibu City), the fires in Ogano could easily be seen. Reacting quickly, the merchants and the wealthy of Ōmiya began to scurry into hiding, or to send off their families and their valuables in anticipation of the impending attack upon the town by the rebels.

In Ogano on 2 November at 6:00 A.M., over 3,000 men and women divided into squads of riflemen, *takeyari* ("bamboo spears"), and *battōtai* ("drawn-sword squad") formed into two long columns, boasting squad and battalion flags, and departed from Ogano to head southeast toward Ōmiya. As they encountered no resistance along the way, they reached Ōmiya by noon and easily overpowered a squad of policemen who were defending the town. They then proceeded to the district government office (*gunyakusho*)—earlier vacated by the district head, known locally as "Daruma" because of his corpulence—where they placed a sign on the building that read: "Headquarters of the Revolution" (*kakumei hombu*).[179] The Kommintō army also immediately captured the town jail, which they partly destroyed, and the courthouse, from which official documents were seized and burned.

Between the evening of 2 November and the morning of 3 November, the Kommintō leadership issued three orders to its army. First, the homes and contents of Ōmiya's more notorious usurers were to be wrecked. Secondly, Ide Tamekichi, "the collector of funds for the army" (*gunyōkin-bōshukata*), who was a Nagano resident and Jiyūtō member, was to take charge of collecting money from the town's wealthiest citizens. Official records show that almost 3,000 yen was acquired from the wealthy, and over 250 yen from the district government office. To at least five of the ten who "donated" money to the Kommintō, "official" receipts were given, showing the amount donated, the purpose for which the money would be used ("military expenses"), the date, and a stamp reading "Headquarters of the Revolution," addressed Ōmiya. Tashiro personally signed four of them.[180]

The third order issued by the command concerned an appeal for aid and manpower from the nearby villages. To this end, small forces of Kommintō were dispatched to the nearby villages of the Bukō Mountain area. Appeals for aid were usually made directly to the vil-

179. *CJSR* II:215; Ide, *Kommintō*, p. 119.
180. The names of the wealthy and the amount of money they "contributed" is listed in the *Yomiuri Shimbun*, 14 November 1884.

lage head, who was asked to send to Ōmiya one person from each household. As a consequence of these appeals, during the next two days people from the region poured into Ōmiya, bringing the total force to at least seven or eight thousand by 3 November. Some newspapers and the Komminto itself, and later the authorities, said that by this date the total Komminto force had reached 10,000. But whatever the correct figure, as several newspapers expressed it, the Chichibu rebellion had become "the largest and most violent movement since the peasant uprisings (ikki) of 1876 in Gifu, Mie, and Aichi prefectures."[181]

From Victory to Defeat

An equally important fact pointed out by the newspapers at the time was that, up until this point, "all of the Chichibu region had been a clear battlefield for the Komminto."[182] It had thus far only experienced victories, albeit minor ones, in its battles against the authorities. Communications being what they were, the very remoteness of Chichibu, the very mountainous and therefore largely inaccessible terrain, as well as the impressive size of the Komminto army, not to forget the unpreparedness on the authorities' part, were all factors ensuring these early victories. There were, however, attempts made by local authorities early on to nip the rebellion in the bud. As early as 1 November, the prefectural governor had requested the Home Ministry, headed by the notorious Meiji oligarch Yamagata Aritomo, to dispatch Imperial troops to quell the rebellion. But no response was made by the Home Minister until the following day. On 2 November, the secretary to Yamagata relayed to him the cables that had been arriving from the Chichibu authorities. He also probably reported to Yamagata that the nation's major newspapers were beginning to send special correspondents to Chichibu, indicating that the rebellion was coming to be regarded publicly as an event of some importance. At 6:00 A.M. on November 3, an assistant to Yamagata telegraphed Urawa, the capital of Saitama:

> The Home Minister has become very anxious about conditions there. But [it seems] there is little danger at this time and he urges caution. He says that by now the [Tokyo garrison] troops should have been dispatched.[183]

181. *Yomiuri Shimbun*, 8 November 1884; *Yūbin Hōchi Shimbun*, editorial, "Bōtō no dōsei," 7 November 1884.
182. Inoue, *Chichibu jiken*, p. 130.
183. Quoted in Inoue, *Chichibu jiken*, p. 120.

By 9:30 A.M., a company of the Imperial Army, led by Major Harada and Second Lieutenant Kumamoto, arrived in Urawa, and their arrival was soon followed by that of two other companies in the late afternoon. All of these troops proceeded to head for Kumagaya, and then on to Yorii (by rail), where a base of operations was set up. On 4 November, the next day, the Third Company of the Third Battalion of the Tokyo garrison had arrived at Kodama Town. Chichibu was sealed off at the north and at the northeast.

Perhaps because they had not anticipated that the Imperial Army would be mobilized so quickly, or perhaps because of rumors circulating around Ōmiya, on 3 November the Komminto leadership panicked. The panic was accentuated by their own "intelligence reports"— never very reliable throughout the entire time of rebellion—which mistakenly reported that the Imperial Army was marching on Ōmiya that very morning.

To minimize the disorder arising among the rank and file because of these reports, the Komminto leadership devised a strategy to replace their earlier one of *shutsugeki* (sortie) into surrounding hamlets for men, weapons, and provisions. Since by then it was obvious that a show of strength alone would not compel the authorities to consider their demands, they concluded that they must utilize and test the strength of their army for the first time. Accordingly, they decided to employ their three battalions. Katō Orihei and Arai Shūzaburō were to take the First Battalion and head toward the Ogano-Yoshida district and repulse the advance supposedly being made by the Imperial troops toward that area. The Second Battalion, under the command of Kikuchi and Iizuka, was to head north to defend Onohara. The Third Battalion, commanded by Tashiro and Ochiai, was to remain in Ōmiya and prepare to defend the city.

Almost nothing went as planned. The Second Battalion disobeyed its orders and went beyond Onohara as far as Yorii, where they were routed and forced to retreat back to Onohara. The First Battalion, numbering only 1,000 men, found no Imperial troops at Yoshida; they remained there, rather than searching out government troops, and carried out sorties in the region. Tashiro, too, was guilty of disobeying (his own) orders. Fearing that an attack on Ōmiya was inevitable, he took most of the Third Battalion and went to Minano, which, he figured, was a less likely target of government attack. While there, Tashiro suffered severe chest pains (he was fifty-one years old), and, for all practical purposes, by the morning of 4 November had withdrawn from the revolt. His abandonment of his responsibility to the rebels, it appears, was precipitated by the arrival of his son Yasa, with whom he subsequently disappeared into the mountains, only to be found and arrested two weeks later.[184] On the same day, Kommintō leader Inoue Denzō also disappeared. Nothing more was heard about him until thirty-five years later, when on his deathbed in a small village in Hokkaidō he revealed his true identity as a "leader of the Chichibu Incident."[185]

Following the disappearance of Tashiro and Inoue on 4 November, the leadership of the Kommintō deteriorated quickly. In quick succession, other leaders also fled: Katō Orihei, Arai Shūzaburō (who had earlier been seriously wounded by a traitor in his battalion), Arai Eitarō, Takagishi Zenkichi, Kokashiwa Tsunejirō, Ide Tamekichi, and Ogiwara Kanjirō all dispersed in different directions. Katō Orihei, second in command under Tashiro, probably typified the sentiments of the other leaders who fled, when he said, upon hearing of the disappearance of Tashiro and Inoue, "I thought to myself, there is nothing to do but flee."[186]

Regardless of their reason for breaking rank, they did so none too soon. Even more troops had been mobilized on the afternoon of 4 November, and had begun to augment their force by recruiting (conscripting, in some cases) local hunters and ex-samurai, and making them the core of "self-defense" forces. By late in the day, an estimated 1,000 policemen, army troops, and local recruits had formed a semicircle from the northeast to the southeast around Chichibu, and were slowly closing in, constricting the movements of the Kommintō. By the early morning of 5 November, the authorities had retaken Ōmiya, "Headquarters of the Revolutionary Army."

At this point, the only effective resistance by the rebels who remained was centered at Minano. From there, Ochiai ordered a unit of eighty to a hundred men to hold the Kainida pass, the most likely point of entry for the government's troops coming over the mountains that separated Minano from Sakamoto village. Near Sakamoto late on 4 November, the two sides clashed in armed combat, and although the Kommintō troops were successful in repulsing the government's advance that evening, they were forced to retreat the next morning after a squad of garrison troops, armed with the new Murata

---

184. *Tokyo Nichi Nichi Shimbun*, 17 November 1884.
185. Inoue died on 18 July 1918.
186. Quoted in Inoue, *Chichibu jiken*, p. 134.

rifles, arrived as reinforcements. During the retreat Ochiai vanished, only to re-emerge two years later as a participant in the Osaka Incident led by Ōi Kentarō.

Defeat followed defeat. At almost the same time that the Kommintō leaders remaining in Minano were learning of Ochiai's retreat, they also learned that one of its best organized units, the Fuppu village Kommintō, had met disaster late on 3 November. Led by Ōno Naekichi, the 300-man Fuppu unit had headed northward into neighboring Kodama district the day before in order to provoke rebellion in that region. Although they had managed to recruit or conscript about 300 villagers during their march, they were nonetheless decisively defeated by a smaller force of army troops, a short distance to the south of Kodama Town.

Learning this news, the Kommintō leaders remaining at Minano—Kikuchi Kanbei, Sakamoto Sōsaku, and Kadodaira Sōhei—concluded that Minano too would soon be lost. They therefore assembled about 100 men, left Minano, and went to Yoshida, where they joined the fifty-man force of Arai Torakichi of Gumma prefecture. After discussing the desperateness of their situation, they elected Kikuchi to serve as their commander, and resolved to take the Chichibu rebellion to Nagano prefecture, Kikuchi's home, by way of a western march through Gumma, Minami-Kanra district, along the Sanchūyatsu Kannagawa basin. They selected this route for its easy access from Chichibu and because it was known to be a highly politicized region, dominated by Jiyūtō activists who since 1881 had been busy organizing the local farmers.[187] Their choice of routes proved to be a good one, for "when the Chichibu Kommintō rose up, the farmers of Sanchūyatsu also rose up."[188] Indeed, before Kikuchi had even crossed the border into Gumma, a large group of villagers from the Hominoyama region were already on the march to join the Chichibu rebellion, and soon the two groups united. But not only for this reason was their choice of routes a good one. Since most of the government's troops and the local police were concentrated around Ōmiya, the Sanchūyatsu road was relatively open to Kikuchi's company.

Along the way toward Nagano, Kikuchi was able to recruit or impress about 125 men and was able to steal enough arms and food to ensure that the march continued. Not until the morning of 7 November, just before they were beginning to cross the mountains that separated Gumma from Nagano, were they attacked from the rear by

187. Ibid., pp. 145–46. 188. Ibid., p. 146.

government troops. They lost twelve men captured and an unknown number of others through desertion, mainly Gumma residents who did not want to leave their own prefecture. Despite these reverses, before they departed from the border town of Shirai they had managed to build up their number to 250–300 men, this time with residents from the Minami-saku district of Nagano, a strong center of Jiyūtō activity, who had crossed the border into Gumma to join them. Despite this welcome aid, Kikuchi's company was thereafter forced to divert their attention and manpower to keep a close watch on the Sanchūyatsu farmers who made repeated attempts to escape once they were in Nagano.

By the evening of 7 November, the Kommintō force had reached the village of Ōhinata, where they camped for the night. That evening they were joined by a number of farmers from the area who had heard of their arrival, and who hoped that by joining they would free themselves from indebtedness. Perhaps in response to their hopes, the next morning (8 November) witnessed uchikowashi campaigns against local creditors by the Kommintō. More than 1,000 yen worth of weapons, artifacts, and money were taken and then distributed to local residents. Through such philanthropic action the Kommintō attracted a large number of new recruits, bringing their total force to about 430. With this new-found strength they marched toward Kaize, attacking usurers, a bank, and a drygoods store along the way. By then, one squad of their army had been designated to serve as the "Smashing Corps" (uchikowashi-gumi), which in turn called itself the "Freedom Corps" (Jiyū-tai). A special "swordsman squad" of twenty men was also organized, led by a haiku poet from Ōmiya. It was separated from the main body and ordered to go north to Usuda; along the way it was to attack government offices, to recruit (or impress) villagers, and to learn whatever possible about the movements of the authorities. This squad only got as far as Takanomachi, where it was met and routed by local police.

Meanwhile, the main force under Kikuchi advanced as far as Higashi-managashi, where they camped during the evening of 8 November. From there, squads were sent out to the surrounding villages to attack banks and usurers, and also to secure recruits.

Unknown to the rebels at this time, however, there were more than 100 troops of the Takasaki garrison (from Gumma) encamped near Usuda, where another 100 local police were mobilized in order to march south to battle the rebels. As these troops moved south, they were spotted near Kaize by a Kommintō recruitment patrol. Four or five of the rebels, riflemen, remained there to fire upon the government troops and delay their advance while their comrades hastened to inform Kikuchi of the bad news. At first, Kikuchi hesitated to withdraw, opting to remain to meet the government troops. A short battle cost the Kommintō the lives of thirteen men (only one policeman was killed) and the aid of many more as a good number turned and fled. At this, Kikuchi assembled his remaining force of about 200 and retreated south from Managashi. By 2:00 P.M. on 10 November, the Kommintō force had gone as far as the foothills of the Hachigaoka mountain range near the village of Noheyamabara, when unexpectedly they were attacked again, this time by a squad of soldiers who had come to meet them from Azusayama. The rebel force was thoroughly routed. Its members fled in all directions, and in a short time the Kommintō army no longer existed. Only isolated individuals and small groups, most of whom went into hiding, remained to await capture by the authorities. The Chichibu rebellion was over.

Conclusion

From the foregoing accounts, the reader may very well be wondering what criteria are called into play to permit these three very differently appearing disturbances to be subsumed under the omnibus term, *gekka jiken*. Examine the obvious differences between them: The Fukushima Incident was largely lawful and nonviolent compared with the Kabasan and Chichibu incidents; the Kabasan was a small-scale plot while the other two were mass-based movements; in terms of the size of the area encompassed and the fighting organization employed, the Chichibu Incident appears to have been a "miniature civil war,"[189] whereas the other two were confined to small areas and not nearly so well organized. The origins of each disturbance, the apparent aims of each, and the effectiveness of each in combating the authorities are also areas where differences seem to overshadow similarities. Although these differences will be treated at greater length in subsequent chapters, for the present, based on what we have learned so far, it seems wise to explain why the three incidents are generally regarded as varied species of the larger, generic classification, *gekka jiken*.

In doing this we rely upon the lead provided by historian Gotō Yasushi.[190] His analysis of the *gekka jiken* revolves around the first

189. Nobutaka Ike, *The Beginnings of Political Democracy in Japan* (Baltimore, 1950), p. 165.
190. Gotō Yasushi, *Jiyū minken: Meiji no kakumei to hankakumei* (Tokyo, 1972), pp. 180-92, especially pp. 180-81.

of them, the Fukushima Incident, which he regards as a prototype of subsequent ones. Gotō sees in the year-long Fukushima struggle four aspects or tendencies of popular opposition that reappeared in later *gekka jiken*. The first of these is the lawful approach adopted by the activists toward the handling of the conflict: the attempt of eastern Fukushima leaders to confine the conflict to the legislature, and Kōno Hironaka's attempt to keep his eastern branch from compromising itself by involvement in the Aizu struggle, as well as the use of petition, litigation, and a nonviolent tax boycott by western liberal activists. Similar kinds of attempts to remain within the bounds of law were made by those Chichibu activists who later became Kommintō organizers. Well over a year before the actual conflict, these early Chichibu activists presented petitions to local officials, they tried negotiating with individual creditors, and they endeavored to hold meetings with other indebted farmers in order to arrive at a collective approach to local problems. This legal and nonviolent approach, Professor Gotō correctly points out, received its strongest support from Jiyūtō President Itagaki Taisuke even though it again and again proved to be ineffective in the face of wide-scale repression. In Fukushima, the property of protesters was seized and auctioned publicly; activists were assaulted and beaten by members of the government's party; and meetings were broken up, and many were arrested. In Chichibu, laws placing restrictions on assembling and petitioning, the aid the authorities gave to creditors, and the forcible breaking up of Kommintō organizational meetings all proved the uselessness of attempting nonviolent political activity.

Since the line separating nonviolent from violent collective action is a very thin one, and since "the range of collective actions open to a relatively powerless group is normally very small," once lawful activity proves to be ineffective there remains only the choice between taking no action at all and taking violent action.[191] Such seems to have been the choice confronting the activists who led the three incidents. In all three cases there emerged a faction which advocated direct action immediately, and another which proposed waiting, either in the hope that legal action would eventually prove effective, or for a propititious moment when direct action would have a good chance of effectiveness. The emergence of a radical faction in the Fukushima Incident is the second prototypical aspect which Professor Gotō dem-

---

191. Charles Tilly, Louise Tilly, and Richard Tilly, *The Rebellious Century, 1830-1930* (Cambridge, Mass., 1975), p. 283; but also see pp. 280-85.

onstrates. He says that Hanaka's Radical Party (*Kyūshintō*) in the Fukushima Incident was mirrored by the "small movement" advocates in the Kabasan Incident, and, I would add, by the founders of the "Headquarters of the Revolution" within the Kommintō. The advocates of violent collective action in the Kamo, Gumma, Iida, and Shizuoka incidents could also be cited as further examples.

A third feature common to several *gekka jiken*, and which took place first in the Fukushima Incident, is the alliance struck between local Jiyūtō branches and the farmers of the region. Jiyūtō and local farmer alliances were also formed in the cases of the Chichibu, Gumma, Kanagawa, and Iida incidents. The last prototypical feature of the Fukushima Incident which Gotō identifies is closely related to the third. Due in part to Jiyūtō leadership, and due in part to certain socioeconomic developments, the farmers in the Fukushima and subsequent incidents began manifesting a collective consciousness of their political rights vis-à-vis the authorities.

Based upon the purely descriptive accounts of the three incidents presented in this chapter, Professor Gotō's analysis of the commonalities existing among the *gekka jiken* seems a fair and accurate one, but only in regard to his first three points. The information supplied thus far is insufficient to allow either confirmation or rejection regarding the farmers' consciousness of their political rights. It is an important point, however, not only because it is basic to Marxist historiography but also because it is crucial to an understanding of the quality, meaning, and historical significance of the rebellions. Eric Hobsbawm|is right when he says that "Revolutions may be made *de facto* by peasants who do not deny the legitimacy of the existing power structure, law, the state and even the landlords."[192] Rebellion is rebellion whether people fight for a new type of society or for the restoration of an idealized version of the old, but the character of the rebellion and its consequences will certainly differ according to the level of political consciousness exhibited by the rebels. The issue is an important one, then, but it makes little sense to pursue it until we have a better understanding of the historical, socioeconomic, and political context of the three incidents.

192. Eric J. Hobsbawm, "Peasants and Politics," *Journal of Peasant Studies* 1:1 (October 1973):12.

2. Background

In the new society they were free to choose their
own fate; to live or die, to remain on the land or
sell out and go to the city.

E. H. Norman
Japan's Emergence as a Modern State

In the course of relating the details of each of the three disturbances
in the last chapter, what may be regarded as the precipitating causes
were indicated. In the case of the Fukushima Incident, they were the
road scheme, Governor Mishima's use of high-handed tactics, the onerous taxes and corvée labor dues imposed on the Aizu people, and
so on. The immediate causes of the Kabasan Incident appear to have
been the repression that most of the participants suffered because of
participation in the Fukushima Incident, the desire for revenge, and
a more general wish to effect drastic changes in government. What set
off the Chichibu Incident can be inferred from the nature of the demands the rebels made: debt deferment, tax reductions, and an end
to high interest loans; in other words, the rebels wanted relief from
the economic depression.

If this adequately sums up the precipitating causes of each of the
disturbances, then we must go beyond and investigate what the underlying causes were. That is the purpose of this chapter, to search for
the historical, social, economic, and political forces which, in providing a context for the revolts, help to explain why they occurred.

Specifically, this chapter will examine the following: First, we will
look at the Tokugawa tradition of peasant rebellion, a legacy uncon-
sciously bequeathed by Tokugawa period (1600–1867) peasants to
Meiji farmers. We study this tradition of rebellion for what it can tell
us not only about rebellion as such, but also for what it reveals about
the changing socioeconomic and political features of the Tokugawa
and early Meiji periods. Secondly, this chapter examines the nature
of the Japanese economy as it was immediately before the distur-

bances of the 1880s and as it was at the time of their occasion. Here, special emphasis will be given to the Matsukata deflation policy as it affected the nation's farmers as a whole and as it affected the farmers of Yama (Fukushima), Chichibu (Saitama), and Makabe (Ibaraki) specifically. Finally, the last section will look at the political climate of the 1870s and 1880s, and especially at the rise of the popular rights movement.

Tradition of Rebellion

In the experience of most nations, it seems that some regions are more inclined toward rebellion than others. In China, for instance, the south more than other regions has been "the hearth of rebellion within the Chinese State."[1] In Mexican history, the north in general and the State of Morelos in the south stand out as rebellious areas. Likewise, one can site Nghe An province in Viet Nam; Kabylia in Algeria; Oriente in Cuba; the Ukraine in Russia; the south (Hampshire, Sussex, and Kent) in early industrial England; and the provinces surrounding Paris in eighteenth- and nineteenth-century France.[2] The reasons for some regions and not others to manifest rebelliousness are both complex and varied: peripheral location vis-à-vis the center of State control; close proximity to urban centers of commerce; linguistic or ethnic differences separating a region from the majority of the population; differences with regard to patterns of agriculture, economy, and kinship; and perhaps even the existence of a folk "custom of rebellion" that relies upon the collective memory of a region's inhabitants.[3]

Now, the existence of such a tradition of rebellion in a particular region cannot be regarded as a *cause* of rebellion. It must, however, be considered in any explanation of the origins of rebellion, if only as a crucial intervening variable that helps to show a tendency or proclivity of the residents of certain areas to employ collective violence as a means to redress wrongs, or even to attempt to reform society itself. If this is so, what, then, can be said about the case of Japan?

1. Eric R. Wolf, "On Peasant Rebellions," *International Social Science Journal* 21:2 (1969):291.

2. Ibid.; and in the cases of England and France, George Rudé, *The Crowd in History, 1730–1848* (New York, 1964), chaps. 1 and 2.

3. See Rudé, *Crowd*, pp. 241–42, and the treatment of Antonio Gramsci in Charles Tilly, "Town and Country in Revolution," in *Peasant Rebellion and Communist Revolution in Asia*, ed. John Wilson Lewis (Stanford, Calif., 1974), especially pp. 271–76.

Patterns of Rebellion

Despite the emphasis in recent years by Western scholars on the importance of the passivity of Japan's peasant population as a key to her successful modernization, the truth is otherwise—Japan modernized in spite of peasant rebellion. As if to emphasize this much under-emphasized point, eminent Japanese social historian Irokawa Daikichi stressed, "Even our country has a history of armed rebellion."[4] During the Tokugawa period, no less than 6,889 peasant uprisings (*ikki*) were recorded; this figure translates into nearly twenty-five disturbances per annum.[5]

An annual average, of course, cloaks the equally important fact of rises and falls within this 267-year era. For instance, during the Tempō period (1830–44), an average of over sixty-seven disturbances occurred annually. This figure was second only to the Keiō period (1865–68), when the annual average was 114 incidents. The Temmei period (1781–89) was another high point; it had a yearly average of fifty-five incidents. By way of contrast, the twenty-year Kyōho period (1716–35) experienced only nineteen risings each year; likewise, there were only nine risings a year during the Kambun period (1661–72).[6]

Just as certain periods witnessed more peasant rebellions than others, so too did certain regions of Japan. If we partition Japan into geographical regions as it has traditionally been done, and look to the number of disturbances each region experienced during all of Tokugawa, then we can see the results in Table 1. The Chūbu region or central portion of the main island of Honshū clearly leads with slightly over 30 percent of all disturbances, and is followed in order by Kinki (19.6), Kantō (16.6), Tōhoku (14.8), and so on. The same kind of figures are likewise indicated for the first decade of the Meiji period, only here we see that the Kinki region drops from second to sixth in rank, and the Tōhoku region advances to second.

4. Irokawa Daikichi, "Kommintō to Jiyūtō," *Rekishigaku Kenkyū* 247:8 (August 1961):1.

5. The average is based on figures taken from Aoki Kōji, *Hyakushō ikki no sōgō nempyō* (Tokyo, 1971), Appendix. I say "no less than" because this is Aoki's most recent finding. In his 1966 book concerning the same topic, he cited 3,804 as the total figure. One can only suspect, therefore, that a future work by Aoki or someone else will discover even more instances of peasant uprisings.

6. These figures were computed using the aggregate data supplied by Aoki, *Sōgō nempyō* (1971). The figures do not differentiate between *hyakushō ikki* (peasant uprising), *murakata sōdō* (intravillage conflict), and *toshi sōdō* (urban or town-type conflict). Aoki defines intravillage conflicts as "tenant conflicts and internal struggles that are not related directly to anti-authority action." Urban type conflicts "are based mainly in the town (*machi*), led by town people; or conflicts that occur in urban areas." These definitions come from his *Hyakushō ikki no nenjiteki kenkyū* (Tokyo, 1966), Appendix, p. 2.

TABLE 1.

Uprisings by Region

Region	No. of Provinces	Rural Uprisings	City Type	Intra village Rising	Total	% of Total	Rank
TOKUGAWA, 1590–1867							
Tōhoku	(8)	664	45	311	1,020	14.8	(4)
Kantō	(9)	349	74	721	1,144	16.6	(3)
E. Kantō	(6)				(660)	(9.6)	
W. Kantō	(3)				(484)	(7.0)	
Chūbu	(15)	735	155	1,187	2,077	30.1	(1)
Chūō	(2)				(747)	(10.8)	
Hokuriku	(7)				(609)	(8.8)	
Tōkai	(6)				(721)	(10.5)	
Kinki	(15)	519	127	706	1,352	19.6	(2)
Chūgoku	(12)	375	40	137	552	8.0	(5)
Shikoku	(4)	260	9	75	344	4.9	(7)
Kyūshū	(11)	303	38	52	393	5.7	(6)
(Unclear)		7			7	0	
Total	(74)	3,212	488	3,189	6,889	99.7	
MEIJI, 1868–1877							
Tōhoku		110	–	10	120	17.8	(2)
Kantō		58	4	41	103	15.3	(3)
E. Kantō					(54)	(8.0)	
W. Kantō					(49)	(7.3)	
Chūbu		98	11	46	155	23.0	(1)
Chūō					(59)	(8.7)	
Hokuriku					(47)	(6.9)	
Tōkai					(49)	(7.3)	
Kinki		43	3	26	72	10.7	(6)
Chūgoku		72	5	11	88	13.0	(5)
Shikoku		29	–	13	42	6.0	(7)
Kyūshū		89	1	4	94	13.9	(4)
(Unclear)		–			–	–	
Total		499	24	151	674	99.7	

Source: Aoki Kōji, *Hyakushō ikki no sōgō nempyō* (Tokyo, 1971), Appendix.

Although this breakdown is revealing in a very general way, it none-theless obscures internal geographical distinctions within each region, as partially noted in the table by the subdivisions of the Chūbu and Kantō regions. Also, we know that each region distinguishes itself from the others by consisting of different numbers of provinces (*kuni*), as well as varying numbers of feudal domains (*han*). To the extent that many uprisings were generated by distinctive provincial or domain problems—and it is impossible to say here when and how often this was the case—then it becomes necessary to go beyond the high level of generalization concerning uprisings by regions, and try at least to distinguish the uprisings by employing a lower level of geo-graphical specificity. Since it is the tradition of rebellion within cer-tain Meiji prefectures that we are interested in studying, then we do what the Meiji government did and amalgamate the seventy-four *kuni* into forty-five prefectures. The results are shown in Table 2.

For the present, the most important point to be taken from Table 2 is the rankings according to prefecture. We see that Fukushima and Saitama prefectures, where the Fukushima and Chichibu Incidents occurred, rank third and second respectively in their number of inci-dents for the Tokugawa period, and first and fourth for the first dec-ade of Meiji. Ibaraki prefecture, site of the Kabasan Incident, does not rank highly in either period. It should also be pointed out that even if we look at a higher level of specificity by separating Fuku-shima into Iwashiro and Iwaki provinces (*kuni*) and look only at the figures for Iwashiro (the larger part being the Aizu region), then we see that its 259 Tokugawa incidents and its fifty-two in Meiji would still place it in the top ten in both periods, and would even rank it first for early Meiji!

Unfortunately, the same cannot be done with Saitama prefecture, since it and Tokyo have historically been lumped together as Musashi province.[7] Nevertheless, it is known that within the Saitama portion of Musashi province, the northern zone—of which Chichibu occupies the largest part—was where most of the peasant disturbances took place during the Tokugawa period.[8] During the eight-year Temmei period (1781–89), for instance, all but two of its disturbances took place outside of Tokyo, and eighteen of them were based in the

7. Actually, it could be done if one were willing to count through 6,889 incidents, cata-logued in nearly 700 pages, and locate the origins of each Musashi disturbance.
8. Ōno Fumio, *Saitama-ken no rekishi* (Tokyo, 1971), p. 165.

northern part of Saitama.[9] Chichibu district as such, with four disturbances, was second only to the Tama region (with six), which, it may be recalled, is not only contiguous to Chichibu but is topographically identical and had, since the sixth century, been regarded as an adjunct of Chichibu.[10]

Also from Table 2 we should notice that of the 432 Tokugawa period disturbances, most probably took place in the rural regions of Saitama, since only twenty-eight of all disturbances were of the "city type."[11]

In any case, Tables 1 and 2 show conclusively that Saitama and Fukushima ranked among the highest of the disturbance-prone regions for the Tokugawa and early Meiji periods. Still, there are a number of important features about rebellion that these two tables do not show: the frequency according to region; the intensity of the disturbances; the forms they took; the number of participants; the duration of the risings; their causes and consequences; and so on. For some of these questions, owing to incomplete data, only tentative answers can be offered. For others, the answers must be sought in the remaining sections of this chapter. Right now, however, we will only attempt to answer the first few.

When talking about a tradition of rebellion existing in certain regions, the question of frequency is important only insofar as it serves as an incomplete substitute for the cultural and anthropological evidence that can demonstrate the endurance among a collectivity of an oral or written tradition of rebellion. If, for example, a collectivity rises in rebellion, say, once every couple of generations, then we may provisionally assume that a collective memory passes on the information of the facts of rebellion to younger generations. For this reason, the question of frequency is an important one. But we also know that as time elapses between rebellions, a collectivity also commits itself to an apotheosis of earlier rebels; that is, like any collectivity, it

9. Aoki, *Sōgō nempyō*, pp. 146–68, 377–86, 477–84. Unless otherwise stated in the text, all figures refer to the total *ikki*, *murakata sōdō*, and *toshi ikki*. (See note 6, above.)

10. Ōno, *Saitama*, p. 30. Today even the Chichibu-Tama National Park attests to the historical and geographical closeness of the two regions. As late as August 1867, farmers from Chichibu and Tama rebelled together in a *yonaoshi ikki*; see Shōji Kichinosuke et al., eds., *Minshū undō no shisō* (Tokyo, 1971), pp. 490–91.

11. Although Tokyo was in fact the only major urban center of the Musashi region, it is possible that *toshi sōdō* could have occurred in the market towns of Chichibu, since Aoki makes the class of the participant one of the main distinguishing criteria of the "city type" of conflict. See note 6, above.

TABLE 2.

Types of Tokugawa (1590–1867) Uprisings by Meiji Prefectures*
and During First Ten Years of Meiji (1868–1877)

Region	Prefecture	TOKUGAWA					MEIJI				
		Uprisings	City Type	Intra village	Total	Rank	Uprisings	City Type	Intra village	Total	Rank
Tōhoku	Aomori	34	9	3	46		4	—	—	4	
	Akita	91	12	28	131		9	—	1	10	
	Iwate	138	8	14	160		22	—	—	22	(9)
	Miyagi	25	8	5	38		4	—	—	4	
	Yamagata	129	5	81	215	(10)	13	—	1	14	
	Fukushima	247	3	180	420	(3)	55	—	8	63	(1)
Kantō	Ibaraki	52	3	45	100		6	—	3	9	
	Tochigi	33	21	66	120		12	1	—	13	
	Gumma	74	12	71	157		18	—	4	22	(9)
	Saitama	94	28	310	432	(2)	16	3	15	34	(4)
	Tokyo	22	7	82	111		—	—	10	10	
	Kanagawa	74	3	147	224	(9)	6	—	9	15	
	Chiba	138	40	128	306	(6)	23	3	2	28	
Chūbu	Niigata										(6)
	Toyama	37	24	4	65		5	5	3	13	
	Ishikawa	54	19	17	90		3	—	1	4	
	Fukui	67	18	63	148		2	—	1	3	
	Shizuoka	40	15	71	126		2	—	1	2	
	Yamanashi	21	3	156	180		7	1	4	12	
	Nagano	173	23	371	567	(1)	28	—	19	47	(2)
	Aichi	74	5	78	157		12	2	3	17	

Kinki	Gifu	104	5	276	385	(5)	13	—	13	26	(7)
	Shiga	67	15	61	143		4	1	1	6	
	Kyōto	102	16	107	225	(8)	6	1	2	9	
	Ōsaka	64	8	200	272	(7)	—	—	12	12	
	Nara	55	16	21	92		1	—	1	2	
	Wakayama	27	12	26	65		3	—	—	3	
	Mie	19	7	17	43		9	1	—	10	
	Hyōgo	180	53	270	403	(4)	20	—	10	30	(5)
Chūgoku	Okayama	96	3	54	153		21	—	4	25	(8)
	Hiroshima	106	20	55	181		15	2	4	21	(10)
	Yamaguchi	69	2	3	74		14	—	—	14	
	Tottori	45	7	9	61		7	—	3	10	
	Shimane	59	8	16	83		15	3	—	18	
Shikoku	Kagawa	26	1	6	33		4	—	3	7	
	Ehime	145	4	30	179		19	—	7	26	(7)
	Tokushima	53	0	4	57		2	—	2	4	
	Kōchi	36	4	35	75		4	—	1	5	
Kyūshū	Fukuoka	37	6	2	45		9	—	—	9	
	Ōita	55	3	4	62		12	—	—	12	
	Miyazaki	71	1	4	76		19	—	—	19	
	Saga	20	1	17	38		6	—	—	6	
	Nagasaki	38	14	9	61		7	1	2	10	
	Kumamoto	68	13	12	91		33	—	2	35	(3)
	Kagoshima	14	0	4	18		3	—	—	3	
(Unclear)		7	0	0	7		3	—	—	3	
Total		3,212	488	3,189	6,889		499	24	151	674	

*Excluding Hokkaidō and Okinawa.

Source: Aoki Kōji, Hyakushō ikki no sōgō nempyō (Tokyo, 1971), Appendix.

creates for itself certain folk heroes.[12] Also, since a collectivity may be defined in either very broad or very narrow terms, a hero-rebel may at first only be remembered by the local community from which he came, but later may be revered by a regional or even the national community, and revered perhaps for reasons totally unrelated to the original experience that catapulted him into the ranks of heroism. In the Japanese experience, folk heroes have traditionally been rebels. Kanno Hachirō of Fukushima, Date district, Kaneharada village, who led a revolt against his domain government in 1866, is one such example. His name was invoked as a legitimizing symbol a decade later by Tama region popular rights advocates.[13] Much earlier, Sakura Sōgorō was initiated into the holy order of martyrdom after he was crucified by the feudal government for illegally petitioning for economic relief for his village.[14] *Gimin* ("righteous man" or, in this context, martyr), *kyōkaku* ("Robin Hood"), and *daimyōjin* ("Divine Rectifier") were terms variously used by peasants to refer to their rebel heroes who had led them against the authorities. Itagaki Taisuke, President of the Liberal Party (Jiyūtō), was oftentimes referred to as a *daimyōjin* for the imagined help he gave to the poor and disenfranchised in their quest for economic and political autonomy.[15]

But cultural rebel-heroes aside, there exists enough evidence on the frequency of risings to lead us to suppose that at least the peasants of Fukushima and Chichibu possessed a collective memory of rebellion. In the Iwashiro region of Fukushima, or western Fukushima, where the 1882 incident was centered, risings of various types broke out fairly regularly, beginning in 1654 and continuing off and on until the Fukushima Incident itself.[16] After the mid-eighteenth century, risings in the Aizu region were rarely separated from one another by more than a dozen years, and in some periods there was even some clustering, especially in the period from 1749 to 1752, and during

12. One need only cite Louis Riel in the case of some Canadians, Crazy Horse for American Indians, Jefferson for Americans, Saigō Takamori for later Japanese, Zapata for Mexicans, etc., etc.

13. See the author's article, "The Politicization of Japanese Social Bandits," in *Asian Bandits and Radical Politics*, ed. Paul Winther (forthcoming). Also see Aoki, *Hyakushō ikki*, pp. 142–43.

14. Yokoyama Toshio, *Gimin: Hyakushō ikki no shidōshatachi* (Tokyo, 1973), pp. 10–19. Also, Inaoka Susumu, *Nihon nōmin undō shi* (Tokyo, 1974), pp. 28–29.

15. See Irwin Scheiner, "The Mindful Peasant: Sketches for a Study of Rebellion," *Journal of Asian Studies* 32:4 (August 1974):588; see note 70, below.

16. Aoki, *Sōgō nempyō*, pp. 34, 38, 76, 88, 107, 110, 114, 127, 130–31, 134, 144, 151, 164, 166, 170, 184, 196, 201, 204, 207, 209, 211, 214–15, 234, 249, 259–60, 270, 276, 280, 283–86, 290, 322, 327, 332–33, etc.

the 1780s and the 1860s. In these years it appears that one revolt was transposing itself into another. It should be noted that the clusterings usually coincided with periods of poor harvests and famine.[17]

Like Fukushima, the Musashi region also experienced risings on a fairly regular basis, and also demonstrated some clustering, notably in the Tempō (1830–44), Temmei (1781–89), and Keiō (1865–68) periods. The 130 uprisings in these three periods alone accounted for 30 percent of all Musashi-based Tokugawa disturbances. Nearly a quarter of the 130 were centered in the Tama region, and nineteen, or about 15 percent, took place in and around the district of Chichibu.[18]

Compared to Fukushima and Chichibu, Hitachi province (Ibaraki) did not experience any clustering until the Bakumatsu period (1853–68). In that period, Ibaraki had twenty-two of its 100 Tokugawa risings, fourteen of which took place in the Tsukuba or Makabe regions, both areas of popular rights activity in the 1880s.[19]

Thus, in all three regions, though somewhat less in the case of Ibaraki, a tradition of rebellion seems to have been sustained throughout the Tokugawa period, and was bolstered by a frequency of occurrence that probably made later generations of residents less hesitant to take collective action whenever an apparent need to do so arose. Equally important, in all three regions the number of incidents of rebellion clustered during the latter years of the Tokugawa period, thereby increasing the chances that a tradition of protest would survive the profound changes that came with the founding of the new Meiji order.

This certainly seems to have been the case with the Aizu region. In the first ten years of Meiji, that area alone accounted for twenty-four risings. In the same period, ten of the thirty-four Musashi risings took place in and around Chichibu. Even Ibaraki, where only nine disturbances were counted in this period, showed continuity with its past by hosting three of them in Makabe district.[20]

---

17. Rudé, *Crowd*, p. 22, makes the same point in the case of late eighteenth-century France.

18. The figures are computed based on the date in Aoki, *Sōgō nempyō*, pp. 222–61, 393–98, 533–57; 147–67; 380–85, 478–82; 297–311; 405–8; 600–607.

19. Figures are based on compilations made from ibid., pp. 276–98, 578–603. For an account, both official and from the newspapers, of the large-scale disturbances occurring in Makabe district between 1876 and 1877, see *Ibaraki ken shiryō*, Vol. 1 of the *Kindai seiji shakai hen* (Ibaraki, 1974), pp. 377–420.

20. Figures are taken from Aoki, *Sōgō nempyō*, pp. 322–57; 613–18; 316–57; 611–16; 409; 355–60; 615–18.

If quantity with special reference to frequency is one index that helps to demonstrate a tradition of rebellion for certain regions, then it is necessary to show the quality of the rebellion as well. Form, intensity, duration, and participation figures are aspects of rebellion that help to differentiate the risings which have thus far only been counted and not explained.

In a large measure, the intensity and duration of, and the extent of participation in, a peasant uprising was a function of the form the rebellion took. What is meant by form here differs minimally from the typologies used by Hugh Borton, Kokusho Iwao, and Aoki Kōji.[21] Each of these specialists more or less subscribe to the same typology, but since Aoki's is the most recent and the most complete, it is the one related here.[22]

Chōsan ("running away") refers to a form of protest used by peasants since the early Muromachi period, whereby they would collectively abandon their farms and leave the area.[23] It perhaps rested on the idea incorporated in the old saying, "Agreement in the village on nonparticipation is one way to coerce."[24] In effect, then, it was a farmers' strike and was therefore potentially harmful to the feudal rulers whose wealth and power was derived from agricultural production. For this reason, it enjoyed considerable success as a way of getting demands met. But with the gradual erosion of village solidarity, a *sine qua non* for this form, the *chōsan* soon became impossible to effect; seldom did it occur after the early eighteenth century.

The other forms, however, lasted well into the Meiji period: (1) The *tonshū*, *chōshū*, and *gunshū* referred to the legal gathering of a crowd intent upon demonstrating its discontent. When these gatherings were unruly and broken up by local officials, they were known as *fuon* ("unrest"). (2) When the crowd manifested enough organization to make a collective appeal by legally petitioning the village officials, the form was known as a *shūso*. (3) Sometimes the protesters would try to bypass or leapfrog their local officials and appeal directly to the domain lord or even to the Bakufu. This form was illegal and was called an *osso*. It had a variant known as the *daihyō osso*, which referred to an illegal appeal made by a village representative(s), usually

21. Hugh Borton, *Peasant Uprisings in Japan of the Tokugawa Period*, Vol. 16 of the *Transactions of the Asiatic Society of Japan* (Tokyo, 1938); Kokusho Iwao, *Hyakushō ikki no kenkyū zokuhen* (Tokyo, 1959); and Aoki, *Hyakushō ikki*.

22. Aoki, *Hyakushō ikki*.

23. Aoki, *Hyakushō ikki*, pp. 33–34; also see Paul Varley, *The Ōnin War* (New York, 1967), p. 213.

24. Quoted in Aoki, *Hyakushō ikki*, p. 139.

the village headman. Sakura Sōgorō and Kanno Hachirō, earlier mentioned as rebel heroes, are two examples. (4) If an *osso* was backed up by threat, intimidation, or violence, then it became a *gōso*. (5) That form easily and oftentimes was transformed into a *bōdō* ("violent movement"); and if it was directed against the homes, property, or persons of officials, wealthy merchants, and farmers, then it became an *uchikowashi* ("smashing"). (6) These latter largely local affairs might sometimes go beyond village or domain borders and then become a *zenpan sōdō* ("all-domain rising"). To the extent that it was organized and had a strong goal orientation, then it was a *hōki* ("rebellion"). In some cases, the large-scale rebellions were characterized by atavistic, religious, or primitive communistic undertones; these were termed *yonaoshi ikki* ("world reform uprising").

As might be expected, usually the intensity heightened, the duration lengthened, and the number of participants increased as the form of rebellion progressed from the first type toward the last. Rarely, it seems, if ever, did a disturbance pass through all six "stages." Many were probably uniform, i.e., began, proceeded, and ended at the same stage or in the same form, and probably just as many jumped from the legal appeal stage directly to the "smashing" stage.

While most of these forms could be found occurring at any time during the Tokugawa period, at certain times one form seemed to predominate.[25] Thus, for the first seventy years, until 1660, the predominant form of social protest was what it had been for the past several hundred years, the *chōsan*, and secondarily, the *bōdō*. The next fifty years witnessed the ascendency of the *osso*, but particularly its variant, the *daihyō osso*. During the following half century, until the early 1760s, the illegal and more violent *gōso* form was the major type of protest. During the last 100 years of Tokugawa and during early Meiji, peasant uprisings were usually of the *bōdō* and *uchikowashi* varieties, although this is when the all-domain risings and the *yonaoshi ikki* also began manifesting themselves.

Accordingly, as the more violent forms of protest became more frequent as the Tokugawa era approached the Meiji, the intensity, duration, and peasant participation also heightened. Even a cursory examination of the figures shows that especially after the mid-eighteenth century, more peasants were involved more often in more violent forms of protest.[26]

25. Ibid., pp. 34–37, 116, 148–51.
26. See the tables in ibid., pp. 84, 92, 99, 118, 136. For a more complete explanation, see the discussion on pp. 73–74, 81, 84.

Why this happened has to do with certain socioeconomic changes that were taking place, changes which were themselves reflected by changes in the form of peasant uprisings. Before viewing these changes in this way, a brief outline of the main socioeconomic changes occurring during Tokugawa would be helpful.[27]

Tokugawa Uprisings: Economy, Society, and Polity

During the seventeenth century, the system of landholding changed dramatically. Large landholdings which were based on the extended family and servant labor—what Professor Aoki Kōji terms the "system of patriarchical slavery" (kafuchō doreisei)[28]—were breaking up, and in their place many small landholdings appeared, some tenant operated and others held by self-cultivators. In some regions, such as the Kinai (Osaka region), which was more urban and commercial than other parts of Japan, this phenomenon of the disintegration of large holdings was already pronounced. Even in less commercialized regions, such as the Tōhoku, although the same process was already discernible as early as 1594,[29] it did not become widespread until the eighteenth century.[30]

Although this process was recorded and made official by government surveys which recognized the de facto operator of a landholding, it was also commonly recorded by the villages themselves in the form of village codes. These codes recognized landownership, established regulations regarding the appropriation of common lands, and set down penalties for violations.[31] The codes were oftentimes the product of the buraku (hamlet) association which would, after a natural disaster or a poor harvest (and the consequent loss of land for some smaller cultivators), rewrite the village code so as to reflect the new realities of land distribution. Those who lost their land would commonly sell their labor for a term of service as a day laborer or servant; so doing, however, meant a loss of whatever sociopolitical rights the code granted landowners.[32]

27. Much of the following summary comes from Thomas C. Smith, *The Agrarian Origins of Modern Japan* (New York, 1966; originally published in 1959).
28. Aoki, *Hyakushō ikki*, p. 65.
29. Ibid., p. 58, for landholding patterns in three Aizu villages, one in Yama district, and two in Ōnuma district.
30. Smith, *Origins*, p. 104.
31. Aoki, *Hyakushō ikki*, pp. 66–67; also see Ishikawa Naoki, *Tonegawa minken kikō* (Tokyo, 1972), pp. 37–41.
32. Aoki, *Hyakushō ikki*, pp. 68–69; and Smith, *Origins*, pp. 9–10.

Still, despite having lost their property and their rights as landhold-ers, they benefited from the close social and familial ties operative in early Tokugawa villages. Whether related by blood, marriage, or in-dentured servitude, the agricultural laborer was treated as a "child" by the large landowner he served. This relationship, known as *oyakata-kokata* ("parent-child"), reflected a condition of social and economic interdependence between the two parties.[33]

Occasionally in early Tokugawa, this relationship took on a politi-cal aspect as well when "the successful farmer, having become a vil-lage official representing the interests of the small farmer, represented the village cooperative body in opposition to the domain authority."[34] In addition to representing his village, he oftentimes led it in rebel-lion. This too was a political act: "Resorts to violence—peasant revolts and jacqueries—was the only other method of intermittent participa-tion in the decision-making process."[35]

Only within such a close, interdependent, and cooperative vil-lage context could the predominant form of peasant protest be the *chōsan*, a form which virtually disappeared after the mid-seventeenth century. Until then the village had retained much of its cooperative spirit, but thereafter began losing it as the breakup of the large land-holdings left in its wake several remaining large landholders and a multiplicity of small-scale subsistence farmers. The resulting un-equal relationship usually enabled the large landholder to occupy a position of authority equal to his economic position. Thus he be-came the headman (*shōya*, *nanushi*, or *kimoiri*, depending on the lo-cation of the village), an office sometimes inherited by his descen-dents, but a position of leadership rather than one of overlordship. He derived his political predominance from the consent of the organic village unit; and in order to keep it, and to be true to the cooperative spirit of the village, he would on occasion have to represent the de-mands of the villagers to the domain rulers.[36]

It was not until the late seventeenth and early eighteenth centuries that local officials became alienated from the village unit. As Thomas Smith and others suggest, this was due to a number of factors: an in-

33. Smith, *Origins*, chap. 3.
34. Ibid., p. 69.
35. Kurt Steiner, "Popular Political Participation and Political Development in Japan: The Rural Level," in *Political Development in Modern Japan*, ed. Robert E. Ward (Princeton, N.J., 1968), p. 220, n. 13.
36. Aoki, *Hyakushō ikki*, p. 70.

heritance system that reinforced an economic hierarchy among land-holders; an expanding population that put extra pressure on fixed land resources and that helped to foster in turn the creation of socio-economic classes; the development of sharper class lines after natural disasters, causing many to borrow heavily from the large landholders; the routinization of certain social customs such as dress, ceremonial seating arrangements, and the increasing importance attached to fam-ily histories; the increasing intrusion into and the control over village government by domain government;[37] and finally, the growth of the market economy, which made land, labor, and wealth into commod-ities, that is, "goods produced not for use, but for sale."[38] Hence, in-creasingly the socioeconomic context was being defined in terms of the unequal encounter between the large landholder *qua* village of-ficial, on the one hand, and the rest of the village small holders, on the other. Village solidarity was slowly eroding, giving way to a polar-ization of classes within the village brought on by the impersonal re-lationships imposed by the cash nexus.

This change was clearly mirrored by the changing form of peasant protest. During early Tokugawa, "when the solidarity of the village had not been widely disturbed by the influence of competitive farm-ing, many peasant uprisings were led, not by outcasts and ne'er-do-wells, but by headmen," despite the fact that siding "with the village against his lord . . . meant almost certain death."[39] But during the latter half of the Tokugawa period, many peasant uprisings were led by the villagers themselves and were frequently directed against the headman *qua* landlord.[40] Some of these, known to later historians as *murakata sōdō* (intravillage conflict), would go beyond the village af-ter peasants disposed of the headman and appealed directly to Bakufu officials.[41] These types of rebellions, usually expressed in the more violent forms of *gōso* or *uchikowashi*, accounted for between 40 and 50 percent of all uprisings of the mid-Tokugawa period.[42]

Even then, however, it was not uncommon in the more economi-cally backward regions for some headmen to lead their villagers in

37. Ibid., and Smith, *Origins*, pp. 43, 59.

38. Eric Wolf, *Peasant Wars of the Twentieth Century* (New York, 1969), p. 277; and Aoki, *Hyakushō ikki*, p. 74. Even though a Bakufu law of 1643 forbade the selling of wet and dry land, the practice continued anyway. In Aizu, for instance, 19.3 percent of the pop-ulation was propertyless as of 1684. See Aoki's Table 16 in *Hyakushō ikki*, p. 77.

39. Smith, *Origins*, p. 60.

40. Aoki, *Hyakushō ikki*, p. 81.

41. Ibid., pp. 79–80.   42. Ibid., pp. 73–74.

rebellion; but this was becoming more and more rare.[43] Since head-men were increasingly also the major landlords and creditors of the village, especially in the Kinai and Kantō regions, they were not very sympathetic to demands for debt deferment, lower prices for com-modities, and, to the extent that they were tied to the domain govern-ment, requests for tax reduction.[44] Consequently, in their place as leaders of village rebellions, the middle-income farmer—oftentimes a minor village official or the head of an old but financially unstable family—who was more vulnerable to the vicissitudes of the market and of nature, rose to lead the poorer villagers.[45] Rebellions led by middle-income farmers in the mid-eighteenth century were as yet small-scale affairs; the large-scale ones were led by the headman. As Professor Aoki observes, the scale of violence "widened considerably" whenever the poorer farmers "formed an alliance with other classes [i.e., headmen]."[46]

An example of the latter case is the Tenma Sōdō of 1764.[47] One of the largest Tokugawa uprisings, it involved an estimated 200,000 peasants, encompassed both Bakufu and private domains, and during its more than three-month existence spread throughout most of the northern Kantō region (Chichibu in Saitama, Gumma, Tochigi, and Eastern Nagano).[48] The uprising takes its name from the issue which set it off originally, the Bakufu's decision to increase the number of post stations (tenma) in the sukegō ("assisting village," responsible for providing men, horses, and other official transportation services between post stations)[49] on the main road between Tokyo (Edo) and Nikkō, shrine of the Tokugawa family, which was about to celebrate the one hundred and fiftieth anniversary of its founder's death. For that reason, and to improve the road for commercial traffic, the Bakufu imposed an onerous tax. It was supported by the merchants who had business in the region, anticipating increased revenue in the future, but it met with violent opposition by the many farmers—

43. For example, see the cases presented in ibid., pp. 81, 83, 95, 96.
44. Ibid., pp. 82–83; and Smith, Origins, pp. 74–149.
45. Aoki, Hyakushō ikki, p. 88.
46. Ibid., pp. 90–91.
47. See Hayashi Motoi, Zoku hyakushō ikki no dentō (Tokyo, 1971), p. 172; Ōno Fumio, Saitama-ken no rekishi, pp. 165–68.
48. Aoki, Sōgō nempyō, pp. 128–29.
49. For more information on the sukegō, see William Jones Chambliss, Chiaraijima Vil-lage: Land Tenure, Taxation, and Local Trade, 1818–1884 (Tuscon, Ariz., 1965), especially p. 145.

including the village headmen—who would have to finance the largest proportion of the *sukegō* system improvement plan. Most villages along the road contributed manpower to the rebellion—villages that were reluctant to join were threatened with destruction—and together they compelled the government to abandon its plans. However, the victory was not without its price. Some 600 village leaders—headmen, elders (*toshiyori*), "group heads" (*kumigashira*), and farmers' representatives (*hyakushōdai*)—were punished; only 113 peasants received sentences, usually much lighter than those given to the leaders.[50] The principal leader of the rebellion, a village headman from Kodama district in Saitama, was executed, only to be resurrected 100 years later as a *gimin* (martyr).[51]

This example of rebellion also points to another index of what Smith terms "the decline of the cooperative group,"[52] that is, the emergence of a new pattern of mobilization for uprisings whereby rebel leaders would compel individuals to participate. One person per household was the usual exaction, and those households which would not comply might be subjected to property "smashings."[53] In the mid-to-late eighteenth century, when trans-domain uprisings took place (like the Tenma Sōdō), entire villages were forced to participate.[54]

During the last 100 years of Tokugawa, peasant uprisings continued to record changing socioeconomic conditions. Most of the large-scale disturbances of this time reflect the increasing numbers of farmers who were turning to specialized commercial production of crops[55] but were finding the consequences of this hard to bear. They were troubled by: variability of farm income and an inelastic cost structure; increased production of cash crops hurt by the variability of the market; fixed taxes in the face of such variability; the steady concentration of landholdings in the hands of a few, which made competition difficult; the rising merchant guilds that manipulated the market; time-consuming and costly government projects for improved transportation systems that depended on the farmer's corvée labor; and so on.[56]

The Tenma Sōdō, for instance, reflected the government's efforts to establish efficient means of transportation between production centers and commercial centers. Seventeen years after that uprising,

---

50. Ōno, *Saitama-ken no rekishi*, p. 167.   51. Ibid., p. 168.
52. Smith, *Origins*, chap. 10.
53. Aoki, *Hyakushō ikki*, pp. 89–90.   54. Ibid., p. 94.
55. See Smith, *Origins*, chap. 6.   56. Ibid., especially p. 157.

the same region experienced another, but this time centered in the sericulture region of later-day Gumma prefecture. This time it was over the government granting permission to merchant guilds and village headmen/wealthy farmers to establish quality controls on silk production, and to issue transport licences and levies on silk.[57] A few years after that incident, an entire series of "rice riots" (*kome sōdō*) broke out in countryside areas which had no rice because they had to sell it all, and in cities denied rice because of a general shortage.[58] Rice shortages again produced rice riots in the Tempō period.[59] Two decades later, in 1865 and 1866, the demand for rice provoked more violence, especially in Edo and in the predominantly cash crop areas of Chichibu and Aizu. Both areas were dependent on the importation of staples to meet basic needs; they were also troubled by a new government stamp tax on silk and other sericulture-related items.[60] Moreover, the staples that the people of these areas required were priced almost out of reach, even if they could get them. Between 1859 and 1867, the price of rice increased 3.7 times; soy sauce, 4.0 times; sugar, 3.2 times; cotton, 4.3 times; and tea, 1.3 times.[61] According to one of the rebels involved in the 1866 uprising:

> Since the opening of the Yokohama port, commodities have become higher priced, gradually causing hardships for village peoples, especially this year when silkworm production was poor. Popular discontent was widespread, and after discussion it was decided to do some housewrecking. In addition to grain stores, we wrecked five houses.[62]

The Chichibu protesters "decided to destroy the homes of officials first" and especially the homes of the headmen. After disposing of them, they attacked silk and tea merchants who were selling their goods to Yokohama merchants. Finally, they attacked "rice dealers, usurers, officials, and others who have authority."[63] From Chichibu, this uprising spread south, almost to Yokohama itself, and later north

---

57. Aoki, *Hyakushō ikki*, p. 149; Hayashi, *Dentō*, p. 173.
58. Hayashi, *Dentō*, p. 173; also, Shōji Kichinosuke, *Yonaoshi ikki no kenkyū* (Tokyo, 1974), p. 123.
59. Shōji, *Yonaoshi*, p. 150.
60. Ibid., p. 140; Aoki, *Sōgō nempyō*, pp. 299–301. For more details on this uprising, known as the Bushū Ikki, see Sasaki Junnosuke, ed., *Yonaoshi*, Vol. 5, *Nihon minshū no rekishi series* (Tokyo, 1974):271–85; Nakazawa Ichirō, *Jiyū minken no minshūzō* (Tokyo, 1974), pp. 10–17; and Ōmachi Masami and Hasegawa Shinzō, eds., *Bakumatsu no nōmin ikki* (Tokyo, 1974), pp. 13–15.
61. Ōno, *Saitama-ken no rekishi*, p. 176.
62. *Chichibu kimpen uchikowashi ikki*, quoted in Shōji, *Yonaoshi*, pp. 139–40.
63. Ibid., pp. 141–42.

as far as Fukushima, but only after reaching a very violent stage in the Gumma area. The rebellion involved tens of thousands of farmers, and finally had to be put down by the newly organized *nōheitai* (farmers' army), armed with rifles supplied by the Tokugawa government. This army was "composed mainly of the sons of middle-income and wealthy farmers."[64] In contrast, the rebel forces were mainly led by middle-income farmers but manned by "poor people—day laborers, servants, craftsmen, tenants, and the like."[65]

This rebellion, especially as it was manifested in Fukushima, developed into a *yonaoshi ikki*, and therefore exhibited a markedly antifeudal character. It opposed merchant guild controls over production, taxes, and special levies on the production of cash crops, and called for free enterprise of commodity production and sale. Politically, it called for the democratization of village government, i.e., an end to hereditary positions in village government, and the use of open and free elections; it also demanded village autonomy from domain administration. Finally, the participants wanted tenant rents decreased and wages for day laborers increased.[66]

Similar types of demands were again made in October 1868, when another *yonaoshi* involving several thousands of Aizu residents broke out. In this one, and in others in different parts of the country, demands for a more equitable distribution of the land, as well as demands for the elimination of certificates of pawned land (*shichichi-ken*), have led later historians to regard these *yonaoshi ikki* as precursors of the democratic movement and/or the "farmers' revolution."[67] Indeed, the "leveling" component of the *yonaoshi* was recognized by observers of their time, who referred to such uprisings as *yonarashi ikki* (literally, "equalize-the-world uprisings"), a radical variant of the *yonaoshi*. As one of the few specialists on the subject characterizes them:

64. Ibid.; also see E. Herbert Norman, *Soldier and Peasant in Japan: The Origins of Conscription* (Vancouver, 1965; originally published in New York in 1943), especially p. 30, for additional information on the *nōheitai*.

65. Shōji, *Yonaoshi*, pp. 141, 143.

66. Ibid., pp. 118–22; methods for filling the office of headman differed according to region, although the three most common means were election, rotation, and inheritance, election being the least common. Smith, *Origins*, p. 58, tells us that election was confined to villages "where traditional status patterns had broken down under the impact of commercial farming." Shōji, *Yonaoshi*, p. 122, tells us that beginning in the eighteenth century, practices of "bidding" (*nyūsatsu*) and "nomination" (*suisen*) were also used in the Fukushima region as means to fill the post.

67. For example, Shōji, *Yonaoshi*, p. 121. Another historian who takes this position is Kano Masanao in his *Nihon kindaika no shisō* (Tokyo, 1972), pp. 62–67; he specifically relates the "revival of the tradition of peasant rebellion" to the Chichibu Incident.

Yonaoshi took as its objective the leveling of economic life and the creation of a [new] universe. Concretely, as the movement expressed its [aims] in action, most sought to recover documents pertaining to pawned land or loans; to distribute food equally in times of famine; and appeared as destroyers of the private property of the wealthy farmers, whose economic status stemmed from holding positions of village authority, or from serving as domain functionaries. Moreover, the participants were all poor farmers, therefore making the risings totally class based.[68]

Since many *yonaoshi ikki* were centered around the sericultural regions of Chichibu, Fukushima, Gumma, and eastern Nagano, where tenancy was minimal and most farmers were small landholders who produced mainly for the market, the "poor farmers" of the *yonaoshi* rebellions must be understood in this light. Moveover, it should also be made clear that leaders of the *yonaoshi* were usually the slightly more wealthy of the community of poor farmers.[69]

Despite the fact that many of the *yonaoshi* rebellions invoked Buddhist millennial notions and occasionally neo-Confucian standards of right and wrong to justify their antifeudal economic and political opinions,[70] it is nonetheless necessary to pay heed to the leveling aspect they exhibited, especially since this aspect later re-emerged in the radical popular right philosophy of Ōi Kentarō and others, as well as in the expressions and slogans used by Meiji farmers belonging to the Jiyūtō and Komminto. Calls for political reform during the Chichibu Incident, for example, were expressed by such slogans as "*Ita-*

68. Tamura Eitarō, *Kindai Nihon nōmin undō shiron*, quoted in Shōji, *Yonaoshi*, p. 348.

69. Aoki Kōji, *Meiji nōmin sōjō no nenjiteki kenkyū* (Tokyo, 1967), pp. 21, 25; and Shōji, *Yonaoshi*, p. 10; also Aoki, *Hyakushō ikki*, p. 143. For evidence relating to Gumma prefecture, with comparisons with other sericulture regions, see Nagatani Yasuo, "Gumma jiken no shakaiteki kiban ni kansuru kenkyū nōto," *Shien* 32:1 (February 1972):81-90.

70. See Scheiner, "The Mindful Peasant." From Professor Scheiner's account of the rebellion, we get the mistaken impression that Chichibu farmers defined their revolt in Buddhist and millennial terms. We get this impression for two reasons: (1) Scheiner indiscriminately places the Chichibu rebellion among other truly millennial movements as if the former represents the acme of millennialism as represented by the latter; he does this by beginning his story with the Chichibu Incident, points to a few *yonaoshi* elements in the incident, and then moves on to discuss unrelated (geographically and temporally) and genuine instances of *yonaoshi*; (2) he incorrectly conceptualizes the 1884 Chichibu rebels as "peasants" rather than as farmers, and hence shows little appreciation for the economic basis of the rebellion. Scheiner is correct, I believe, in taking the comparative approach to the study of Japanese rebellion, and is also correct in saying that chiliastic and revolutionary movements share some features in common; but it is a mistake to ignore the secular aspects of a revolutionary tradition by overemphasizing the religious. It is also worth pointing out that Yasumaru Yoshio (whom Scheiner cites), in his essay "The Thought of Popular Movements" ("*Minshū undō no shisō*," in Shōji et al., *Minshū undō*, pp. 391-436), emphasizes that some so-called *daimyōjin* (divine rectifiers) were motivated by secular Confucian principles and displayed a sense of political consciousness in their activities.

gaki no yonaoshi" ("World reform of [Jiyūtō President] Itagaki"), and "aid the poor, equally distribute the wealth."[71]

Meiji Uprisings

If the various types of Tokugawa peasant uprisings were not an important cause of the disintegration of the Tokugawa government and system, then they certainly may be regarded as an index of the extent to which the feudal system was collapsing. A feudal system based theoretically upon the wealth derived from the land the peasants worked was being increasingly subjected to ever more violent attacks by the farmers themselves. Even after traditional village leaders were co-opted by the system, thereby taking from the peasants one of their more important means to plug into the decision-making structure, the farmers continued to employ the only other means left open to them—rebellion. Moreover, this system which so denigrated the merchant by placing him last in the feudal social hierarchy was being undermined by the many farmers who turned increasingly to commerce as a subsidiary or even as the main source of their income. The peasant uprisings, then, and the penetration of the market economy down into the depths of peasant society, revealed clearly the socioeconomic contradictions besetting the feudal system.

But even when the old system fell and a new set of feudal elites replaced the old, peasant uprisings continued to plague the new government just as much as they did the old, and to make just as apparent the contradictions inherent in the new order. It could hardly have been otherwise. For the vast majority of farmers, conditions prevailing during at least the first five years of Meiji, until the land tax reform, were no different than those of late Tokugawa.[72] Neither should it be surprising, therefore, that the bulk of peasant violence in early Meiji occurred during the first five years.

In the first year of Meiji, at least eighty-five disturbances occurred, eleven of them large *yonaoshi ikki*.[73] During the first decade (see

71. Inoue, *Chichibu jiken*, pp. 76–81. For information concerning the emphasis placed on "leveling" by the Akita *Risshisha*, see Masumi Junnosuke, *Nihon seitō shiron* 1 (Tokyo, 1965):274.

72. Aoki, *Meiji nōmin sōjō*, pp. 20–40; also, Kokusho Iwao, "Meiji shonen no hyakushō ikki," in *Meiji isshin keizai shi kenkyū*, ed. Honjō Eijirō (Tokyo, 1930), p. 713. For an instance where the financial plight of farmers became even worse as a result of the new Meiji tax and land reform, see Fukuda, *Sanmin sōjō roku*, pp. 23–24.

73. Aoki, *Meiji nōmin sōjō*, p. 36. I say "at least eight-five disturbances" because it is likely that, as with Tokugawa *ikki*, more Meiji conflicts are probably being discovered by scholars other than Aoki. Also, in his 1971 *Sōgō nempyō* (see Table 1, p. 107), Aoki shows a considerably higher number of disturbances occurring for early Meiji than he does in his

Table 1), 674 incidents took place, a yearly average of 67.4 (a median of about fifty per annum), considerably higher than the rate for almost any decade during the Tokugawa period. Most reflected economic conditions not unlike those which existed in late Tokugawa. For example, due to a succession of poor harvests in the first three years of Meiji, nineteen "rice riots" broke out. Likewise, even as the government was making appeals to merchants to stop speculating on commodities, violent "smashings" and *bōdō* were occurring in the name of cheaper food or tax relief or debt exemption. Nearly 50 percent of all disturbances during the first ten years were of this type.[74]

Some disturbances of this period, however, were different from Tokugawa ones, but only in terms of the immediate cause and not in terms of the form they assumed. For example, after the Restoration, domain borders formerly closed to outside commerce were now opened; this cut into profits made in the local market, producing some rebellion.[75] Once prefectures were established (1871), differences in the tax rates between prefectures, or rather the knowledge of this, provoked some rebellion.[76] Other early reforms enacted by the new government also produced discontent. Conscription, the school system, the census, and the telephone and telegraph systems were all, to quote E. H. Norman, "sparks which ignited the uprisings."[77] But probably the most resented of all the new reforms was the land tax reform of 1873. It recognized private ownership, issued land deeds, changed the form of tax payment from rice to cash, and fixed the land tax at 3 percent of the land's assessed value.

The new land tax regulations were regarded as excessive by many farmers, especially those from regions where immediately after the Restoration the domain rulers had reduced annual land taxes (*nengu*) by half in order to placate a rebellious peasantry.[78] For most farmers, however, several years were needed in order for them to understand and be affected by this reform. Its most immediate effect was "the establishment of the landlord system."[79] Large numbers of small- and

---

Meiji nōmin sōjō. It is also necessary to note that only one other *yonaoshi ikki* was recorded for the entire Meiji period, that one in 1870.

74. Aoki, *Meiji nōmin sōjō*, p. 35.

75. Kokusho, "Meiji shonen," p. 716.

76. Ibid., p. 717.

77. E. H. Norman, *Japan's Emergence as a Modern State* (New York, 1940), p. 73.

78. For example, in Aizu. See Shōji, *Yonaoshi*, pp. 141–43; also, Kokusho, "Meiji shonen," p. 717.

79. Aoki, *Meiji nōmin sōjō*, p. 61.

medium-sized landholders began losing their land because they were unable to pay the tax or the mortgage that they took out the year before in order to meet that year's land tax payment. Hence, they fell into tenancy. In 1872, the amount of land under tenant cultivation was an estimated 29 percent. By 1888, the figure was over 40 percent.[80] The records of subsequent protest also record the effects of the land tax reform. During the decade 1877 to 1886, 29 percent of all disturbances were tenant-landlord conflicts, up 23.3 percentage points from the decade earlier; 17 percent of all incidents for 1877 to 1886 were fights against creditors, a type of disturbance virtually unrecorded in the previous decade. In contrast to these types of disturbances, between 1877 and 1886 the percentage of anti-government conflicts had dropped about 41 percentage points, to a mere 9 percent of all incidents.[81] It seems that in a very short time, the main enemy of the farmer had changed from the government to the landlord and creditor.

In the next section, where the rising rate of tenancy and dispossession of land is discussed, it will become apparent why the number of anti-landlord conflicts jumped dramatically after the 1873 land tax law had a chance to effect changes in patterns of landownership. On the other hand, why the number of anti-government conflicts dramatically decreased requires explanation immediately. Briefly, it has to do with the growing power and authority of the Meiji government. In an incredibly short period, the leaders of the Meiji Restoration embarked on a program of "centralization of power by means of taxation and conscription [that] rendered rebellion well-nigh impossible."[82] In the name of the Emperor, the forces of "oligarchic absolutism"[83] organized a conscript army capable of suppressing peasant *and* samurai uprisings. Nowhere was this capacity better demonstrated than in 1877, when the conscript army easily and quickly put down the large samurai army of Saigō Takamori. A year before, it had done the same in the case of the huge Mie and Gifu peasant uprising.

Up against a veritable brick wall of military strength, the Meiji farmer learned quickly that he could not knock it down. Instead, he joined lawful struggles (gōhō tōsō)—"This is one characteristic that

---

80. Shimoyama Saburō, "Meiji jūnendai no tochi shoyū kankei o megutte," pp. 176, 183.

81. Aoki, *Meiji nōmin sōjō*, pp. 36, 64; anti-creditor disturbances, if there were any, were not shown in the table for 1868–77 disturbances.

82. Robert A. Scalapino, *Democracy and the Party Movement in Prewar Japan: The Failure of the First Attempt* (Berkeley, 1967), p. 61.

83. Ibid., p. 63.

separates the Meiji period from the Tokugawa feudal period"[84]—to oppose national policy. Chief among these lawful struggles was the *jiyū minken undō*. In joining it, the farmer changed from the essentially nonpolitical being he was during the Tokugawa period, having no political rights outside the village (providing, of course, that he held land), to a political being out to define what was meant by the 6 April 1868 Imperial Oath, especially Article One: "An assembly shall be widely covened and all issues shall be resolved by public opinion."[85]

Strengthened by the legacy of protest bequeathed to him by his Tokugawa forefathers, and given direction by the Freedom and People's Rights Movement, the Meiji farmer sought to make government honor the Imperial Oath. To this experience we will turn shortly, but before doing so we will look first at the economic background to the "incidents of intense violence" of the 1880s.

The Economic Basis of the *Gekka Jiken*

The "incidents of intensified (violence)" took place against an economic backdrop of severe depression, the acceptance of which was made all the more difficult since the five preceding years (1878–82) were a period of unprecedented prosperity for most landowning farmers. What brought on the depression was Finance Minister Matsukata Masayoshi's deflationary policy. This policy was adopted in late 1881 in order to strengthen the unstable Japanese economy, beset by a weak currency at home and a too heavy reliance on imported goods. What exactly the policy entailed and even its effects on the farming population in general have been well-documented elsewhere.[86] Here let it suffice to outline the consequences of the deflation policy on the general farming population and then, more specifically, on the farming populations of the regions where the *gekka jiken* occurred.

84. Aoki, *Meiji nōmin sōjō*, p. 67. In their study of collective violence in France, Italy, and Germany between the years 1830 and 1930, the Tillys make the point, "Despite hopeful liberal mythology to the contrary . . . violent repression works" (*The Rebellious Century, 1830–1930* [Cambridge, Mass., 1975], p. 285). We will substantiate the point further in Chapter 5, below, where we discuss the nature of Meiji repression.

85. Quoted in Scalapino, *Democracy*, p. 52.

86. Probably the best treatment of its effects remains Chapter 12 of Nobutaka Ike's *The Beginnings of Political Democracy in Japan* (New York, 1969; originally published in 1950), pp. 138–47. Also see Thomas C. Smith, *Political Change and Industrial Development in Japan: Government Enterprise, 1868–1880* (Stanford, Calif., 1955), pp. 81–85, 95–100; E. H. Norman, *Emergence*, pp. 144–48; K. Ohkawa and H. Rosovsky, "A Century of Economic Growth," in *The State and Economic Enterprise in Japan*, ed. William Lockwood (Princeton, N.J., 1965), pp. 63–66.

Depression in the Countryside

Following the Satsuma Rebellion of 1877, Japan's farming population prospered. In that year the rate of taxation was lowered from 3 percent to 2.5 percent. This was done partly in response to peasant uprisings over the land tax, and partly in response to pressure applied by the popular rights movement on the government to keep its 1873 pledge of lowering the land tax.[87] At the same time, the commodity price index rose appreciably, thereby increasing the incomes of farmers. Increased income encouraged increased consumer spending, as well as efforts to expand production and commercial enterprise. This situation, however, helped improve only the lot of the landowner; it hurt the tenant and wage workers, whose low and fixed incomes were insufficient to afford the higher-priced commodities.[88] Still, for most farmers, the post-1877 period was one of prosperity.

We can see that this was the case by looking at the situation in more detail. One journalist who toured the Chichibu region around this time wrote an account of the growing wealth of the region's farmers; it was entitled "A Diary of Prosperity in the Countryside" (*Inaka hanjōki*). He wrote: "The people of Chichibu have sericulture. They will live in comfort for a hundred years." He also observed the trend of increased consumer spending, noting that even "young wives and young girls have enough money to buy fine dresses and silks."[89] Silk farmers and their families enjoyed this newborn prosperity because their product was the number one income earner of all exports for

87. An indication of the peasant's joy of victory over the government is recorded in a poem appearing in Inaoka, *Nihon nōmin*, p. 61; "Farmers of various regions/celebrated their own victory,/When we thrust our spears/we get 2½%." For a general discussion of the farmers' uprisings of 1876 and their effect on bringing down the tax rate, see Inoue Kiyoshi, *Nihon no rekishi* 2 (Tokyo, 1965):168–69. Also see Ienaga Saburō, *Ueki Emori kenkyū*, (Tokyo, 1960), p. 359, where it is shown that Ueki believed the 1876 uprisings were instrumental in getting the land tax lowered; Ueki also believed them to be early manifestations of later farmer involvement in the popular rights movement. On the government's pledge to lower the land tax: Paragraph Six of the original land reform law said that when taxation on commodities reached 2 percent, then the land tax would be reduced to 1 percent of the land's assessed value. According to Shimoyama Saburō, that point had been reached by 1883. See his "Meiji jūshichinen ni okeru Jiyūtō no dōkō to nōmin sōjō no keikyō," in *Jiyū minkenki no kenkyū*, eds. Horie Hideichi and Tōyama Shigeki, Part 3: *Minken undō no gekka to kaitai*, Vol. II (Tokyo, 1959):12. Corroborative evidence is found in an article in the *Jiji Shimpō*, reprinted in translation in the *Japan Weekly Mail*, 29 March 1884: "Ten years ago it was announced that the land tax, although fixed at 2½%, should gradually be reduced to 1%." Also, in Paul Mayet, *Agricultural Insurance in Organic Connection with Savings Bonds, Land Credit, and the Commutation of Debts*, trans. Reverend Arthur Lloyd (London, 1893), p. 59: "From the year 1873 the government has been under a promise to lower it [the land tax] to 1% of the estimated value of agricultural land."

88. Ike, *Beginnings*, p. 139.

89. Quoted in Inoue, *Chichibu jiken*, pp. 7–8.

nearly twenty years after the Restoration. But not only silk farmers benefited from the post-1877 boom: between 1877 and 1880, producers of cotton watched their product increase in value by 28 percent on the market, and rice growers enjoyed a doubling in value for their crop.[90] Another indication of prosperity was the growth of producer societies, in Chichibu and elsewhere, organized in order to modernize and expand production. But in order to do this, most farmers were forced to borrow from either the government or private loan dealers.[91]

The government recognized that much of the increased wealth the countryside was enjoying was in fact illusory, that it was the product of inflation, beneficial to the farming population in the short run, but detrimental in the long run to the establishment of a solid industrial, modernizing economy; for this reason, the government embarked on a stringent policy of deflation. Immediately, it attacked one of the major causes of inflation, cheap money, by withdrawing nearly 35 percent of the depreciated paper currency then in circulation. Consequently, the paper money left in circulation appreciated considerably, causing commodity prices to decline drastically, and causing the real value of taxes to increase substantially. "To express this increase more concretely, the peasant was obliged to sell 42 percent more of his crop to pay his land tax in 1885 than in 1881."[92] Not only did the real cost of land taxes increase the financial burden of the cultivators, but many who had converted production to cash crops during the inflationary period were now afflicted with new duties on such items as *sake*, lacquer, tobacco, and soy sauce. These duties, coupled with more expensive money, priced their cash crops out of the range of the buying power of most consumers. Local tax rates were also increased in many areas, mainly because as part of its retrenchment policy the central government ceased to provide in whole or in part subsidies for such local needs as hospitals, roads, schools, prisons, and government offices.[93] The figures support this: Between 1880 and 1883, all prefectural taxes increased on the average of 22 percent. The prefectural land tax increased by 39 percent, and town and village taxes rose by 19 percent.[94] Finally, the deflation program called for the

90. Ōe Shinobu, *Nihon no sangyō kakumei* (Tokyo, 1968), pp. 74–76.

91. Inoue, *Chichibu jiken*, pp. 10–11.

92. Smith, *Political Change*, p. 81. The quotation concludes: "assuming that his crop was the same in both years and calculating its money value at Tokyo prices."

93. Aoki Keiichirō, *Nihon nōmin undō shi* 2 (Tokyo, 1958):295–96.

94. Ōe, *Sangyō kakumei*, p. 87.

stopping of liberal granting of funds for local agricultural improvement and expansion schemes, thereby preventing many farmers from pursuing a positive means to break free from their financial difficulties.

Since they lacked positive means, large numbers of farmers were compelled to adopt negative ones to free themselves from indebtedness—heavy borrowing at usurious rates, mortgaging their land, and nonpayment of taxes. Bankruptcy and tenancy soon followed, or, even worse, "having lost their land, many farmers would desert their families, disappear or commit suicide; others would flow toward the mines and cities, creating a class of lumpen proletariat."[95] Equally destructive socially, as the February 1886 issue of the *Nihon keizai sha kai hōkoku* (Report of Japanese Economics and Society) tells us, "Presently there are great numbers of debt disputes and gangs of tenants and paupers whose hardships push them into our prisons."[96] Similarly, we read in the newspapers of October 1884 of "the great increase of paupers in many districts, and in more than one instance so desperate were these people that they would resort to violence."[97] Not all resorted to violence. Some simply escaped from it by emigrating, many to British Columbia or to Hawaii.[98]

It is impossible to say exactly how many emigrated, were imprisoned, committed suicide, or fled to the cities or mines as a consequence of poverty and the loss of their lands, but we can gain some idea of how many did in fact lose their land. Hirano Yoshitarō says that between 1883 and 1890, those who lost their land because of tax defaults numbered 367,744. Seventy-seven percent of these, he says, lost their land because of true impoverishment (as opposed to neglect), owing a total amount of about 31 *sen* (.31 yen) apiece.[99] The amount of land involved was 47,281 *chō*, having a total value of 4,944,393 yen!![100] Aoki Keiichirō further computes that the value of the land lost was twenty-seven times greater than the value of the average debt that each person owed in taxes.[101] Based on these fig-

95. Ibid., p. 296.
96. Quoted in ibid.
97. From the *Mainichi Shimbun*, reported in the *Japan Weekly Mail*, 25 October 1884.
98. *Japan Weekly Mail*, 20 December 1884. The same article says that those desiring to emigrate to Hawaii will be guaranteed free passage and employment once they reach the islands. The *Jiji Shimpō*, according the the *Japan Weekly Mail*, advised ex-samurai to go to America rather than Hawaii so that their talents would not be wasted on "insignificant sugar cane fields."
99. Hirano is quoted in Aoki Keiichirō, *Nōmin undō* II:296. Smith, *Political Change*, p. 83, n. 33, mistakenly says "31 *yen*." Ike, *Beginnings*, p. 144, cites the correct figure of 31 *sen*.
100. Aoki Keiichirō, *Nōmin undō* II:296.
101. Ibid.

ures, Thomas Smith calculates that "something in the order of 11 percent of all peasant proprietors were dispossessed for nonpayment of
taxes in a seven year period [1883–90]."[102] And as Smith also notes,
it was probable that "only in exceptional cases was land surrendered
for back taxes"; that in most cases the peasants borrowed from local
usurers and consequently "it seems all but certain that more land was
taken by foreclosure than was sold for taxes."[103] Hence, we learn that
on 7 August 1884, seven local creditors in the village of Togashira,
Kambara district, Niigata prefecture, foreclosed on 513 villagers
whose total debts amounted to 10,000 yen.[104] Elsewhere we read:
"A large number of householders in the province of Harima—900, it
is said—have declared themselves insolvent, in order to escape paying
the autumn taxes."[105] Or: "During the last year—and the same condition seems likely to apply in the course of the present year—he
[the farmer] has found too often that, after laboring the whole year,
he is unable to pay the tax on his farm."[106]

The problem of indebtedness was further complicated by government intransigency in allowing deferred payment of taxes. Earlier regulations set by the Finance Ministry in 1874 and 1876 imposed heavy
interest payments for late taxes, and a short period of grace before
the farmer's land would be auctioned publicly.[107] As if this were not
tough enough, in 1880 the government abolished the earlier "rules
for deferred payment" (ennō kisoku) and increased the interest
charges applied to the deferred payment period to over 50 percent of
the amount owed.[108] Tough rules like this one explain in part why
the number of incidents of farmers selling their land jumped so high.
In 1887, there were 680,000 incidents of land sales; in 1888, there
were 1,230,000; by 1891, the figure exceeded 1,710,000.[109]

Not only was the government less than lenient with regard to payment of the land tax in depressed times, but it also wrote laws which
encouraged usury. The Interest Limitation Law of 11 September
1877, for instance, set the legal maximum interest chargeable for private loans of under 100 yen—an amount applicable to the vast major-

102. Smith, *Political Change*, pp. 82–83. Smith's figures come indirectly from Mayet, *Agricultural Insurance*. Hirano's and Aoki's probably come from the same source.
103. Smith, *Political Change*, p. 83.
104. A *Jiji Shimpō* report printed in the *Japan Weekly Mail*, 23 August 1884.
105. *Japan Weekly Mail*, 8 November 1884.
106. Ibid., 25 October 1884.
107. Smith, *Political Change*, p. 83, n. 33.
108. Aoki Keiichirō, *Nōmin undō* II:298.
109. Ibid. For additional figures on instances of forced land sales, pawning, and bank-ruptcy between 1883 and 1885, see ibid., p. 152, Table 2.21, and p. 154.

ity of farmers seeking credit—at 20 percent per annum. Article Two of the same law, however, forbade litigation in cases where "people exceed these limits,'" thereby giving the creditor the right to exploit with impunity tight market conditions whenever he was able. Paul Mayet, the German economist employed by the Meiji government to study conditions of agriculture in Japan, commented on this law: "Hence we see the government takes no action against creditors for overstepping the various rates of interest."[110]

Besides the wide-scale loss of property, increasing amounts of land were falling into tenancy: "The increase of 1.42 percent between 1883 and 1884 was probably the greatest annual increase for the entire Meiji period."[111] Also, since there existed restrictions on voting rights according to the amount of taxes that were paid, the number of people qualified to vote in local elections also dropped: If the year Meiji fourteen (1881) is taken as 100, by 1884 the voting index was ninety-three, by 1887 it was eighty-two, and by 1894 it was fifty-nine.[112] Another common occurrence during the depression was commodity speculation by large merchants. As prices fell, they would buy up large quantities of a product in anticipation of a later rise in prices. Thus we read: "Considerable purchases of rice by Yokohama firms are reported to have been effected. It is supposed that the buyers intend to hold for a rise in the Japanese markets."[113] The market was indeed down: In 1881, one *koku* (4.96 bushels) of rice was selling for 11.2 yen; in 1884, it cost less than half its 1881 price at only 5.14 yen.[114] Still, money was more expensive in 1884 than in 1881, and therefore commodities were less affordable. Moreover, as rice and other commodities were removed from the market by speculators, people could neither find nor afford to buy basic food staples; consumption rates therefore declined drastically.[115] This occurred despite the fact that, as one source has it, rice production rose by 27 percent in the period from 1878 to 1885.[116]

In view of all these facts, it is difficult to overemphasize the catastrophic consequences produced by the Matsukata deflation policy

110. Mayet, *Agricultural Insurance*, pp. 110–11.

111. Namatame Yasushi, *Kabasan jiken no ikkōsatsu* (Takahagi, 1962), p. 18. Also see Ike, *Beginnings*, pp. 145–46; and Aoki Keiichirō, *Nōmin undō* II:300.

112. For figures on the number of people qualified to vote, see Aoki Keiichirō, *Nōmin undō* II:299.

113. *Japan Weekly Mail*, 11 October 1884.

114. Aoki Keiichirō, *Nōmin undō* II:302.

115. Endō, *Kabasan jiken*, p. 126.

116. Morris D. Morris, "The Problem of the Peasant Agriculturalist in Meiji Japan," *Far Eastern Quarterly* 15:5 (May 1956):361–62.

in the early eighties. Although the complete account of the human suffering caused by this policy will probably never be known, the question of who were the victims can be. According to a certain merchant named Kurihara:

> [The depression] has not hurt the nobility, the bureaucrats, the scholars, priests, and industrialists. Those who are suffering most are the farmers. Their wives scream they are cold because they have no warm clothing. Their children yell they are hungry because they have no rice to eat. Such is the terrible lot of the farmers. They have to suffer the laws and the courts because of creditors. They have to sell their homes and land, that which has been the source of their lives and the lives of their ancestors. . . . Farmers cannot afford to buy manufactured products either—they who ought to be our best customers.[117]

These are supposedly the words that Kurihara spoke to an audience in attendance at a cotton and silk producers convention in June 1885. Most likely, they are not an exaggeration. In a market economy, merchants like Kurihara serve as nerve centers of society, and when the pain which comes from losing their best customers because they have sunk into poverty is expressed as ingenuously as Kurihara has expressed it, then we should be inclined to believe them.

What also can be known is the violent reaction of thousands of farmers to the suffering they endured because of a policy that sought to create a solid industrial base on the backs of the agricultural population. Smith maintains that this had to be the case:

> Without an agriculture capable of producing a sizable surplus year after year, the whole Meiji programme, including industrial development, would undoubtedly have been impossible. *The peasant had to be relentlessly exploited for the modernization of the non-agricultural sector of the economy* [emphasis added].[118]

Let us now look at the nature of the exploitation in the local areas of Fukushima, Saitama, and Ibaraki.

Depression in the Regions

In Chapter 3, we will see that the patterns of landholding relations, at least among the rebellious farmers of Chichibu and Aizu, were characterized by a comparatively low rate of tenancy and a high level of landownership, especially of the general type known as "middle" farmers who owned one to two *chō* (2.45–4.90 acres) of land. Details

117. Quoted in Ōe, *Sangyō kakumei*, pp. 151–52.
118. Smith, *Political Change*, p. 85.

are also offered to show that a good percentage of the middle-level farmers had mortgaged their land at the time of their rebellions. Paul Mayet's figures for 1881, in fact, show that in terms of numbers of mortgages, the farmers of Saitama ranked sixth in the nation, right behind the cultivators of Ibaraki; the farmers of Fukushima ranked thirteenth.[119] There is, then, little question that indebtedness was widespread in these areas, but equally important is the reason for it, a question which we shall examine briefly here.

Fukushima was an economically segmented prefecture that demonstrated various levels of economic development existing among its different regions. (Economic development, for our purposes, is measured by the extent to which agricultural production is commercial, i.e., the amount of cash crop production relative to staple production.) The mid-northern region (Shinobu, Date, Adachi, and Asaka) was clearly the most developed region of the prefecture, devoting more than 50 percent of its agricultural production to such cash crops as cocoons, raw silk, and eggworms.[120] In contrast, the mid-southern region (Iwase, Tamura, Ishikawa, Nishi-Ishikawa, and Higashi-Ishikawa) was mainly a rice and staple-producing area and, except for Tamura and Higashi-Ishikawa, devoted more than 80 percent of all production to such foods. The Aizu region, along with Tamura district where the Fukushima Incident was centered, stands in contrast to both the other two regions. If the middle-northern region can be called developed, and the middle-southern region undeveloped, then the Aizu region and Tamura district can be termed "developing."

Cash crops accounted there for roughly a quarter to a third of all agricultural production, although some variation existed within the six districts. Yama (30.9%) and Onuma (29.7%) districts, located near the major centers of trade and commerce, Kitakata and Wakamatsu, led in cash crop growing, along with the huge district of Minami-Aizu (34.3%); all three were principally involved in raw silk and cocoons. The diminutive districts of Kita-Aizu (9.3%) and Kawanuma (11.9%), along with Higashi-Kabahara district (21.6%), made part of Niigata prefecture in 1888, concentrated agricultural production on staples. In terms of productivity as measured by average household production (1879), Yama district was far ahead of the other five districts,

119. Mayet, *Agricultural Insurance*, p. 65.
120. The following statistics are taken from Ōishi Kaichirō, "Fukushima jiken no shakai keizaiteki kiban," in *Jiyū minkenki no kenkyū*, Part 2: *Minken undō no gekka to kaitai*, Vol. 1, ed. Horie Hideichi and Tōyama Shigeki (Tokyo, 1959), pp. 1–119. Ōishi also uses percentage of cash crop production as an index of economic development.

but still ranked far behind the household production of the developed middle-northern region.[121]

Another feature of importance is that as a developing region, Aizu was a latecomer. Yama, Kawanuma, and Onuma districts dramatically expanded cash crop production after 1877, when the country was enjoying an era of prosperity. Yama district, for example, reacted to the demands of the market and more than doubled its production of cocoons and raw silk in the three-year period from 1877 to 1880.[122] Likewise, during the same period, when the cheaper imported cotton was causing a drop in the public's demand for domestic cotton, Yama farmers in 1880 produced barely a third of the amount they produced in 1877.[123] Yielding to the same kinds of market demand of these three years, Yama farmers increased tea production by 40 percent and paper mulberry by more than 500 percent; they decreased rice production by nearly 100 *koku*.[124] Also, in order to increase production of cash crops, particularly sericultural items, they borrowed new techniques from the more advanced districts like Shinobu and Date.[125]

Expanded production of cash crops, and therefore growing financial dependence on income from cash crops, coupled with a system of landholding dominated by small-scale individual proprietorships which, because of their smallness are more vulnerable to dramatic changes in the market than large-scale landlord-dominated areas like Shinobu, Date, Kita-Aizu, and Minami-Aizu, together made the effects of the Matsukata deflation policy—and such extra financial burdens like road labor—especially hard to bear for the farmers of the regions where the Fukushima Incident was centered.[126]

121. The percentage of household income derived from cash crops was 34% for Yama, 14% for Kita-Aizu, 18% for Ōnuma, 39% for Minami-Aizu, and 8% for Higashi-Kabahara. Though Minami-Aizu ranks higher than Yama in this regard, it should be noted that the average household income for a Minami-Aizu family is less than half that of a Yama district family.

122. Ōishi, "Shakai keizaiteki," pp. 36–37.

123. For commentary and figures regarding the decline of the Japanese cotton industry vis-à-vis foreign imports, see Norman, *Emergence*, pp. 162–63.

124. Ōishi, "Shakai keizaiteki," pp. 36–37. Yet it should also be pointed out that the farmers cultivated one more *chō* of land in 1880 than they did in 1877.

125. Ibid., p. 50.

126. Shimoyama Saburō, "Fukushima jiken oboegaki," in *Jiyū minken undō*, Vol. 3, comp. Meiji Shiryō Kenkyū Renraku Kai (Tokyo, 1956), pp. 148–86. Aoki Kōji, *Meiji nōmin sōjō*, p. 73, says that the effects of the deflation policy first struck the farmers in 1882. Based on his analysis of bankruptcies and liabilities, Ōe (in *Sangyō kakumei*, p. 156) says about districts like Yama and Tamura: "In areas where self-cultivating proprietors were the mainstay along with the wealthy farmer strata, the economic changes [of the early 1880s] were extremely serious." He claims the small self-cultivating farmer was affected the worst by the depression, but adds that many *gōnō* also suffered the loss of their land. He discerns a correspondence between areas where middle farmers predominated and the Liberal Party

Farmers in many areas, such as the Aizu region and Nagano, Yamanashi, and Gifu prefectures, turned to the production of silk after the Restoration because of its high market value and because it was one domestic product that was not in competition with any foreign imports. The expansionist boom after 1877 had especially favorable effects on the already thriving silk industry; silk alone accounted for as much as 42 percent of Japan's total exports during the period from 1868 to 1893.[127] So important was this industry, especially immediately after the Restoration, when Japan was suffering from an unfavorable balance of trade, that the government intervened in an effort to establish controls over what in early Meiji had been essentially a cottage industry. One of the first areas affected by the new policy was Chichibu. In 1872, when land deeds were being issued, the government established at Ōmiya and Ogano (Chichibu) a "raw silk improvement center" (*Ki-ito kai kaijō*). There, in an effort to standardize the quality of silk for export, government officials inspected production methods of export silk, stamped those roles of silk eligible for export, and kept records on the producers.[128] Cultivators complied with this interference because they knew that export silk brought a higher market price. They also went along, even to the extent of tolerating the building of local factories, with the government's control over the introduction of a plan to universalize new techniques of machine production, hoping that it too would mean additional revenue. Of course, since small-scale producers could not easily compete with the factories, the owners of the latter were increasingly able to appropriate an ever greater share of the means of production. Hence, around 1880 to 1881, a whole series of *ton'ya* ("wholesale houses," but they actually were combines that owned land, controlled production, processed it in their factories and marketed it themselves) sprang up throughout Chichibu and other silk-growing regions.[129] It is not just coincidence that around this time such men as Shibusawa Eiichi, "the father of Japanese capitalism,"

---

was strong, and areas where landownership was concentrated in the hands of a few landlords and Teiseitō (party) dominance. See ibid., pp. 154–57, especially Table 2.26 on p. 157.

127. Chambliss, *Chiaraijima*, p. 18.

128. Inoue, *Chichibu jiken*, p. 9.

129. Ibid.; the government's "intention was to transplant the machine industry of the advanced countries into Japan with the factory as the unit, completely regardless of the actual conditions of existing industries" (Niwa Kunio, "The Reform of the Land Tax and the Government Programme for the Encouragement of Industry," *Developing Economies* 4:4 (December 1966:466).

and his son Sōsuke made their fortunes in the area neighboring Chichibu by playing the silk and indigo market of the region.[130]

In Chichibu, silk was not merely an attractive agricultural item because of its export value, but also because it could be cultivated almost anywhere; in a region where only 6 percent of the land area was arable and where most of it was mountainous, this was an important factor. Also, since the dry land (as opposed to the paddy) was valued less, and therefore land taxes were less, Chichibu farmers found silk a very suitable product. In fact, it had been regarded as such since the middle of the Tokugawa era, so that by the early 1880s nearly 80 percent of Chichibu's population was connected in some way with the sericulture industry.[131]

Like the majority of Aizu farmers, again a point elaborated on in the next chapter, most of the Chichibu sericulturalists were middle-level farmers—small scale, self-owning, and self-cultivating proprietors of about one *chō* of land.[132] And they too, like their Aizu counterparts, had gone into debt during the expansionist boom of 1877 to 1881 in order to expand production to meet the growing domestic and international demand for silk. Moreover, besides having to meet traditional consumption needs that required the importing of twice the amount of rice and one-third the amount of wheat produced prefecturally,[133] they also, as was observed earlier, had to satisfy a consumption level for luxury items that was on the upswing. To complicate matters further, small-scale silk producers in Chichibu were slow in abandoning their traditional handreeling (*zaguri*) method for the new, more productive and efficient mechanized methods adopted by most post-Restoration newcomers into the sericulture industry. As a result, whatever edge they had on the market because of the traditional popularity of Chichibu silk was lost in the competitive market to the newcomers who could produce silk more economically. It is worth adding that Ōe Shinobu, one source for this information on production methods in Chichibu, argues that *ton'ya* in Chichibu may have been responsible for the retention of backward production

130. Chambliss, *Chiaraijima*, pp. 19–23.

131. Computed from the figures supplied by Inoue Kōji, "Chichibu jiken: Sono shakai-teki kiban," in *Jiyū minken undō*, Vol. 3, comp. Meiji Shiryō Kenkyū Renraku Kai (Tokyo, 1956), p. 79. Also see Chambliss, *Chiaraijima*, pp. 16–22, for an impressive account of the importance of the silk industry to the farmers of Hanzawa district, which neighbors on Chichibu.

132. Wagatsuma et al., *Seiji saiban shi* II:71.

133. Inoue, *Chichibu jiken*, p. 4.

methods: Because they engaged in the market manipulation of prices, they could profit from backwardness as much as they could from progress.[134]

The effect the Matsukata deflation policy had upon Chichibu farmers was not felt until 1883. Then the price of mulberry leaves, one of Chichibu's principal items of production, fell from 3.5 yen per horseload (*ichida*) to 1.25.[135] Likewise, the value of silk fell 50 percent between 1881 and 1884, as the following table shows.

Just as the Chichibu sericulturalist's income was declining—so too, of course, was the purchasing power of many silk buyers[136]—simultaneously, his taxes increased to three times the 1881 amount in real terms.[137] To make matters even worse, other government policies added to the burdens of the already overburdened farmer: Regional subsidies, earlier given in order to encourage production, were withdrawn; residents were compelled to work on a new road linking Chichibu to Takasaki (Gumma); regional government increased its taxes by nearly 20 percent; and finally, government ignored the appeals of Chichibu farmers to curtail loan dealers from recalling loans during these hard-pressed times.[138] Together these developments caused many to fall into a Dickensian state of poverty.[139] It was that poverty, according to the eminent chronicler of Meiji peasant uprisings, Aoki Kōji, following on the heels of prosperity, that was at the bottom of the Chichibu Incident.[140]

Impoverishment alone is not sufficient cause to rebel. Due to the deflation policy, we know, over three million people across Japan suffered bankruptcy,[141] but far from all of these expressed their frustration (or, prior to the fact, their *fear* of bankruptcy) by rebelling. Certainly the farmers of Makabe district in Ibaraki prefecture, to whom the Kabasan rebels appealed for support in the rebellion, for the most part refused to acknowledge the rebels' appeal. It is necessary to ask why. To anticipate later findings somewhat, it appears that the answer lies mainly in the type of insurrection the Kabasan rebels planned, and also perhaps in the nature of the patterns of landhold-

134. Ibid., pp. 158–59.

135. Wagatsuma et al., *Seiji saiban shi* II:71.

136. An index of the declining purchasing power of the consumer is that in 1884 he could buy less rice with one yen than he could in 1877.

137. Wagatsuma et al., *Seiji saiban shi* II:71.

138. Ibid., pp. 71–72; and Inoue, *Chichibu jiken*, pp. 16–17.

139. Sawada Shūjirō, "Innovation in Japanese Agriculture, 1880–1935," in *The State and Economic Enterprise in Japan*, ed. William Lockwood (Princeton, N.J., 1965), pp. 340–41.

140. Aoki, *Meiji nōmin sōjō*, pp. 83–84.

141. Endō, *Kabasan jiken*, p. 23.

TABLE 3.
Market Value of One Roll
of Silk by Year

Year	Raw silk cloth	Coarse silk
1878	2.60 yen	4.80 yen
1879	3.50	5.58
1880	4.50	6.50
1881	5.20	8.00
1882	5.40	8.50
1883	3.50	6.00
1884	2.26	4.50
1885	2.35	4.00

Source: Inoue Kōji, "Chichibu jiken: Sono shakaiteki kiban," in *Jiyū minken undō* 3, ed. Meiji Shiryō Kenkyū Renraku Kai (Tokyo, 1956), p. 86.

ings and agricultural production peculiar to Makabe district. Both points will be elaborated upon in subsequent chapters. Here we will briefly examine only the economic developments of early Meiji and those stemming from the deflation policy to see whether they affected the farmers of Makabe differently than they did the farmers of Yama and Chichibu.

At the outset it is necessary to point out that the farmers of Makabe district were neither passive toward poor economic conditions nor reluctant to rise in rebellion against the authorities whom they regarded as responsible for them. As late as 1876, for instance, the farmers of Makabe and neighboring districts, especially Naka district, were chief among those areas violently involved in one of the larger peasant uprisings of the early Meiji period. In late November and early December, Makabe farmers joined in what constituted the tail end of a revolt earlier begun in Gifu, Mie, Wakayama, and Aichi over the government's land tax policy. The participation of the Makabe farmers stemmed from dissatisfaction over the local government's handling of petitions for tax relief and tax reform. A one-time wealthy farmer and village headman, Honbashi Jirōsaemon, led about 2,500 farmers in rebellion against the local authorities, but the unorganized army of farmers was soon dispersed by troops called in from a nearby garrison.[142]

142. *Ibaraki-ken shi: shi, machi, mura hen* 1 (Mito, 1972):626–30; *Ibaraki ken shiryō: Kindai seiji shakai hen* 1 (Ibaraki, 1974):377–516; Aoki Keiichirō, *Nōmin undō* II:233–43.

If it was not for want of fighting spirit that Ibaraki farmers failed to respond to the call for revolution issued at Mount Kaba in 1884, neither was it because they had escaped the disastrous effects of the Matsukata deflation policy. Between 1884 and 1885, a substantial 3.5 percent increase in the land area falling under tenancy was recorded for Ibaraki as a whole; the year before, a 2 percent rise in the tenancy rate was recorded for the farming population. In some villages, more than a 6 percent rise was said to have occurred. Moreover the source for these statistics tells us that particularly hard hit were the farmers of Makabe district.[143]

A rise in the tenancy rate is a significant index of the toll that the depression was taking on Ibaraki farmers. But also, as in the cases of Chichibu and Yama farmers, we must wonder whether the type of agriculture the Makabe farmers were engaged in might help to explain how vulnerable they were to the violent fluctuations in commodity prices then affecting the market.

Compared to the Yama and Chichibu farmers, and to the farmers of other Ibaraki districts, the Makabe farmers were "overwhelmingly producers of staples."[144] Secondly, the figures for 1884 show that the vast majority of Makabe farmers were either tenants or part tenant and part small landholder. Tenants worked usually on very large-scale rice and/or barley farms and took home an average of 32 percent of the crop yield. Tenants composed 23.5 percent of the Makabe farming population and part tenants/part landowners 44.7 percent;[145] tenant-worked land amounted to only 31 percent of the total agricultural land area of the district.[146] Those figures, of course, translate into a very large landlord class having very large landholdings. In fact, in 1879, Makabe district ranked third among the prefecture's seventeen districts for the size of its landlord class.[147] Moreover, compared to the other districts in the prefecture, Makabe was relatively "undeveloped" with regard to cash crop production. Yet despite that, it was the prefecture's leading producer of raw silk and cocoons (but by an amount negligible compared to Chichibu or Yama), the second-ranked producer of cotton, the third-ranked in red beans (azuki), and the fourth-ranked tea producer.[148] Since we know that most of Makabe's agricultural land area was in the form of large staple-producing landholdings, we can infer that probably much of the cash crop production was done by the large class of part tenant/part small land-

143. Namatame, Kabasan, pp. 20, 27.   144. Ibid., p. 38.
145. Ibid., pp. 27, 50, 58.   146. Ibid., p. 25.
147. Ibid., p. 23.   148. Ibid., p. 50.

holder, that 45 percent of the population which owned less than one *chō* of land.[149]

For this group, at least, the drastic drop in commodity prices and the more expensive taxes and money that attended the deflation policy together must have been catastrophic. Very likely, its effects were indicated in the rising tenancy rate mentioned above. Many part owners probably became full tenants, and although the fall into tenancy for these already part tenants was not as far or as steep as it was for the small landowner of Chichibu and Yama, we can nonetheless imagine it to have been equally painful.

To conclude this section, we can say that although the financial losses encumbered by many farmers of Yama, Chichibu, and Makabe districts because of the Matsukata deflation policy were indeed difficult to bear passively, in themselves they were not sufficient to cause rebellion. People who suffer economic misery without having an understanding of its basis, without having a clearly laid out program of how to escape from it or how to build the type of society where producers reap the full harvest of their efforts and production, will merely remain miserable. It was up to the popular rights movement to make the condition of economic misery meaningful to the sufferers and to offer them a means by which they could end it.

The Movement for Freedom and Popular Rights

The title of this section is the customary translation for *Jiyū minken undō*, the term for the movement initiated in the early- to mid-1870s by the upper-class anti-government forces (or more precisely, anti-the-government-in-power forces) but which was later transformed in the early eighties by lower-class democrats, some of whom were involved in the *gekka jiken*. Those involved in both the early and later stages of the popular rights movement were known as *minkenka* (advocates of popular rights), but in terms of the ideology which each supported they were substantially different types. The reason for this difference stems in part from the different class backgrounds and in part from the different extent to which each group was tied to the central and local governments. Briefly, the early *minkenka* were samurai who played a role in the Meiji Restoration and for a short period,

149. Ibid., p. 21. Although not touched upon explicitly in our account, an important related point about the increase in tenant-cultivated land is one made by F. M. L. Thompson: "A greater number of tenant farmers, or simply a greater area of tenanted land, would mean that an increased proportion of total agricultural output moved into the orbit of the market" ("Landownership and Economic Growth in England in the 18th Century," in *Agrarian Change and Economic Development*, ed. E. L. Jones and S. J. Woolf [London, 1969], p. 43).

prior to consolidation of the new regime, a role as leaders of the new government. The later *minkenka* for the most part played no part in the Restoration (Kōno Hironaka is one who did), nor in the central government, but who were oftentimes active in local government. A few déclassé samurai could be found among their ranks, but most were *gōnō* (wealthy farmers), primary school teachers, priests, petty merchants, or even small landholding farmers.

How great the differences were between the two groups can be demonstrated by making an in-depth comparison of them. Part of this will be done in the next chapter, where we examine the kinds of people who comprised the three incidents, and in Chapter 4 where we show how these people were tied by organization and ideology to the popular rights movement. Here we will look at the movement in its early years, between 1874 and 1881, and at the changes which transformed it into a predominantly rural and increasingly mass-based movement.

To this end, we divide the movement into three parts:

1. "The formative period," 1874 to 1878, covers the time between the establishment of the *Aikokukōtō* (Public Party of Patriots) and the *Risshisha* (The Society to Establish One's Ambitions) in 1874, and the movement to re-establish the *Aikokusha* (Society of Patriots, founded first in 1875 after the Osaka Conference, but abandoned the same year by its leaders who joined the government).
2. "The period of promotion and organization," 1878 to 1881, begins with the proliferation of local popular rights societies and culminates with the establishment of the *Jiyūtō* (Liberal Party) in October 1881.
3. The third period, herein called "the period of activism," began with the *Jiyūtō* and ended with its breakup in late October 1884. This period is the subject of most of the remainder of this work and will therefore be dealt with in subsequent chapters.

The Formative Period

The first five years of the movement was characterized by the formation of several political societies. Most of the founders of these societies were samurai coming from old Tosa domain, or Kōchi prefecture as it was then named.[150] The rank-and-file membership also largely consisted of samurai, so it was in name only that these early

150. Scalapino, *Democracy*, p. 62.

societies were called "public parties" (*kōtō*). In fact, they did not
seek popular support. As Robert Scalapino says, "The term 'people'
was to be limited for the time being to these groups [ex-samurai and
wealthy commoners], and was not intended even by the liberals to
include the obviously unequipped lower classes."[151] Examples of
such "parties" include the *Aikokukōtō*, the *Risshisha*, and the *Aikokusha*; all either emerged in Tosa or were established by Tosa samurai,
and were led by such figures as Itagaki Taisuke, Kataoka Kenkichi,
Furuzawa Uro, Ueki Emori, and Okamoto Kensaburō. Other ex-
samurai activists involved in these groups but coming from different
areas of the country include Kōno Hironaka, Etō Shimpei, Gotō
Shōjirō, and Komuro Nobuo.[152]

During this early period, all were active as political "outs" in calling for the government to establish a representative assembly,[153]
a demand made repeatedly in the petitions and memorials they submitted to the government.[154] Besides calling for representative government—their "panacea" to remedy the evils of misgovernment, the
concentration of power in the hand of a select few ex-samurai from
the old domains of Satsuma and Chōshu, conscription, heavy taxes,
mismanagement of foreign affairs, etc.[155]—the other principal features common to most of these documents was a notion of natural
right that would have as its positive expression the institutions of
self-government, local autonomy, and the equality of the classes.[156]
"We, the thirty millions of people in Japan," a *Risshisha* statement
of principles read, "are all equally endowed with certain definite
rights, among which are those of enjoying and defending life and liberty, acquiring and possessing property, and obtaining a livelihood
and pursuing happiness. These rights are by Nature bestowed upon
all men, and, therefore, cannot be taken away by the power of any
man."[157] If this was an expression of the rights of the individual that
natural law demanded, then a representative assembly, guaranteed by
a constitution, was the least demand the popular rights advocates were
duty-bound to make of the government, the writers of positive law.

151. Ibid., p. 56.
152. Ibid., p. 45; and W. W. McLaren, ed., "Japanese Government Documents, 1867–
1889," *Transactions of the Asiatic Society of Japan*, Vol. 42, Part I (Tokyo, 1914):426–27.
153. Scalapino, *Democracy*, pp. 40–60; Ike, *Beginnings*, pp. 60–71; Norman, *Emergence*,
pp. 174–80.
154. Some of these can be found in McLaren, ed., "Documents."
155. Ike, *Beginnings*, p. 67.
156. Ibid., p. 61.
157. Quoted in ibid. An equally liberal statement of party principles was made by the
Aikokukōtō on 12 January 1874; see Scalapino, *Democracy*, pp. 45–46.

The principles of most political societies of this time were not as explicit as those of the *Risshisha*. Most spoke more about "universal principles" than about rights and freedoms.[158] But in either case, the men who headed these societies employed such principles in a very Machiavellian manner, interested more in gaining political power than in educating the people in the principles of natural right. Itagaki Taisuke, President of the *Risshisha* and later head of the Jiyūtō, was one such man. E. H. Norman seems to be correct when he characterizes Itagaki as having "the instinctive sensitivity of a chameleon to the colouring of his political environment."[159] So too was Scalapino probably right in his assessment that despite a few dedicated and principled men, "the liberal movement was being used partly as a tool with which to bring personal power to certain ex-members of a warrior class who could no longer rely upon military force or social and intellectual prestige."[160] As noted earlier, the *Aikokusha* folded the very year of its establishment when its leaders were co-opted by the government by being promised high government posts; Itagaki was one of those leaders.[161]

Itagaki's colors are also clearly shown in the principles he espoused. His well-known address "On Liberty," delivered in Kōchi in 1882, shows clearly that his conception of equality and liberty was a very restrictive one. He makes a clear distinction in his speech between the value of the political opinions of "the lettered and unlettered classes," that is, between the samurai and most commoners, and implies that political power should be held only by the upper and monied classes.[162] Only this group, he believed, should have the franchise: "We would only give it in the first instance to the samurai and the richer farmers and merchants, for it is they who produced the leaders of the revolution of 1868."[163] In his way of thinking, these people were the "public" that should be allowed to be involved in "public debate."[164]

Itagaki can hardly be faulted for being an illiberal liberal. He was merely a politician in search of political power, then being concen-

158. McLaren, ed., "Documents," p. 430: "Memorial on the Establishment of a Representative Assembly," 17 January 1884.

159. E. H. Norman, "Feudal Background of Japanese Politics," Ninth Conference of the Institute of Pacific Relations, Hot Springs, Virginia, January 1945 (Secretariat Paper No. 9), International Secretariat, Institute of Pacific Relations, New York, p. 65.

160. Scalapino, *Democracy*, p. 69; also see pp. 70–72.

161. Ibid., p. 59.

162. McLaren, ed., "Documents," p. 445.

163. Scalapino, *Democracy*, p. 56.

164. Ibid., p. 51.

trated in the hands of a small number of oligarchs. Instead of having other politicians as opponents in the contest for office, he had the government to contend with, and it had the Emperor on its side. Although Itagaki and other early popular rights leaders also invoked the name of the Emperor, they were at a disadvantage because the government had the advantage of administering the country in the name of the Emperor. That left the discontented samurai and the wealthy commoners as the most natural allies in the battle to capture political power; they had, after all, been the official and unofficial powers, respectively, during the old regime. However, the wealthy were too busy seeking more wealth to bother with politics (except from behind the scenes), and the discontented samurai were in many cases too strongly tied to traditional elitist values to align themselves with a liberal movement. This situation during the early period of the movement's development left remaining, ironically, the 80 percent or so of the population to whom the principles of equality and liberty that Itagaki and others were preaching would naturally appeal. But Itagaki was not a democrat. He wished to "broaden the popular base of the movement," but only enough to enable him to unseat the government, assume power, and embark on his own plans for "national defense and commercial and political expansion."[165] His quandary was inescapable: how to broaden his base of support without broadening it too much? His answer was to talk equality to the dispossessed samurai and the wealthy—and the government as well: It had to understand the nature of the popular rights threat in order to be responsive to Itagaki—and that meant invoking natural right, the "natural" ideology to be employed against the government's "divine right."

An historical parallel (which shall be discussed at greater length in Chapter 4) that might help to explain Itagaki's and the predominant samurai position in the early stages of the popular rights movement would be the political thought of the leaders of the English Revolution, especially that of Cromwell and Ireton. Simply stated, despite the force of events and because of the exigencies of securing and maintaining political power in a milieu of rapid change, Cromwell and Ireton did not show themselves as social revolutionaries, but only as constitutional liberals and reluctantly as republicans. Both clearly opposed universal suffrage and the granting of any political rights to the people beyond the basic constitutional ones of life, liberty, and the pursuit of property. For Cromwell, Parliament could be composed

165. Ibid., p. 58.

only of men "who had opposed the King and possessed property" and could "represent the worthy alone, and, among the worthy, only those who have a stake in the country"; in his terms, that meant ownership of property valued at £200 or more.[166] Ireton concurred, warning that a franchise not limited by wealth would result in a state of general anarchy.[167]

In these respects, Itagaki's beliefs differed little from Cromwell's and Ireton's; they were liberal but not democratic: All three men chose to exclude the vast majority of the population from participation in the public realm. But like the English case, the Japanese liberal movement contained within it the seeds of democracy whose growth represents an unintended consequence of opposing the government in the name of liberal values. Japanese Levellers, and even a few Diggers, began making themselves heard in the local popular rights societies which began springing up in ever greater numbers around 1878. These societies, like the Levellers, took to heart the proclamations of liberty and freedom issued by the early leaders of the popular rights movement, and in some instances endeavored to give them a truly democratic coloring.

The Period of Organization and Promotion, 1878 to 1881

Despite the fairly heavy repression which the political societies suffered at the hands of the government at the outset of this period,[168] the movement to re-establish the *Aikokusha* met with a warm reception by commoners throughout the countryside. Not only was "the economic and political unrest of the old *heimin* [commoner] classes, especially among the agrarian group . . . growing,"[169] but the movement's call for "revision of land taxes" brought more and more farmers into the local political societies that were beginning to be formed. Still, "It is clear that in spite of this national growth the 'civil rights movement' was still predominantly in the hands of the southwest ex-samurai, more especially the men of the *Risshisha*; not only did they hold the majority of high offices, but their views were the determinants of policy."[170]

---

166. Quoted in G. P. Gooch, *Political Thought in England, Bacon to Halifax* (London, 1960; originally published in 1915), p. 71. Also see his *English Democratic Ideas in the Seventeenth Century*, 2nd ed. (New York, 1959; originally published in 1927), pp. 192-204.
167. For a treatment of Ireton's thought, see Gooch, *Political Thought*, p. 67; and *English Democratic Ideas*, pp. 134-40.
168. Gooch, *Political Thought*, p. 61.
169. Ibid.
170. Ibid., p. 62.

The situation was quickly changing, however, as growing numbers of local political societies began bringing larger numbers of commoners into the movement. Although, as Nobutaka Ike says, "Exactly how many societies were formed in this period and how big a membership they boasted is not known,"[171] he also tells us that "local societies affiliated with the Risshisha sprang up in almost every city and county" and that "numerous groups were organized, particularly at the village level."[172] One more recent study claims that there were more than 150 "well-known political societies at this time."[173] Another shows that as of October 1881, when the Jiyūtō was formed, there were 149 political societies which then became Jiyūtō affiliates; as of November 1880, these same 149 societies were able to mobilize over 135,000 people for participation in a petition campaign for the establishment of a national assembly.[174]

Another recent study, this one by Shimoyama Saburō, provides us with a clear picture of the extent of popular rights growth during this period.[175] The growth of rural political societies was a result of, and concurrent with, a campaign originally spearheaded by the *Aikokusha* to petition for "the establishment of a national assembly" (*Kokkai kaisetsu kisei*). By the fourth general convention in March of 1880 (when it changed its name to the "Association for the Establishment of a National Assembly"—*Kokkai kisei dōmeikai*), 114 delegates present claimed to represent 96,900 members of organizations spread over twenty-eight prefectures throughout Japan.[176] In the same year, over 246,000 people in twelve different petitions and forty-two memorials had signed their names, demanding the establishment of an assembly.[177] Contrary to what Robert Scalapino claims—that it was still controlled by the early popular rights leaders of Kōchi at this time—Shimoyama's more recent evidence reveals otherwise, at least regarding the geographical origins of the later leadership. Even by the time of the second *Aikokusha* conference in December 1879, the members

171. Ike, *Beginnings*, p. 68.
172. Ibid., pp. 65, 68.
173. Irokawa Daikichi, "Freedom and the Concept of People's Rights," *Japan Quarterly* 14:2 (April–June 1967):176. One local history shows that in the Tsukuba area of Ibaraki prefecture alone, at least eleven popular rights societies were started between 1879 and 1880 (Tsuchiura-shi shi hensan i-iinkai, comp., *Tsuchiura-shi shi* [Tsuchiura City, 1975], p. 726).
174. Gotō Yasushi, *Jiyū minken: Meiji no kakumei to hankakumei* (Tokyo, 1972), p. 95.
175. Shimoyama Saburō, "Jiyū minken undō—sono chiikiteki bunseki," *Tōkei Daikai Shi* 37 (February 1962):199–224.
176. Ibid., p. 203; Scalapino, *Democracy*, p. 62, using a different source dated 1927, cites the figure of 87,000 people and only twenty-four prefectures.
177. Shimoyama, "Chiikiteki," p. 204.

of local societies from Eastern Japan accounted for 60 percent of the national membership. The fastest growing region, in fact, was the Kantō (Tokyo area prefectures); its political societies could claim 24,166 members by late 1879.[178] Tokyo alone with twelve societies was second only to Kōchi with seventeen.[179]

As regards the class leadership of the movement, Scalapino is probably mistaken as well. Ike, for one, maintains that after 1878, leadership of the popular rights movement shifted to the *heimin*, the "rural aristocracy" in particular (by which it is assumed he means the *gōnō* or "wealthy farmer"), due mainly to the greater wealth they had at their disposal to fund the movement, as opposed to the declining fortunes of ex-samurai.[180] Ike is not alone in taking this position. Gotō Yasushi tells us that a substantial change in the class basis of the leadership of the *minken* movement occurred in the half year separating the *Aikokusha* conference of March 1880 and the second meeting of the Association for the Petitioning of a National Assembly in November 1880. In the March meeting, 66 percent of the representatives were ex-samurai (*shizoku*); but at the November conference, 53 percent of the sixty-four delegates (representing 130,000 political society members) were *heimin*, most of whom came from the "wealthy farmer" class of rural society, holding such positions as prefectural assembly representative or village headman. Of course, the ascendency of the commoners in the movement meant a corresponding decline of *shizoku* power. An index of this decline is the fact that the predominantly *shizoku*-composed Kōchi *Risshisha* was able to collect only about 48,000 signatures on one of its petitions in March 1880, and on another in November less than half that, only about 20,000.[181]

The growing trend for commoners to take a leading role in the popular rights movement continued after the Jiyūtō was founded in October 1881. By November 1882, there were 769 known party members; 80 percent were commoners.[182] In some regions, commoner predominance in the party was even more pronounced. For example, again by November 1882, all seventy-six of Kanagawa's Jiyūtō members were *heimin*; sixty-one of Saitama's sixty-two were as well; twenty-six of Ibaraki's twenty-seven, and sixty-seven of seventy-one

178. Ibid.
179. Gotō, *Kakumei*, p. 95; Kōchi's membership, however, was far greater than Tokyo's.
180. Ike, *Beginnings*, pp. 69–71.
181. Gotō, *Kakumei*, pp. 105–6, 109.
182. My figures are taken from the several tables appearing in Satō Seirō, "Meiji jūshichinen gogatsu no Jiyūtō-in meibo ni tsuite," *Rekishigaku Kenkyū* 178 (December 1954): 31–38.

in Gumma were commoners.[183] In terms of geographical dominance, by this time the Kantō region accounted for 59 percent of the party's total membership.[184] By the time the party dissolved in October 1884, the seven prefectures that compose the Kantō region still predominated with 46 percent of the party's total membership.[185] Finally, in anticipation of subsequent chapters, it might also be mentioned that certain districts (*gun*) within the prefectures that make up the Kantō region had especially large memberships: Chichibu and Makabe ranked first in Saitama and Ibaraki prefectures respectively.[186]

Thus we can conclude that at least by 1880, the shifts in the class makeup and in the geographical center of activity had transformed the popular rights movement into a Kantō-centered and commoner-led affair. But besides these two shifts, another occurred as well; an ideological shift, one more of emphasis than of content. As commoners wrested control of the movement from the early *shizoku* leadership, they also took the demand for a national assembly, and the principles of natural right which supported that demand, from the power seekers and made these their own. Commoners coming especially from the Kantō region and contiguous prefectures (e.g., Nagano and Fukushima) appear to have seriously believed that a national parliament was needed in order to implement the principles of natural right.

Conclusion

A great deal of territory has been covered in this chapter, as we have leaped through nearly 280 years of historical, socioeconomic, and political changes with fifty- and one-hundred-year bounds, forever anxious to direct ourselves "back" to the more familiar terrain of the 1880s. In traversing the sometimes dark countryside of Tokugawa and early Meiji Japan, however, we were able, first of all, to discern what for our understanding of subsequent rebellion seemed to be the most consequential developments and, secondly, to begin to clarify the point of uncertainty with which we concluded the last chapter—namely, the idea that the rebellions of the 1880s serve as evidence of a farmer consciousness of possessing certain political

183. Ibid.   184. Ibid.   185. Ibid., p. 31.

186. Ibid., p. 32. No reliable figures are available either for Fukushima as a whole or for its districts. Shimoyama, "Chiikiteki," explains that for some provinces, complicated membership rules meant that the membership of many district parties was either not recorded at all or not recorded properly. See especially pp. 209–11. We can say, however, based on the data that we use in Chapter 3 and the information regarding party activity in Chapter 4, that the Jiyūtō in Fukushima appears to have been as active and as large as that in any other region of the country.

rights vis-à-vis the authorities. You will recall that we ended the last chapter by saying that to claim the existence of such a farmer consciousness would be premature until we first understood the background of the *gekka jiken*. Now that we have that information, as well as the details of the incidents themselves, we are in a better position to provide an explanation to the question concerning the awakening of a new political consciousness among Japanese farmers. To answer that question completely, it will be necessary to review the evidence and enlarge upon it in the form of an extended argument on how this political consciousness developed.

The development of an agrarian political consciousness in Japan can be conceptualized as having come about in four stages, with each stage identifiable according to certain socioeconomic changes and the opposition or resistance these changes engendered. It is necessary to add that the four stages do not lend themselves to any kind of strict periodization, nor do they represent absolute and uniform changes in society and economy; as much as anything, they represent trends or "historical forces" which can at best be identified only by their changing content. For any but the Tokugawa specialist, it would be foolish to try to pinpoint their origins or to describe the bewildering complexity of their varied effects on all the agriculturalists of the different regions of Japan. For our purposes it is enough merely to describe their broad contours so as to make it clear that history is not a series of *non sequiturs*, but is instead the constantly changing product of past experiences, and to show that the rebellions of the 1880s were in some way connected with past historical developments.

During the first stage of the development of farmer consciousness of his political rights, the feudal, precapitalist peasant did not seem to believe he possessed any substantive political rights vis-à-vis the Tokugawa rulers, nor did the Tokugawa and domain rulers really recognize any such rights as belonging to peasants. The only substantive "quasi-political" rights that peasants possessed during this first stage stemmed from their economic "right of subsistence."[187] At a time

187. The term "quasi-political" used to describe peasant rights in early Tokugawa comes perilously close, I realize, to social science "jargonese." Hopefully, however, its meaning will become clear in the remaining part of the conclusion to this chapter. Regardless, the term does take on definite meaning when compared historically to a similar right in eighteenth-century England. E. P. Thompson, in "The Moral Economy of the English Crowd in the Eighteenth Century," discusses the function of certain oftentimes traditional "legitimizing notions" or rights that informed the activities of the crowd involved in food riots. These notions or rights were the mainsprings of the people's "moral economy"; they were moral notions that distinguished between fair and unfair, legitimate and illegitimate practices in mar-

when the attitude and the policy of officialdom toward the agriculturalist were expressed by such sayings as "Peasants are like sesame
seeds—the more you squeeze them, the more they produce" and
"Peasants should be allowed neither to live nor die," peasant surplus
production was the property of the landowners of Japan, the government;[188] peasants held only the rights of bare subsistence. Stemming
from this most basic of economic "rights" was the quasi-political right
of appealing to a supposedly "benevolent government" for ameliorative action in times of severe dearth, when flood or famine or a dishonest local tax collector infringed on their "right to subsist." At such
times, the Japanese peasant's only political role was that of "supplicant," entreating the authorities to show mercy and to act on his behalf, to restore the condition of subsistence *ante*-crisis. If their peaceful but not necessarily legal entreaties (the *tonshū, shūso, osso,* and
daihyō osso) failed, then the only other means open to them to influence the authorities was violent rebellion (the *gōso, bōdō, uchikowashi,* etc.). As rebellion in this context was ultimately little more
than an *appeal* through violence rather than a *demand* based upon
the government's recognition of individuals or collectivities possessing political rights, it shows clearly the essentially feudal *cum* Confucian nature of Tokugawa political culture: While feudal in *form*,
like the European version, having certain established relationships involving rights and obligations between rulers and ruled, it was nonetheless Confucian in *substance* and therefore highly restrictive of the
manner by which the ruled could press the rulers to honor traditional
feudal obligations.

Chief among the ruler's obligations was the guarantee of the peasant's right of subsistence. In James C. Scott's view, this right constitutes the heart of the precapitalist "moral economy" of the peasantry. The *modus operandi* of this "moral economy" was security over
surplus: "Living close to the subsistence margin and subject to the

---

keting and could therefore serve to legitimate direct action. Thompson writes: "While this
moral economy cannot be described as 'political' in any advanced sense, nevertheless it cannot be described as unpolitical either, since it supposed definite, and passionately held, notions of the common weal—notions which, indeed, found some support in the paternalist
tradition of the authorities; notions which the people re-echoed so loudly in their turn that
the authorities were, in some measure, the prisoners of the people" (*Past and Present*, No.
50 [February 1971] :79). In this sense, these rights or moral notions in the Japanese moral
economy were neither political or unpolitical; I therefore use the term "quasi-political."

188. See W. Donald Burton, "Peasant Struggle in Japan, 1590–1760," *Journal of Peasant
Studies* 5:2 (January 1978):135–71.

vagaries of weather and the claims of outsiders the peasant household has little scope for the profit maximization calculus of traditional neoclassical economics."[189] In the precapitalist moral economy, rebellion occurred not because the peasant was deprived of a profit accruing from his surplus production of crops, but rather because additional exactions or usual exactions at times of scarcity infringed upon his perceived right to subsist. The "right to subsistence," argues Scott, was "a moral principle" informing the unwritten code of ethics in peasant society. Justice in such a society referred to the seemingly static condition in which the peasants' right to subsist received at least *de facto* recognition by the authorities.

Conditions in the peasant economy were, however, hardly static. By the close of the first hundred years of Tokugawa rule, the breakup of large landholdings, at least in part in response to the intrusion of the market into peasant villages, resulted in the unequal encounter between the few larger landholders and the many smaller ones. This development, which marks the second stage in the development of rural political consciousness, brought about the fragmentation of village solidarity, or as Smith expressed it, the "decline of the co-operative group." As the larger landholders assumed political power equal to their growing economic power, the "absconding" (*chōsan*) type of resistance necessarily gave way to types that reflected the alienation of peasants from village leaders, and indeed were not infrequently directed against the village officialdom. The change was not, however, a zero-sum differential; a new "moral economy" of impersonal market relations did not supplant the old moral economy of subsistence. Instead, there arose an incongruous *community* of fully *competing* economic units wherein competition consisted of antagonistic claims on scarce resources, and where the two antagonists were a commercializing and increasingly wealthy village *farmer* stratum on the one side, and on the other a peasantry struggling to protect its right of subsistence, and likewise resisting the centripetal pull of market forces. The "moral economy," therefore, in this second stage was the contradictory one(s) of the unequal encounter of those devoted to the accumulation of wealth and power, and those trying to hold on to a secure existence of subsistence farming. In this situa-

---

189. James C. Scott, *The Moral Economy of the Peasant: Rebellion and Subsistence in Southeast Asia* (New Haven and London, 1976), p. 4. This is in my opinion the most important study to date on the topic of precapitalist peasant rebellion. I am grateful to Ms. Anne Walthall for bringing this book to my attention.

tion, "justice" oftentimes had to support two different conceptions: One, the old notion, referred to the condition wherein a detached ruling power accepted the right of the ruled to subsistence; the other, newer notion argued for an economic morality based on inequality of landholding and hence inequality in human relations; in this latter case, "justice" represented the outcome of contracts of exchange in money, property, labor, and goods. Naturally enough, in this period of coexisting and competing "moral economies," intravillage conflict would occur whenever the outcome of exchanges between the two groups appeared "unjust" according to one or the other's sense of justice. Though not always victorious in any particular contest, the capitalist farmer, the advocate of greater productivity, could rely on his wealth and power and the support which, out of self-interest, domain lords lent to the greater producers, to defeat the marginally productive peasant in the end. Yet in conflicts whose origins were extravillage, that is, which stemmed from claims coming from above (claims made by the authorities on the village's resources as an undifferentiated *unit*, as in the Tenma Sōdō), the proponents of the two different moral economies could unite momentarily in resistance against the government *qua* outsider. Because in such instances the extractive powers of government did not differentiate between market and subsistence producers, the two disparate groups were forced into a temporary coalition and were able to mount greater levels of resistence.

Such was increasingly proving to be the exception, however. During the latter half of Tokugawa, the commercialized village *gōnō* leadership more often than not ruled the political and economic life of the village in splendid isolation, usually free from the *extraordinary* claims made by supravillage government.[190] As their local rule lengthened in years and as productivity in agriculture increased, larger numbers of peasants were drawn into the local market economy, either as self-cultivators selling their surplus production, or as dispossessed landholders who as agricultural laborers sold their labor on the open market. Many, in other words, necessarily had to reconcile their lives as producers with a moral economy that changed landholding and labor from social functions benefiting the cooperative group into objects to be appropriated in a competitive economy that in practice placed no restrictions on the acquisition of land, labor, and wealth.

190. Nowhere is the fact of village isolation from central control more suggestively advanced than in Thomas C. Smith's marvelous comparative study, "Pre-Modern Economic Growth: Japan and the West," *Past and Present*, No. 60 (August 1973):127–60.

This development towards a more complete form of a market economy and its accompanying morality of unlimited and unequal appropriation was the third stage in the broadening of the farmers' political consciousness of their rights. Best expressed, perhaps, in those risings occurring at the very end of Tokugawa, and discussed earlier, the third phase was the antifeudal and procapitalist stage of development wherein rebels called for the destruction of guild controls over production, the end of special levies on cash crops, and the demand for official support of a free enterprise system of commodity production and sale. No longer did the *plea* for the right of subsistence play a central role, but instead it was the *demand* for the right of unimpeded commercial production and sale.

In a recent and extremely suggestive article that explicitly compares Japan's and Europe's pre-industrial economic growth, Thomas C. Smith provides evidence which shows that in contrast to Europe, where capitalism originated in urban areas, Japanese capitalist growth was "rural-centered," especially after the mid-eighteenth century, reflecting a process which Smith terms "de-urbanization." Wealth and population growth occurred in the countryside, he argues, and moreover accelerated because the declining power of the Tokugawa government was insufficient to turn the tide of a rural market economy that was increasingly autonomous and increasingly free from government attempts to intervene with effect. "Farmer and tradesmen have exchanged positions," says one statute of the mid-eighteenth century that Smith quotes, because farmers "enjoyed the advantage of lower production costs and freedom from guild and municipal restrictions. . . . [They] were able to *make and sell 'just as they please.'* "[191] The free *rural* market of late Tokugawa, Smith shows, likewise demonstrated such aspects of capitalistic society as occupational migration and mobility; employment contracts; competitive hiring practices; competition to secure adequate supplies of raw materials; a small-producer hatred of government-supported monopolies; the concentration of wealth and political power in the hands of large landholders; and wide-scale commercial farming. In this situation of a "rural-centered" market economy, it was not the rural producer

191. Ibid., p. 140 (emphasis added). In referring to the requests by townsmen for compassionate, Confucian intervention by the government, which Smith (ibid., p. 151) characterizes as "pleas . . . anything but demanding," their requests for relief were made "not as a matter of right or justice but out of sympathy for their sufferings and in consideration of past loyalty, obedience and payment of taxes." Again, this type of supplication stands in contrast with the demands made by rural producers.

who made *pleas* for government benevolence, but rather the townsmen. Similarly, it was not the bourgeois townsman *demanding* that
government refrain from interfering in commerce, but rather it was
the rural farmer-merchant. "Such men were far from being peasants
with an abacus," Smith writes. Instead, "we . . . find them in conflict
with government over its intervention in local affairs, in matters concerning village common land, irrigation rights and the selection of
headmen. . . . "[192] Local political autonomy, "a more open system
above," and unrestricted rights of commerce were the "liberties" *demanded* by the rural beneficiaries of the expansion of the market
economy.

Yet at the same time, the rebellions in the closing years of Tokugawa also revealed the social tenacity of the old moral economy of
subsistence. At times of economic crisis, the small agricultural producer sometimes yielded to the temptation to invoke the ideas of the
old moral economy because the economic security they argued for
seemed preferable to a market system which, besides promoting surplus production, also encouraged profiteering, usury, and monopoly.
The security offered by the equal right of all to subsist, and ideally
to produce a small surplus, and an older notion of a "just price" un-
affected by market fluctuations and manipulations of supply and demand, and the hope of persuading a "benevolent government" to pay
heed to their calls for benign intervention, and finally a conception
of a general good as taking precedence over the economic freedom of
a few rapacious entrepreneurs were all ideals which even at this late
stage of market growth could be invoked by the *yonaoshi* rebels who
called for a "leveling" of economic life and the *re-creation* or "remak-
ing" of an older, idealized economic world based on an older economic morality. That these rebels could simultaneously and seemingly
contradictorily call for free enterprise *and* an equalitarian society
composed of small producers of small surpluses—it was too late, they
recognized, to return completely to the old moral economy of subsistence—bespeaks their dissatisfaction with the unbridled market economy and their desire for the retention of at least some of the old values favoring "fair" prices and "fair" distribution of wealth. Yet if the
yonaoshi ikki were rearguard reactions against the forces of the market run wild, they were nonetheless rebellions waged by swivel-headed
men who alternately marched looking backward before turning to

192. Ibid., p. 152.

face forward toward the market economy with the rest of the growing army of Tokugawa farmers.

The backward-looking intent of some late Tokugawa rebels, frustrated with the economic insecurities of the market economy, was to
equalize wealth rather than be pauperized by it. Within the first ten
years of Meiji, when roughly the fourth stage in the development of
agrarian political consciousness commenced, there occurred structural
changes so consequential as to make extremely difficult a backward-
looking vision. If the ultimate victory of the market society had ever
been in question, the political and economic reforms of the new
Meiji government removed any doubt. Swivel-heads became stiff-
necked as a consequence of these reforms and as a result of the salu-
tary effects that the continued expansion of the domestic market and
the opening of the international market had upon their livelihood.

Although the Meiji reforms in fact really only made legal some
practices long in existence, their official sanction seemed to propel
a more rapid growth of market forces and morality whose ultimate
effect was to grant all individuals the *de jure* rights of unlimited appropriation of wealth. The reforms constituted the "capitalist revolution," underscoring Bertolt Brecht's well-known dictum that it is
capitalism, not communism, which is revolutionary. Legal differenti-
ations between classes were ended; restrictions on land sale and ownership were removed, giving industrious samurai and merchants the
right to develop land, and farmers the right to *own* the land they
formerly just *held* and also to acquire as much additional land as they
were able; *han* monopolies were abolished with the effect of making
commercial enterprise freer and more competitive; and occupation
for the first time in several hundred years was left to freedom of
choice.[193] These reforms, as well as the development of an infrastructure for commerce, government loans to private enterprise, and the
creation of a central banking system, amounted to a governmental
endorsement of the liberal-market society. If the Tokugawa peasant

193. Once again Thomas Smith seems to be preeminent for recognizing the import of
these reforms. See his "Landlords and Rural Capitalists in the Modernization of Japan,"
Journal of Economic History, 16:2 (June 1956):165–81, especially pp. 172–73. The reforms
and the changes Smith recognizes would have meant little if the agriculturalist had not developed "new pre-industrial values" during the period of "pre-modern growth" of capitalism.
In referring to the rural textile industry, Smith argues that general economic conditions favored the rise of "pre-industrial" but nonetheless capitalistic values: "The growth of the
modern textile industry [in the countryside] was made possible by the specific skills, attitudes, roles, capital accumulation and commercial practices brought into being mainly during
the period of 'pre-modern growth' " (Smith, "Pre-Modern Economic Growth," p. 128).

derived psychological security from subsistence production, the Meiji farmer felt no less secure working the land to which a title deed now gave him proprietory claim. He was liberated because *his* land had been liberated.

But only partially, as it turned out. The extractive claims of government on the farmer had not ended with his acquisition of newly granted freedoms. With new rights came new obligations, particularly the fixed land tax. His freedom was limited to that extent and, moreover, to the extent that the workings of the market economy set intrinsic bounds on his expectations to profit from surplus production and his right to appropriate greater amounts of land, labor, and capital. But in the case of governmental limitations on his freedom, the Meiji farmer understood, as did his ancestors, that the extractive claims of government rested on its political authority; he likewise understood that there existed a close relationship between political authority and the distribution of wealth. To maintain his new-found freedom to acquire theoretically unlimited wealth, he would have to be able to influence political power-holders; or, in other terms, to reduce the state's claims on his wealth, he must perforce control the state or at least modify its authority to extract arbitrarily or to interfere in the commerce which benefited him. (Here, it should be added, I do not believe the recognition by farmers of this relationship between wealth and political power represents a new development of their deductive powers of reasoning, but it does represent, I believe, a better or higher level of understanding of the relationship, if only because government, especially at the national level, was more visible in Meiji, more easily identifiable than in Tokugawa: A national land tax and ownership certificates issued by the national government showed at one and the same time who held authority and who would determine the distribution of wealth.)

How, then, did this development of a liberal economy affect the farmers' consciousness of their political rights, and how was this consciousness expressed?

The answer to this very important question has to do in large measure with the change in the way individuals and collectivities made grievances in market society and the moral justification used in making these grievances. We saw that in precapitalist Confucian society, where the moral economy of subsistence predominated, grievances took the form of supplication before an authority that usually recognized only the peasants' quasi-political right to appeal, which in turn stemmed from their perceived economic right of subsistence. In the *de jure* capitalist society of the Meiji period, when all enjoyed unlimited economic freedoms to strike the best bargains they could manage in the open market of labor, land, and capital, grievances were not surprisingly expressed in the market form of bargaining through demand and counterdemand, eventuating in an outcome or settlement or relationship expressed explicitly in contractual terms.[194] In market society, explicit contracts of these types reflected the relative power positions of theoretically equal and free parties in terms of stated rights and duties; this stands in opposition to the tacit feudal "contract" based on the ascribed ordering of society according to the fixed status of legally unequal and unfree parties.

Now equal and free to enter into contractual relations, the early Meiji farmer transferred the new economic principles of the market to the political realm.[195] Just as the moral economy of his forefathers legitimized the right of subsistence, and the rebellion necessary to reaffirm this right, the moral economy of Meiji capitalism no less informed the political consciousness of the market-oriented farmer who judged political and economic relationships as contractual. Market principles of freedom of ownership of property; freedom to appropriate a greater share of land, labor, and capital; free access to the market; free contracts between free and equal parties; in short, those economic conditions together comprising "justice" in the new morality of liberal market society were principles transferred to politics in the form of a demand for the right of each person to participate freely and equally in the political arena. The early market liberalism of Meiji, in other words, formed the basis of the rise of a liberal-democratic consciousness. Institutionally this consciousness found expression in

194. For those familiar with the recent work of Irwin Scheiner, it should be obvious that my idea of "contract" is patently different from his. He employs the notion of contract in a metaphoric sense to refer to the feudal (Tokugawa) "covenant" binding lord and peasant in a relationship not unlike that between God and man in Judeo-Christian tradition, albeit the language of the Japanese "covenant" is strikingly Confucian. Scheiner's argument is persuasive, and to the extent that it is a correct analysis of the Tokugawa relationship between lord and peasant, it helps explain in part why later Tokugawa and early Meiji farmers could have interpreted political relationships in contractual terms. See Scheiner's "Benevolent Lords and Honorable Peasants: Rebellion and Peasant Consciousness in Tokugawa Japan," a paper presented at the Colloquium, Center for Japanese and Korean Studies, University of California, Berkeley, 19 February 1975. (This paper was in a draft form when I read it, and its author asked that I not quote from it.)

195. See C. B. Macpherson, *The Real World of Democracy* (Toronto, 1965); Barrington Moore, Jr., *Social Origins of Dictatorship and Democracy* (Boston, 1966); and S. N. Eisenstadt, *Modernization: Protest and Change* (Englewood Cliffs, N.J., 1966), pp. 15–16, for comparative perspectives and theoretical explanations on how this transfer came about.

the popular rights movement which, as we saw, was increasingly attracting greater numbers of rural commoners. *Heiminshugi*, or "commonerism," was one shorthand characterization of the period used to refer to the ideological and social underpinnings of wide-scale commoner participation in the popular rights movement; democratic populism, perhaps, no less captures the essential meaning.[196] Buttressed by a tradition of popular resistance and, as I shall show later, by a "new" philosophy akin to European natural right doctrine which imparted moral legitimacy to the fight for free and equal *political* rights equivalent in power to their already established economic ones, Meiji commoners gave demonstrable proof of possessing a political consciousness of their rights in the *gekka jiken* of the eighties.

This argument requires further elucidation, but before resuming it in Chapter 4, it seems wise to paint faces onto the many abstract bodies of the Meiji rebels, that is, to show exactly who was drawn into the battle for greater political rights in the 1880s.

196. For example, Taoka Reiun (pseud; real given name was Sayoji), *Meiji hanshin den* (Tokyo, 1953; originally published in 1909), pp. 22, 30, 33. Also see Peter Duus, "Whig History, Japanese Style: The Minyūsha Historians and the Meiji Restoration," *Journal of Asian Studies* 33:3 (May 1974):415–36. Duus suggests that the term *heiminshugi* (which he translates as "popular democracy") reflects a tendency among "Whig" historians of Japan to rewrite history for political reasons, i.e., to help advance the fight for democracy. But to the extent that the rebels of the 1880s were fighting for democratic reform, then Duus's "Whig" historians (like Tokutomi Sohō, Takekoshi Yosaburō, etc.) were describing events and interpreting them for what they were, and not prescribing the course history should take.

3. Participants

We profess that we never had it in our thoughts to
Level mens estates.

John Lilburne, 1650

It is clear that during the late seventies and early eighties commoners were joining political parties and "societies" in increasing numbers. In his seminal work, *The Beginnings of Political Democracy in Japan*, Nobutaka Ike acknowledged this fact, but added: "Without the extensive use of archival material and local histories, one cannot make a statistical analysis of the membership of these societies."[1] Nor, I would add, of the political parties. Using just the sort of material Ike suggested, such an analysis will be attempted in this chapter. But before commencing, a few words of caution are required.

The reader is asked to remember that the purpose of this chapter is to identify the participants who were involved in the three incidents according to a number of commonly used criteria. But even when this identification process is completed, the task still remains unfinished. The next chapter will finish the process by examining the participants in terms of political society and/or party membership. This chapter can, however, stand by itself insofar as we can appreciate that simple participation in the various incidents is perhaps a better means to trace the collective action of *heimin* than is membership in an established political party or society.[2] Though in many individual instances the latter was temporally anterior to the former, it was far from being the rule. A broader strata of people could be mobilized for, say, attacking a wealthy rice merchant than they could for membership in a society or party. Indeed, ofttimes such membership was exclusive, restricted to those with education, wealth, and social and political standing, while participation in a rebellion lacked such restrictions.

---

1. Ike, *Beginnings*, p. 69.
2. Charles Tilly, Louise Tilly, Richard Tilly, *The Rebellious Century, 1830–1930* (Cambridge, Mass., 1975), especially pp. 287–90.

Consequently, by looking at these three incidents of collective action, we gain exposure to a larger number of people; we sacrifice, however, due to that very fact, the degree of precision that comes from studying a limited sample. Similarly, as with any study dealing with large numbers of people coalesced into a movement of some size, the best historical records tend to be those that tell of a movement's leadership; this study is no exception. Indeed, to make the study manageable, there is little other choice. It is hoped, however, that by including a number of those arrested in the various incidents who were classified by the authorities as "blind followers" (*fuwa zuikōsha*), as well as by utilizing some aggregate figures concerning those involved, we will gain a better understanding of the social breadth of the movements.

Membership in a political society and/or party has been mentioned as one of the characteristics that will be used to identify the incidents' participants. The other characteristics used in the analysis are residence, age, occupation, status (i.e., official status—*shizoku* or *heimin*), land ownership/financial status, arrest record, and literacy. Also, where applicable, a distinction is made between party and/or society leader and followers. In addition, information concerning the nature of an individual's connection with other participants; the prison sentence he received; and certain post-incident biographical data that seem relevant are used to identify the participants further. Most of the basic biographical information comes from police interrogations or from court records; much of the rest comes from secondary sources: contemporary accounts, recent studies, biographies, and the like. All these details appear in Appendices B, C, and D.

Although an effort has been made to provide the same information for all of the participants in each of the incidents, in some cases it was either not attainable or it was simply not relevant. In the former instance, for example, in the cases of literacy and prior arrests, frequently these questions were simply not asked by the prosecutor during his interrogation of the suspects. In the latter instance, there is the example of Chichibu, where local political societies were virtually nonexistent and hence this category of identification is irrelevant.

The biographical information of the participants is employed in order to determine relationships and patterns among variables. By showing exactly who was involved in the incidents and how factors such as residence, age, economic status, and so on related to participation, the way is cleared for a deeper understanding of the nature of their organization, ideology, targets, goals, and the reaction by the authorities to the rebels. For at the lowest level of analysis it is clear that who was involved significantly determines the what, why, and wherefore of their collective activities. Identification of the participants will also help to show how deeply into society notions of freedom and popular rights penetrated.

The Samples

In Chapter 1, where the story of each of the incidents was told, mention was made of the large number of participants in both the Fukushima ("several thousand") and Chichibu ("seven or eight thousand") incidents. (The Kabasan Incident, as was shown, is a special case.) For obvious reasons, it would be impossible to treat the biography of each of the participants individually. The problem would be slightly eased if we were to work only with those arrested in each case, but even then not only are the figures unmanageable (Fukushima—from one thousand to several thousand, depending on the source;[3] Chichibu—one source counts over 3,100 either arrested or having surrendered; another, almost 4,500 of those caught in Gumma and Nagano prefectures are included)[4] but also sufficient biographical information is missing for the vast majority of the participants. (Most were merely fined and therefore not as thoroughly interrogated as suspected "ringleaders.") Even if the study were to focus only on those arrested who came from the two most active districts in each of the incidents, Yama and Chichibu, the figures are still unwieldly, amounting to 518 and 234 respectively.[5]

Since it is clearly necessary to arrive at some figures that are manageable, that have substance, and that in some way are representative of larger numbers of participants, the samples were derived in the following way. In the case of the Fukushima Incident, the fifty-eight individuals charged with treason (kokujihan, literally, "a crime [against] national affairs") and sent to the High Crimes Court (Kōtōkō-in) in Tokyo make up the sample. (See Appendix B: Fukushima Activists.) There are two weaknesses in this sample and possibly a third: (1) a disproportionately high number of the activists, thirteen in all, are

---

3. Takahashi, Fukushima jiken, p. 189; Shōji, ed., Nihon seisha, p. 307.
4. CJSR I:509: Inoue, Chichibu jiken, p. 194.
5. Takahashi, Fukushima jiken, p. 189; CJSR I:632–39. All but ten of the 234 arrested were natives of Chichibu district.

from outside Fukushima—six from Gumma, four from Kōchi, and one each from Miyagi, Yamagata, and Ehime. This definitely overrates the real percentage of non-Fukushima people who participated in the incident; (2) only eight of the forty-five Fukushima participants came from the Aizu region; this figure underrates the high percentage of activists coming from Aizu; (3) of the fifty-eight indicted for treason, only six were convicted; the other fifty-two were released in March and April 1883, for lack of sufficient evidence. This last fact causes us to query: If so many were found innocent, and therefore falsely charged, then surely the charges were trumped up, making us wonder whether these fifty-two "activists" were as active in the incident as the treason charge led us to believe. The facts seem to indicate that the charges were, if not fabricated, then at least inaccurate. This is suggested by the number of times, four in all, between 13 January and 4 February 1883, that the government made alterations, i.e., additions and deletions, to the list of those to be tried for treason.[6] In any case, those who made the "final list," for whatever reason, were ultimately prosecuted as the real "ringleaders" (*shukai*) of the disturbance; and, not incidentally, thirty of them, as it turns out, had a direct relationship with the great popular rights leader of the region, Kōno Hironaka, who was in fact convicted of treason. Whether or not it can be termed a "political trial"—Takahashi among others claims that it was[7]—it is clear that most of those tried were political activists, the government's accusations notwithstanding, and this fact makes the sample relevant to this study. Also relevant is the information regarding a number of other major figures who were not tried as "traitors" in Tokyo, but who were prosecuted locally at Wakamatsu and elsewhere; this information will supplement the core sample. Finally, in an effort to learn about the "followers," we will make use of government reports on the villages and villagers involved in the anti-road construction movement.

Similar kinds of limitations also help to determine who is included in the Chichibu sample, e.g., insufficient biographical information stemming from sketchy interrogations of the individuals. In this case, however, the sample is not restricted to those officially considered activists, i.e., those publicly tried, but includes most of those whom the Kommintō itself regarded as activists. The sample consists of those forty-seven men (concerning whom more-or-less complete data exist

6. Takahashi, *Fukushima jiken*, pp. 224–25.   7. Ibid., p. 225.

for thirty-eight) whose past activism earned them a Komminto army post just prior to the outbreak of the incident.[8] (See Appendix C: Chichibu Activists.) Although these individuals form the core of this section of the study, in order to provide a wider perspective of the participants' identity, supplementary data will also be utilized. General, aggregate data will be used for: (1) the 115 people who "instigated the masses into joining prior to the outbreak of violence"; and (2) the 103 people classified as "members of the Komminto" who destroyed the homes of "wealthy farmers and merchants and instigated violence in their villages."[9] Among the other supplementary data to be used is Inoue Kōji's analysis of 261 people prosecuted in Gumma prefecture, which he took from the fourteen-volume *Criminal Records of Chichibu Rioters* (*Chichibu bōtō hanzai ni kansuru shoruihen*). His findings may also serve as a check against, and as a standard by which we can judge, the representativeness of the strictly Saitama data marshaled here. Finally, it should also be pointed out that in the next chapter interrogation records of several participants, categorized by the government as "blind followers," will be used in order to gain an appreciation of the type of "followers" who involved themselves in the rebellion.

The limitations of the Chichibu and Fukushima data are absent from or, rather, different from those connected with the Kabasan Incident, largely due to the latter's being a very different type of disturbance. In addition to the twenty principal conspirators, the Kabasan sample will also include information on thirteen others who were, for a variety of reasons, implicated in the abortive rebellion, thus bringing the total sample to thirty-three. (See Appendix D: Kabasan Activists.)

Before examining the data, it is necessary to caution the reader once more about the problem of how representative of the larger population are the individuals included in the three samples. For the most part, the individuals who comprise the samples were local elites— socially, economically, and politically. Most came from one of the older and wealthier families of their village, and many of them held positions of leadership in the local political society or party. These facts obviously set them apart from the larger local population. Yet, at the same time, as far as their position in the incidents or in the

---

8. These are listed in *CJSR* I:640–43.
9. Ibid., pp. 643–56. Other relevant aggregate data can be found on pp. 204, 292, 312, 329, 343–45, 464.

popular rights movement is concerned, these local elites were serving as *representatives* as well as leaders of the local population. The social, economic, and political status advantages they held over the local population may have been responsible for their having been able to assume leadership of the incidents and of the movement, but only inasmuch as their views and actions genuinely reflected the aspirations of those whom they led. They were elites, yes, but at the *local* level; also, as the next chapter will show, they were the elite of a movement whose goals transcended the traditional status considerations of parochial politics, and, more important, the goals they sought were shared by many of their followers.

Residence

The principal question being asked here is to what extent the geographical origins of the participants clustered around some areas (and not others). Did certain areas tend to turn out more activists than others? In what way, and how much, did residence affect participation? Once these questions are answered and once these findings are correlated with other characteristics of the participants, then it is hoped that in the following chapter these variables will provide insight into questions concerned with the participants' organization.

If we abstract the information on residence which appears in Appendix B, we see that of the fifty-five names of Fukushima Incident activists for whom we have residence information, forty-two are from Fukushima. If broken down according to district (*gun*), Tamura accounts for over half, totaling twenty-four in all, followed by Yama (seven), Ishikawa (four), Atachi (three), with one apiece for Soma, Kawanuma, Shinobu, and Futaba districts; in all, only eight of Fukushima prefecture's twenty-one districts are represented.[10] (See Table 4.)

If this breakdown is compared with the list of people originally accused of treason, dated 31 January 1883, we see a somewhat different distribution, albeit once again Tamura district continues to rank highest. (See Table 4.) On that date, not only were fifteen of the districts of Fukushima represented, but also the difference between Tamura and Yama—the latter commonly regarded by the authorities

10. There were twenty-one administrative districts as of 1882. In 1896, the prefecture was reorganized to include only seventeen districts. See Kobayashi Seiji and Yamada Akira, *Fukushima-ken no rekishi* (Tokyo, 1973), pp. 24–33.

TABLE 4.

A Comparison of Residence of Fukushima Activists
Originally Listed for Crime of Treason with
Those Actually Tried

	ORIGINAL LIST	TRIED
	(13 January 1883)	*(March and April 1883)*
PREFECTURE		
Kōchi	6	4
Gumma	7	6
Yamagata	2	1
Ehime	1	1
Tochigi	1	—
Fukushima	55	42
DISTRICT		
Tamura	14	24
Yama	11	7
Kawanuma	5	1
Minami-Aizu	1	—
Futaba	1	1
Kita-Aizu	1	—
Adachi	2	3
Sōma	1	1
Asaka	1	—
Iwase	4	—
Ishikawa	2	4
Shirakawa	1	—
Shinobu	9	1
Iwaki	1	—
Ōnuma	1	—
Total	82	55

Source: For the "Original List," Shōji Kichinosuke, ed., *Nihon seisha seitō
hattatsu shi* (Tokyo, 1959), pp. 560–62. For those "tried," see Appendix B
for references.

as the hub of the anti-road construction activity[11] —is reduced to only three. If those activists from Kawanuma, Yama's neighbor and ally
in the anti-road fight, are added to the Yama figure, then we have
a better idea of that area's participation in the incident relative to the
other areas.

11. Shimoyama Saburō, "Fukushima jiken oboegaki," in *Jiyū minken undō*, comp. Meiji
Shiryō Kenkyū Renraku kai, 3 (Tokyo, 1956):144–51.

The discrepancy between this original list of traitors and the list of those who were finally sent to the Tokyo trials is probably accounted for in an observation made by Takahashi. Speaking of the unusually large percentage of Tamura district "traitors," he writes: "This fact clearly indicates that the Aizu disturbance [Kitakata Incident] was merely a pretext for the [subsequent] large-scale arrests; that the real aim [of the government] was the extermination of the Jiyūtō within the prefecture, which was then under the influence of Kōno [Hironaka]."[12] And, it is necessary to add, the strength of the eastern Fukushima Jiyūtō, and many of the political societies supporting it, was concentrated mainly in Tamura district, Miharu Town, where, importantly, Kōno was its most distinguished popular rights advocate. All other things being equal, this fact, more than others, appears to account for the high number of Tamura district residents appearing in our sample.

But regardless of the reason for the arrest of (relatively) so many Tamura residents, there exist other data which show that the vast majority of the participants in the Kitakata/Fukushima incident did in fact reside in the western region of Fukushima, that is, in the six districts that comprised the Aizu region. Of those having leadership positions in the *Aizu Rengōkai* (see Chapter 1), only two, Uda Seiichi and Miura Bunji, were sent to the Tokyo trials (and appear therefore in our sample). Most of the others—Hara Heizō, Kojima Chūhachi, and Monna Shigejirō, for example—described by the authorities as "ringleaders and instigators," were tried in the local courts of Fukushima and Wakamatsu towns.[13] These activists came from the Aizu districts of Yama, Kawanuma, and Ōnuma.

As with the leadership, most of the followers in the incident resided in the western part of the prefecture. Shimoyama Saburō cites Yama, Kawanuma, and Ōnuma as the three most active districts.[14] In fact, if we examine the figures provided by the authorities at that time, it appears that a plurality if not a majority of the followers were residents of Yama district. Using as the total number involved in the Kitakata Incident that imprecise figure "several thousand" as a basis of comparison, we see in "A Report on Those Who Support the Litigation [against the government] and Who Protest Against the Road Building" that twenty-seven Yama district villages involving 2,120 peo-

12. Takahashi, *Fukushima jiken*, p. 225.

13. *Fukushima-ken shi*, 11 (Fukushima, 1964):482–83 (hereafter abbreviated *FKS*); Takahashi, *Fukushima jiken*, pp. 165, 227.

14. Shimoyama, "Oboegaki," p. 151.

ple were regarded as the most active areas.[15] After the wholesale arrests in December, it is known that at least 500 villagers were fined,[16] among whom 214 were charged as having been "blind followers who massed for rebellion" (Kyōto shūshū fuwa zuikō). All but three of the 214 were residents of Yama district.[17]

Again referring back to Appendix B, if we look at an even lower level of administration, the village/town/city level, the most striking fact, not surprisingly, is the large number of participants, twenty in all, who resided in the town of Miharu, the principal urban area of Tamura district, and in its surrounding villages. The other interesting finding to be extracted from the sample, again not particularly surprising, is the absence of any significant clustering in Yama district. Of the seven residents listed, only Atsushio-kano village, located about ten kilometers due north of Kitakata, had more than one person—in fact, only two people—sent to the Tokyo trials.

Once again, however, by looking at other data, certain patterns emerge. In the list of Yama district "ringleaders" (kyokai) provided by district head Satō Jirō to Governor Mishima on 29 November 1882 (the day following the Kitakata Incident), we see that in addition to Akagi Heiroku, who was later sent to Tokyo for prosecution, Wajima Akigo and Ueda Kiyomaru both came from Shinai village.[18] In the case of Atsushio and Kano villages (later consolidated), Uryū Naoshi, prosecuted in Tokyo, was joined by Yama "ringleader" Endō Yūhachi.[19] We also see that the very villages from which these people came were among the most active in terms of the number of residents mobilized. Atsushio-kano accounted for 221 participants, Shinai for 95;[20] respectively, these two villages ranked first and fourth in Yama district.

To summarize, then, what has been said about residence and participation in the Fukushima Incident: First, based upon our sample, it is clear that urban-based activists—namely, those from Miharu of Tamura district—were regarded by the authorities as having been most responsible for instigating the disturbance of November 1882. Secondly, relying on other evidence, it appears that those leaders from the Aizu region, and especially from Yama district, were just as active

15. FKS, pp. 483–84. The average village participation was slightly less than eighty; the range was seven to 128.

16. Takahashi, Fukushima jiken, p. 227.

17. FKS, pp. 941–49. The report was dated 13 January 1883.

18. Ibid., pp. 482–83.   19. Ibid.   20. Ibid., pp. 483–85.

as those from Miharu, but that, for whatever reason—probably princi-pally a political one—they were omitted from the government's "list of traitors." Thirdly, perhaps a majority of "followers" involved in the incident were concentrated in the Aizu region, principally Yama district and secondarily Kawanuma and Ōnuma districts. Finally, at the lowest level of administration, the village/town/city, there appears to exist a close relationship between the village from which a "ring-leader" came and the number of participants coming from the village. This final point, however, must be considered as a tentative one for the present, as its ideological and organizational implications will be explored further in the next chapter.

Before moving on to look at the relationship of residence to partic-ipation in the Kabasan Incident, a few words are needed about the thirteen individuals in the Fukushima sample who came from outside prefectures.

We know from Chapter 1 that Satō and Sugiyama, from Miyagi and Ehime prefectures respectively, were sent by Kōno Hironaka to investigate the situation in Aizu prior to the Kitakata Incident. Since there exists no other information on these two, it might be guessed that sometime earlier they must have abandoned their native prefec-tures to live, and probably to study, at one of the popular rights acad-emies in eastern Fukushima. Matsumoto, from neighboring Yamagata prefecture, appears to have been a primary school teacher who relo-cated in order to teach in Miharu; it is known that he was a Jiyūtō member, so very likely he moved in order to involve himself in the most active of the popular rights centers of the Tōhoku region. In the case of the four men from Tosa (Kōchi prefecture), the fountain-head of early popular rights activity, they undoubtedly were popular rights activists. All that is known for certain, however, is that one was a Jiyūtō member who was in Fukushima visiting its Jiyūtō headquar-ters. The other three quite possibly could have been teachers of pop-ular rights thought at one of the local academies (see Chapter 4), for it is known that several Tosa popular rights advocates were in their employ as teachers. About the six who came from Gumma we can be more definite. They were all members of the most prominent of the political societies of Gumma, the *Yūshinsha*, and went to Fukushima, in the words of the leader of the expedition, Nagasaka Hachirō, "be-cause it was clear that [Governor] Mishima's road construction plan was unjust; therefore, we went in order to instigate the people to take court action."[21] It is necessary to point out, however, that they did not even arrive in Fukushima until 9 December, well after the Kitakata Incident and the start of the wide-scale arrest campaign against the local Jiyūtō members.

An understanding of how residence related to participation in the Kabasan Incident is even more crucial—and certainly more obvious—than it was in the case of Fukushima. The most significant and consequential fact about residence is that of the twenty principal activists who plotted and participated in the incident, twelve were natives of Fukushima prefecture.[22] (See Appendix D.) Two of the twelve, in fact, Kōno Hiroshi and Miura Bunji, appeared in the previous sample, having been accused of "treason" for their part in the Fukushima Incident. Several of the other Fukushima people as well were involved in that incident, but were tried at lower courts and subsequently released: Monna Shigejirō, Yokoyama Nobuyuki, and Isokawa Motoyoshi. Several others, such as Hara Rihachi and Kotoda Iwamatsu, had either escaped arrest or were simply disregarded by the Fukushima police after the incident. In any case, as Takahashi has said, "Most of them were active in the Fukushima Incident."[23]

Of the other eight principal conspirators in the Kabasan Incident, Ibaraki and Tochigi prefectures each accounted for three, and Aichi and Ishikawa for one each. Moving to the lower levels of administration, all three of the Ibaraki participants were from Shimodate Town, Makabe district, while two of the three from Tochigi (information is missing for Hirao Yasokichi) came from Shimotsuga district, but from different villages. Ten of the twelve conspirators from Fukushima were either residents of Tamura (five) or Yama (five), and all of those from Tamura were Miharu Town residents; village residence was different for each of those from Yama district.

Twelve of the other thirteen people appearing in the sample were activists who were later arrested for complicity in the incident. The remaining activist, Fukao, on whom no biographical information exists, disappeared prior to the incident, thereby lending support to the

21. Fukuda Kaoru, *Sanmin sōjō roku: Meiji jūshichinen Gumma jiken* (Tokyo, 1974), pp. 50–51.
22. Takahashi, *Fukushima jiken*, p. 264, states that the number was thirteen instead of twelve, having added Kobayashi Tokutarō, who was officially listed as a resident of Aichi prefecture. He was in fact born in Fukushima, but his family moved to Aichi when he was only six years old, and it is therefore problematic how strong his loyalties were toward Fukushima prefecture.
23. Ibid., p. 259.

contention of Yokoyama and others that he was a police spy.[24] (Actually, large numbers of reputed *minken* advocates, of Fukushima especially, were later arrested for suspicion of involvement; more about this will be mentioned in Chapter 5.) Six of the twelve accomplices were Tochigi residents; two were from Fukushima; and one each were from Ibaraki, Tokyo, Iwate, and Aichi prefectures.

In order to comment here on the importance of residence as it relates to participation in the Kabasan Incident, it is necessary to anticipate some of the findings that will appear in the next chapter on organization and ideology. Briefly stated, other than in the case of the twelve principal conspirators from Fukushima, and even here to a large extent, participation in the incident appears to have been due more to a common desire to overthrow the government than to the fact of common place of residence. To be sure, common geographical origins were important to the growth of the conspiracy, mainly because it made for easier communication among the rebels. Yet even with that, as we saw in Chapter 1, many of the rebels first became acquainted with one another not in their home districts, but in Tokyo at one of several Jiyūtō meetings or organizational functions. Common residence might have been a necessary condition that favored participation, but alone it certainly was not a sufficient one. More important, it would seem, were the facts of shared experience in a prior incident (i.e., the Fukushima Incident), membership in the same political societies (in Tochigi, Ibaraki, and in Fukushima), and the belief shared by all conspirators that the government should be toppled. Hence, while it was not unimportant, ultimately it was the superimposition of other characteristics of the rebels upon the factor of residence that gave it whatever importance it had.

The situation is entirely different in the case of the Chichibu Incident, as a glance at Appendix C will show. Of the forty-seven names appearing on this list—representing the leadership of the Kommintō army[25]—forty are Saitama residents and thirty-seven of these are from Chichibu. With such a preponderance of Chichibu residents, district residency becomes virtually insignificant in helping to locate particularly active political areas, making it necessary therefore to

---

24. Nojima, *Kabasan jiken*, p. 58.

25. Most studies of this incident reproduce this list, though frequently some names are added and some omitted. Mine comes from the original document, appearing in *CJSR* I:640–42, identified as "Those Appointed Positions by Tashiro Eisuke at Hinozawa [*sic*] Village, Chichibu District, on October 31, 1884."

use the village/town administrative unit as a basis of reference. (See Table 5.) Upon doing this, we see that of the twenty-one villages and one town (Ōmiya) shown on the list, only nine had more than one Kommintō army leader representing them; in fact, if we combine the "Upper" and "Lower" Yoshida villages and do the same for the "Upper" and "Lower" Hinozawa villages, then the figure is reduced to seven. Thus amalgamated, these "two" villages had the highest representation, with seven and six respectively. They are followed by Isama and Fuppu, each having four; by Akuma with three; and by Ōmiya and Shiroku with two each. It is perhaps also significant that those villages with the greater representation were also those whose leaders held some of the higher ranks within the Kommintō army.

If arrests can be regarded as an indication of activism, then the very same villages also rank high for producing activists, as seen in a government document entitled "A table of those defendants charged with massing to riot."[26] (See Table 5.) It shows that with sixty-one Chichibu residents coming from a total of twenty-eight villages, the villages that ranked highest were Hinozawa (seven), Yoshida (seven), Isama (six), Fuppu (six), and Sanzawa (five). In yet another government document, entitled simply "Names of Rioters" (Bōto jimmei), listing 224 people from Chichibu, again ranked highest was Hinozawa (thirty-one: "Upper" and "Lower"), followed by Yoshida (thirty: "Upper" and "Lower"), Fuppu (twenty-seven), and Isama (fifteen).[27] These villages, it is important to note, were all located within ten kilometers of one another and were situated in the northwest corner of Chichibu district, near the Gumma prefectural border. It was in this area that many of the Kommintō members resided, and in which during November much of the fighting occurred.[28]

That these villages predominated in the Chichibu Incident is confirmed by the final count of the number of rioters involved, according to village, that was calculated by the courts at the end of the year.[29] (See Table 6.) This table shows that in terms of the absolute number of participants, Yoshida ("Upper" and "Lower"), Hinozawa ("Upper" and "Lower"), Isama, Iida, Sanyama, and several others ranked

26. CJSR I:378–83.
27. Ibid., pp. 632–39. This document is dated 28 November 1884.
28. Inoue, Chichibu jiken, p. 89.
29. The issue date of the court report is 30 December 1884. These figures represent only the number of people prosecuted for involvement. It seems safe to say that a good many others escaped prosecution. See CJSR I:340–43.

TABLE 5.

Comparison of Residence of Kommintō Army
Leaders by Town and Village with Residence of Those
Charged with "Massing to Riot"

Town/Village	Army Leaders (no.)	"Massing to Riot"
Shimo-yoshida	5	7
Kami-yoshida	2	
Shimo-hinozawa	3	7
Kami-hinozawa	3	
Akuma	3	1
Isama	4	6
Fuppu	4	6
Ōmiya	2	2
Shiroku	2	1
Ōta	1	1
Yokose	1	2
Iida	1	3
Misawa	1	5
Shimo-ogano	1	1
Sanyama	1	3
Ikoda	1	
Honnogami	1	2
Onohara	1	
Nakino	1	
Nishinoju	1	
Makinichi	1	1
Nagaru		1
Minano		1
Komori		2
Nogamishimogo		1
Hio		1
Sakamoto		1
Kanezawa		1
Kawaharazawa		1
Terao		1
Toyaen		2
Yoshigekubo		1
Total	40	61

Source: Data for "Army leaders" is abstracted from Appendix
C; for "Riot," CJSR I:378–83.

TABLE 6.
Number of Participants in Chichibu Incident by Village,
Relative to Village Population, for Villages Contributing More
Than Fifty "Direct" Participants

| Village | No. Participants | | Total | Village Pop. | % Pop. Mobilized (rounded) |
	Direct	Indirect			
Shimo-yoshida	324	360	684	2,516	27
Kami-yoshida	236	155	381	1,612	24
Shimo-hinozawa	139	139	378	986	36
Kami-hinozawa	77	120	297	565	52
Fuppu	35	63	98	411	24
Isama	111	174	285	865	21
Ōfuchi	57	126	183	330	55
Nomaki	72	79	151	454	33
Hisanaka	76	78	154	436	35
Akuma	50	50	100	375	27
Hio	92	82	174	598	30
Fujikura	130	159	289	944	30
Iida	142	190	332	888	37
Sanyama	162	222	384	1,150	33
Kawaharazawa	94	96	190	584	33
Susuki	134	152	286	2,446	12
Shimo-ogano	159	151	340	1,325	25
Hanni	74	74	148	658	23
Nagaru	141	164	305	1,062	28

Source: CJSR I:340–43. Population figures are based on government figures cited in ibid.; no criteria are given to distinguish "direct" from "indirect" participants. Total number of participants is shown as 6,017; total number of "direct" participants is 2,644; "indirect" is 3,373.

highest. (The significance of the final column, showing the number of participants relative to village population, will be commented upon in the conclusion of this chapter and also in the next chapter.) In general, because these findings compare favorably with those of our sample, and with the other Chichibu data thus far presented, we can conclude that the above-mentioned villages were the principal centers of activism at the time of the incident, both in terms of the number of individuals mobilized from them, and the number of Kommintō leaders representing them.

To summarize, in each of the three cases, certain areas produced more activists than others: Tamura district in eastern Fukushima and Yama district in western Fukushima in the case of the Fukushima Incident; Fukushima prefecture itself in the case of the Kabasan Incident; and the villages of Yoshida, Hinozawa, Isama, and Fuppu in the case of the Chichibu Incident. All these areas contributed an inordinate number of both leaders and followers to the common body of participants in each of the incidents. Moreover, in both the Fukushima and Chichibu incidents, not surprisingly, the local areas that boasted the more activistic of the incident's leadership also vaunted a larger number of followers. In both cases, this fact probably reflects the endurance of a tradition of local cooperative spirit, relatively strong communal ties, and the organizational prowess of the incident's leaders. Yet at the same time, as we shall see in the next chapter, high rates of participation also reflect the increasing extent to which farmers were receptive to the ideology of the popular rights movement.

Age

It has been frequently observed that the leaders of rebellion and revolution are comparatively young men.[30] We know, for instance, that in the case of the Meiji Restoration, or "revolution" as some would have it,[31] most of the principal rebels were in their twenties or thirties.[32] With minor qualifications, the same observation applies to the leaders of the Fukushima, Kabasan, and Chichibu incidents.

Again abstracting from our Fukushima sample (see Table 7a), we can see that if the age breakdown were graphed, it would closely resemble a bell. Of the thirty-nine Fukushima residents on whom we have information, twenty-eight fall between the ages of twenty and thirty-nine. Seven persons were in their late teens, three in their forties, and only one was in his fifties. The overall sample exhibits an average and a median age of twenty-nine and a range of seventeen to

30. See, for example, Carl Leiden and Karl M. Schmitt, *The Politics of Violence: Revolution in the Modern World* (Englewood Cliffs, N.J., 1968), pp. 78–89, especially p. 86; also see Rudé, *Crowd*, pp. 209–10.

31. W. G. Beasley, *The Meiji Restoration* (Stanford, Calif., 1972).

32. W. G. Beasley, "Political Groups in Tosa, 1856–68," *Bulletin of the School of Oriental and African Studies* 30:2 (1967):382–90; Albert Craig, *Chōshū in the Meiji Restoration* (Cambridge, Mass., 1961); and Sakata Yoshio and John W. Hall, "The Motivation of Political Leadership in the Meiji Restoration," *Journal of Asian Studies* 16 (November 1956):31–50.

TABLE 7.

Age Structure of Sample Participants of Fukushima,
Chichibu, and Kabasan Incidents

Age group	a. Fukushima (residents only)			b. Kabasan (all participants)			c. Chichibu (residents only)		
	Number	Average Age	Median Age	Number	Average Age	Median Age	Number	Average Age	Median Age
-19	7			7			1		
20-29	13			12			8		
30-39	15			10			10		
40-49	3			1			12		
50-59	1			0			3		
60-69	0			0			0		
	39	29	29	30	26½	24	34	35	36+

Source: Abstracted from Appendices B, C, and D.

fifty years. It is youth, however, which appears to be conspicuous. There are other data that lend support to this impression.

Takahashi has analyzed the age structure of the forty-four leaders—consisting of thirty-four from Fukushima, five from Kōchi, and five from Gumma—arrested after the Kitakata incident on 28 November at the home of Aizu Jiyūtō leader Akagi Heiroku. The youngest person present was seventeen (Yasuda Keitarō), the oldest thirty (Iga Wanato), and the average age was only twenty-two.[33] Takahashi also records, in combining both leaders and followers into a sample of one hundred participants (including those sent to the Tokyo trials), that the average age was twenty-eight.[34] In all, the data force the conclusion that youth and activism were closely associated, at least in the case of the leadership of the Fukushima Incident; the absence of evidence relating strictly to followers prevents us from making a similar conclusion.

If youth characterized the participants of the Fukushima Incident, it was even more conspicuous in the Kabasan case. (See Table 7b.) Here the range was eighteen to forty-three, and showed an average age of about twenty-six-and-a-half, and a median age of twenty-four. Those under thirty predominated, nineteen persons in all, while the thirty to thirty-nine range accounted for ten. Tanaka Shōzō, who gained notoriety in the 1890s for the fight he led against the pollution caused by the Ashio copper mines, was the "old man" of the group at a frisky forty-three. The youth of the Kabasan participants places them very neatly, therefore, into that universal category known as "young revolutionaries."[35]

Compared to the youthful participants of the Fukushima and Kabasan incidents, those who led the Chichibu Incident were "middle-aged." (See Table 7c.) The average age of the thirty-five individuals comprising the Chichibu sample is slightly over thirty-six. If graphed, the age structure more closely resembles a two-dimensional mountain, gradually rising on one side and dropping steeply on the other. At the summit would appear those in the forty to forty-nine age group, the largest group, with twelve members. On the line up to the summit are the twenty to twenty-nine age group (eight) and the thirty

33. Takahashi, *Fukushima jiken*, p. 187; Takahashi, *Fukushima jiyū minken undō shi* (Tokyo, 1954), pp. 177-80.

34. Takahashi, *Fukushima jiken*, pp. 61, 226-27.

35. For an interesting comparison, see Sidney R. Brown, "Political Assassination in Early Meiji Japan: The Plot Against Ōkubo Toshimichi," in *Meiji Japan's Centennial: Aspects of Political Thought and Action*, ed. David Wurfel (Lawrence, Kansas, 1971), pp. 18-35.

TABLE 8.

Age Structure, with Graph, of Seventy-seven
Defendants Charged with Rioting

Late teens	5	no.	
20–29	27	25	
30–39	25	20	
40–49	15	15	
50–59	5	10	
60–69	0	5	
Total	77	0	
		Age 0 10 – 20 – 30 – 40 – 50 –	

Average Age: 33 years (rounded)
Median Age: 31 years

Source: Abstracted from Appendix C.

to thirty-nine age group (ten). At one base is a single individual in his late teens, and at the other base are three who are in their fifties. The range is from age nineteen to fifty-six.

The age structure of this sample can be compared to the ages of those appearing in an earlier-used document, "A table of those defendants charged with massing to riot,"[36] in order to assess its representativeness; since this was a lesser crime, we can assume that many of the individuals included were followers. The collated results and a graphic representation of them appear in Table 8.

By again using the analogy of a two-dimensional mountain to describe the age structure of the followers, we see that the data in this case shape up to be just the reverse of the former sample. Here the mountain rises steeply on the first side, peaks at the twenty to thirty age grouping, and slopes gradually on the second side, thereby indicating a younger group of participants. The picture derived from the second set of data, however, is somewhat deceptive, much like the steepness of a mountain is to someone standing at its bottom, since only three years separate the average age of the first set from the average age of the second set of participants.[37]

To summarize, the average age of the Kabasan participants at around twenty-six was lowest, and Chichibu's at around thirty-three to thirty-six was highest; the average age of the Fukushima participants at twenty-eight or twenty-nine fell in between.

36. *CJSR* I:378–83.   37. Inoue, *Chichibu jiken*, p. 91.

A final important point to make about age as it concerns participation is how it affects organization. Given the well-known role that age plays in ordering personal relations in Japanese society—the dictum of the Confucian value system instructing the young to show deference to their elders[38]—did this social fact affect the ordering of organizations? A quick glance at our Chichibu sample, especially at the column indicating the rank of the individual within the Kommintō army, indicates that many, but not all, of the higher ranks were held by older men. The exceptions, however, stand out, such as Arai Shūzaburō, Inoue Denzō, and Ogiwara Kanjirō. Very likely, such exceptions—and they are present in the other two incidents as well—are explained by the fact that such notions as *jinzai* ("capable man"), *meibōka* ("man of high repute"), and *minkenka* ("advocate of people's rights") were accorded greater value than age in assigning rank within *heimin* organization during the early- and middle-Meiji periods.[39]

Status

Like residence and age, status was fixed, or rather, "nearly fixed," for upon performance of some meritorious deed for the community or state a *heimin* could be elevated to *shizoku* status.[40] (The opposite was also true, as will be shown presently.) For most, however, to be born a *heimin* usually meant to die a *heimin*. This is not to say that there were no *heimin* who prospered; nor does it mean that commoner status prevented social, economic, or political upward mobility, or that *shizoku* status meant automatic prosperity. The point is merely that with *shizoku* status one's life chances were better. *Shizoku* referred to the ex-samurai who until 1877 received stipends from the government—free money in effect—and by virtue of their status had connections with those in high places, had avenues open to them that were denied to the vast majority of commoners. The omnibus classification *heimin* referred to all those who occupied the lower orders during Tokugawa—some *gōshi* ("rural samurai"; two important examples of déclassé *gōshi* are Kōno Hironaka and Tashiro Eisuke), but

38. Bellah, *Religion*; Scalapino, *Democracy*.

39. See, for example, Sidney R. Brown, "Kido Takayoshi: Meiji Japan's Cautious Revolutionary," *Pacific Historical Review* 16 (May 1956):152–62, for a general treatment of the concept of *jinzai*; for *meibōka*, see Takahashi, *Fukushima minken*, pp. 181–297; for the importance of *minkenka*, see Chapter 4, below. Also see Irokawa, "Survival Struggle," pp. 479–80.

40. For example, see Kee-il Choi, "Tokugawa Feudalism and the Emergence of the New Leaders of Early Modern Japan," *Explorations in Entrepreneurial History* 9:1 (1956):72–84.

mainly farmers, artisans, and merchants, most of whom entered Meiji with meager assets. An official classification as *heimin* merely increased the chances that one's assets were likely to remain meager.

Like the other "fixed" characteristics, an official status of *heimin* was no guarantee that one would participate in the popular rights movement or in any of the three incidents examined here. The purpose, therefore, of identifying the participants in terms of status is to test the proposition that the movement and related incidents included a growing number of commoners, and to use the findings later in order to determine whether status was a factor that contributed to participation and, if so, to what extent.

The breakdown by status according to incident appears in Table 9.

From this table we can say that the percentage of *heimin* among the participants in the three incidents was respectively two-thirds, one-half, and one-hundred percent. But since our samples really reflect only the leadership strata of each of the incidents, it remains necessary to inquire into the status composition of the followers as well.

To treat the most obvious first: One Chichibu document, dated 2 December 1884, that helps in determining the status composition of the followers in this incident is entitled "A list of names of those charged with rioting who surrendered themselves to the authorities between November 4 and November 30, 1884."[41] The list consists of 160 people coming from seven different villages in Chichibu district. All 160 people were *heimin*. If we again use the "Table of those defendants charged with massing to riot" as a rough index of those who were followers, we see that all seventy-seven persons were classified as *heimin*.[42] Using the even larger sample of 254 persons, including leaders and followers—Tashiro Eisuke's appointed officers, those charged with "instigating the masses," and those accused of membership in the Kommintō—it is significant that there are no *shizoku* listed among them.[43] This evidence supports the contention that the Chichibu incident was a *heimin* disturbance. The only exception to this generalization might be Tashiro Eisuke, the Commander of the Kommintō army. Though born a *gōshi*, his family failed to receive *shizoku* status after the Restoration.[44]

Although not as marked as the Chichibu sample, the Fukushima one does show that *heimin* predominated by a ratio of two to one

---

41. *CJSR* I:403–8.   42. Ibid., pp. 378–83.   43. Ibid., pp. 640–56.
44. Inoue, *Chichibu jiken*, pp. 50–52. Kikuchi Kanbei of Saku district was a self-declared *shizoku* (*CJSR* I:49, and *CJSR* II:431), but all official records show him to be a *heimin*.

TABLE 9.
Official Status of Participants in
the Three Incidents

	Fukushima (N–45)	Kabasan (N–31)	Chichibu (N–35)
Heimin	30	15	35
Shizoku	14	16	0
Unclear*	1	0	0

*"Unclear" refers to one case where an individual was classified by the authorities as *shizoku* but who, during interrogation, classified himself as *heimin*. Except for the Kabasan, the other figures include only residents of the area where the disturbances broke out.
Source: Abstracted from Appendices B, C, and D.

over the *shizoku* involved in the incident. If we look again, however, to the first indictment list of 13 January 1883,[45] then the percentage of *shizoku* involved is even smaller. Assuming that only leaders in the incident were indicted for "treason" and/or for "instigating the masses," then we see that of the sixty-four leaders so charged, only ten of them were *shizoku*. Also, importantly enough, no *shizoku* appear among the 285 Fukushima residents charged with "blindly massing to riot." From this we may gather (1) that the *heimin* dominated the leadership at least by a ratio of two to one over the *shizoku*; (2) that most or all the followers in the incident were probably *heimin*; and (3) that if a *shizoku* were to play a part in the incident, not only would he likely be a resident of Tamura but he would also hold a position of leadership (Tamano, Aizawa, Sawada, and Hanaka are just some of the more important figures).

Shizoku were especially important in the Kabasan Incident as well; so much so, in fact, that it would be fair to ask why this incident is included in a treatise concerned with *heimin* revolts. For of the twenty principal participants, only six were *heimin*; and of the total sample, as we saw, not quite half were *heimin*. Now that the question has been posed, it seems appropriate to respond.

The Kabasan Incident was included for three main reasons. First, ostensibly at any rate, the participants conspired to overthrow the existing government in order to erect a new government more responsive to the needs of the vast majority of Japanese, who were, of course, commoners. Secondly, the intent of the conspirators was to mobilize the people to achieve this. That the response of local farm-

45. FKS, pp. 939–49.

ers to the call for rebellion was poor bespeaks several things, not the least of which was the poor organization of the rebels and probably the good sense of the local farmers not to involve themselves in an apparently futile attempt at revolution, which they regarded, perhaps, as a vendetta against Governor Mishima. (See Chapter 1.) This relates to the third reason for including this disturbance in our study. *Even if* the Kabasan Incident was in part a *tomurai gassen* or "battle of revenge," as it is frequently regarded,[46] the point still remains that the participation of *heimin* vitiated the *shizoku* class basis of the affair. This becomes all the more obvious when it is recalled that the prime mover of the entire scheme was Koinuma, a *heimin*. Moreover, as we shall see in the next chapter, the participants themselves explicitly stated in their manifesto that they regarded class as unimportant insofar as recruitment was concerned.

A final remark about the importance of status considerations as they relate to the three incidents is necessary. It would be a mistake to regard the distinction between *heimin* and *shizoku* as anything akin to the Marxist proletariat/bourgeoisie dichotomy that is usually made in terms of the "consciousness" each class has of itself as a class. Though one might profitably talk about the existence of a "*shizoku* consciousness,"[47] it was premature at that time, despite such notions as "commonerism," to talk about a "*heimin* class consciousness." Indeed, *heimin* and *shizoku* are not terms denoting economic classes; they are descriptive terms used to refer essentially, on the one hand, to the many who were *not* of samurai origin and, on the other, to the few who *were*. The principal criterion for differentiation was simple— the place in the feudal hierarchy of one's Tokugawa ancestor. If *class* as a descriptive term is at all useful, it is in how it relates to occupation and to the income and social status derived from it. To this we now turn.

Occupation

For several reasons, identification of the participants by occupation is not as straightforward as it was by residence, age, or status. First, there are many instances where an individual has more than one occupation, the most frequent example being the farmer/merchant, i.e., one whose farm produces a surplus of cash crops sufficient to allow

46. Endō Shizuo, *Kabasan jiken* (Tokyo, 1971), p. 19.
47. See Brown, "Assassination."

him to market directly a sizable portion of his crop in either raw or processed form. In the case of processed goods, such as silk clothing, dye, paper, and the like, the farmer may bypass the merchant and sell locally. There are also examples of farmer/"lawyer," where "lawyer" (*daigennin*) may refer, for example, to the practice of mediating between debtors and creditors and receiving a "fee" for the service, usually in the form of a favor or some commodity. Farmer/village head (*shōya, kimoiri, nanushi*), farmer/priest, farmer/teacher, and farmer/craftsman are additional examples. Secondly, there is the problem of individuals who are unemployed, bankrupt, or who simply have "no occupation" (e.g., due to youth). And thirdly, there is the further problem of discrepancy between different sources concerning the facts about individuals. Hence, in identifying the occupation of individuals, it has occasionally been necessary to make a choice, based on what appears to have been their principal occupation. In many cases, however, what the individual himself identified as his occupation during the course of police interrogation has served as the source of our classification.

The breakdown of the Fukushima sample shows that for the thirty-five people on whom we have information, farmers constituted a clear plurality of the participants, numbering fourteen in all. Following them were what could be termed the "local intelligensia," namely teachers (five) and priests (Shintō four, and Buddhist one). Next came merchants and those who responded "none" during interrogation, each with three. There were also two doctors, one druggist, one assistant in village government, and one lawyer's aide.

Takahashi has shown that in the Fukushima case there existed a close correlation between the occupation of a participant and his residence.[48] Most popular rights leaders from the Aizu region, for example, were farmers, mainly small landlords and well-to-do, self-cultivating farmers. The question of the nature of landholdings aside, our sample lends support to his findings: All of the Yama residents were in fact farmers (and *heimin*). They were also, as Takahashi claimed about most of the leadership from this area, *kimoiri* or village heads. There were sufficient numbers of village heads in this region involved in the Aizu Jiyūtō—more than the 80 percent of the party membership, he says—that it almost warrants calling it the *kimoiritō*, "party of village heads."[49] In our sample, eleven individuals were village heads.

48. Takahashi, *Fukushima jiken*, pp. 39–42.   49. Ibid., p. 58.

Our sample also shows a few village heads coming from the Tamura-Ishikawa region, but most of the individuals from this area were teachers, priests, and merchants. Again, this finding squares with Takahashi's own investigations.[50] So too in the case of those coming from the coastal region—Sōma and Futaba districts: Activists from these areas, such as Aizawa and Kariyado Nakae, were on the whole either ex-samurai who had returned to farming, or priests and teachers.[51]

Most of the followers in the Fukushima Incident, we saw earlier, came from the Aizu region and Yama district in particular. Since it was a farming district, it seems safe to assume that most of the followers were farmers. More about the scale and type of farming in that region will be discussed in the section immediately following this one.

More participants in the Kabasan Incident, nine in all, engaged in farming at one time or another than in any occupation. But of the nine, it appears that only three or four made it their sole vocation. Of those claiming to be farmers, for example, Koinuma was more a merchant/landlord than he was a farmer; Kokugi derived most of his income from the railroad, even though he farmed part-time; and Tamamatsu served as a bodyguard to Tomimatsu.[52] Indeed, there were probably as many "intellectuals"—four journalists and one teacher—as there were full-time farmers. The category into which most of the participants fall is "unemployed/no occupation," accounting for eight, all of whom were *shizoku*. This fact tends to lend additional support to the widely held belief that a large floating body of unemployed ex-samurai were becoming political activists in the post-Restoration period.[53] Also included in the sample were two village heads (one *kimoiri* and one *kochō*), and three ex-policemen, one of whom—Monna Shige-jirō—began to be active in the movement during the period in his police career when he was required to attend and spy upon popular rights lecture meetings.[54]

As might be expected, there is not the same variety of occupations among Chichibu Incident participants. Twenty-four, or nearly all of those appearing in our sample, were farmers. Although some individuals engaged in subsidiary sericultural work such as silk weaving, the vast majority spent most of their energies in the cultivation of mul-

50. Ibid., p. 39.
51. Ibid.
52. Nojima, *Kabasan jiken* (Tokyo, 1966; originally published in 1900), pp. 207–8.
53. See Brown, "Assassination"; Scalapino, *Democracy*.
54. Ishikawa Naoki, *Tonegawa minken kikō* (Tokyo, 1972), pp. 170–78.

berry or in the raising of silkworms.[55] Even the seven individuals who are listed as having nonfarming jobs—craftsman, blacksmith, dyer, merchant, "lawyer" (*daigennin*), priest (Shintō), and teacher—were probably closely tied to the agricultural community. The previously used "Table of those charged with massing to riot" again supports the representativeness of our Chichibu sample. Of the sixty-one names for whom occupation data exists, fifty-five were listed as farmers. The other six included a seaman, a day laborer, a soldier, a carpenter, a mortician, and a (bamboo) craftsman.[56]

In Inoue Kōji's study of the occupational structure of the 261 people arrested in Gumma prefecture for their participation in the Chichibu Incident (among whom ninety-two were Chichibu residents), we see that 70 percent were farmer-cultivators, a figure lower than we would expect, given the evidence just presented. However, he also notes that of the other 30 percent, "very few of them were not tied to agriculture in some way,"[57] and he lists "lawyers" (*diagennin*), charcoal makers, roof thatchers, forest laborers, day laborers, servants, dyers, plasterers, silk weavers, etc., as examples of this close tie.

Given the conditions of the Meiji economy at that time (as outlined in Chapter 2), it is not surprising that so many of the participants should have been farmers. At the same time, however, unlike many teachers and priests (members of the "intellectual class"), whose participation in an anti-government movement finds many historical parallels elsewhere,[58] the fact of the farmers' ties to an essentially liberal and, at the same time, anti-government movement was certainly new

---

55. Assuming that the occupational structure remained fairly stable after the incident, the following breakdown for 1888 is of interest:

Occupations Related to Sericulture, 1888

Occupation	No. of Households
sericulturists	9,123
silk thread manufacturers	563
specialty silk manufacturers	86
weavers	7
cocoon and silk merchants	586
Total	10,365
Total no. households Chichibu dist.	13,071

Source: Inoue, *Chichibu jiken*, p. 12.

56. *CJSR* I:378–83.
57. Inoue, *Chichibu jiken*, p. 91.
58. See, for example, Crane Brinton, *The Anatomy of Revolution* (New York, 1956); Harry Eckstein, "On the Etiology of Internal Wars," *History and Theory* 4 (1965):433–63.

to Japan and probably relatively rare historically when compared to other parts of the world.[59] Certainly a partial explanation for this development lies in a study of the property relations existing at the time of these rebellions.

Financial Status/Land Ownership

In the second section of Chapter 2, it was shown how farming in Fukushima had come to be increasingly devoted to production of commodities strictly for the market. It was shown that the impetus behind increased production was the inflation of the late seventies, and the rising demand domestically for *sake*, pottery, lacquer ware, wax, etc., and internationally for silk. Farmers of Fukushima (and of Chichibu in the case of silk) responded to this demand by devoting more and more land and energy to the production of such items.[60] It was also shown in Chapter 2 that due to the success of the Matsukata deflationary policy, and to new quality control standards imposed by the government, prices for such products fell drastically. That fact, coupled with the constant pressures of taxation and demands by creditors for repayment of the loans taken out earlier during the expansionist boom, brought on the bankruptcy, or the threat of it, of innumerable farmers. We can imagine as well that farmers from some areas—for instance Chichibu, where crop production was not diversified—were more affected by such changes in fortune than were farmers in Fukushima, where crop diversification was a long-established practice.

Within this rapidly changing economic context, the *gekka jiken* broke out. Given the depressed state of the economy, the following questions arise: Were those who rebelled the downtrodden, the disinherited, the dispossessed? Were they the tenants, wage laborers, or subsistence farmers? Was it poverty that signaled the call for rebel-

59. The reason for this was perhaps described by Karl Marx in "The Eighteenth Brumaire of Louis Napoleon," *Selected Works* 1 (Moscow, 1969):478: "The small-holding peasants form a vast mass, the members of which live in similar conditions but without entering into manifold relations with one another. Their mode of production isolated them from one another instead of bringing them into mutual intercourse. The isolation is increased by France's bad means of communication and by the poverty of the peasants. . . . The great mass of the French nation is formed by simple addition of homologous magnitudes, such as potatoes in a sack form a sack of potatoes." Applying the same structural analysis to Japanese agricultural society, we might hypothesize that their principal mode of production, i.e., cooperative rice production, allowed them the interaction denied to the French peasants.

60. Ōishi Kaichirō, "Fukushima jiken no keizaiteki kiban," in *Jiyū minkenki no kenkyū*, Part 2, *Minken undō no gekka to kaitai*, Vol. I, eds. Horie Hideichi and Tōyama Shigeki (Tokyo, 1959):36–37.

lion? Popular conceptions would have it so. But the question requires investigation.

This section intends to examine the income and land ownership distinctions that existed among those belonging to the farmer class, for, as has already been shown, the farmers were the group that predominated in the Fukushima and Chichibu incidents. Moreover, inasmuch as the Kabasan conspirators directed their revolutionary energies at the mainly rural population of Ibaraki prefecture, it would be instructive to look at relations of landownership there as a possible means to explain why its farmers, unlike the people of Fukushima and Chichibu, did not rise in rebellion when the opportunity presented itself.

A second reason for investigating distinctions of wealth among the participants is to test the claim that the leadership of the popular rights movement was changing hands from the *shizoku* to the *heimin* class (which claim, from the evidence presented in the section on "status," we saw was true), and to the *gōnō* or "wealthy farmers," in particular. We will look at this last point first.

In the Fukushima sample of leaders, fourteen individuals were identified as farmers; and of these, information on property holdings exists for ten. Here we will supplement this sample with the same kind of information on nine others who were active in the Fukushima popular rights movement, and also in the Kitakata Incident, as attested by their later arrests.[61] Fifteen of the nineteen farmers, it should be pointed out, were residents of Yama district. (See Table 10.)

Based on this sample, it appears that most of the leadership, at least that part of it coming from the farming contingent, was drawn from landowners having more than two or three *chō*. It was this group, collectively referred to as *gōnō*, that "participated in the Aizu Jiyūtō [branch]; they were small landlords having about ten *chō*, or prosperous self-cultivators having two or three *chō*."[62] The question remains, however, that if this amount of land ownership characterized the *gōnō* as the rebellion's leaders, what amount characterized their followers? In terms of their property holdings, how are the followers to be distinguished from the *gōnō*?

61. The additional individuals are Watanabe Ichirō, Kojima Chūhachi, Miura Shinroku, Endō Naoyuki, Hara Heizō, Saji Kōhei, Saji Kumimatsu, Maeda Kōsaku, and Iijima Kōtaro. The data come from Takahashi, *Fukushima minken*, pp. 173–74, and from Takahashi, *Fukushima jiken*, p. 60.

62. Takahashi, *Fukushima jiken*, p. 60.

TABLE 10.
Size of Landholdings of Twenty-four Fukushima
Men Involved in the Fukushima Incident

Land Area	Number of Farmers	Others
landless	1	2
below 1 chō	0	1 (priest)
1–2 chō	2	0
3–5 chō	4	1 (priest)
6–10 chō	7	1 (sake manufacturer)
11–20 chō	3	0
above 21 chō	2	0
Total	19	5

Source: Abstracted from Appendix B.

Most students of this period generally distinguish between the various economic strata within the farmer class in the following manner: landlords, landlord/self-cultivator, self-cultivator, self-cultivator/tenant, tenant, tenant/wage laborer, and wage laborer.[63] In this way, distinctions are made in terms of each person's place (role) in agricultural society. But since it is clear that those individuals encompassed, for example, in the categories of landlord/self-cultivator and self-cultivator/tenant may, because of their "split roles," share much in common with either the stratum directly above or below—depending upon to what extent their property holdings place them more in one category than in the other—the even broader but perhaps more pertinent distinction is made between strata of farmers according to the extent of their landholdings. The strata include: (1) jōnōsō, or "upper-level farmers," referring to those whose cultivable landholdings are two chō or more; chūnōsō, or "middle-level farmers," those who have between one and two chō of land; and genōsō, or "lower-level farmers," those owning less than one chō of land.[64] To gain an understanding of how such a breakdown related to Fukushima prefecture, the reader is referred to Table 11.

63. Though the distinction between wage laborer and servant is usually made, it is not relevant here since neither category provided any leaders in these incidents. On the distinction, see, for example, Nagatani Yasuo, "Gumma jiken no shakaiteki kiban ni kansuru kenkyū nōto," Shien 32:1 (February 1972):81–90.

64. A chō equals 2.45 acres or .992 hectares. The three categories are applicable to landholders across Japan, although the amount of land equivalent to each size of holding will vary slightly according to region. They certainly are applicable to Fukushima; they come from the source cited in note 65.

TABLE 11.
Average Area of Land Managed in Fukushima
Prefecture, by Strata (1875)

Farmer Level	Wet Field Average	Dry Field Average	Forest Average	Total Land Average	% of Total Farming Population	Total Cultivated Land (excl. Forest)
Upper	1.4 *chō*	.93	1.83	4.26	8.0%	2.33 *chō*
Middle	.8	.68	1.2	2.74	28.0%	1.48
Lower	.3	.3	.43	1.03	64.0%	.6

Source: Shōji Kichinosuke, "Jiyū minken undō no keizaiteki haikei," in *Jiyū minken undō* 3, comp. Meiji Shiryō Kenkyū Renraku Kai (Tokyo, 1956), p. 189.

Several comments need to be made about this table. First, its title tells us that the figures therein represent *not* the average amount of land *owned*, but only the average amount of land managed. Secondly, as the author of the article in which this table appears says, the two strata, middle level and lower level, include self-cultivating farmers, self-cultivating tenant farmers, and tenant farmers.[65] And, thirdly, it may safely be assumed that the 8 percent representing the upper-level farmers—included are 199 households with total family property in excess of 4,000 yen, the so-called *funō*, or "rich farmers"—were actual owners of property and, it is important to add, were probably landlords.[66]

This last point is an important one, for it clearly shows that within the upper strata there existed distinctions of wealth not adequately represented by the categorization as it appears in Table 11. Hence, in speaking of this group, collectively known as *gōnō*, the modifiers "small," "medium," and "large" are usually employed. Returning for a moment to those individuals coming from our sample, we can say, first, that sixteen of the nineteen individuals were clearly *gōnō*, i.e., among the upper 8 percent of Fukushima farming society; but, secondly, that the majority, the eleven who held between three and ten *chō*, were "small" *gōnō*. The three owning between eleven and twenty *chō* were "medium" *gōnō*; and the two possessing more than twenty *chō* were "large" *gōnō*.

65. Shōji Kichinosuke, "Jiyū minken undō no keizaiteki haikei," in *Jiyū minken undō*, comp. Meiji Shiryō Kenkyū Renraku kai, Vol. 3 (Tokyo, 1956), p. 189. The same table but accompanied by more elaborate analysis can be found in Ōishi, "Shakai keizaiteki," pp. 108–9.
66. Shōji, "Jiyū minken undō," p. 189.

Most Japanese specialists on the subject view this phenomenon of *gōnō* leadership as a "contradiction" in the popular rights movement because the "class" interests of the *gōnō* were squarely in conflict with the "revolutionary tendencies" found within the small-scale farmer class who, in their capacity as followers, comprised the vast majority of the movement. Ultimately, this "contradiction" is usually cited as the principal cause for the failure of the incidents in particular, and the popular rights movement in general.[67] This thesis is propounded despite the knowledge that the comparative history of rebellion and revolution is replete with examples of such movements being headed by members of a class or strata ranking above those from which most of the movement's followers came.[68] The thesis is also advanced despite its conflict with much of the data coming from the *gekka* rebellions, which indicate if not prove that in terms of property relations (and even values)[69] those who were most likely the followers in these incidents were not very far removed from the leadership. "Most likely," because the data on the property holdings of individual followers are very poor; we can only guess at who they were by looking at the general, aggregate data on property relations within a given geographical area. Since, in the case of the Fukushima Incident, we know that the vast majority of the following were residents of the Aizu region, we shall focus our attention there.

A fair index of how landownership was distributed within Fukushima prefecture can be seen in Table 12. Keeping in mind the facts that the payment of between five and ten yen in land tax meant ownership of between .86 and 1.7 *chō*, and that payment of more than ten yen meant holding more than 1.7 or 1.8 *chō* of land,[70] what is most striking is, first, the high percentage of individuals owning land in the Aizu region (Yama, Kawanuma, Ōnuma, Kita-Aizu, Minami-Aizu, and Higashi-Kabahara) and especially Yama district, where, as it will be recalled, the Kitakata Incident was centered; and secondly, the predominance of middle- and upper-level farmers among landowners there. Shimoyama, in fact, tells us that the average area of land held by the average household in Yama district was 1.7 *chō*, or trans-

---

67. For example, see Gotō, *Jiyū minken*. Also see Ōishi, "Shakai keizai," p. 118; and Hirano Yoshitarō, *Minken undō no hatten* (Tokyo, 1948).

68. Cf. Rudé, *Crowd*, p. 248; Arendt, *On Revolution*, p. 112; Hobsbawm, "Peasants and Politics," pp. 12, 19, 20; Moore, *Social Origins*, pp. 464, 473–74.

69. *Value* in the sense that production of cash crops and the corresponding tendency to merchandise as well indicate some belief in capitalistic values.

70. Shimoyama, "Oboegaki," p. 158.

TABLE 12.
Strata Structure by District Using Land
Tax Payments (1883)

District	Percent of Population by District Paying Land Taxes			
	Less than 5 yen	5 yen to 10 yen	more than 10 yen	(more than 5 yen)
Shinobu	65%	17%	18%	(35%)
Date	59	19	22	(41)
(AIZU REGION)				
Yama	41	34	25	(59)
Kawanuma	59	14	27	(41)
Ōnuma	57	23	20	(43)
Kita-Aizu	48	17	35	(52)
Minami-Aizu	90	9	1	(10)
Higashi-Kabahara	86	12	2	(14)

Source: Ōishi Kaichirō, "Fukushima jiken no shakai keizaiteki kiban," in *Jiyū minkenki no kenkyū*, Part 2, *Minken undō no gekka to kaitai* Vol. 1, ed. Horie Hideichi and Tōyama Shigeki (Tokyo, 1959), p. 21.

lated into land tax terms, an annual payment of five to ten yen.[71] Finally, one *assumption* which can be drawn from this table relates to the question of political consciousness: Fifty-nine percent of Yama district residents were qualified to vote; and even though it is not known how many took advantage of this privilege, it might nonetheless be assumed that their right to vote made them politically conscious of local affairs.

The observation that the middle-income farmers predominated is reinforced by the data provided in Table 13, which show the land ownership relations for a more or less typical village of Yama district.

A high rate of individual landownership, of course, necessarily means a low rate of tenancy. How this rule applied to Fukushima prefecture is shown in Table 14.

The districts which provided most of the manpower in the incident —Yama, Kawanuma, and Ōnuma—stand out from the rest as having a low rate of tenancy and a high percentage of self-cultivating farmers, most of whom, we may infer from Tables 12 and 13, were "middle-level" farmers. It might be observed that the figures for Asaka district are very similar to the three above-mentioned districts; why Asaka's

71. Ibid., and Ōishi, "Shakai keizai," p. 20.

TABLE 13.

Farmer Strata According to Size of
Landholdings, Fukuzawa Village,
Yama District, Fukushima
Prefecture (1872)

Land Area (chō)	Number of Households	
2.5–3.0	1	8%
2.0–2.5	1	
1.5–2.0	8	67%
1.0–1.5	11	
.7–1.0	3	17%
.5– .7	2	
.3– .5	0	8%
.1– .3	1	
.0– .1	1	
landless	0	
Total	28 households (100%)	

Source: Ōishi Kaichirō, "Fukushima jiken no shakai keizaiteki kiban," in *Jiyū minkenki no kenkyū,* Part 2: *Minken undō no gekka to kaitai,* Vol. 1, ed. Horie Hideichi and Tōyama Shigeki (Tokyo, 1959), p. 64, Table 18.

farmers were not active in the Fukushima Incident is not altogether clear. However, one very plausible explanation for this has to do with the great financial benefits the people of the district received from the government the year before in the form of the Asaka land reclamation project. Quite possibly this disposed them favorably toward the intrusion of the central government into local affairs, and hence they were not very sympathetic to the protests coming from Aizu.[72]

Since, as we have seen in Chapter 2, the Aizu farmer had only since the late seventies begun to enjoy unprecedented prosperity on account of a switch from staple to cash crop production, we may suppose that the threat of losing his newly acquired wealth seemed all the more odious a prospect to him. It is interesting to note that de Tocqueville, and more recently, George Rudé, observed a similar pattern in prerevolutionary France: Rebellion does not come merely when times are hard, but instead it comes when a period of prosperity

72. Shimoyama, "Oboegaki," pp. 55–58.

TABLE 14.

Percentage of Households and Land by Type of
Cultivation for the Sixteen Districts of Fukushima (1883)

District	% of Households (1883)			% of Land (1883)	
	self cultivator	self tenant	tenant	self cultivated land	tenant land
Shinobu	55.5%	23.2%	21.3%	79.9%	20.1%
Date	55.9	26.2	17.9	25.5	24.5
Atachi	69.0	21.8	9.3	91.1	8.9
Asaka	81.0	17.8	1.2	88.9	11.1
Iwase	64.5	31.0	4.5	85.8	14.2
Nishi-Shirakawa	62.4	29.4	8.3	83.8	16.2
Higashi-Shirakawa	58.8	36.2	5.1	82.1	17.9
Ishikawa	61.1	29.0	9.8	85.0	15.0
Tamura	79.0	19.5	1.5	93.7	6.1
Yama	80.6	10.0	9.4	88.4	11.6
Kawanuma	82.8	13.2	3.9	97.0	3.0
Ōnuma	81.7	15.0	3.3	88.2	11.8
Kita-Aizu	52.3	43.6	4.1	85.0	15.0
Minami-Aizu	64.1	34.7	1.2	91.4	8.6
Higashi-Kabahara	70.0	27.1	2.9	85.8	14.2

Source: Ōishi Kaichirō, "Fukushima jiken no shakai keizaiteki kiban," in *Jiyū minkenki no kenkyū*, Part 2: *Minken undō no gekka to kaitai*, Vol. 1, ed. Horie Hideichi and Tōyama Shigeki (Tokyo, 1959), p. 20, Table 3.

begins to collapse.[73] When this happened in Aizu, those individuals most closely tied to the market, and hence most vulnerable to it, namely the small self-cultivator and self-cultivator/tenant, rose to protest against the economic forces of the market of which they were part but over which they had no control.

For similar reasons, in part, the farmers of Chichibu revolted. Their close ties to the market were described in Chapter 2: (1) a very sizable dependency on the import of staples from outside the district, stemming from a shortage of arable land (only 6 percent of the total area); (2) the almost total devotion to producing silk for the market, engaged in by at least 80 percent of all farm households in Chichibu; and (3) the growth of market towns—Ōmiya, Ogano, Shimo-yoshida,

73. Alexis de Tocqueville, *The Old Regime and the French Revolution* (New York, 1955), pp. 176–77; and Rudé, *Crowd*, p. 20.

and Nogami—since the mid-Tokugawa period to handle the processing and sale of their silk.

It is necessary to note the strong ties to the market as a preliminary to identifying the participants in the incident according to their financial status. There are several reasons for this. First, since data on land ownership by individuals are scanty, only by showing the relationship of the market to general patterns of land ownership and type of crop cultivation can we infer their economic status. Secondly, one reason for a paucity of data relates to what was one of the main objectives of the incident's participants, i.e., the destruction of all documents relating to indebtedness; this in turn tells us indirectly of the financial status of many of the farmers involved. And thirdly, most discussions of the participants' resources are usually vague and ill-defined, speaking primarily in terms of "bankrupt," "near-bankrupt," or "indebted" farmers as those who composed the vast majority of participants in the incident.

Like Yama district in Aizu, Chichibu district displayed a relatively low rate of tenancy and a fairly high rate of landownership; but interestingly enough, unlike Yama, there were very few *gōnō*. In 1885, one year after the rebellion, almost 60 percent of all households were self-cultivators, as is shown in Table 15. Two further points need to be extracted from this table: (1) Even allowing for a measure of statistical error, the jump in tenancy—11.6 percent—in one year is extraordinary; (2) this happened in a region where "there were no great landlords; most people in the mountain village were self-cultivators; there was no such thing as a landlord-tenant problem."[74] According to one contemporary observer, a Shintō priest named Tanaka Senya, there were only three families that could be called landlords, and they held only two to four *chō* of land.[75]

Though undoubtedly an underestimate, the priest's testimony does point to a significant fact about landowning relations within the district. Unlike the Aizu area, where we saw a relatively high percentage of landowners paying land taxes exceeding five yen, the figure for Chichibu was an inconsequential 4 percent of the population (1885); those paying more than ten yen in land taxes were a diminuative 0.8 percent.[76] If we consider this fact along with the high rate of land-

74. Inoue Kōji, "Chichibu jiken: Sono shakaiteki kiban," in *Jiyū minken undō* III:67.
75. Ibid., and Ishikawa, *Tonegawa*, p. 212; and *CJSR* II:551-88.
76. Gakushūin Hojinkai Shigakubu, comp., *Chichibu jiken no ikkōsatsu* (Tokyo, 1968), p. 70.

TABLE 15.
Percentage of Households by Type of Landholding
for Chichibu District and Saitama Prefecture

	1885 Chichibu	1885 Saitama	1883 National Average	1886 Chichibu	1887 Chichibu
Self-Cultivator	59.5%	28%	39.8%	50%	50%
Self-Cultivator/Tenant	32.1%	57%	38.6%	29%	25%
Tenant	8.4%	13%	21.9%	20%	25%

Source: Inoue Kōji, Chichibu jiken: Jiyū minkenki no nōmin bōki (Tokyo, 1968), p. 13; and Shimoyama Saburō, "Minken undō nōto," in Jiyū minken 10, Nihon rekishi series, ed. Sakane Yoshihisa (Tokyo, 1973), p. 302.

ownership and the low rate of tenancy, we find that the average area of land owned by self-cultivators was small, certainly less than one *chō*. In fact, if we glance at Table 16, we see that the average area of wet and dry fields cultivated by one Chichibu farm household (which averaged 5.2 family members) in 1884 was, respectively, .05 *chō* and .59 *chō*.[77] Of course, as we saw in Chapter 2, it could hardly have been otherwise: With only 6 percent of its territory arable, and with a population over 50,000, landholdings had to be small. Not only were the landholdings small, they were also the least valued in all of Saitama prefecture, worth only about forty yen and nine yen per *tan* (.245 acre; one tenth of a *chō*) for wet and dry fields respectively.[78] About all the land was good for, as we saw earlier, was the cultivation of mulberry, the principal crop of the district, which, once harvested, was used to feed the silkworms, the other main "crop."

Since the land area under management or ownership of the cultivator was small, the scale of production of the farmers was also small —too small for many farmers to serve as their own merchants (as did many of the farmers of Yama district).[79] It appears that this situation encouraged merchants under the aegis of several large *ton'ya*— five in all that sprang up from 1880 to 1881—to handle the mulberry and silk trade of the many small producers.[80] Once the farmer sold

77. Inoue, Chichibu jiken, p. 9. Another source claims that the total wet and dry field cultivation average area was .63 chō (Gakushūin Hojinkai Shigakubu, comp., Ikkōsatsu, pp. 17–18). The discrepancy may be due to which year's statistics the different sources relied upon.

78. Gakushūin Hojinkai Shigakubu, comp., Ikkōsatsu, p. 17.

79. Shimoyama, "Oboegaki," p. 165: "There was a preponderant tendency for direct producers—middle level farmers—also to act as small merchants."

80. Inoue, Chichibu jiken, pp. 10–11.

TABLE 16.
Selected Statistics for Saitama Prefecture
and Chichibu District (1885)

Category	Chichibu District	Rank among 18 districts	Saitama Prefecture
Type of holding (% total land area)	self 88.3% tenant 11.7%		self 58% tenant 42%
Average area cultivated by household	wet .05 *chō* dry .59 *chō*	15th	wet .37 *chō* dry .73 *chō*
Land in mulberry	3,389 *chō*	1st	
Percent of land area in dryfield	32%		12%
Amount of silk-worm production	9,736 *koku* (1 *koku*=4.96 bu.)	1st	
Average silkworm production per household	.95 *koku*		
Value of same	28 yen		
Average annual land tax	2.1 yen		
Number of residents paying more than 5 yen in land tax	687	15th	
Percent of same of all households	4%		
Number paying more than 10 yen in land tax	138	18th	
Percent of same of all farm households	0.8%		
Raw silk production	6,963 *kan* (1 *kan*=8.3 lbs.)	1st	

Source: Shimoyama Saburō, "Minken undō nōto," in *Jiyū minken* 10, *Nihon rekishi series*, ed. Sakane Yoshihisa (Tokyo, 1973), p. 302.

his mulberry leaves, or cocoons, or raw silk to an agent of the ton'ya, which of course existed to make a profit, his income in 1884 was only about twenty-eight yen.[81] This was not nearly enough to pay taxes, repay debts, buy rice, and generally survive.

A quick glance at our participant sample will clearly show just how meager that annual income was. For the six individuals for whom we have data, the range of indebtedness is 25 to 225 yen, with an average of 75 yen per person, although the median indebtedness of about 50 yen is probably a more representative figure. Indebtedness as such, however, was no stranger to the Chichibu farmer; indebtedness had been necessary during the seventies in order to finance expanded production to meet the rising demand for silk. What was in the end disastrous for him was the type of indebtedness he was frequently compelled to bear. One type, *getsu shibari* ("bound by the month"), the predominant type used by loan companies, had a 15 percent interest rate per three-month period, or 60 percent annually. Another type, the *kirikanegashi*, or "limited (i.e., short-term) loan," often meant an interest rate of 20 to 30 percent per month; thus, if a farmer borrowed ten yen in January, by November he would owe between twenty and thirty yen.[82]

Tashiro Eisuke, leader of the Chichibu Kommintō, was himself an indebted small silk farmer; he owed money to two or three loan companies and had a mortgage on his small plot of land.[83] Tashiro, according to one source, paid land taxes on his .6 *chō* of (dry) land amounting to 2.4 yen (about the district average; see Table 16) and was representative of the majority of "lower-middle-level" farmers of Chichibu.[84]

Although we lack figures on the financial status of most of the other individuals included in our sample, there is reason enough to believe they suffered similar misfortune. The very demands made by the Kommintō—tax reduction, loan exemptions, closure of the schools, etc.—probably bespeak the financial distress of its members. Collateral evidence seems to support this contention. As we saw in the last chapter, Saitama prefecture was among the nation's highest in terms of the total amount of loans made to its residents, and the number of properties mortgaged.[85] Also, data on the financial status

81. Ibid., p. 12.   82. Ibid., pp. 19–21.   83. Ibid., p. 28.

84. Shimoyama Saburō, "Minken undō nōto," in *Jiyū minken*, Vol. 10, *Nihon Rekishi* series (Tokyo, 1973):304; also Gotō, *Jiyū minken*, p. 182.

85. Paul Mayet, *Agricultural Insurance in Organic Connection with Savings Bonds, Land Credit, and the Commutation of Debts*, trans. Reverend Arthur Lloyd (London, 1893), p. 65.

of members of the Hachiōji Komminto, a neighbor of the Chichibu party, reveal that most of its members were either bankrupt or approaching bankruptcy.[86]

These facts, considered along with the small land area cultivated by the average Chichibu farmer, the extremely high proportion of farmers engaged in producing silk, and the depressed state of the silk market, together characterize the financial status of the participants in the Chichibu rebellion. It is important to note, however, that while the deteriorating financial status of the farmers appear to have been an important contributing factor in bringing about the revolt, it was, nonetheless, only one of several. It seems instructive to repeat that economic misery is a necessary but not a sufficient cause for revolt. There existed then (and still exist today) too many examples of people passively living in a state of poverty to think otherwise. As was indicated in the last chapter, the farmers of Ibaraki, Makabe district, stand as an example of this passivity.

In Chapter 1, we told of how hundreds of farmers from neighboring Gumma prefecture, especially from Minami-Kanra district, and also from Minami-Saku district of Nagano prefecture, used the Chichibu rebellion as an opportunity to join in property smashings against local landlords, loan institutions, and individual creditors. We also observed that historically this instance was merely one of a number of rebellions that had spread to encompass entire areas, crossing prefectural boundaries and behaving much like a "chain-reaction" effect. Recognition of this pattern, however, requires that we ask why the same did not occur in the case of the Kabasan Incident. We must ask why the Ibaraki villagers, unlike the Gumma and Nagano participants in the Chichibu rebellion, did not use the Kabasan revolt as an opportunity to rise up. As we know, they were not immune to the economic misery of the depression that was plaguing much of the rest of the country. Was there something, then, about local conditions that prevented them from responding to the call for rebellion? The answers to these questions, I believe, lie elsewhere than in the single feature of landholding relations, probably in the type of revolt the conspirators planned. The rebellion was mainly intended to be *for*, rather than *by*, the people. This discussion, however, has more to do with ideology and organization and shall therefore be postponed until the next chapter for a fuller consideration. Here our attention will

---

86. Irokawa Daikichi, "Kommintō to Jiyūtō," *Rekishigaku Kenkyū*, 247:8 (August 1961):1–30.

TABLE 17.
Landholding Relations, Makabe District,
Ibaraki Prefecture (1884)

	(Makabe district) % of total population	Ibaraki prefectural average	National average	% of total land area (Makabe district)
Self-Cultivators	31.7	38.0	39.8	69.1
Self-Cultivators/Tenant	44.7	41.0	41.0	
Tenant	23.5	21.0	21.9	30.9

Source: Namatame Yasushi, Kabasan jiken no ikkōsatsu (Takahagi, 1962), pp. 20, 23.

focus upon the landholding relations and economic status of those farmers who resided in the immediate area of Mount Kaba in Makabe district, Ibaraki prefecture.

As might be recalled, despite the original intention of the rebels to begin the revolution in Tochigi prefecture at Utsunomiya Town, the conspirators were ultimately forced to make their appeal for revolution to the farmers of Makabe district.[87] Except for several hundred poorly organized local farmers, who were quickly intercepted by the authorities before they could join the conspirators atop Mount Kaba, the people of this district were unresponsive. What, then, differentiated the farmers who tried to answer the call for revolution from those who did not? At least part of the answer seems to be related to the type of landholdings. In looking at this, Tables 17, 18, and 19 will serve as the basis for analysis of the landholding relations in Makabe district.

From these tables, a number of conclusions can be drawn. First, for the district as a whole (Table 17), it is apparent that compared to the percentage of farmers cultivating their own land in Yama (Fukushima) and Chichibu (Saitama) districts, the Makabe rate is very low, revealing a difference of 48.9 percent and 27.8 percent respectively. Accordingly, Makabe district also displays a much higher rate of tenancy than do the other two districts: respectively, 14.1 percent and 15.1 percent higher. Makabe, then, unlike the other two, comes very close to the national average, as well as to the prefectural average. It also follows that the amount of land under self-cultivation and under tenancy is, respectively, less and more than in the case of Yama and

87. Endō, Kabasan jiken, p. 9, suggests it might be wise to rename the Incident the "Utsunomiya jiken" for this reason.

TABLE 18.

Landholders by Strata According to Size
of Holding, Makabe District (1879)

Category	Amount of Land Held	Percentage of Total
Poor Farmers	less than one *chō*	45.8
Middle Level	1–2 *chō*	24.3
Upper Level	2–5 *chō*	22.8
Landlords	5–10 *chō*	5.2
Large Landlords	10 *chō*	1.9

Source: Namatame Yasushi, *Kabasan jiken no ikkōsatsu* (Takahagi, 1962), p. 23.

Chichibu. They each had about 18 percent more land under self-cultivation and 20 percent less under tenancy than Makabe.

Table 18 shows several things, but in order to make sense of it, it is first necessary to recall from the last chapter that the principal crops of Makabe were rice and barley and hence it was primarily a staple-producing region.[88] This is significantly different from Yama and Chichibu, where cash crops such as silk, lacquer, tobacco, and the like predominated in the primarily dry-field areas. There, although the land was not very valuable in terms of its assessed tax rate, the crop was. In Makabe, the land was valuable since much of it was in wet-field areas, but relatively speaking, the crop was not valuable. This meant that the net income from one *chō* of Makabe rice-producing land would be worth less than, for example, that from one *chō* of Chichibu or Yama mulberry-producing land. Hence, the Chichibu farmer with little land was probably better off financially than the Makabe farmer with more land—especially since tax rates on rice-paddy land were more than on dry-field land, and in a cash economy that often meant the difference between solvency and insolvency.[89] Consequently, the classification "lower-strata" farmer has a different meaning depending on the area in which the term is applied.

This said, it seems necessary to "weight" Table 18 in order to make it comparable to the figures for Yama and Chichibu. To do this we add roughly half of the figure for "middle-level" farmers to the figure for "poor farmers" and estimate the "poor" or "lower-strata" farmers

88. Namatame Yasushi, *Kabasan jiken no ikkōsatsu* (Takahagi, 1962), p. 20.
89. *Jiji Shimpō*, 29 March 1884, has a report on the effects of the new tax regulations of 15 March. *Japan Weekly Mail*, 31 May 1884, has a special supplement on taxation. Also see Chambliss, *Chiaraijima*.

TABLE 19.

Landholding Relations in Two Villages of Makabe District:
Number 1 Responded to Call for Revolution; Number 2 Did Not (1879)

Size of Landholding	chō 0–0.1	0.1–0.5	0.5–1.0	1.0–1.5	1.5–2.0	2.0–3.0	3.0–5.0	5.0–	Total
1. Village Kadoi:									
Number of households	1	9	21	21	12	3	2	0	69
Percent	1.5	13.0	30.4	30.4	17.4	4.3	2.9	0	100% (rounded)
2. Village Teraueno:									
Number of households	6	30	12	4	2	6	3	1	64
Percent	9.4	46.9	18.8	6.6	3.1	9.4	4.7	1.5	100% (rounded)

Source: Namatame Yasushi, *Kabasan jiken no ikkōsatsu* (Takahagi, 1962), p. 24.

to comprise around 57 to 60 percent of the total Makabe farm population—which of course puts it considerably higher than the percentage in Yama district, where wealth was concentrated among the middle-level strata, and in Chichibu district, where wealth was very diffuse
and no great disparities in property-holding or income existed.

The implication of this argument is, of course—and it receives considerable support from comparative historical works—that somehow
the poor, or at least the poor relative to a given population, are not
the ones who join in rebellion.[90] A glance at Table 19 lends support
to this hypothesis. There we see that the village (Teraueno) which did
not heed the call of the Kabasan rebels exhibits a very marked disparity in land holdings: The moderately wealthy, with more than three
chō of land, constituted 6.2 percent of the village population; the relatively poor, who owned less than one chō, made up 75.1 percent of
the population; and there was a very small "middle stratum." The
other village, Kadoi, in contrast, which was active in the popular
rights movement, and which responded to the rebels' call, shows
a strong middle stratum and weak upper and lower strata. It should
be kept in mind that, based upon the landholding relations for the
district as a whole, Kadoi village was the exception, and not Teraueno village.

The absence of a strong middle stratum of landowners residing in
the area seems to help explain why the rebels were unable to mobilize
the local population, and, ultimately, why the revolution failed. Yet
at the same time it is probably less important than other factors, such
as weak planning, mistaken policy, factional infighting, and fanciful
notions about how to capture political power. The next chapter will
treat these other factors; but now, before continuing, it would be
wise to summarize the findings presented in this chapter.

Conclusion: Leaders and Followers

The participants in the Fukushima, Kabasan, and Chichibu incidents have been identified according to five characteristics—residence,
age, occupation, status, and property holdings. The other characteristics shown in the three samples—literacy, arrest record, and membership in political societies and/or parties—properly require consideration elsewhere. Using, then, the findings presented thus far, what can
be said of the participants?

---

90. See Rudé, *Crowd*, pp. 199–201; Eric R. Wolf, *Peasant Wars of the Twentieth Century*
(New York, 1969), pp. 290–92; and Kathleen Gough, "Peasant Resistance and Revolt in
South India," *Pacific Affairs* 41:4 (Winter 1968–69):540.

First of all, from the *conventional* perspective, they were what the newspapers of that time reported them to be. The leaders were called "pettifoggers," "banditti and common jailbirds," "broken-down gentlemen, indigent burghers, and professors of vice," and "desperadoes." The followers were depicted as "slow-thinking masses," "insignificant mobs," and the like.[91] Such epithets, however, do little to provide an accurate identification of the participants; what they probably do provide is an accurate account of official opinion of those people suspected to have been most active in the various anti-authority disturbances. The Kabasan rebels, for example, were portrayed as a "band of thieves"[92] who "disgraced the cause of liberty by an exhibition of mad licence,"[93] and were mistakenly identified as "six *shizoku*, five professional gamblers, and eleven *heimin*."[94] The Fukushima Incident was described as a case where "a few reckless radicals succeeded in persuading the farmers that the taxes they were required to pay for local purposes were quite superfluous. . . ."[95] The Chichibu activists were called "gamblers and harebrained radicals"[96] and "members of the old Jiyū party, gamblers, and low-level legal practitioners."[97]

Somewhere in all this invective there is a measure of truth: Robbery (or banditry) was committed in the course of these incidents; a few activist individuals had sometime in the past been convicted of gambling, e.g., Tashiro Eisuke; some participants were radical liberals; and so on. But from the perspective of the participants themselves, from the point of view of those so labeled by the press, "robbery" would probably have been regarded as the mere act of retrieving articles of value out of which they had earlier been cheated; "gambling" would probably have been treated as a harmless means of supplementing an otherwise meager income; and "radicalism" perhaps would have been interpreted as belief in an ideology which happened to be contrary to that of the government.

Such language is of course evaluative, and outside of the objective criteria that have been used thus far in this chapter to identify the participants of the three incidents. To point out the past use of such

91. These characterizations come from a variety of newspapers: *Jiji Shimpō*, *Tokyo Nichi Nichi Shimbun*, *Mainichi Shimbun*, *Yūbin Hōchi Shimbun*, *Chōya Shimbun*, and the *Japan Weekly Mail*, covering the period from 14 April 1883 to 13 December 1884.

92. *Japan Weekly Mail*, 27 September 1884.

93. *Jiji Shimpō*, 2 October 1884.

94. *Jiyū Shimbun*, 8 October 1884.

95. *Japan Weekly Mail*, 21 April 1883.

96. *Nichi Nichi Shimbun*, 9 December 1884.

97. Ibid. Compare the use of this kind of evaluative language with that in French history; see Rudé, *Crowd*, pp. 198–212.

language is, however, important at this stage, for in the final analysis evaluative language is what is used by opposing sets of political actors in real conflict situations; and it undoubtedly reflected the image that one set of actors had of its opponents. But more to our present purpose is the distinction made by such language between the few leaders ("agitators") and the many ("blind") followers. This distinction will be employed for the remainder of the summary.

Leaders, those who appear in the three main samples, generally came from only a certain few geographical regions of the many areas encompassed by each of the incidents. Yama and Tamura districts accounted for most of the activists involved in the Fukushima Incident; the conspirators of the Kabasan Incident came mainly from Fukushima, from Shimotsuga district of Tochigi, and from Makabe district in Ibaraki; and within Chichibu district, certain villages such as Hinosawa, Yoshida, Fuppu, and Isama turned out the greatest number of activists. The geographical distribution of followers, not surprisingly, pretty much coincided with that of the leaders. This applies all the more in cases where political organization was a function of residence in a village community (as we shall see in the next chapter). Though not uniformly so, this was more the case with Chichibu than with Fukushima. With Chichibu we saw that the very same villages which produced most of the leaders—Fuppu, Isama, "Upper" and "Lower" Yoshida, and "Upper" and "Lower" Hinozawa—also were ranked among the highest for the number of followers they turned out. Sanyama, Iida, and Shimo-Ogano villages were among several exceptions to that rule, although the explanation for this might lie in the factor of organization; this also appears to be the case where the following from some villages was not great in absolute terms but did show a large participation relative to the small number of village inhabitants. (See Table 6.)

The factors of organization and ideology also appear to be relevant in explaining how so many leaders of the Fukushima Incident came from areas, principally Tamura district, other than those where most of the followers resided. The area where residence of leaders and followers most closely corresponded was the Aizu region, and chiefly Yama district where the Kitakata Incident occurred.

Because the demographic factor pertaining to the leadership in the Kabasan Incident was not local but interregional, in fact interprefectural, and because the appeal by the conspirators to the farmers was made at a place where most of them had no local following, residence was of little importance as a factor in participation among the relatively few farmers who did heed their call. In fact, from the outline of the incident as it was presented in Chapter 1, it can easily be inferred that two of the other factors, age and status, were also of little significance in moving local residents to join in the Kabasan disturbance. It was shown that if any of the five factors were important, then it was the relations of landholdings that existed in Makabe district, and only coincidentally the further factor of occupation, since their call to arms was made in an area largely agricultural.

The age of the participants was the second characteristic treated. The leaders of all three incidents were fairly young. We saw that the Kabasan leaders were the youngest, the Chichibu leaders the oldest, with the Fukushima leaders falling somewhere in between, but closer to the Kabasan than to the Chichibu leaders. Regardless of incident, most leaders were either in their twenties or thirties, and therefore we are allowed to conclude, with minimal reservation, that our age data do not contradict and perhaps even support the whole notion of the "young rebel." About the followers it can be said that in the case of Fukushima the evidence is scanty, but that, based on Takahashi's sample of 100 participants, there was little difference between the ages of leaders and followers. The Chichibu evidence on followers, using the lesser crime of "massing to riot" as a crude index of position in the movement, was more complete, and hence it is likely that most were in the twenty to forty age group. Especially in the Chichibu case, however, the factor of age as it relates to participation in rebellion should be regarded as an empirical observation rather than as a causative explanation of why individuals rebelled.

Official social status, i.e., *shizoku* versus *heimin*, was the third factor treated, and was chosen in order to test, in part, the proposition that the popular rights movement and related disturbances, such as the three under study here, were increasingly coming under the leadership of commoners. The evidence for the leadership of each incident strongly suggests that the proposition is a true one, even though this conclusion must be regarded as tentative until the next chapter establishes to what extent each of the incidents was ideologically and organizationally related to the popular rights movement.

Occupation was the fourth characteristic of the participants that was examined. We saw that the leadership of the Fukushima Incident was characterized by a variety of occupations—farmers, merchants, teachers, priests, doctors—and that a close relationship existed between the type of occupation and the residence of the individual. Most of the leaders coming from Yama district, for example, were farmers; most from Tamura were merchants, teachers, and priests. The Kabasan principals also held a variety of occupations, but the most striking fact about these rebels was the relatively large number of unemployed *shizoku*, or, as they would have been characterized during the Tokugawa period, *rōnin* ("masterless samurai").

The occupations of the Chichibu leaders showed much more uniformity than in the other two cases. Most were farmers, sericulturalists in fact, and even many of those who were not farmers per se were somehow tied to sericulture. The same can be said not only for the occupations of the followers in the Chichibu Incident, but for the followers in the other two incidents as well. Of course, it could hardly have been otherwise, since not only did the incidents take place in rural areas but also because of the simple fact that the population of Meiji Japan of the 1880s was overwhelmingly rural and agricultural.

This last fact chiefly determined the focus of inquiry in treating the last characteristic of the participants that was looked at in this chapter, namely, relations of land ownership. An attempt was made to determine whether members of certain economic strata, and not others, were more inclined to rebel; and secondly, in order to build upon the earlier tentative finding that the *heimin* were rapidly taking over the leadership of the popular rights movement from the *shizoku*, we sought to discover whether it was the *gōnō* stratum of the *heimin* that were predominant among the new leaders.

In going about this task, we decided that it was useful to distinguish between strata of farmers according to the extent of their landholdings. Accordingly, the distinction was made between "upper," "middle," and "lower" strata farmers. But because within the "upper" category there was considerable variance in the extent of landholdings, a further distinction was made between "small," "medium," and "large." When this distinction was checked against the Fukushima sample, it was shown that the largest percentage of leaders came from the "small *gōnō*" stratum. This fact obviously squared well with the thesis that the *gōnō* stratum was assuming leadership in the popular rights movement (subject, of course, to the establishment of a link between the incidents and the movement). But when we examined the landholdings of the leadership of the Chichibu Incident, we were unable to find anyone among the leadership approaching *gōnō* status.

Instead, what was found was a great number of small self-cultivators, many of whom were apparently in considerable debt; and in terms of landholdings, there was very little difference between leader and followers. The crucial variable, it would seem, that separated the Chichibu participants from the Fukushima ones, again in terms of landholdings, was the type of agriculture that the Chichibu residents engaged in. It was a predominantly single-crop area—by necessity, as we saw—that because of a very limited arable land area permitted very few large landholdings. This fact also resulted in a very low rate of tenancy.

The Aizu region also had a very low rate of tenancy, but what appeared to distinguish it from Chichibu was the larger area of cultivatable land, the greater variation of crops, and consequently the greater comparative wealth of its farmers. Although the farming of both areas was similar in the sense that cash crops represented most of the agricultural production of each, ultimately the Aizu farmer was less vulnerable to the vicissitudes of the market because of the diversification in his farm produce and, secondly, because of his greater wealth stemming from his larger landholding. Still, regardless of the landholding differences between both areas, *within* each area, relative to the landholdings of others, most of the followers in each incident came from the "middle-level" strata of farmers. The same, we saw, was the case with the Makabe district farmers who responded to the call for rebellion made by the Kabasan conspirators. This finding lends support to the thesis that it is not the very poor who involve themselves in rebellion and revolution, but instead "some sector of the middle classes that is upwardly striving and finds its way blocked."[98] If "middle classes" is understood in a very precise fashion, then specifically, within the farmer or peasant class as a whole, as Eric Wolf points out, it is the "middle peasant," the person "most vulnerable to economic changes wrought by commercialism," who is revolutionary.[99]

The last point is an important one, but it needs to be qualified in one respect: It must be emphasized that most of those people who participated in the three incidents we are examining were *not* peasants; they were not agrarians engaged in subsistence production who believed that poverty was inherent to the human condition. We have come across indebted or bankrupted *farmers* in the course of our study, rural producers of commercial goods who were temporarily suf-

98. Leiden and Schmitt, *Politics of Violence*, p. 87.
99. Wolf, *Peasant Wars*, pp. 289–94, especially p. 292.

fering from debts and taxes which came after a period of prosperity, but we have not encountered any peasants, to my knowledge. The rebels we have been looking at were participants in the "moral economy" of the market, farmers who produced for the market certain goods from the sale of which they expected a fair profit; they were farmers who sought to increase their holdings of land and capital by employing their own labor and/or the labor of others. Awareness on their part that their depressed economic condition might have its origins in politics rather than in Nature spurred them to fight for the political rights which might assist them in holding on to the advantages of production for profit.

Many Japanese historians, Marxists for the greater part, have acknowledged these facts with enthusiasm, and they have accordingly seen in these three *gekka jiken* all the makings of a bourgeois revolution. The objective conditions, they maintain, necessary to foster a bourgeois-democratic revolution were present at the time of these rebellions: wide-scale commercial farming; the beginnings of landlordism and the emergence of a class system; and the primary accumulation of productive capital. The class nature of the rebellions themselves, they argue, lends persuasive support to their thesis. Ōishi Kaichirō, for example, after performing a very detailed and impressive analysis of the economic basis of the Fukushima Incident, concludes that it was "a bourgeois-democratic movement which derived its principal impetus from wide-scale small farmer participation," and he adds that "the *gōnō* (especially the petty bourgeois small *gōnō* as small landlords) composed the leadership." Parenthetically, he says, the Fukushima Incident "was fundamentally a real bourgeois revolution." That it was a revolution that failed, Ōishi claims, was due to the contradiction inherent to a class alliance between small farmers and landlords—the latter type of rural capitalist realized only too well that his interests would be protected by the absolute state.[100]

Ōishi's analysis is in many respects an echo of the thesis advanced by the influential Hirano Yoshitarō, whose explanation of the Chichibu rebellion rings some of the same polemical bells. It represents, he argues, the high point of the growth of Jacobinical tendencies within the bourgeois-democratic movement, having clearly revealed "the revolutionary action of agricultural laborers and small farmers from below" who had come under the influence of radical democrats

100. Ōishi, "Shakai keizaiteki," p. 118.

like Ōi Kentarō.[101] This high point, says Marxist historian Gotō Yasushi, can be compared with the Kabasan Incident. Though composed of "revolutionary democrats," their battle for the democratic revolution unfortunately comes off as "the reckless opposition of revolutionary petty-bourgeois intelligensia who forgot about the existence of the revolutionary masses."[102] If the prescribed terminology can be separated from their basic thesis for a moment, and if we can only bring ourselves to consider the very impressive array of facts which these very talented historians have marshaled, then the central finding seems to be that the *gekka jiken* reflect the growth of liberal or bourgeois economic and political forces in Japan during the 1880s.

Western students of Japan's political and economic development have repeatedly tried to disprove this thesis, but they have not faced it head-on. Instead, they have bypassed it altogether in "modernization studies," or they have ignored it by focusing on great Meiji leaders, or they have segmented the thesis in order to challenge merely one aspect of it. Some have even resorted to *ad hominem* arguments, saying that Japanese scholars support this thesis because they are in "revolt against the whole prewar regime in which they grew up."[103] There may exist among Western scholars an understandable bias against the heavy Marxist jargon, but there is certainly a less acceptable Western bias in the commonly held belief which says that "unique Japan" could not have experienced anything akin to *Western* liberalism.[104]

Yet what has been shown thus far in the cases of the three incidents would in general seem to support the Japanese Marxist thesis. But it is only supportive insofar as it has been shown that certain regions—Chichibu and Aizu mainly—exhibited economic, social, and political features which could have engendered a liberal revolution

---

101. *Bourgeois minshushugi kakumei* and *Nihon shihonshugi shakai no kikō* are two of Hirano Yoshitarō's better-known works dealing with this thesis. The passage cited comes from his *Minken undō no hatten* (Tokyo, 1948), p. 292.

102. Gotō, "Meiji jūshichinen," pp. 246–47.

103. R. P. Dore, "The Meiji Landlord: Good or Bad?" *Journal of Asian Studies* 18:3 (May 1959):355. The article is a review of Japanese Marxist scholarship concerned with the beginnings of landlordism in the 1880s, and although Dore demonstrates familiarity with the literature, he never answers the question he posed in the title to this article. Instead he only suggests that landlords may have been "good" because so many Japanese historians have said they were "bad."

104. The position is a popular one: Jansen, "Ōi Kentarō"; Scalapino, *Democracy*; and Pittau, *Political Thought in Early Meiji Japan, 1868–1889* (Cambridge, Mass., 1967), could be listed as several examples.

after the pattern of England, France, or America. Briefly, these features include: heavy and arbitrary taxation following on the heels of a period of prosperity; the commercialization of agriculture to a significant extent;[105] a sharp drop in demand for commercial products, accompanied by indebtedness, bankruptcy, loss of landownership, and the corresponding fall into tenancy; the consciousness of agricultural producers that they lack the political rights necessary to defend their economic rights as producers; the rise of an opposition movement whose platform promises producers the political rights they lack; and the social fact that the leaders of the opposition movement are generally educated, relatively wealthy, and, for the moment at least, believe that their interests coincide with those of the uneducated and relatively poor but nonetheless small capitalist producers.

These elements at least seemingly must be present before anything resembling a bourgeois revolution, or the tendency toward one, can occur. The purely economic prerequisites listed above have already been treated; the political ones and the one concerning the farmers' consciousness of their plight will be treated in the next chapter. In going about this, we shall try to clarify the necessary political conditions by making some comparative observations between the Japanese case and the American and European parallels. We shall also try to place the individuals examined in this chapter into a social context—that is, into the political groups of which they were a part and through which, in terms of ideology and organization, their actions took on purpose and definition.

105. Extent, of course, implies measurement, but I know of no magic formula by which it can be determined at what point agriculture becomes sufficiently commercialized to ignite a bourgeois revolution; at best, a whole constellation of conditions must be present first. The point is made best by Thomas H. Greene in his *Comparative Revolutionary Movements* (Englewood Cliffs, N.J., 1974).

4. Ideologies and Organizations

> The rugged face of society, checkered with the extremes of affluence and want, proves that some extraordinary violence has been committed upon it, and calls on justice for redress.
>
> *Thomas Paine,*
> *Agrarian Justice, 1795–96*

Introduction

The Fukushima, Kabasan, and Chichibu incidents were not riots, nor blind expressions of rage, nor were they mere repetitions of traditional peasant uprisings. They were not the spontaneous explosions of an angry "mob," randomly attacking whomever or whatever. On the contrary, behind each incident there existed one or more organizations, held together by customary and political ties, which had formulated their immediate targets and long-term goals with an exactitude not usually recognized by most North American students of the period.

Past treatments of the political history of this period have generally not been very sensitive to commoners and the organization and ideology behind their rebellions. When Robert Scalapino, for instance, speaks of a "peasant class, whose activities . . . took the form of scattered violence under the impetus of economic misery,"[1] whether intended or not, the picture given is one of impoverished peasants involved in aimless violence and acting as unthinking links in the (simplistic) "direct causal chain from hardship to anger to action."[2] E. H. Norman does better, admitting that some organization existed among the "peasants," but at the same time he sees the rebellions as a result of political agitators who "stirred them up." He likewise sees the "isolated village peasant" as being too far removed to play anything

1. Scalapino, *Democracy*, p. 114.
2. Tillys, *Rebellious Century*. Their entire book represents an assault upon this type of simplistic theorizing. The particular passage quoted appears on p. 271.

more than an intermittent role in the liberal movement.[3] Nobutaka Ike recognizes the heavy dependence of the rebels on commercial agriculture (and he stands alone in this regard), but when he describes the Chichibu Incident, for example, he forgets that they are farmers and falls into the old terminology of "peasants" assembling as a "mob."[4] From the more recent work of Irwin Scheiner, one gets (I believe) the mistaken impression of "peasants" rebelling in Chichibu *because* they believed in millennial Buddhist dogma.[5] But whichever account of Meiji rebellion one might consult, the lasting impression that is derived is one of a "mob" of peasants "as a disembodied abstraction and not as an aggregate of men and women of flesh and blood"[6] who, I would add, are organized as a political movement based on political principles.

This chapter is an attempt to define the ideologies that underpinned the political organizations involved in the Fukushima, Kabasan, and Chichibu incidents. It is an inquiry, first of all, into those principles which the participants of the incidents employed to define their goals and to order themselves; and secondly it is an inquiry into the makeup, workings, and tasks of the organizations themselves.

It is well to note here that the plural form of the nouns *organization* and *ideology* is used, for although there were certain similarities between the organization and ideology found in each of the incidents, there were also differences. The organization of the participants encompassed such widely differing forms as: political parties; "political societies" (*seisha*) and the private schools operated by these societies; "circles," or small local groups consisting of a few "like-thinking men" (*dōshinsha*); "friendship associations" (*shinbokukai*); "cells" (*saibō*), or local units of a larger organization; lecture societies; and the like. Moreover, not only did such forms of organization serve to order the relationships and purposes of those involved, but they also served as vehicles or as agencies for the further expansion of other organizations. They performed a function basic to the viability of organization, that is, the task of recruitment. For this, in addition to the organizations themselves, a variety of means were used: lectures, de-

---

3. Norman, *Emergence*, pp. 173, 182. Both quotes are rewritten for the sake of comprehension, but the meaning is retained: In the first, the word *them* is interposed; in the second, the phrase is contracted from "peasants living in outlying, isolated villages to take active part in politics."

4. Ike, *Beginnings*, pp. 160, 164.

5. Scheiner, "The Mindful Peasant."

6. Rudé, *Crowd*, p. 9.

bates, demonstrations, petition campaigns, and familial and extra-fa-
milial relationships such as, respectively, marriage and "parent-child"
(*oyabun-kobun*) links; speaking tours aimed at various villages and
their agricultural associations; political party and society newspapers
and bulletins; handbills; and even songs and poems. Thus, not only
could and did organizations take on a variety of forms, but so too
did their methods of recruitment.

The forms which organizations and the recruitment function took
varied in degree, type, intensity, and place. Not all forms or recruitment patterns could be found in any one place. In some areas, such
as Chichibu, people tended to coalesce more around traditional village forms of organization than they did around "political societies"
or "circles." There, "parent-child" relations between individuals, or
familial connections arising from marriage, tended to predominate as
vehicles of organization. In other areas, however, such as eastern
Fukushima, the political society, or "circle," found fertile soil to nurture organizational growth. Recruitment was often impersonal, and
interpersonal relations were less traditional, with people being united
more by shared ideas than by shared in-laws or by common place of
birth.

The role of ideology in uniting individuals also differed according
to place. It was, for instance, more important to the organizations in
Tamura than to those in Chichibu. Ideology also differed according
to the level at which it was expressed. If it was expressed at the level
of day-to-day concerns—food, housing, and capital expenditures in
general—then it appealed to, and served to organize, those who were
in financial difficulty; therefore, the demands expressed by such people were particular and immediate ones. On the other hand, ideology
at the more general level, as an expression of a desire for a certain kind
of society, reflected concerns other than the issue of economic security. The point is that the same ideology, albeit expressed differently
at different levels, was manifested by different forms of organization,
recruitment patterns, demands, issues, and the like, according to who
voiced it and where it was voiced.

For this reason, it seems appropriate to speak in terms of ideologies
rather than ideology. For instance, the demands made by the Chichibu farmers, as outlined in Chapter 1, were mainly at the level of day-
to-day concerns—tax reduction, debt exemption, etc. But in order to
secure a remedy for such economic problems, the farmers believed
that a representative constitutional system of government was re-

quired. Political reform, they thought, would provide a cure for economic ills. Although it is not without hesitation that we refer to these farmers as proponents of a democratic ideology, or even as "constitutionalists," because of their strictly economic reasons for desiring such a system, they remain, nonetheless, democrats of a definable type.

By way of historical comparison, the reasons they had for supporting constitutional government are not altogether different from those which served the American colonists as a rationale for demanding the same kind of system a hundred years earlier. The theme of "no taxation without representation" can be found in both cases.

Although similar in this respect, the American and Japanese cases differed with regard to the political tradition that the proponents of constitutionalism in each case had inherited. Unlike the Japanese case, the Americans had inherited the English political tradition of "natural rights," which they drew upon in order to underpin their essentially economic reasons for supporting constitutional government. "Natural right" doctrine, as expounded long ago by John Locke, and as underscored by Thomas Paine and Thomas Jefferson, was, or could be when deemed necessary, used as a rationale for revolution.[7] But even before "natural right," England had had a tradition of revolt. Speaking of England—and Americans, of course, inherited much of English tradition—Elie Halevy wrote: "The right to riot or as it was termed by the lawyers, 'the right of resistance,' was an integral part of the national traditions."[8]

Largely Confucian Japan, of course, had no "natural right" doctrine to draw upon as a rationale for revolt, although, as we saw in Chapter 2, Japan did have its own tradition of revolt, and, as we also saw, the tradition was stronger in some areas, namely Kantō and Fukushima, than in others. Evil rulers and bad government, as evidenced oftentimes by economic distress attendant upon natural disasters, was reason enough in the Confucian value system to provide the pretext for the revolt;[9] but probably more important were the

---

7. Jefferson wrote in a letter to James Madison, 30 January 1787: "I hold it that a little rebellion now and then is a good thing, and as necessary in the political world as storms in the physical. Unsuccessful rebellions indeed, generally establish the encroachments on the rights of the people which have produced them. . . . It is a medicine necessary for the sound health of government." Quoted in Adrienne Koch, ed., *Jefferson* (Englewood Cliffs, N.J., 1971), pp. 36–37.

8. Elie Halevy, *England in 1815* (New York, 1961), p. 148, and quoted by Charles Tilly, "Collective Violence in European Perspective," in *Violence in America*, ed., H. D. Graham and Ted R. Gurr, (New York, 1969), p. 6.

9. Irokawa Daikichi, "Freedom and the Concept of People's Rights," *Japan Quarterly* 14:2 (April–June 1967), 181.

values emanating from, first, the older moral economy of subsistence, and then subsequently from the newer moral economy of capitalism. The older system legitimated rebellion that sought to force the authorities to acknowledge and respect the right to subsistence, and the newer system justified resistance against those authorities who would arbitrarily interfere in the workings of the market economy. The question then arises: Within the changing economic, political, and social context, as earlier outlined, when Confucian and subsistence values were being supplanted by capitalist ones, was it not then necessary for the Japanese to discover new and different rationales for revolt? Is it not likely that, as with England and Europe where natural right doctrine was formulated to explain and justify the acquisitive principles of capitalism, Japan as well would require a similar philosophy to legitimize its emerging market economy? Did not they too need something akin to "natural right," or even "natural right" itself, to provide philosophical, political, and moral support for revolts arising from purely economic causes?

The answer to these questions differs according to the incident. Resistance to change, and hence the viability of tradition and the values of the older moral economy were clearly stronger in Chichibu than in the other two cases. Very likely, the traditional Confucian right to revolt served to pave the way for the acceptance of, and perhaps to reinforce, the right to revolt as it was expressed in the natural right doctrine then being adopted by many market-oriented farmers. This is not surprising and can find support from comparative history, such as that of post-revolutionary France, where even after the notion of natural right had more or less become the official ideology of the state,[10] there were still many instances of revolt that conformed to traditional modes of organization and justification.[11] But even when they did so, the fact that they occurred against a changed political, social, and economic backdrop, different from the one against which they had traditionally been expressed, gave them a greater intensity or impact, or a new direction.[12]

In the cases of the Fukushima and Kabasan disturbances, the "new" notion of "natural right" was indeed influential, not only as a justifi-

10. It was "official ideology" in the sense that the "Declaration of the Rights of Man" (27 August 1789), the Constitution of 1791, and the Jacobin Convention of July 1793 endorsed the principles of natural right.

11. For example, see Charles Tilly, The Vendée (New York, 1967), for instances in the French case. Also see Rudé, Crowd, especially pp. 241–42.

12. Rudé, Crowd, p. 219.

cation for revolt in particular, and collective action in general, but also as a principle by and around which the participants of the two incidents organized themselves. The people involved in these incidents, like the American colonists, drew upon the principles of natural right in order to justify their opposition to the government, to protect their economic interests, and to give purpose to their collective action. This comparison, and others, will be discussed in due course.

Natural Right and Literacy

In Chapter 2, the point was made that prior to the founding of the Jiyūtō in late 1881, the leadership of the popular rights movement, as well as much of its following, was largely commoner-composed and Kantō-centered. It was also stated that the new leadership had adopted natural right doctrine to serve as the ideological basis of the movement and that they embraced its principles more strongly than had the early popular rights advocates. Here we will attempt to substantiate the latter point by discussing the nature of the natural right component as it appeared in late 1870s and early 1880s *minken* thought and action at the local level of politics. Following that, we will look at literacy rates in the countryside in order to see whether rural folk were able to comprehend such a system of thought as natural right. Before doing so, however, we will discuss natural right doctrine at some length in both the Western and Japanese contexts.

Natural Right: Western

There exists no one spokesman for natural right in the sense that one "thinker" has codified its principles and listed its rights. But without too many qualifications, it would be safe to say that "natural right," as it is understood today and as it was understood in Japan of the 1880s, consists of many of the principles enunciated by John Locke in his *Second Treatise* as well as the way his ideas were operationalized in the American Declaration of Independence, Constitution, and Bill of Rights. Implicitly or explicitly, natural right consists of a number of propositions:

1. Nature bestows on man *qua* man certain inalienable rights, such as life, liberty, property, security, and the right to take measures to protect these rights.
2. Natural right is anterior to the establishment of the state.
3. The state comes into existence when men contract with one an-

other to establish an agency (the state) whose sole purpose is to protect and guarantee these rights.

4. The authority of the state is derived from its duty to promote and protect these rights. Laws should reflect the recognition of natural rights.

5. If the state fails to perform this duty properly, then revolution is justified.[13]

These five points, of course, only represent a digest of a much more complicated system of ideas, which at the very least involves a number of propositions corollary to these main five. For example, a corollary to proposition Number 3 would be popular representation, essentially a check on the state to insure that man's fundamental rights are protected. Corollary to proposition Number 1 is the notion of equal rights—that is, no distinction of wealth, status, etc. should be made between men in terms of their natural rights.

The right of revolution, proposition Number 5, is the ultimate right and the logical conclusion to be drawn from the rest of natural right doctrine. Because the doctrine conceives of government as a *trustee* chosen by the people to protect their natural rights, the people retain the ultimate right to dismiss the government in the event it violates their trust, i.e., whenever it fails to protect their natural rights sufficiently. Supreme power or sovereignty rests with the people therefore; government's power is purely fiduciary. Needless to say, this view of government represents a radical departure from earlier absolutist conceptions of government, such as Divine Right.[14]

John Locke was one of the earliest and most thorough propounders of natural right doctrine, but only in the sense that he was one of the first who recorded and interpreted in a systematic manner the new political ideas which dominated the turbulent politics of seventeenth-century revolutionary England. His writings, which were only completed near the close of the century, cannot themselves be regarded as a reason for the English Revolution, but instead should be thought of as an *ex post facto* philosophical justification of the revolution.

13. A. P. d'Entrevès, *Natural Law* (London, 1951); Kingsley Martin, *French Liberal Thought in the Eighteenth Century* (New York, 1962; originally published in 1927); Bernard Bailyn, *The Ideological Origins of the American Revolution* (Cambridge, Mass., 1967), especially pp. 77–86.

14. Theorists who have made the right of revolution into a natural right are Locke (*Second Treatise on Civil Government*, pars. 127, 130, 133, 222); Jefferson (see note 7, above); and Rousseau (*Social Contract*, Book II, chaps. 1, 8; Book III, chaps. 8, 10).

Later revolutionaries in America and France, however, can fairly be said to have invoked a Lockean version of natural right, if only indirectly, and perhaps were even moved to rebel because of it. It is Sir Ernest Barker's contention that Locke's political thought "passed through Rousseau into the French Revolution; it penetrated into the North American Colonies, and passed through Samuel Adams and Thomas Jefferson into the American Declaration of Independence."[15] This view, moreover, has received reinforcement from such authorities as John C. Hall in his *Rousseau*, from Carl Becker in his *The Declaration of Independence*, and more recently from Bernard Bailyn in his prize-winning *The Ideological Origins of the American Revolution*. G. P. Gooch, in his classic treatments of seventeenth-century English democratic ideas, and Vernon Parrington's monumental work on the American political thought lend additional support to this view.[16]

Natural right doctrine, therefore, in any of its variants, whether expressed by Locke, Rousseau, or Jefferson, has strong revolutionary implications, not only because it invests sovereignty in the people, but also because it makes the government's fulfilling of its fiduciary obligations the grounds of political obedience. In fact, revolutions and rebellions fought in the name of natural right, by their very occasion, proffer a *new* answer to the age-old question, "Why obey?" They answer, "I will obey only if I am free to disobey."

The connection between natural right doctrine and the three classical revolutions is clear enough then; but in order to be able to relate the doctrine to the Japanese rebellions we are examining, it is also necessary to explain in very general terms *why* the doctrine had the revolutionary force it did in England, France, and America. What, it must be asked, was the appeal of the doctrine to seventeenth- and eighteenth-century revolutionaries? What was its socioeconomic and

15. In the "Introduction," p. xvi, of *Social Contract: Essays by Locke, Hume, and Rousseau* (London, 1969).

16. John C. Hall, *Rousseau: An Introduction to his Political Philosophy* (Cambridge, Mass., 1973), pp. 43–45; Carl L. Becker, *The Declaration of Independence: A Study in the History of Political Ideas* (New York, 1942), pp. 7–10, 27, 30, 79, 240; Bernard Bailyn, *Origins*, pp. 30, 45, 47, 59, 77, 184–88, 201; G. P. Gooch, *Political Thought in England, Bacon to Halifax* (Oxford, 1960; originally published in 1915) and his *English Democratic Ideas in the Seventeenth Century*, 2nd ed. (New York, 1959; originally published in 1927); Vernon L. Parrington, *Main Currents in American Thought: The Colonial Mind, 1620–1800*, 1 (New York, 1927), 274–75, 284–362. The work of Eric Foner is yet another source, and perhaps one of the most pertinent in terms of the argument that follows. Foner has made creative use of the notion of "moral economy" in his study of eighteenth-century American thought, especially the natural right thought of Thomas Paine. See his stimulating *Tom Paine and Revolutionary America* (London, Oxford, and New York, 1976), especially Chapter 5, "Price Controls and Laissez-Faire: Paine and the Moral Economy of the American Crowd."

political foundations? Was its proclaiming of the right of revolution somehow related in a fundamental way to changes in society and economy? These questions require answers if we are to avoid the simplistic assumptions which say either that doctrines or ideas are mere inventions which in no way reflect a larger social reality, or contrariwise are forces which can alone determine socioeconomic and political configurations. Herein we take the position that to move people to act, and to justify or legitimize their actions, meaningful actions and the doctrines which explain their purpose must necessarily have derived their meaning and force from a larger socioeconomic context.

Between the seventeenth and nineteenth centuries in England, France, and America, the overwhelming consequential development in society, economy, and polity was the rise of liberalism. "Hardly less a habit of mind than a body of doctrine,"[17] liberalism slowly developed into a political philosophy through the writings of a variety of thinkers who sought to explain as well as to legitimize a new, emerging set of socioeconomic conditions and relations that we refer to today as capitalism or the liberal market society. Its effect was not felt suddenly, but it was revolutionary. In place of the old feudal society which had been based on custom, status, and the authoritarian allocation of work and rewards, liberal market society substituted individual mobility, contracts, and the impersonal market allocation of work and rewards. As "men began to doubt that poverty is inherent in the human condition,"[18] notions of freedom from subsistence and freedom to unlimited acquisition of wealth, the motive forces of liberal market society, seized the minds of Europeans no less than it liberated their capacities in the never-ending search for profit.

In the market society, the working principle around which socioeconomic relations were centered was the individual's freedom to employ his labor, his land, and his capital to strike whatever bargains, to enter into whatever contracts, and to benefit from whatever socioeconomic relations that would serve to increase his wealth or to raise his social status. Naturally, there were preconditions which had first to be met before market society could function smoothly enough to allow the individual the necessary freedom to seek greater wealth and status—namely, land, labor, and capital had to be widely regarded as marketable commodities, as alienable commodities produced not for

17. Harold J. Laski, *The Rise of European Liberalism: An Essay in Interpretation* (London, 1962), p. 13.
18. Hannah Arendt, *On Revolution* (New York, 1963), p. 15.

use but for sale. Once these preconditions were met, as they were in England by the late seventeenth century and in America and France roughly a hundred years later, then social relations previously governed by custom and status were increasingly converted into market relations.

Since liberal market society worked on the principles of unlimited production and unlimited personal acquisition, it served to unleash incomparably greater productive capacities than had feudal society with its principle of subsistence. For the many who benefited from this new economic growth, their greater wealth meant greater freedom and mobility. For the many who were not quickly integrated into the market system, there was nonetheless a net gain in personal freedom, because upon entering the market, even if it was only to sell their labor, they gained the chance to improve their lot.

Both in England and France the spread of the market economy throughout the cities and the countryside took place under feudal or arbitrary systems of government. The realm of politics, in other words, worked on principles exactly contrary to the principle of freedom in market relations which governed the economic realm. In one very real sense, the English Revolution can be regarded as one instance where these opposing principles clashed. Then the government-supported monopolies and enclosures, wage and price controls, and the arbitrary taxation policies of Charles I served to alienate large sections of the population who had wed themselves to the principles of commercial liberty, which, of course, implied a minimum of government interference in the affairs of commerce. Arbitrary taxation rubbed no less roughly on the liberal-minded commercialism of the American colonists a hundred years later, and on the notions of free trade held by the French physiocrats just a few years after that. There were other equally important reasons for these three revolutions, but for the present it is only necessary to observe that in all three cases the post-revolution political settlements represented victories for the liberal market society. All had been struggles against arbitrary government, and all were victories for greater freedoms and rights of citizens to secure their property against government interference. As Hannah Arendt has characterized this struggle, "In the eighteenth century, and especially in the English-speaking countries, property and freedom still coincided; who said property, said freedom, and to recover or defend one's property rights was the same as the fight for freedom."[19]

19. Ibid., p. 180.

In all three of these revolutions, governments that had been unresponsive to emerging market society were replaced by ones which subscribed to minimum government interference in the workings of the market and maximum protection of private property.

In post-revolution politics a complementary development took place. Government became "the supplier of certain political goods . . . [and] the kind of laws and regulations, and tax structure, that would . . . allow [the market society] to work, and the kind of state services . . . that were thought necessary to make the system run efficiently and profitably."[20] Post-revolution governments assumed this new function because the new liberal state was under the control of an electorate consisting of property owners. In none of the three countries was the government democratic, because the franchise was limited to property owners, but they were by all means liberal. Post-revolution governments guaranteed freedom of association, speech, and publication, equality before the law, the inviolability of private property, and other freedoms and rights. They guaranteed these through a liberal constitution, "not the act of a government," as Thomas Paine phrased it, "but of a people constituting a government."[21] Those constituting the government were men of property, and although the constitutions they wrote did not prevent any individual from entering their ranks—all possessed the basic rights of equal opportunity to life, liberty, and property—only those meeting the property requirements were entitled to participate fully in the public realm. The people at large were at this point no more trusted than they had been under the ancient régime. Moreover, the new constitutions reflected not only a mistrust of political power as such, but also a mistrust of both authoritarian government controlled by a handful of aristocrats or oligarchs and the authoritarian governments that were expected to evolve if the masses were permitted an equal say in the making of public policy. In liberal market society it was assumed

20. C. B. Macpherson, *The Real World of Democracy* (Toronto, 1965), p. 8. Many of the ideas concerning natural right doctrine and its relationship to the rise of the liberal market society which I have tried to convey in this section reflect my understanding of this work by Macpherson and his earlier work *The Political Theory of Possessive Individualism* (London, 1962). Macpherson's basic thesis, the bourgeois class basis of natural right doctrine, was first advanced in his article "The Social Bearing of Locke's Political Theory," *Western Political Quarterly*, 7 (1954):1–22, and is reprinted in Gordon J. Schochet, ed., *Life, Liberty, and Property: Essays on Locke's Political Ideas* (Belmont, Calif., 1971). Many of the essays in the Schochet volume are responses to Macpherson's ideas; it is interesting to note that even Macpherson's detractors (e.g., see the Alan Ryan article in the same volume) agree that his thesis is fundamentally a sound one.

21. Quoted in Arendt, *Revolution*, p. 143.

that those without property were (or would be) irresponsible toward the onerous obligations of maintaining the security of the property, life, and liberty of others, because in market society, life and liberty were regarded as functions of property. Without property and hence a respect for the rights of private property, a respect for life and liberty would be absent. In its extreme version it was expressed in terms similar to the Kansas Constitution of 1857: "The right of property is before and higher than any constitutional sanction."[22]

Although among the leadership of the revolutionary parties in the three classic cases there were true democrats who preached egalitarian ideas, the dominant factions in each were composed of men who believed in a natural hierarchy which in market society was defined in terms of wealth and property. And the dominant faction suppressed more or less violently those who sought to make the revolutions into truly democratic movements. The Levellers in the English Revolution and Babeuf and his supporters in the French were suppressed because of their egalitarian views; and in the American Revolution, the radical democrats such as Jefferson and Paine had ultimately to reconcile themselves to a system which declared all equal (except slaves), but only in having the most basic political liberties necessary to maximize their wealth. What Harold Laski said about the proponents of liberalism in revolutionary France seems to apply equally to liberals in post-revolution England and America:

> Its exponents were demanding in effect the emancipation of the whole nation, but when they applied themselves to the details of their programme their imagination limited its range to the freedoms sought by men of property.[23]

Cromwell deserted the Levellers and imprisoned the Diggers.[24] Robespierre glorified the poor, the *peuple*, but crushed their *societas populaires* because their devolutionary tendencies seemed to threaten the requirements of a strong central government.[25] The leaders of the

22. Quoted in Becker, *Declaration*, p. 240, n. 2. Also see Bailyn, *Origins*, pp. 282–83; and Parrington's discussion of the debate among the Founding Fathers over the role of property in the new republic, in *The Colonial Mind*, pp. 283–96.

23. Laski, *Rise*, p. 144.

24. The better descriptive account is Gooch, *English Democratic Ideas*, chaps. 5 and 7, and his *Political Thought*, chap. 4; the better treatment of the political thought of the Levellers is Macpherson, *Possessive Individualism*, chap. 3, especially pp. 117–36. Also see Christopher Hill, ed., *Winstanley: The Law of Freedom and Other Writings* (Middlesex, England, 1973); and Pauline Gregg, *Free-born John: A Biography of John Lilburne* (London, 1961).

25. Arendt, *Revolution*, pp. 242–49. For the most dramatic instance where a natural right thinker tried to see the democratic component of the doctrine to its logical end, but was suppressed for trying, see John A. Scott, ed. and trans., *The Defense of Gracchus Babeuf Before the High Court of Vendome* (Boston, 1967).

American Revolution feared no less than their English and French counterparts what colonial leader William Drayton termed "the exuberances of popular liberty," the fear that democracy was really mob rule whose "ultimate purpose" was "the denial of all property rights."[26] Bernard Bailyn makes it clear that the American Revolution was not a social revolution: It was a political revolution waged against an arbitrary government that threatened freedom of commerce and the rights of property through its policies of unlawful and excessive taxation.[27] Yet, as Laski points out in reference to the Levellers, "We must not miss the significance of the social revolution which failed. . . . They make it clear that the victory which was achieved was not their victory."[28] The victories in each went not to the proponents of democracy but rather to the supporters of the liberal market society. Nonetheless, the existence of the radicals shows that within the womb of liberalism, the seed of democracy resided, waiting only for nature (and a good deal of agitation by democrats) to take its course before emerging as liberal-democracy.

Natural right doctrine legitimated the liberal revolutions, and in principle promoted democracy. In part out of principle, in part out of the difficulty to apportion liberty according to property holdings, except for the franchise all came to enjoy as a result of the revolutions the freedoms of thought, speech, publication, petition, assembly, religion, and so on. The constitutions which grew out of the revolutions did not differentiate between classes of people in regard to most basic rights, but they did make property owners the chief beneficiaries of the revolution. Only property owners constituted the government, and as justification for this arrangement John Locke himself could be cited:

> The great and chief end, therefore, of mens uniting into commonwealths, and putting themselves under government, is the preservation of their property.[29]

Radical democrat Samuel Adams, however, could use the same passage of Locke to justify the right of revolution against the English sovereign's policies of unlawful taxation:

> Men therefore *in society having property*, they have such right to the goods, which by the law of the community are theirs, that no body hath the right to

26. Bailyn, *Origins*, p. 283; Parrington, *Colonial Mind*, p. 279.
27. Parrington, *Colonial Mind*, pp. 283–96; and Bailyn, *Origins*, pp. 232–34.
28. Laski, *Rise*, p. 70.
29. *Second Treatise*, par. 124.

take *any part* of their subsistence from them without their consent: Without this, there could have been no property at all [italics in the original].[30]

The right of private property, therefore, justifies revolution no less than it permits limitations to be placed on the franchise. This was basic to the natural right doctrine that served as the ideology of the liberal revolutions and as the working principle which governed the post-revolution constitutional eras. According to natural right theorists such as Locke, property was a pre-political right and the securing of it the very basis of the founding of the state: Hence, the government's ability to protect the right of property becomes the basis of political obligation. Men are only obliged to obey the laws and rules of society and government as long as their natural rights, and especially the right of property, are protected. Under the ancien régime, arbitrary taxation had infringed upon this supposed right; and to those who had suffered as a result, it had become clear that the economic freedoms of market society meant very little in the absence of the political liberties which could protect them. Thus, in the name of natural right doctrine, seventeenth- and eighteenth-century revolutionaries centered their demands around the natural right of property owners to have political liberties equal to the economic ones they already possessed. Life and liberty became ends nearly indistinguishable from the chief means which was to guarantee them—the right of property. To repeat Arendt's words: "Who said property, said freedom, and to recover or defend one's property rights was the same as the fight for freedom."[31] In strict political terms, the fight for freedom was a fight for responsible government, government by consent of the governed, constitutional government, a government which paid homage to the doctrine of natural right and its respect for private property.

An understanding of the development of the liberal market society, the relationship of this development with the rise of natural right doctrine, and the relationship of both to the revolutions which occurred in England, America, and France, is needed in order to place in comparative perspective the use to which Japanese liberals of the 1880s put natural right doctrine. The development of the market society from Tokugawa into Meiji was shown in Chapter 2. It was also shown that many of the early rebels were the same ones who had close commercial ties to the market and that this was in part reflected by the changing manner in which demands upon the political system were

30. Quoted in Parrington, *Colonial Mind*, p. 243.
31. Arendt, *Revolution*, p. 180.

made, moving from a Confucian *cum* feudal form that defended the right to subsistence to one that reflected the bargaining situation of the market. It was further shown that, after a decade into the Meiji period, commoners of all sorts were beginning to staff the popular rights movement in increasing numbers. Then in Chapter 3 it was shown that the individuals who participated in the Fukushima, Kabasan, and Chichibu rebellions were precisely those middle- and upper-income farmers (with the aid of local teachers, priests, and a few merchants) who were tied to the market economy but lacked the political means necessary to gain a measure of control over those public policy decisions which affected market conditions.

At the bottom of the political reforms they sought, there existed a Japanese variant of natural right doctrine. Economic conditions favored the growth and spread of the doctrine; the rebellions are established facts; it thus remains to show that there existed a relationship between the two.

Natural Right: Japanese

Within the popular right movement, there were a number of influential thinkers who subscribed to the western versions of natural right doctrine. Among them were Nakae Chōmin, Yano Fumio, Baba Tatsui, Sugita Teiichi, Ueki Emori, and Ōi Kentarō. In a serious study of this period's intellectual history, all of these thinkers would warrant individual treatment for the intrinsic value of their writings and would need to be studied comparatively in order to make clear the differences in their approach to and understanding of natural right doctrine. Here, however, we are interested only in those natural right thinkers whose activities and writings have some connection with the *gekka jiken* in general and with the Fukushima, Kabasan, and Chichibu incidents in particular. We therefore immediately eliminate from consideration Nakae Chōmin and Yano Fumio, for although they undoubtedly had some influence in the popular rights movement, they appear to have had little impact on or connection with the *gekka jiken*.[32]

Baba Tatsui, as Eugene Soviak has shown, was an important intellectual figure in the popular rights movement and was even involved on the fringes of one of the *gekka jiken*. But his main contribution was a purely intellectual one: He aided such early liberal societies as

---

32. Ike, *Beginnings*, pp. 124–29, discusses the life and thought of Nakae Chōmin; Joseph Pittau, S. J., *Political Thought in Early Meiji Japan, 1868-1889* (Cambridge, Mass., 1967), chap. 4, treats Nakae, Yano, Baba, Ueki, and several other natural right thinkers.

the *Ōmeisha* and the *Kōjunsha* in the areas of doctrine and organization. The principle reason we eliminate him from consideration is because he was openly contemptuous of, in his own words, "the uneducated and illiterate" commoners whom he felt were unable to understand or appreciate Western ideas.[33] The other intellectual who will not be treated here is Sugita Teiichi, an early popular rights leader and author of "A New Theory on Administration" (*Keisei shinron*). Sugita, too, was content to stand outside the activist part of the movement, busying himself mainly with making observations about the state of local Jiyūtō branches during his travels throughout Japan.[34]

There thus remain Ueki Emori and Ōi Kentarō, two of the leading advocates of natural right doctrine in this period and, more to the point, the two thinkers whose activities *and* ideas had the greatest impact on our three rebellions and their leaders. In one way or another, both Ueki and Ōi were connected with the Fukushima, Kabasan and Chichibu rebellions.

Ueki spent nearly two months in Fukushima during 1882, between early August and late September, when the confrontation between popular rights activists and Governor Mishima was becoming ever more intense. Ueki was in Fukushima at the invitation of the Fukushima Jiyūtō branch to oversee its new party organ, the *Fukushima Jiyū Shimbun*. Ueki left when he did only because he had been called back to Tokyo to replace Baba Tatsui on the staff of the central party's organ, the *Jiyū Shimbun*.[35] It must be imagined that Ueki's witnessing of the Fukushima Incident firsthand embittered him all the more against the tyranny of absolutist government, for immediately after the mass arrest campaign of December, he and several others (including Ōi Kentarō) counseled escaped Fukushima activists Hirajima Matsuo and Yamaguchi Chiyosaku; and Ueki alone helped them to write a memorial to the Emperor in protest against the oppression the Fukushima Jiyūtō had suffered under Mishima.[36]

While Ueki lent his writing talents to the Fukushima party, Ōi Kentarō, a skilled lawyer and Vice-Chairman of the Tokyo Lawyer's

33. Quoted in Ienaga Saburō, *Ueki Emori kenkyū* (Tokyo, 1960), p. 363. Eugene Soviak makes much the same point in his "The Case of Baba Tatsui: Western Enlightenment, Social Change, and the Early Meiji Intellectual," *Monumenta Nipponica* 18:1-4 (1963):191-235, especially pp. 227-28.

34. Ienaga, *Ueki*, pp. 284-85; Fukuda, *Sanmin sōjō*, p. 95.

35. Ienaga, *Ueki*, pp. 215-21; and also his *Kakumei shisō no senkusha: Ueki Emori no hito to shisō* (Tokyo, 1955), pp. 31-38.

36. These two Fukushima activists had escaped arrest in December, fled to Tokyo, met with Ueki and Ōi, only to be subsequently apprehended. Ienaga, *Ueki*, pp. 227-28.

Association in 1882–83, lent his legal skills to Tamano Hideaki by serving as his defense attorney in the treason trial of early 1883.[37] After the acquittal of fifty activists for the crime of treason, Ueki attended a congratulatory banquet held in their honor on 15 April 1883.[38] For Ōi's client Tamano, who was not acquitted and who died in prison on 29 November 1883, Ueki took charge of arrangements for the funeral service. At the funeral, Ueki delivered an oration in *waka* (thirty-one syllable ode) form, the last lines of which read:

> Take comfort, spirit of departed friend Tamano.
> Though you are gone, we will be true to your life's purpose:
> The light of liberty will not grow dim.[39]

Among the Kabasan rebels, both Ueki and Ōi could count several as close friends or associates. Tomimatsu Masayasu, later leader of the Kabasan Incident, was a good friend of Ueki and Ōi, and associated himself with the Ōi strategy of "large movement" (see Chapter 1). Tomimatsu and his *kobun* Tamamatsu Kaiichi, moreover, besides having met with Ōi on numerous occasions, shared with Ōi the distinction of being among the membership of the "Revolution or Death" faction within the Jiyūtō. Tamamatsu's brother was also an intimate of Ōi, having joined him in the ill-fated Osaka Incident of November 1885.[40] Kōno Hiroshi, nephew of Hironaka, was also an intimate of both Ōi and Ueki—with Ueki probably because Kōno had known him when he (Kōno) was a student at the *Risshisha*, and with Ōi probably because of Ōi's friendship with his uncle. When several of the Kabasan rebels were sentenced to death, Ueki editorialized: "These death sentences given to these patriots, these friends of our party, must be condemned. Let's petition [for commutation] and inscribe our names deeply!"[41]

Except for Murakami Taiji,[42] an early organizer of the Chichibu Jiyūtō, Ueki had no other known relations with Chichibu rebels.

37. Hirano, *Ōi*, pp. 40–42.
38. Ienaga, *Ueki*, pp. 228, 754.
39. Quoted in Ibid., p. 228.
40. Hirano, *Ōi*, pp. 83, 85–89, 92–93; Ienaga, *Ueki*, p. 754, says that Ueki met with Tomimatsu in Shimodate on 12 February 1884.
41. Quoted in Nojima Kitarō, *Kabasan jiken* (Tokyo, 1966; originally published in 1900), p. 394. The article appeared in the *Doyō Shimbun* on 17 July 1886 and was entitled "The Court Verdict of Tomimatsu Masayasu and the Eighteen." Also, it is quoted in part in Ienaga, *Ueki*, pp. 432–33. On p. 754, we also learn that Ueki's relations with Kōno Hiroshi began by at least 21 October 1883.
42. See Jun Shiyoda, "Murakami Taiji no saiban," *Rekishigaku Kenkyū* 186 (August 1955):28.

Ueki's main connection with the region is the series of political speeches he gave in Saitama as well as Chiba, Kanagawa, Ibaraki, Tochigi, and Gumma prefectures between 1882 and 1884. Ōi Kentarō, however, was an influential force in Chichibu liberal politics (which will be treated further later in this chapter). His speaking tour in Ōmiya in February 1884 is credited as having been responsible for getting at least seven local activists to join the Jiyūtō; six of them later served as organizers of the Poor People's Party. One of them, Ochiai Toraichi, later joined Ōi in the Osaka Incident.[43]

Ōi and Ueki also had ties with several of the other *gekka jiken*. Leaders of the Gumma Incident, Miyabe Noboru and Nagasaka Hachirō (who was also implicated in the Fukushima Incident), shared administrative positions with Ōi in the central Jiyūtō headquarters and were good friends of his.[44] Among Ueki's acquaintances who were instrumental in organizing a *gekka jiken* was Okunomiya Kenshi. Okunomiya was a young Jiyūtō member who helped organize the Rickshamen's Party (*Shakaitō*) and was imprisoned for his leadership role in the Nagoya Incident (August 1884); years later, as a socialist, he was involved in the plot to assassinate the Meiji Emperor.[45] During the early stages of organizing the Rickshamen's Party, Ueki responded to a request for help made by Okunomiya, attended several of the organizational meetings, and on 24 November 1882 was scheduled to give a talk to the members entitled "The Many Oppressive Theoreticians Among Today's Popular Rights Thinkers." Before he had a chance to speak, however, the meeting was broken up by the police.[46]

Ueki has also been tied to the Iida Incident of December 1884. Centered in the Sakū region of Nagano prefecture, the same area where Ueki and Ōi had lectured to popular rights groups in July of the same year,[47] the incident involved an elaborate plan to unite popular rights advocates of Nagano, Aichi, and the Kantō plain in a movement to overthrow the government.[48] Largely due to the urgings of

43. Hirano, *Ōi*, pp. 110–12.
44. Ibid., pp. 98–100.
45. Ike, *Beginnings*, p. 108, gives an alternate rendering of his name—Okumiya Kenji—but the Japanese authorities I have consulted (Hirano, Ienaga) render it as given in the text; see, for example, Ienaga, *Kakumei shishō*, p. 40.
46. Ienaga, *Ueki*, p. 226; Ike, *Beginnings*, p. 109, says, presumably referring to the same incident, that Ueki's speech was interrupted halfway through.
47. Hirano, *Ōi*, pp. 77–80.
48. Ike, *Beginnings*, pp. 165–67, provides a short but nonetheless good account of the incident's main features.

three of the incident's leaders, Muramatsu Aizō, Kawazumi Tokuji, and Yagi Shigeharu, Ueki agreed to write them a manifesto for the revolution. Only because Muramatsu covered for Ueki by claiming authorship of the manifesto did Ueki escape arrest.[49]

Ōi's activism, unlike Ueki's, led ultimately to organizing his own *gekka jiken*, the Osaka Incident. Basically it was a scheme to provoke a democratic revolution in Korea as the first step of a longer-term plan to bring the revolution to Japan. Very likely, the peculiar direction this incident took is explained by the fact that, having witnessed so many failures at revolution within Japan during the early eighties, Ōi concluded that another such attempt would prove to be equally ineffective. This assumption seems a more plausible one than that made by Marius Jansen, for example, who asserts that the plan to "invade" Korea could easily be converted into a "rationalization of imperialistic aggression."[50] Ōi's intent, after all, was to ally his small party of less than a hundred men with the Korean progressive movement under the Independence Party; if that party could assume power, they reasoned, then Korea could serve as a base of democracy in East Asia from which other such movements could be launched. The conception was not a novel one. Ōi probably appropriated the idea from Kōno Hironaka. During the treason trial, Ōi heard Kōno explain that when he and other Fukushima liberals discussed the overthrow of the Japanese government, they discussed it in terms of laying "a great foundation for freedom" which would then be used "to benefit all of Asia," referring specifically to Korea and China.[51] For both Ōi and Kōno, however, the primary objective remained the democratization of Japanese politics. Kobayashi Kusuo, one of Ōi's

49. Ienaga, *Kakumei shisō*, p. 45; also Ienaga, *Ueki*, pp. 716–23, especially, pp. 720–23, where Kawazumi's court testimony relating to the manifesto is provided. One important paragraph of the manifesto is given by E. H. Norman in his "Feudal Background of Japanese Politics," which appears in John W. Dower, ed., *Origins of the Modern Japanese State: Selected Writings of E. H. Norman* (New York, 1975), pp. 446–47.

50. Jansen, "Ōi Kentarō," p. 309; also see Hirano, *Ōi*, p. 140. Unlike Hirano, Professor Jansen is consistently skeptical of Ōi's liberalism. While it is impossible to deny Ōi's early nationalist sentiments or his later chauvinism, it is possible nonetheless to emphasize his high regard for liberal-democratic values, which seem to have tempered his nationalism. Professor Jansen sees Ōi's liberalism and nationalism as contradictory, though at the same time he does say, "Nationalism and chauvinism are not historically incompatible with democratic liberalism" (p. 306). He wisely concludes his essay on Ōi by suggesting the need for further research into this difficult question.

51. Quoted in Hirano, *Ōi*, pp. 204–05. In his "Ōi Kentarō," p. 308, n. 17, Professor Jansen rather unfairly, I believe, refers to the Fukushima Incident as "*mob violence* [that] broke out in protest against forced labour for public works which the liberal leaders had opposed in Fukushima" (emphasis added).

lieutenants in the Osaka Incident, testified: "We sought first to effect the principles of liberty and equality in our government, and then to try to spread them to other countries. But anyway, these are not principles which should be limited to one particular man or country; they should be carried out throughout the entire world."[52] And to carry out that idealistic plan, Ōi recruited only those with strong liberal credentials: Kanagawa activist Ōya Masao (and his more famous literary friend, Kitamura Tōkoku, who assisted in the planning of one related robbery);[53] the son of Jiyūtō leader Ishizaka Masatsuga; Murano Tsuneemon (who later became a famous Seiyūkai politician);[54] Kabasan accomplices Tateno Yoshinosuke and Arai Shōgo; Chichibu Incident leader Ochiai (mentioned earlier); and early women's rights activist and writer Kageyama Hideko.[55]

Considering for the moment only the careers of Ueki and Ōi as activists, it is obvious that Ōi was the more radical of the two. Most Japanese historians subscribe to this view and are quick to place the two men into categories according to their respective contributions to the popular rights movement and, more important, to the bourgeois-democratic revolution. Not surprisingly, Ōi is regarded as the superior figure; he is credited with having been one of the principal leaders of the "Revolutionary Democratic Faction" (kakumeiteki minshushugi ha), while Ueki is denigrated for having been a member of the "Law-abiding Faction" (gōhōshugi-ha).[56] It does seem true that Ōi was the more radical of the two men, but it is doubtful whether he had a greater impact on the popular rights movement. Both Ueki and Ōi were radicals, members of the anti-mainstream element of the popular rights movement, but Ueki stands out as being the more representative of this element. He was hardly a "middle-of-the-roader," as Hirano Yoshitarō calls him. The appellation might be a fit description of, say, Fukuzawa Yukichi, who believed in gradual reform and the slow implantation of democracy from above, but it would not be an ac-

---

52. Quoted in Hirano, Ōi, p. 207.
53. Ibid., pp. 126–27.
54. See Irokawa Daikichi and Murano Renichi, Murano Tsuneemon: Minkenka jidai (Tokyo, 1969), p. 51, for information regarding Murano's indirect connections with the Kabasan Incident, and Chapter 7 of Irokawa's Shimpen Meiji seishin shi (Tokyo, 1973) for a short biographical treatment of Murano.
55. Hirano, Ōi, pp. 173–75.
56. For example, see Gotō, "Meiji jūshichinen," pp. 206–07, and Hirano, Ōi, p. 102. Gotō makes a simple dichotomy between the two types, while Hirano places Ueki midway between the extreme right-wing represented by Itagaki and the extreme left-wing represented by Ōi.

curate description of Ueki's thought. "His [notion of democracy] was different from the democracy of men like Fukuzawa," Ienaga Saburō informs us, "because Emori believed democracy ought to be seized forcibly, taken from below through popular struggle."[57] Ueki was a radical without doubt, but he was also a journalist, a political theorist, a pamphleteer, and a propagandist who believed his chief duty was to educate the people about their inherent natural rights. Ōi, in contrast, was a radical activist, a revolutionary in search of a revolution. Like the Levellers, however, they both were members of a revolution that failed.

This last comparison can be strengthened and extended. The Levellers, too, were the anti-mainstream group in their country's revolution, and within this group there existed divergent views on important matters. Lilburne, for example, went beyond Cromwell and Ireton to assert that the inherent natural rights of man invest the people with political and economic liberties which cannot be restricted by any save themselves because they are sovereign. Winstanley went even further, calling for a social revolution that would equalize property and eradicate classes. He also favored making land into community property and called for the proscription of buying and selling.[58] Generically, both Lilburne and Winstanley are Levellers; natural right doctrine was at the basis of their ideas. In many ways, Ueki is a figure comparable to Lilburne, and Ōi to Winstanley. What separates the two Englishmen from the two Japanese is the position each takes on what Hannah Arendt has termed "the social question."

An apt illustration of what is meant by this in Ueki's and Ōi's case is the different program espoused by each toward the question of the poor, a burning issue among liberals during the depression of the eighties.

Ueki approached the question in a series of editorials published in the *Doyō Shimbun* between 20 September and 11 October 1885, under the title *Hinmin ron*, or "The Poor People Question."[59] Early in

57. *Kakumei shisō*, p. 195.
58. Gooch, *Political Thought*, pp. 60–65, 93–101; Macpherson, *Possessive Individualism*, pp. 137–59. Also see Gregg, *Free-born John*, chap. 18, and Hill, ed., *Winstanley*, "The Law of Freedom in a Platform." An excellent work dealing with the historical context in which these ideas emerged, and which also shows Lilburne's practice of pragmatic politics, is John R. MacCormack's *Revolutionary Politics in the Long Parliament* (Cambridge, Mass., 1973), especially pp. 169–76, 201, 290. My thanks to Professor MacCormack for discussing the politics of this period with me.
59. The complete article appears in Ienaga Saburō, ed., *Ueki Emori senshū* (Tokyo, 1974), pp. 115–46; Ienaga comments on the import of the article in *Kakumei shisō*, pp. 145–51.

the essay, Ueki lays the groundwork of his argument: "If we understand that the purpose of existence is in having happiness, then no person ought to be denied whatever means necessary to secure happiness." The way to achieve a state of happiness, he says, is through freedom, and since "there are no differences among men in their natural state, which is one of equality, then all ought to have equal rights and freedoms." In today's society, Ueki argues, disparity in wealth acts as an obstacle to a condition in which all may enjoy equal freedoms and rights, but he adds that it is "a social force which cannot abruptly be leveled in a day or a night." Given this social fact, he advocates "getting rid of the inequalities of rights and freedoms which are the causes of inequalities of wealth." Economic inequality and the poverty that results, he is saying therefore, are political phenomena and contrary to nature's equality. Inequality of wealth exists because "the right of political participation belongs only to the few wealthy members of society." Ueki's solution to correct this injustice is a franchise qualified *only* by the payment of taxes, however small the amount. His reasoning goes like this:

> If you compare the amount of taxes paid by the rich and the poor on an individual basis, then of course the rich pay more than the poor. But if you divide the entire nation into the two groups of the rich and the poor, then the rich pay much less than the poor. In fact, in terms of basic capital supporting the government, the poor provide most of it.[60]

To reinforce his argument for the franchise, Ueki inverts a traditional argument: "If you have a duty to pay taxes to the government, then don't you also have the duties of conscription and voting?" With the franchise in hand, Ueki assumes, the poor will better be able to protect themselves against "the oppressive rich." He believes that once the poor have a measure of control over the government, then what wealth they now possess will be secure. But this is the second best situation, suitable to a society that has abandoned reason. If reason ruled the world, then "we would have equality of property"; but "since reason is denied, we ought to aim for a society that guarantees equal rights and protections to all: such a society would be in accord with Nature's reason," he concludes.[61]

Ueki's approach to "the social question" is singularly reformist and lawful, and probably for this reason he has earned the disapprov-

60. Ienaga, ed., *Ueki Emori senshū*, p. 141.
61. Ibid., p. 146.

ing appellation of "middle-of-the-roader," attached to him by Japanese Marxist historians. Yet, given the historical context in which his appeal for a taxpayer's franchise was made, his proposal seems remarkably democratic if not revolutionary, particularly when it is recalled that he believed the ideal condition to be one of equality of property and wealth. Still, although Lilburne would have welcomed Ueki as a kindred spirit, neither Winstanley nor Ōi would have.

Had Ōi been near St. George's Hill in 1649, he would probably have taken a spade in hand, joined in the digging, and nodded his head in assent when Winstanley declared: "The great creator Reason made the Earth a common treasury for beasts and man."[62] That statement, in any case, is a good summation of Ōi Kentarō's belief as he expressed it in his *Jiji yōron*, or "Treatise on the Needs of Our Time," which he wrote in 1886 while in prison serving his sentence for his role in the Osaka Incident.[63] Ōi sought, in his own words, "a new society of equality and liberty," a society in which small, private, autonomous commercial interests are protected against government-supported enterprise[64] and in which "every household is guaranteed an equal amount of property, where its resale is forbidden, and is held in perpetuity." Such an arrangement he calls "a good policy which would prevent anyone from sinking under misfortune."[65] A "land equalization law" (*tochi heibun hō*) is the solution, Ōi maintains, to the main problem in society whereby "the wealthy are aiming to appropriate more and more wealth and property without the least concern for the common good and, moreover, [creating] a situation of greater and greater suffering for the poor." The end result of this situation is clear: "The poor become poorer and poorer, the rich become richer and richer, and the gap between the rich and the poor gradually widens."[66]

Such empirical observations served to buttress Ōi's basic philosophical position: "You cannot evade the point that land ownership is illegal. Since land ultimately is the common property of the community (*shakai kōkyō no zaisan*), there is no reason we ought to recognize

62. Quoted in Gooch, *English Democratic Ideas*, p. 183.

63. Gotō, "Meiji jūshichinen," p. 246, tells us that the ideas advanced by Ōi in *Jiji yōron* are based on the observations he made about social conditions as they existed in 1884.

64. Although the idea of protecting small commerical interests was first expressed by Ōi in his *Jiyū ryakuron* (Short Treatise on Liberty), it is echoed in his other writings. See Hirano, *Ōi*, p. 63.

65. Quoting from *Jiji yōron*, in Hirano, *Ōi*, pp. 64–5.

66. Quoted in ibid., p. 67.

property rights, however many years may pass."[67] As Hirano Yoshitarō points out, Ōi's basic beliefs are an unconscious echo of the
French revolutionary Babeuf's, made a hundred years earlier: "Land
does not belong to anyone; it belongs to everyone."[68] Winstanley
made much the same point a hundred years before Babeuf, when he
charged: "Break to pieces the bands of property."[69] But all three of
these radicals, separated by time and place, raised "the social question" well before there existed an audience willing to respond favorably to their solutions. They remain in history as the unheard voices
of social revolutions that failed.

Ueki was on the fringes of the failed revolution, but it appears that
many of his ideas did not go unheeded. Though still a radical by the
conventional standards of his day, Ueki was clearly not as radical as
Ōi, and for this reason he stands as the more representative figure of
his time—at least, that is, as regards the many popular rights advocates
who subscribed to natural right doctrine. Consequently, in the remainder of this section, only the thought of Ueki Emori will be examined, and this will be done in terms of its western origins, its content, and the means Ueki used to popularize it.[70]

Several Japanese historians—Irokawa Daikichi and Kano Masanao,
to name two of the more prominent—have treated in detail the intellectual debt that early popular rights advocates owed to such Western
thinkers as Tocqueville, Bentham, Rousseau, Mill, Spencer, and others,
while at the same time warning that it would be a mistake to overesti-
mate the extent of that debt. Irokawa, for example, in discussing the
thought of a Hachiōji activist named Hosono, stressed that many liberals at that time understood "the thought of Rousseau and Spencer
through the medium of the revolutionary ideas of Confucius and
Mencius." Irokawa cites a specific example: "Rousseau's treatise on
natural rights, which said Nature gives men equal rights, was under-

67. Quoted in ibid., pp. 69–70. Compare that statement of Ōi's with one made by the
French communist Babeuf: "If the earth belongs to none and its fruits to all; if private ownership of public wealth is only the result of certain institutions that violate fundamental human rights; then it follows that this private ownership is a usurpation" (Scott, ed. and trans.,
Defense of Graccus Babeuf, p. 54).
68. Quoted in Scott, *Babeuf*, p. 69. The similarities in thinking have prompted Hirano to
label Ōi's thought as a form of "Jacobinism"; Inoue, *Chichibu jiken*, claims that similar Jacobin features appeared in the thought of the Chichibu rebels.
69. Quoted in Gooch, *English Democratic Ideas*, p. 184.
70. It is worth pointing out that neither Ike (*Beginnings*) nor Pittau (*Political Thought*)
has given serious consideration to the attempts of popular rights thinkers to communicate
their ideas to the people.

stood in Confucian terms.''[71] Other popular rights activists of the same region, who were not as well read in Western theory as Hosono, understood the right of revolution, Irokawa says (and Kano supports him in this regard), through the Japanese tradition of "spirit of rebellion" (*hangyaku seishin*).[72] Yet other activists, such as Chiba Takasaburō who oversaw the writing of a draft constitution by an Itsukaichi village liberal political society, could draw upon both their past experience in rebellion (Chiba took part in the Boshin War) and upon their readings of Western political theorists, as Chiba did with Rousseau.[73] But in any case, whatever was the source of their belief in natural right and the right of revolution, Irokawa claims that "the spirit [behind the fight for freedom] was definitely not an import.''[74] Rather, it was indigenous in origin: "Those grass roots [of democracy] were nurtured within feudal society, stemming from primitive forms of democratic practices. . . . If not from there," Irokawa asks rhetorically, "then must we not then assume that democracy and modernism are rootless?''[75]

The roots of democracy in Japan, Irokawa suggests, lie in the sense of local self-government that villagers at the *buraku* (hamlet) level came to acquire over several hundred years of relative isolation from upper levels of government. The emphasis that the Itsukaichi constitution drafters put on the rights of local self-government is evidence of the existence of this tradition.[76]

In his "Draft Constitution of the Japanese Nation" (*Nihon kokka kokken an*) of August 1881, Ueki placed the same strong emphasis on the rights of local self-government as did the Itsukaichi drafters.[77] If the order in which sections and articles of a constitution appear is any indication of the drafter's priorities, then Ueki regarded the rights of provinces or states (*shū*) in his *federal* system of government as more important than any other type of right, save perhaps for the in-

---

71. Irokawa Daikichi, Ei Hideo, and Arai Katsuhiro, *Minshū kempō no sōzō: Uzumoreta kusa no ne no ninmyaku* (Tokyo, 1970), pp. 97–98, 136–37; the quotation appears on p. 98 and was written by Irokawa.

72. Ibid., p. 28; Kano Masanao, *Nihon kindaika no shisō* (Tokyo, 1972), p. 65: "The popular rights movement was superimposed upon the tradition of peasant uprisings and spread among the commoners as a result. . . . The revival of uprisings was connected with the origin and spread of the popular rights movement."

73. Irokawa in *Minshū kempō*, pp. 114–15, 138–42.

74. Ibid., p. 137; also see pp. 152–56.

75. Ibid., p. 159.

76. Ibid., pp. 159–62.

77. Ueki's draft constitution appears in Ienaga, ed., *Ueki Emori senshū*, pp. 89–111.

dividual's, which, it should be noted, he believed would be best protected if state rights were paramount.[78] His reason for promoting the
rights and powers of local government vis-à-vis the central regime may
have sprung, as with the Itsukaichi drafters, from a tradition of local
autonomy in his native Kōchi (Tosa), from the part he played in the
self-government movement in Kōchi during the 1870s,[79] or from his
understanding of the crucial importance of self-government to securing the foundations of democratic government, which he learned
from Western political theorists. Most likely, all of these factors were
important. But the main point is this: Although in the succeeding
pages we will be focusing on Ueki's debt to Western theorists, we do
not wish to imply that his receptivity toward Western theory was
groundless, that it lacked a native, traditional foundation.

Ueki fortunately kept a dairy concerned with the books he read,
beginning before 1873 and continuing until 1884.[80] The number and
range are impressive, although all the Western works he read were in
translation. His list began with Young's *A Short Study of American
Politics* (*Gassbūkoku seiji shōgaku*) and ended with Tocqueville's
Democracy in America, which was translated as *Jiyū genron* (Principles of Liberty). Some twelve works he read were exclusively concerned with American history or politics or the federal system of
government, and one specifically with the American Constitution.
English and French political history and the revolutions of those
countries were topics of other books Ueki read. Among the political
theoreticians he read, several authors especially stand out: Vissering,
Mill (*Representative Government* and *On Liberty*), Tocqueville,
Rousseau (*Social Contract*), More (*Utopia*), Burke, and Spencer (*Social Statics* and *Representative Government*).

A detailed exegesis of Ueki's writings may very well show that his
own ideas profited from all these readings; but simply in terms of
his primary intellectual commitment to natural right doctrine, such
a study will show conclusively that his biggest debt was to Herbert
Spencer, and especially to one of Spencer's earlier works, *Social Statics* (1850). Ienaga Saburō, Ueki's modern biographer, claims this to
be the case but seems to rest his claim on a reading of Ueki only (and
not Spencer) and on the further fact that Ueki is known to have read

78. Ienaga, *Ueki*, p. 344.
79. Ibid., pp. 158–68.
80. The list appears in ibid., pp. 349–51.

more Spencer than any other Western theorist except for Vissering.[81] In any case, Ueki first read Ozaki Yukio's abridged translation of *Social Statics* in 1879, under the title *Kenri teikō*, or "A Proposed Morality of Rights, With Reasons." However awkward the translation, it does nonetheless convey Spencer's own objectives behind writing the book and is echoed in the subtitle chosen by Spencer himself: *The Conditions Essential to Human Happiness Specified, and The First of Them Developed*.[82] Ueki reread the book in 1882, but this time he had an unabridged version entitled *Shakai heiken ron* ("A Treatise on Social Equality"), translated by Matsushima Ko; this latter title better expresses the nature of the content of the book and Ueki's understanding of it.

In this early work of his, Spencer shows himself to be a different type of thinker from the Spencer of later years, the one who gave Mori Arinori "conservative advice," who said he supported the absolute sovereignty of the Japanese Emperor, who was used by Katō Hiroyuki as an apologist for absolutism, and who was a highly respected authority for theories of evolution and survival-of-the-fittest (*yūshō reppai*).[83] The Spencer whom Ueki relied upon in his own writings was the "early Spencer" of *Social Statics*, the one who rejected utilitarianism "because it permits all actions"; the one who promoted the natural right *a priori* truth that says "human happiness is the Divine will"; and the one who claimed that the people have a right to resist unlawful authority.[84] Only the teleology of the early Spencer shows continuity with the older Spencer. Progress is the catchword of both Spencers, but whereas the older Spencer saw the end of progress as a highly organized organic state with totalitarian dimensions, the younger Spencer, Ueki's teacher, believed that progress meant ". . . less government. Constitutional forms mean this. Political freedom means this. Democracy means this."[85] As civilization advances, Spencer argued, government inexorably decays and should

---

81. Ibid., pp. 351–52.

82. All references to *Social Statics* are taken from the 1873 edition, published by D. Appleton and Company in New York.

83. Ike, *Beginnings*, pp. 113–14, and Pittau, *Political Thought*, pp. 119–22. For further supporting evidence of the argument that follows, see J. D. Y. Peel's "Introduction" to Herbert Spencer, *On Social Evolution, Selected Writings* (Chicago and London, 1972): Peel makes it quite clear that *Social Statics* is a treatise in moral philosophy, bearing the imprint of Ricardian socialist ideas and William Godwin's radical *Political Justice* (1792), and therefore stands apart from Spencer's later, strictly sociological works.

84. *Social Statics*, pp. 12, 91.

85. Ibid., p. 24.

remain only powerful enough to insure "equity, freedom, safety."[86] He reasoned that these conditions will be fulfilled if man fulfills his "duty to exercise his faculties," which is the same as "fulfilling the Divine will." To do this "presupposes freedom of action"; it is the *duty* of government to ensure that the individual has

> the liberty to go and to come, to see, to feel, to speak, to work; to get food, raiment, shelter, and to provide for each and all of the needs of his nature. He must be free to do every thing which is directly or indirectly requisite for the due satisfaction of every mental and bodily want.[87]

Spencer believes that without these liberties man is incapable of fulfilling his duty or God's will, which are one and the same. If he is without liberty—and here Spencer endorses the natural right of resistence—"then God commands him to take it. He has Divine authority, therefore, for claiming freedom of action. God intended him to have it; that is, he has a right to it."[88] This right to liberty, and the corresponding right *and* duty to take it, Spencer asserts, "is not the right of one but of all," because "all are endowed with faculties."[89] The groundwork is now laid for Spencer to state his First Condition "essential to human happiness": "Every man may claim the fullest liberty to exercise his faculties compatible with the possession of like liberty by every other man." And as freedom is the right of each individual, "equal freedom becomes the prerequisite to normal life in society."[90] These basic rights of equal liberty, he adds in pure natural right dictum, "are claims antecedent to those endorsed by governments."[91]

This "first condition" he calls "the law of equal freedom," "an elementary truth of ethics" which, he says, is no less true than geometric theorems.[92] How Spencer applies the law of equal freedom to public policy is varied and far-reaching. To name several applications of the law: "Equity does not permit property in land"; property belongs to society in the form of a "joint-stock ownership of the public"; and all are tenants and all are landlords, but tenants may enjoy the fruits of surplus production, that part which society does not appropriate.[93] Other applications of his first principle of equal freedom include free

---

86. Ibid., p. 36.   87. Ibid., pp. 92–93.   88. Ibid., p. 93.   89. Ibid.
90. Ibid., p. 94; also see p. 121, where the idea is reinforced.
91. Ibid., p. 111.   92. Ibid., pp. 121–22.
93. Spencer emphasizes that he is not a socialist, in league with "Messrs. Fourier, Owen, Louis Blanc, and Co." (ibid., pp. 138–51). Ueki too, I believe, would have denied any ties to socialism.

speech, sexual equality ("Equity knows no difference of sex");[94] equal rights for children, especially the right of equal education; equal political rights, legal rights, commercial rights (in endorsing a strict policy of *laissez-faire*); and the right "to refuse to pay taxes," "the right to resist," and "the right of the citizen to adopt a condition of voluntary outlawry." "No human laws," he adds, "are of any validity if contrary to the law of nature."[95] Government is after all "simply an agent employed in common by a certain number of individuals. . . ." The people are "the only legitimate source of power."[96]

Few of Spencer's lessons were not learned and used by Ueki in his own writings. We have already seen in Ueki's "The Poor People Question" an argument remarkably similar to Spencer's "law of equal freedom." When Ueki called for the franchise for the poor, he based it on the *a priori* assumption that "there are no differences among men in their natural state," which is one of equality. Ueki drew upon the same assumption, although in this instance he quoted liberally from Spencer, in his 1888 essay "Equal Rights for Men and Women" (*Danjo no dōken*).[97] Similarly, in his April 1879 essay entitled "Treatise on Popular Rights and Freedom" (*Minken jiyū ron*), Ueki echoes Spencer when he writes:

> If a man is free and existing as a man, then he ought to have freedom of action. Man in order to be man must necessarily use his natural gifts to obtain everything which the laws of society permit. If man's natural gift of freedom is not used by man, then he commits a great crime against nature.[98]

In the same essay, Ueki states that several instances in which man did use his "natural gift of freedom" were America's War of Independence against England, the Magna Charta, and the French Revolution. He adds that in each instance "the people gained their freedom by overthrowing unresponsive governments."[99] Following Spencer, Ueki as-

---

94. Ibid., p. 173.   95. Ibid., pp. 229–30.   96. Ibid., p. 231.

97. The entire essay appears in Ienaga, ed., *Ueki Emori senshū*, pp. 149–86; see especially pp. 158–59, where Ueki quotes liberally from Chapter 16 of *Social Statics*, entitled "The Rights of Women," pp. 175–76.

98. Although the language clearly seems Spencerian, Ueki in fact maintains that he is quoting from Rousseau's *Social Contract* (Ienaga, *Ueki Emori senshū*, p. 24). It should be noted, however, that Spencer may very well have been indebted to Rousseau for many of his ideas. Consider the following passages from *Social Contract*: "When a man renounces his liberty, he renounces his essential manhood, his rights, and even his duty as a human being" ("On Slavery," chap. 4); or "no man is under an obligation to obey any but the legitimate powers of the state" ("Of the Right of the Strongest," chap. 3).

99. From *Minken jiyū ron*, in Ienaga, ed., *Ueki Emori senshū*, p. 25.

serted the right of revolution is the ultimate natural right derived from the first principle of equal freedom.

One of the clearest examples of Ueki's intellectual commitment to Spencer's version of natural right doctrine is a song which Ueki composed in 1879 entitled "Country Song of Popular Rights" (*Minken inaka uta*). It is an important document, not only because it demonstrates his debt to Spencer, but also because his purpose behind writing the song was to communicate to rural folk the doctrine of natural right, which he clearly hoped they would adopt as their own. Perhaps some did, for Yoshino Sakuzō, the outstanding Taishō period democrat and the editor of this song for later publication, wrote: "This song was said to have been exceedingly popular among peasants and common people."[100] Because of its importance, we quote the song in full:

"Country Song of Popular Rights" (*Minken inaka uta*)
by Ueki Emori

Man is free.
The head thinks and the heart feels;
The body moves and runs;
Man surpasses all other wonderful creatures.
The heart and body are
Comparable to the universe.
Man's freedom does not allow a dearth of liberty;
We are free; we have rights.
The people of Japan must claim their rights;
If we do not, then our companion is shame.

Though the birds have wings they cannot fly;
The caged bird can see the outside.
Though the fish have fins they cannot swim;
The netted fish sees the sea beyond.
Though the horses have hooves they cannot run;
The tethered horse sees the grass out of reach.
Men are endowed with arms and legs,
We have hearts and minds
But today we have no liberty or rights.
If we call ourselves men
Then each person must himself stand up and say,
"Man has rights."

100. Yoshino Sakuzō, comp., *Meiji bunka zenshū*, 24 vols., *Jiyū minken hen* 5 (Tokyo, 1928) 513.

The mind must think and the mouth must say,
"Whether freedom continues or ceases
We all hear and feel its call."

The rights of freedom are possessed by everyone;
Freedom is a gift of heaven.
Men have both intelligence and strength;
There is no gain in not using them.
Living without freedom, not having freedom
Is the same as being dead.

Think of the salt: salt is salt because it is salty;
If it's not salty then it is the same as sand;
Sugar is sugar only because it is sweet;
If it's not sweet it might as well be dirt.
Man is man only if he is free.
If he is not free, he is like a puppet.

From ancient times government has been oppressive and tyrannical.
It destroys homes and kills people,
It suppresses speech and prohibits discussion.
Does it do anything that is good?
For this kind of government
The granting of rights and liberty is seen
As swallowing a bitter mixture of salt and sand,
Not sweet like the earth.
Whether rich or poor, strong or weak,
All men are the same under heaven.
No one is above another and no one is beneath another.

The people of Japan call for the extension of rights,
But there are no methods to extend our rights,
Because the law allows us no freedom.
If a government is evil,
If it checks the freedom of the people,
If it checks their wealth and takes their money,
If it does these wicked things without good reason,
Then it makes a great mistake.

The people's welfare is unobtainable.
Let's resolve for constitutional laws
And for the early popular election of an assembly.
Onward! Onward! People of our country.
Let's push for the rights of liberty.
Work diligently, thirty million people,
All together;

Rise up, be prosperous and go forward.
A political system of constitutional freedoms
Is the pressing need of today.
Cultivate wisdom and pursue scholarship.
Become enlightened people and
Let's make brilliant the majesty of our country.[101]

The substance and the language of the song clearly reflect Ueki's understanding of Spencer's natural right doctrine. Man's innate capacities or faculties, which separate him from the beasts in all respects save an instinct to seek freedom, compel him to make a duty of securing his freedom. His right to freedom is identical to his duty to take his freedom; not to do so is to deny his own humanity. Although Ueki did not explicitly urge his rural audience to take up arms in rebellion, he defined the nature of man and the nature of the contemporary political situation in such a way that listeners could not fail to draw the conclusion that they had a Spencerian right to rebel.

There is even clearer evidence that Ueki followed Spencer's principle of equal freedom and rights in the way that Ueki applied the principle to public policy. In his draft constitution, Ueki listed some thirty-five "rights of human liberty" which he believed basic to a just political system. Among them are the freedoms of thought, speech, publication, communication, travel, petition, assembly, public association, religion, commerce, arts, education, residence, and protection of self and property. Moreover, his constitution guaranteed equality of the sexes, freedom from unlawful search and seizure, and freedom from having to quarter the militia, and it forbade the death penalty in all cases except treason. Strong judicial guarantees were also included as well as significant limitations on the powers of the emperor and the federal government.[102]

Since Ueki regarded government as a trust, as an agent of the people that was duty-bound to ensure that the rights of all men and women would be protected, he concluded his list of individual rights with the ultimate one of revolution.[103] There were four rights in all,

101. Ibid., pp. 194–95.
102. Most of these rights appear in Chapter 4 of his draft constitution ("Rights and Freedoms of the Japanese People and Citizens," or *Nihon kokumin oyobi Nihon jimmin no jiyū kenri*), although I have listed several rights which appear under different sections, such as those relating to the judiciary and the Emperor (chaps. 8 and 5, respectively). From Ienaga, ed., *Ueki Emori senshū*, pp. 93–108. Also see Pittau, *Political Thought*, pp. 102–04, and Ike, *Beginnings*, pp. 130–37.
103. See Ienaga's commentary in *Kakumei shisō*, pp. 87–96.

which might be generally termed the right to resist; these four rights demonstrate conclusively that Ueki believed that sovereignty resides in the people:

Art. 64: The Japanese people may resist general lawlessness.

Art. 70: The Japanese people may choose to disobey any act contrary to the Constitution.

Art. 71: The Japanese people may remove (*haiseki*; literally, "expel") government officials who act oppressively.

Art. 72: When the government acts arbitrarily, contrary to the principles of the Constitution, and interferes with the rights and freedoms of the people, then the Japanese people may overthrow (*fukumetsu*) it and establish a new government.[104]

Spencer was in fact nowhere as explicit as Ueki in claiming for the people the right of revolution, so it is not surprising to learn that in writing his constitution and the above articles, Ueki relied upon sources other than Spencer's *Social Statics*. It is claimed by Ienaga that Ueki also consulted the 1791 and 1793 French Constitutions (especially Article 35 of the latter, which provides for the right of revolution) and Thomas Jefferson's Declaration of Independence, perhaps the closest philosophical link to John Locke's *Second Treatise* and early natural right doctrine.[105]

Whatever the main source behind Ueki's endorsement of the right of revolution, the conception itself came from natural right doctrine, a creed whose origins sprung from the rise of liberal market society but whose logic and principles were intrinsically democratic, resting on the belief, as Ōi Kentarō phrased it, that "Freedom is the essence of human nature," "an inherent natural thing" (*tempu koyū no mono*). When Ōi declared, "To live you need liberty; if liberty is diminished, you will die," he was merely echoing Ueki's basic belief, "Living without freedom, not having freedom, is the same as being dead."[106] For man to be able to live to his fullest capacities, Ueki (and Ōi) believed that man's natural rights had to be protected by constitutional guarantees, not least of which was the right of revolution.

But did the Japanese people of the 1880s believe they had this right? Did the message Ueki sent to the people in the form of his "Country Song of Popular Rights" reach them, and were they con-

104. Ienaga, ed., *Ueki Emori senshū*, pp. 94–95.
105. Ienaga, *Ueki*, pp. 354–55; and his *Kakumei shisō*, pp. 91–96.
106. Quoted in Hirano, *Ōi*, p. 60; and Ueki's "Country Song of Popular Rights," above.

vinced of its truth? Were the efforts of Ueki and others to educate
the people about natural rights successful? Unfortunately, no iron-
clad case can be made, nor can it be shown that Ueki's particular understanding of natural right doctrine was shared by other popular
rights activists of the period. Of the thirty-odd private draft constitutions drawn up by individuals or by political societies at the time,
Ueki's is unique for its espousal of popular sovereignty and its extensive listing of rights and freedoms.[107] Among the many rebels of the
1880s whom we are examining, there were of course many who supported a liberal constitution which would guarantee popular rights,
but few seem to have endorsed all the principles of natural right doctrine as Ueki or Ōi did. A typical example is the 7 December 1880
petition sent to the Emperor by four Aizu activists, Endō Naoyuki,
Hara Heizō, Okada Kenchō, and Kuroda Yutaka. They wrote:

> In reflecting upon present-day conditions in our country, we have reached
> a point where all the people sincerely and completely wish for a national as-
> sembly. *Compared to giving free play to the menace of a Western type of rev-*
> *olution which would strip [your majesty] of sovereignty and give it to the*
> *people*, the strengthening of cooperation between those high and low by al-
> lowing [an assembly] would be better. . . .
>   In these times we must first ask what is the proper road to take. If we ask
> what are the people's wishes for the future, then it is the convening of a na-
> tional assembly; the establishment of constitutional laws; the declaration of
> the rights of both the monarch and his subjects; the expansion of the liberties
> of citizens; and, in general, the advancement of the prosperity and the good
> health of the country based on the development of spirit [*seishin*].[108]

This passage clearly shows its authors to have been respectable liberals (neither Tories nor Whigs) who in general wanted the same kind
of political reforms advocated by Ueki but who nonetheless strongly
rejected Ueki's notion of popular sovereignty. At the same time, their
petition also shows they were cognizant of the fact that Western revolutions have resulted in political systems based on popular sover-

---

107. Irokawa et al., *Minshū kempō*, p. 304, Table One, compares all the private draft
constitutions of the period according to the number of articles they contained; and on p.
305, Table Two, there is a comparison of the Itsukaichi draft with one written by the political society the Ōmeisha according to the categories; on pp. 311–313, Ueki's draft is compared
with the Itsukaichi draft and is found to be the more democratic of the two. Ienaga, *Ueki*,
pp. 342–48, compares Ueki's draft constitution with two other private drafts, again showing
the singularity of Ueki's.
108. Quoted in Shōji, *Nihon seisha*, pp. 154–55 (emphasis added).

eignty. Although it would be a mistake to make too much out of this, it is important to observe that they understood fully the implications of natural right doctrine (and were perhaps bold enough to inform the government that *they knew*). It might also be recalled that these same men were involved in the Fukushima Incident just over a year later.

Specific instances where it appears that at least some of the ideas incorporated in natural right doctrine filtered down to the lower levels of society will be provided in subsequent sections of this chapter. But before concluding this section, we will look at several general pieces of evidence, anecdotes really, which show that an attempt was made to inform rural folk of their natural rights.

In the song *Jiyū no uta* ("Song of Liberty"), one of several that were aimed at the countryside audience and that Nobutaka Ike says "became very popular in this period," we read:

> Follow the path of the English Revolution
> Yesterday a King, today a rebel.
> Cromwell's beckoning with a flag of Liberty in his hand
> Almost upset Heaven.
> By putting King Charles to death
> The basis of liberty was laid.[109]

Another song that was aimed at the rural public, probably written by Ueki around 1878, was *Minken kazoe uta*, or "Counting Song of Popular Rights."[110] Published in serial form in several of the liberal newspapers at that time, its simple but poignant language was well received by all classes of people. The song is divided into twenty very short stanzas, each one telling about some aspect of liberty, or else bemoaning the absence of freedom in Japan. One recorded instance of the "Counting Song" being sung occurred in connection with the Gumma Incident. In April 1884, at a Jiyūtō-sponsored lecture meeting in a small hamlet south of Matsuida village in Gumma prefecture, the gathering sung several stanzas, among them Number Six:

> Let's remember long ago;
> America's flag of Independence;
> Let us be brave now![111]

109. Translated in Ike, *Beginnings*, p. 106; the original appears in Ienaga, *Kakumei shisō*, p. 52.

110. Ienaga, *Ueki*, pp. 170–73, n. 31, provides four different versions of the song; also see pp. 139–40, for commentary. Parts of it are quoted in Hirano, *Ōi*, pp. 56–7.

111. This episode is related in Fukuda, *Sanmin sōjō roku*, pp. 117–18.

According to the historical records of Gumma prefecture, this song was very popular in nearby Chichibu district, spurring liberal activists in the Kanra districts of Gumma, perhaps because of provincial rivalry, to compose a slightly different version of the song for themselves.[112]

These songs (Ueki's two and *Jiyū no uta*) reached the attention of many in the countryside who lacked the education necessary to be able to read Jiyūtō petitions and manifestoes written by the leaders of the popular rights movement. It is impossible to know whether such oral means of communicating liberal ideas affected country folk, let alone whether they were important in moving people to rebellion. For most farmers, names of historical figures and events such as Cromwell and the American War of Independence were probably just that—names, and probably therefore not at all meaningful. The thoughts expressed by Ueki—intended for rural people—probably were meaningful, although this may not be obvious to the reader because much of the simplicity of the song is lost in translation. Nonetheless, it seems fair to assume that the likelihood of rural people comprehending the meaning of such songs (or manifestoes, petitions, memorials, etc.) was increased to the extent that the people either (1) were literate, or (2) were members of, or had connections with, political societies or parties. We will examine the instance of literacy first.

Literacy in the Countryside

Innumerable students of Japan have cited the relatively high rate of literacy among the Japanese population at the time of the Restoration as a partial explanation of how Japan was able to modernize so efficiently and quickly after that date. By the end of the Tokugawa period, there were some 17,000 different schools in Japan, 15,000 of which were *terakoya* ("parishioners' schools") that served the common people in towns and villages;[113] and an estimated 40 to 50 percent of the male population and about 15 percent of the females were literate.[114] This legacy from the Tokugawa period, moreover, was enhanced when, in 1872, the Education Code was enacted by the government, calling for the eradication of illiteracy. By 1875, 40 percent of all boys and 15 percent of all girls were attending elementary school; by 1883, the figures were 67 percent and 34 percent.[115] Al-

112. Ibid., p. 118.

113. Herbert Passin, "Japan," in *Education and Political Development*, ed. James S. Coleman (Princeton, N.J., 1965), pp. 274–75.

114. Ibid., p. 276.   115. Ibid., p. 272.

though up to this time the content of schooling was largely Confucian and nationalistic, and hence showed largely "utilitarian"[116] motives (one index of its "utilitarianism" was the proscription upon teachers from joining political movements), it did nonetheless provide a great many people with the basic tools needed to learn and absorb new ideas. Also, its emphasis on "merit," "success," "talent," and so on, though utilitarian in motive, created values universal in effect and therefore easily adopted by the movements in opposition to the government. In any case, from this brief outline we may assume that many of the activists involved in the popular rights movements would likely have been literate. How, then, does this generalization square with the data presented in the participant samples for the three studies in Chapter 3?

We will look at the Chichibu case first, for if any of the three incidents could be suspected of having a leadership and a following that were largely illiterate, it would be this one. The data appearing in the sample are far from conclusive, but when they are supplemented by other collateral data, a clearer picture emerges.

The most immediate limitation of the data stems from the fact that usually the question of literacy was never asked during interrogation (for this reason there appears no special column in the sample for this characteristic, but it is contained under "other": see Appendix C). Only five people questioned by the authorities were expressly asked about literacy. Four of these five claimed to be literate. (It might be noted that Ochiai Toraichi was not literate at the time of the rebellion but later taught himself reading and writing while serving a prison sentence for his involvement in the Osaka Incident [November 1885].) If, however, we use as probable signs of literacy such information as whether or not a person acted as a petitioner at some time, whether his business required reading and writing skills, whether he was known to have done writing of one sort or another, whether he was a former *gōshi* (as was Tashiro), and so on, then within the sample there are ten others in addition to the above-mentioned five individuals who could be classified as literate. About the rest of the leadership appearing in the sample it is impossible to say, although we can make some educated guesses if we use certain other bits of evidence.

116. Ibid., p. 277; and Ronald P. Dore, "Education: Japan," in *Political Modernization in Japan and Turkey*, ed. Robert E. Ward and Dankwart A. Rustow (Princeton, N.J., 1964), p. 179; and Ronald P. Dore, "The Legacy of Tokugawa Education," in *Changing Japanese Attitudes Toward Modernization*, ed. Marius B. Jansen (Princeton, N.J., 1965), p. 105.

In 1874, when many of the rebellion's participants would have been of school age, the percentage of Saitama children in school was 29.4 percent; the breakdown by sex was 47.1 percent for boys and 11.7 percent for girls. By 1879, the figure for boys increased to 63.6 percent, and for girls to 21.6 percent.[117] It is also known that Chichibu ranked among the highest of Saitama districts in terms of the number of children in school as of 1884–85.[118] That education in Saitama progressed so quickly, moreover, is not surprising when it is realized that during the Bakumatsu period (1853–68) about fifty private schools and about 600 "parishioners' schools" were in existence.[119]

In Inoue Kōji's sample of 261 Chichibu Incident participants arrested by the Gumma prefecture police (who during interrogation did question the suspects on this point), 202 individuals or 77 percent claimed they could at least write their name and position. Among these 202 persons, Inoue was only able to distinguish between the barely literate and the completely literate; respectively, the figures were about 60 percent and 40 percent.[120]

Another piece of evidence pointing to a fairly high rate of literacy in Chichibu has to do with its close ties to the silk market. Inoue tells us that it was not unusual for Chichibu residents to read newspapers frequently in order to gain information about the conditions of the Yokohama and (even) American markets.[121] "Even villages located in the deepest valleys were aware of how close Tokyo and Yokohama were."[122] Also, the prosperity of the region prior to 1884 served to bring merchants, politicians (Ōi Kentarō, for instance, visited Chichibu in early 1884),[123] and even artists to Chichibu. "At this time Chichibu was not a closed society; and its openness was accompanied by a political awakening."[124] To whatever extent a political awakening did occur in Chichibu, based on the evidence presented thus far it seems likely that the fairly high literacy rate prevailing in the region was partly responsible for it.

All twenty-five of the Fukushima individuals for whom we have information were literate, and most of them, it appears, could be termed highly literate. Newspaper reporters, former and present *shizoku*, town and village chiefs (who had to file monthly reports to their government superiors), doctors, students of private political society schools or party schools, lawyers' aides, and so on, can be expected to have

---

117. Ōno, *Saitama*, p. 195.   118. Ibid., p. 196.   119. Ibid., pp. 154–55.
120. Inoue, *Chichibu jiken*, p. 90.   121. Ibid., p. 22.   122. Ibid., p. 23.
123. Ibid., p. 38.   124. Ibid., p. 23; and Hirano, *Ōi*, pp. 111–12.

been highly literate. Even the one individual (Ishii Teizō) who, during interrogation, said he was "barely [literate]," was known to have formed his own local study circle. Also, other leaders, mainly from Yama district, whose names were frequently mentioned in the last chapter—Hara Heizō, Uda Seiichi, Endō Naoyuki, Nakajima Yūhachi, Watanabe Shūya, etc.—appear to have been highly literate, as is indicated not only by the petitions they wrote, but also by the village government posts they held.

There is some reason to believe that many of the followers in the incident were also literate. In addition to the high national literacy rate, as shown earlier, it is known that in the last years of Tokugawa, there were 521 *terakoya* in Fukushima prefecture, of which over 90 percent were operated by wealthy farmers.[125] We may also assume that a fairly high rate of "political literacy" existed among the followers. In one document, dated 20 November 1880 and entitled "Facts relating to the delegation of Hara Heizō, representative of Yama district, for the petitioning for a national assembly," we see that 271 people, all *heimin*, from twenty-eight different villages, affixed their signatures.[126] Although it may be argued that some or even many of these people had little idea of what they signed, it seems more likely, given the evidence presented thus far, that it was otherwise. Moreover, it is easily imagined that even if they were unable to read the document, someone, probably the local organizer, explained the significance of the document to them.

Take, for instance, the testimony of Ishii Teizō, who earlier during interrogation responded "barely" to the question of literacy:

Q. Had you earlier [before the incident] joined the Jiyūtō?
A. Yes, I had.
Q. What do you believe to be the purpose of the Jiyūtō?
A. To establish a constitutional form of government.[127]

Like the Fukushima case, it seems that most of the individuals of the Kabasan Incident appearing in the sample were literate. Most either responded positively during interrogation to the question of literacy or were known to have attended either a domain, prefectural, or *seisha* ("political society") school. Several even were probably "highly literate," as is seen by their occupations—teaching, writing, government, and politics.

125. Irokawa, "Freedom," p. 177, quoting a study done by Shōji Kichinosuke.
126. Shōji, *Nihon seisha*, pp. 151–54.   127. Ibid., p. 332.

Literacy as such, however, means only that the individuals of the three incidents were capable of reading, talking intelligently, and presumably understanding political ideas such as natural right, freedom, representative government, and constitutionalism. Still, not all political activists need be literate, even though, as we have just seen, many of those who are included in the three samples were. As was intimated earlier, an understanding of political notions—that is, "political literacy"—is augmented by membership in or a connection with some type of political group. Here, we will look at two such groups that came into existence during the second period of popular rights development, referred to earlier as "the Period of Organization and Promotion."

Both of these groups are political societies of Fukushima prefecture. One, the *Sanshisha* ("Society of Miharu District Teachers"), was, as its name suggests, based in Eastern Fukushima, and was probably representative of a good number of other political societies that emerged elsewhere in the late 1870s. The other is the *Aishinsha* ("Society for Mutual Regard"), which was based in the Aizu region. Since both were forerunners of the Fukushima Jiyūtō, and since the members of both were deeply involved in the Fukushima Incident several years later, they are therefore important for understanding organizational and ideological antecedents. Also, as we shall see later, a good number of the Kabasan participants were earlier tied to one or the other of these two societies. Finally, before examining these two societies, it is necessary to mention that during this second stage of popular rights development, most of Chichibu's residents seem to have been inactive politically and do not emerge as relevant political actors until the early 1880s.

Natural Right and Political Societies

Sanshisha

In January 1878, on his way from Ishikawa district to take up a new government post at the Fukushima prefectural government office, Kōno Hironaka, ex-samurai (*gōshi*) of old Miharu domain, stopped in Miharu Town to renew relations with several old friends. While there he contacted the village head of the town, Noguchi Kazushi, Shintō priest Tamano Hideaki, ex-samurai Matsumoto Shigeru and Sakuma Shōgen, druggists Asaka Gihei and Kageyama Masahiro, sake manufacturer Matsumoto Yoshinaga, and headmen Iwasaki Seigi and Miwa Shōji. Together they established the *Sanshisha*.[128] (Note that five of

128. Takahashi, *Fukushima jiken*, pp. 16–17.

these individuals appear in our sample, and were therefore tried for "treason" in 1883.)

Just two years earlier, inspired by the formation of the *Risshisha* of Tosa, Kōno had organized the *Sekiyōsha* ("Open Society of Ishi-kawa") in Ishikawa district while serving there as *kuchō* ("ward chief").[129] As legend would have it, however, or as Kōno himself would have it in his biography, it was not just the formation of the *Risshisha* that served as the inspiration, but, rather, his reading of J. S. Mill's *On Liberty*. Kōno wrote:

> Until then [March 1872] I had been nurtured on Confucian and Kokugaku [native Japanese] studies . . . but then [after reading Mill], I realized the importance that should be placed on the rights and the liberties of the people.[130]

In the statement of principles and the rules of organization of the *Sekiyōsha*, we are able to see the influence of Mill and of democratic notions in general. Free speech as the best means to arrive at enlightened decisions on important matters, the importance of the political education of youth, the importance of a representative assembly to express the aspirations of the people, and so on, tell of the influence of Mill and other democratic thinkers on the society, and on Kōno himself, who served as the first President of both the *Sekiyōsha* and the *Sanshisha*. The principles, rules, and organizational structure of the two societies are virtually indistinguishable, and therefore an in-depth examination of either would be equally profitable. But since the *Sanshisha* appears to have had more influence on both the Kaba-san and Fukushima incidents and their participants, we will examine it.

A document entitled "The Principles and Rules of the Sanshisha" (*Sanshisha shishu oyobi shasoku*) best characterizes the nature of the society.[131] In its "Statement of Principles," we see a very sophisticated treatment of the essential argument of natural right doctrine. It reads in part:

> Society consists of a union of people who have both rights [*kenri*] and duties [*gimu*], which run parallel to one another. They cannot be separated even for a short time, because they are the important truth of human existence. Even though they are steadily assaulted by placing excessive importance on wealth and honor, they cannot be beaten. They are *inherent natural rights* [*tempu*

---

129. Ibid., p. 14.
130. *Kōno Banshū bensai kai, Kōno Banshū den* 1 (Tokyo, 1924):186–87, and quoted in Takahashi, *Fukushima jiken*, p. 14. A longer version and translation can be found in Ike, *Beginnings*, p. 112.
131. Shōji, *Nihon seisha*, p. 13–18.

koyū no ken] . . . . They are the true road of nature, of heaven, and of earth, and in truth are both private and public. Although these rights and duties have always existed [in nature] they have not yet been settled to a sufficient degree, and can only be determined by energetic public debate and discussion. *To fail to do this is to deny our nature as men.* . . . The people of Japan today perform their duties. . . . A settled policy is needed to advance in a direction that will benefit society by enlarging the natural rights of the people. . . . To this end, having concluded that a permanent and widely held public debate [is needed] like-thinking individuals have formed a compact [emphasis added].[132]

Following this preamble is a statement of the rules of the *Sanshisha*, which consists of forty-eight articles, divided into five sections. The five sections concern: (1) general rules; (2) meetings; (3) definitions and duties of Society officeholders; (4) rules of debate and discussion; and (5) Society finances. Although the last four sections are of some interest, it is Section One dealing with general rules that tells most concerning the principles of the Society and their operation. It consists of eleven articles, five of which seem the most pertinent:

Article I: This Society will be called the Sanshisha, taking its name from Miharu *machi* of Tamura district, where it will be established.

Article II: There will be no distinction made between the high and the low [or rich and poor—*kisen*] for membership in this society. All have equality of rights [*dōtō no kenri*]; no one will lose his rights so long as he performs his duties.

Article III: Those who become members of this society are expected to perform the duties assigned to them by the headquarters and branches with a docile devotion [*wajun mame*]. They are expected to study the principles we practice; to take them seriously; to find and correct their weak points; to nurture conditions for self-government; and to work to extend the rights of liberty.

Article V: Members must obtain the permission of the Society head before joining another society.

Article VI: All positions other than "head of the Society" [*shachō*] and conference head [*gichō*] will be elected by ballot. All officers may stand for re-election, and a period of one week every year will be set aside for elections. [The *gichō* is elected at each general meeting by those in attendance: Article VIII.][133]

The natural right and democratic contents of this document speak for themselves—the notions of equal rights, critical thinking, self-

132. Ibid., pp. 13–14.   133. Ibid., pp. 14–18.

government, extension of rights and liberties, and an open ballot. The only questionable parts of the document are the expectation in Article III that the members serve with "docile devotion," and the restriction in Article V on the freedom of members. The former case can be written off as the Japanese version of "party discipline," especially since in the same article we see that members are encouraged to study and improve themselves. This stricture is also merely an extension of the idea pronounced in the Society's "Statement of Principles": Obligations must necessarily accompany rights if organization is to work effectively. This is probably the case with Article V as well. After all, Kōno himself served two societies at once, and the *Sanshisha* was in correspondence and had relations with twenty-seven different political societies of fourteen prefectures, among them four from Fukushima itself (*Sekiyōsha, Aishinsha, Kōfusha,* and the *Hokushinsha*). In fact, probably because of Kōno's dual leadership, the relations between the *Sekiyōsha* and *Sanshisha* were very close.

There is also one other rule of the society that may cause some doubt as to how democratic it was. That is the first sentence of Article VI, which removes the office of "Society head" from election. In Section 3, Article 34, defining the office and its responsibilities, we read: "The Society head presides over all general affairs of the Society, oversees correspondence with other societies, punishes members who break the rules of the Society, and interprets the laws in cases where members bring disgrace to the Society; he has this authority until he retires from office."[134] Since no rationale is provided for permitting Kōno to wield such strong executive and judicial authority, the reason can only be conjectured. Possibly it represents an instance of historical continuity, taking as its precedent the tendency prevalent during Tokugawa (and before) to elevate a single individual to an all-powerful position of authority, e.g., the *Shōgun* or the *daimyō*. Or possibly it was the fact that Kōno Hironaka himself held the post; he was, after all, a nationally recognized *minken* leader and a man of charismatic qualities to whom people naturally looked for leadership. "His personal charm brought into the movement all sorts of men irrespective of class or age."[135] In this sense he was like Ita-

---

134. Ibid., p. 16.

135. Takahashi, *Fukushima jiken*, p. 40. Instances of individuals who were influenced by Kōno to join the movement include Kariyado, Shirai, and Matsumoto Yoshinaga. See Takahashi Tetsuo, *Fukushima jiyū minken undō shi* (Tokyo, 1954), pp. 277, 288; also Shōji, *Nihon seisha*, p. 334.

gaki, a drawing card for the movement and therefore of such importance that it was difficult to conceive of someone of sufficient renown
to replace him. Also, his views were recognized by most as democratic
and populist, and hence probably produced little apprehension among
his following that he would abuse his authority.[136] For Kōno himself,
the rule certainly was not the result of a fear of not being elected, because the head of the *Sekiyōsha*, which position he held, was an elec-
tive post.[137] But whatever the reason for the decision not to elect the
President, the more important point of the Society's essentially democratic nature should not be overlooked.

Besides the objectives laid out in the aforementioned statement of
principles, the *Sanshisha*, like the *Sekiyōsha* before it, had as one
of its main purposes "the political education of the youth" of the
area.[138] The *Sekiyōsha*, in order to achieve this goal, built the *Sekiyōkan*, a "hall" for the Society where lectures, meetings, and discussions concerning politics could take place. Although used by all of its
200-odd members—most of whom were farmers and *heimin* of Ishikawa and Shirakawa districts, according to one police report[139]—it
was intended mainly as an education institute, an "academy" for the
youth of the region. The *Sanshisha*, for the same reason, established
the *Seidōkan* ("Academy of the Right Road"), probably around 1881.
A handbill circulated to advertise its formal opening (scheduled for
9 January 1882) said its purpose was "the study of scholarly materials

---

136. In Shōji, *Nihon seisha*, pp. 203–26, Kōno's lecture notes are reproduced. The content of the notes which he used for speeches on freedom and rights strongly suggest that he
subscribed to some version of natural right doctrine. He notes, for example, that "Freedom
is something from Nature [*tenpu no mono*]," in one instance, and makes references to Herbert Spencer and the American and English revolutions in several other instances. This observation, however, should be taken only as a tentative one, particularly in view of the fact that
Kōno himself seems to have subscribed to the utilitarianism of Mill. But at the same time, it
should also be remembered that the Utilitarians themselves, protestations notwithstanding,
are "closet natural right theorists," a point Spencer enjoyed making in his *Social Statics* (pp.
33–35, 111–12) by examining the utilitarian conception of justice. Also see Kingsley Martin,
French Liberal Thought, p. 8. On the other side of the coin, a utilitarian strain of thinking
can be detected in the writings of natural right theorists. Spencer is one example himself—his
geometric approach to ethics and politics comes close to the utilitarian (à la Mill) attempt to
make politics and morality measurable through the pleasure calculus. The point is that the
two theories share certain premises, and that therefore one can subscribe to natural right
doctrine, for example, without dismissing utilitarian notions *in toto*. Tom Paine's thought is
an example of this, particularly as it was manifested in his little-known *Agrarian Justice*. See
Parrington, *Colonial Mind*, pp. 338–42. Also see Peter J. Stanlis's critique of the utilitarian
strain in natural right thought in his *Edmund Burke and the Natural Law* (Ann Arbor, Mich.,
1965), especially pp. 22–28.

137. Article VI of the *Sekiyōsha* charter, appearing in Shōji, *Nihon seisha*, p. 15.
138. Ibid., p. 16.
139. This police report was dated 3 July 1880 and can be found in ibid., p. 7.

dealing with politics, law, economics, and history."[140] On the same handbill appeared "a summary of its aims"—"to further educate men of talent (*jinzai*) and to study scholarly materials broadly related to our region."[141]

The *Seidōkan* was headed by Sakuma Shōgen, Matsumoto Yoshinaga and Asaka Saburō. (All were later tried for "treason"; see Appendix B.) It was housed in an old domain school building and provided dormitory rooms and dinners for three yen a month to those students coming from outside Miharu. For those residing in the town, only six sen a month were charged for fees. The *Seidōkan* also brought in lecturers, some, such as Hirozaki Masao and Nishihara Keitō, from as far away as the *Risshisha* of Kōchi prefecture. Although lectures were the primary mode of education, debates were also organized. Another interesting feature was that instructors and students ate together, a somewhat "democratic" feature in those times.

Although it is not known for certain what the topics of study were, it can be assumed that they resembled those emphasized at the *Sekiyōkan*. There, students were divided into three "organs," each of which specialized in the study of certain subjects. "Organ One" studied "the spirit of the laws," science, theories of social equality, and methods of thinking. "Organ Two" dwelled on the history of England, the origins of freedom, the basis of law, social contract, notions of right, morality, theories of political economy, and theories of representative government. "Organ Three" studied the French Revolution, comparative political systems, principles of politics, the economics of wealth, and the political history of the West. Each Saturday evening, representatives of the various organs would lecture and discuss the past week's research, and everyone was obliged to attend.[142]

Most students, it appears, were seventeen or eighteen years old and were the sons of "small *gōnō*," headmen, and ex-samurai of the region.[143] Many from the *Seidōkan* were later active in the Fukushima and Kabasan incidents. Kotoda Iwamatsu, Isokawa Motoyoshi, Yamaguchi Moritarō, Amano Ichitarō, and Kōno Hiroshi (nephew of Kōno Hironaka), for example, were all students at the *Seidōkan* who later rebelled at Mount Kaba. (See Kabasan sample, Appendix D.) Kōno,

---

140. Takahashi, *Fukushima jiken*, p. 24.
141. Ibid.
142. Ibid., p. 23. Given the topics of study, these "academies" may very well have been the first schools that taught Political Science in Japanese history.
143. Ibid., pp. 26–27.

Yamaguchi, and Isokawa had also studied at the *Risshisha* school before entering the *Seidōkan*.[144]

The authorities, naturally enough, counted such schools as subversive. At least one attempt was made to close down the school, in March 1882, and it is known that one of its leaders, Matsumoto Shigeru, was imprisoned and fined for refusing to obey a court injunction to close the school.[145] In one government report about the *Seidōkan*, it was said: "There are no rules in the organization, no one who manages it. Consequently, the conduct of its students is likely to become exceedingly violent. Its members agitate ignorant people. . . . It is like a poison slowly flowing into the veins of society."[146] On the lines of this metaphor, Governor Mishima tried to play the role of "doctor" by neutralizing the effect that the *minken* "poison" had on the body politic.

The political education of the region's youth, however, was a policy with long-term consequences. In the short term, the *Sanshisha* sought to bring about a national assembly. It therefore was continually involved in petitioning the government. Perhaps the most interesting and most telling point regarding its democratic nature was a draft of a petition to establish a national assembly. Written by Sakuma Shōgen, member of the *Sanshisha* and head of the *Seidōkan*, and dated 1880, it provides a scheme for convoking a constitutional convention that would write a provisional constitution, which would in turn provide for a national assembly. Paraphrased, Sakuma's scheme worked in this way:

1. All males over twenty-two years who are family heads elect five representatives from their district (*gun*).
2. All *gun* representatives elect three representatives from the prefecture.
3. The prefectures' representatives meet in Tokyo and elect forty members to sit on a constitutional convention. They study the laws of various countries and rely on the expertise of public and private citizens knowledgeable in this area.
4. The members then elect seven from among themselves to draw up a provisional draft of the constitution.
5. Upon completing it, the (forty) members discuss, debate, and decide on sending it to the government.
6. The government sets up a national assembly based on the provisional constitution and discusses and debates its merits and decides on making it the Constitution of Japan.[147]

144. Ibid.   145. Ibid., pp. 25–26.   146. Ibid., p. 26.
147. Reproduced in Shōji, *Nihon seisha*, pp. 156–57.

In some respects this scheme is reminiscent of the American experience,[148] although perhaps it is even more democratic in the sense that the Japanese Constitution would be the product of a male franchise that was free of any property qualifications. In any case, it underscores the essentially democratic nature of *minken* societies of eastern Fukushima. As a basis of comparison, we now turn to western Fukushima and examine the *Aishinsha* of the Aizu region.

Aishinsha

Just as the *Sanshisha* and several other such societies were the forerunners of the Jiyūtō branch of eastern Fukushima, the *Aishinsha* was the political antecedent of the Aizu branch of the Jiyūtō. Yet despite this commonality, there were distinct differences between these two political societies. If a contemporary parallel can be made, then we could compare the differences between the *Aishinsha* and the *Sanshisha* with the differences between, say, the Democratic Party of Indiana and the Democratic Party of New York. Historical, geographical, and sociological factors separated the two societies, though members of each would claim allegiance equally strong to the principles espoused by the greater *minken* (and later, the Jiyūtō) movement.

The Aizu region had consisted of different domains during Tokugawa, most of which were loyal to the Tokugawa rule and hence opposed to the new Restoration government. Even as late as 1869, Aizu loyalists had continued fighting against the Imperial forces being sent from Tokyo *and* from Eastern Fukushima as well, in what historians have come to term "The Boshin War."[149] A number of individuals appearing in our sample, for example, were victims of that war, either having themselves fought or having lost fathers who did.[150] In either case, they lost much of their property and fortunes, and several were reduced to penury. Takahashi asserts in this regard: "The dissatisfaction stemming from such experiences was probably the reason they attached themselves to a new political movement."[151]

---

148. "The state ratifying conventions were elected by voters who themselves constituted only a small fraction of the American population. To that extent, the process of ratification [of the U.S. Constitution] was not a democratic action." From Louis H. Pollack, ed., *The Constitution and the Supreme Court: A Documentary History* 1 (Cleveland, 1966):116. Also see Pollak's discussion on literacy and property qualifications as revealed in the "Randolph Plan" and the "Patterson Plan," pp. 60–63.

149. Takahashi, *Fukushima jiken*, pp. 31, 45. On the "Boshin War" as a source of later Aizu enmity towards the East, see Kobayashi and Yamada, *Fukushima rekishi*, pp. 158–77; and Haraguchi Kiyoshi, *Boshin sensō* (Tokyo, 1963).

150. Takahashi, *Fukushima jiken*, p. 46.

151. Ibid.

Geographically, Aizu was situated far to the west, part of it border-ring on Niigata and Yamagata prefectures. It was also cut off from eastern Fukushima by high mountains, which made communication a slow and difficult ordeal. Also, the centers of political activism, which encircled Kitakata Town in Yama district, were mainly agricul-tural areas, thus further distinguishing the region from the centers of activism in eastern Fukushima, where trade and commerce dominated.

Sociologically, as the above point suggests, most of Aizu's inhabi-tants were farmers who, as we have already seen, composed the body of participants in the Fukushima Incident. In the less commercialized farming districts, organization for any purpose, including political, tended to center around the already existing village structure. At the apex of the village structure was the village head, who tended to be a hereditary holder of this office and, coincidentally, one of the larger landholders in the region.[152] From this superior political and econom-ic position, he would traditionally be in charge of village affairs, po-litical or otherwise. As the linchpin for community solidarity and so-cial harmony, he could either promote or hinder political organization.

It would be expected, then, that those political, geographical, and economic conditions might make the ideology and organization of the *Aishinsha* different from that of the *Sanshisha*. We could expect, for example, the *Aishinsha* to employ either a more traditional ide-ology as a rationale for its activities, or perhaps a modified version of natural right, or even a complicated combination of the two. Yet, pre-viously in our discussion of natural right doctrine and its relation to the *minken* movement, we quoted at length the 7 December 1880 petition by four Aizu region representatives that called for a national assembly as the best means to give vent to popular opinion, and there-by to avoid a "Western type of revolution."[153] Although this docu-ment provides some indication of the ideological basis of the *Aishin-sha*, other supporting evidence is required. Unfortunately, as Shōji Kichinosuke informs us, the same kind of detailed information earlier provided for the *Sanshisha*—a statement of principles with rules of organization—is simply nonexistent today. Still, the following docu-ment does provide good insight into the nature of the principles gov-erning the *Aishinsha*:

"A Statement of Aims" (10 November 1878)
Man is separated from birds and animals by the protection he provides for himself through his miraculous intelligence to produce articles for his survival.

---

152. Ōishi, "Shakai keizai," p. 112.   153. Shōji, *Nihon seisha*, pp. 154–55.

We can say that using his intelligence, which secures for him the ability to use his powers for self-protection, is in the end a self-duty, one of several. If he does not understand that he must protect his own liberty in order to extend his right to realize this basic duty, then in fact nothing separates him from the birds and animals.

Today, people are resigned to servility, because servility means peace, and take all of this from those under the Emperor [i.e., the government] ; but the time has come when we ought to consider our own happiness, and demonstrate a spirit of self-government [*jichi*]. Like the Yangtze and Yellow rivers that consist of the drops of water from many roofs, the State consists of individuals.

If we all cooperate and work together, even though we bear the insults of foreign countries, we will come together into one body as do the Yangtze and Yellow rivers.

There are both foolish and wise people, though even the foolish may become wise, and through communication with one another, all ought to see to their best interests. Accordingly, we promise to try to spread wisdom in this country, and to get together and meet with the people to share our views. Talking and lecturing about where rights and duties reside, in other words, teaching regard for oneself as one would regard his country, is our purpose, so we will call our society the "Society for Mutual Regard."[154]

What appears most important about this document is that while it lacks a strong, explicit statement against government abuses of power, it also is a clear and somewhat sophisticated pronouncement of the rights of men as a consequence of their duty to preserve themselves. In this sense, it is unlike the Lockean principles of natural right as outlined by the *Sanshisha*, and closer to the Hobbesian concept of natural right. At the same time, however, its attack on servility—or as Hobbes would have had it, obedience to the Leviathan as the best means to secure life and property—and the attendant call for self-government, brings it back closer to Lockean natural right. This fact suggests what many theorists have noted about Hobbes and Locke, namely, the philosophical debt that Lockean natural right owed to Hobbes.[155] Although interesting, this observation seems less important than the Spencerian import of the document. The sharp distinction between the faculties of man and beast, the natural duty of man to use his natural faculties, the idea that this duty is also a right, the emphasis on the state as being the product of the citizens who com-

154. Ibid., p. 44.
155. For example, see Raymond Polin, "John Locke's Conception of Freedom," in *John Locke: Problems and Perspectives*, ed. J. W. Yolton (Cambridge, England, 1969), pp. 1–18.

pose it, and the importance attached to self-government, all point to at least a basic understanding of either Spencer's thought or Spencer's thought as interpreted by popular rights thinkers such as Ueki Emori. In short, the ideas and the language used in this document indicate something more than mere coincidence.

As well as this intimation of the right and duty to secure self-government, there exists additional evidence that helps to define more precisely the ideological coloring of the *Aishinsha*. It is known, for instance, that Uda Seiichi, later tried for "treason," and Anse Keizō, village head of Kitakata where the society was founded, wrote the *Aishinsha* charter, which consisted of four sections and twenty-five articles, and that the names of fifty-four individuals appeared on the document as founding members. It is known that the *Aishinsha*, founded one year after the *Sanshisha*, bore some resemblance in terms of principles and organization to the latter, particularly so since Anse was a native of Tamura district, Tsuneha village, where Kōno Hironaka once served as vice-head, and during which time they became good friends.[156] Other than Anse and Uda, the other principal movers behind the *Aishinsha* were Nakajima Yūhachi, Yamaguchi Chiyosaku, Kojima Chūhachi, Akagi Heiroku, Endō Naoyuki, and Igarashi Takehiko, all of whom, incidentally, were later prosecuted for "treason." (See Appendix B.)

It is further known that these same individuals, and others such as Hara Heizō and Watanabe Shūya, were later the leaders of both the *Aizu Rengōkai* and the Aizu Jiyūtō.[157] With this knowledge, and since the *Aishinsha* "Charter" is lost, it has become customary to infer the ideology and organization of the *Aishinsha* from that of subsequent organizations, especially its Jiyūtō branch (which will be examined in the next section).

There exists justification for doing this, over and above the fact that pertinent *Aishinsha* documents are missing. First, only four years separate the founding of the *Aishinsha* and the Aizu Jiyūtō branch (February 1882). Secondly, during this time it appears that no dramatic change in the leadership composition of the local popular rights movement occurred. Anse became the first head of the Aizu Jiyūtō, and the other party officials were Miura Tokujirō (V.P.), Uda Seiichi,

156. Takahashi, *Fukushima jiken*, p. 17; and Kobayashi and Yamada, *Fukushima rekishi*, p. 181.
157. "[The Aishinsha] served as the womb for the formation of the Aizu Jiyūtō" (Takahashi, *Fukushima jiken*, p. 18).

Nakajima Yūhachi, and Miura Nobuyuki. All but the two Miuras were signatories to the "Statement of Aims" quoted above. Also, a police report concerning the *Aishinsha*, dated 3 July 1880, says that it was composed mainly of "prefectural assembly men, wealthy farmers, and village heads coming from the various villages."[158] Checking this against the Aizu Jiyūtō membership, we see that prefectural assemblymen Endō Naoyuki, Uda Seiichi, Kojima Chūhachi, Nakajima Yūhachi, Watanabe Ichirō, and Yamaguchi Yoshisaku were all members of the Aizu Jiyūtō.[159] The same individuals, plus Hara, Miura Shinroku, Miura Bunji, Igarashi Takehiko, and Akagi Heiroku, among others, were *gōnō*; and finally, as we saw in the last chapter, most of the above-mentioned individuals were "village heads," prompting one specialist on this incident to characterize the Aizu Jiyūtō as the "party of village heads."[160]

A third and final justification for inferring the ideological character of the *Aishinsha* from the Jiyūtō branch subsequently formed in Aizu has to do with what appears to have been the existence of ideological continuity, and also with the Society's collaborative work with the *Sanshisha* and other natural right organizations of eastern Fukushima. In March 1881, fourteen individuals from different political societies from all over Fukushima, including Endō and Hara from Yama district in Aizu, signed "A Draft of the Principles of the 'Society of Resolve' of the Tōhoku Region" (*Tōhoku Yūshikai no shishu sōan*). It represented a reaffirmation of the principles enunciated in July 1879, when the *Kyōaidōbōkai* ("Society Aiming at Mutual Respect") was founded as a secret alliance of all the political societies in Fukushima and as a means to strengthen their region's ties to the national *Aikokusha*.[161] This document began:

> Man is a creature deriving freedom from heaven. He therefore has the rights of freedom. On this depends his happiness. . . . When he loses his rights he cannot secure the safety of his life or his property; he cannot have nor enjoy prosperity; it does not take a scholar or a genius to know this. . . . To protect our [natural] rights we need [legal] rights in our country and in our society.[162]

158. In Shōji, *Nihon seisha*, pp. 6–7.
159. Takahashi, *Fukushima jiken*, p. 73; Shimoyama Saburō, "Fukushima jiken shōron," in *Jiyū minken*, vol. 10, *Nihon rekishi series*, ed. Sakane Yoshihisa (Tokyo, 1973), pp. 167–68.
160. Takahashi, *Fukushima jiken*, p. 40.
161. Ibid., p. 20.
162. Shōji, *Nihon seisha*, pp. 161–62.

This might appear to confirm only Hara and Endō's personal belief in natural right, were it not for the fact that they were acting as representatives of the entire membership of the *Aishinsha*. Underscoring this contention that the predominant ideology of the *Aishinsha* was natural right is the knowledge that at the lecture meetings of the *Aishinsha*, Hara and Endō, along with Miura Shinroku and Uryū Naoshi, were the most frequent speakers, teaching "a simple straightforward, pure natural right doctrine."[163]

Hence we can conclude that despite the peculiar historical, geographical, and sociological factors of the Aizu region that would tend to have made its political society, the *Aishinsha*, impervious to the natural right notions characterizing the eastern Fukushima societies, it was nonetheless reliant on some version of natural right, though, as we saw, it was less anti-government and more Hobbesian than that of the eastern Fukushima societies.

Where these historical, geographical, and sociological facts had some influence on the character of the *Aishinsha* (and later on the region's Jiyūtō branch) was in the particular way it organized itself. Put very simply, "as opposed to the [eastern] Fukushima branch which assembled representative personalities of various districts, aiming its recruitment primarily at *meibōka* ["men of renown"], the Aizu branch organized itself around villages which served as the basic organizational unit."[164] By using this more traditional means of organization, Takahashi adds, "the Aizu branch was stronger as a result."[165]

Several years before "The Period of Activism," therefore, Fukushima prefecture boasted of a number of political societies that shared the belief that natural right doctrine was the best ideology to govern their activities. Now, to continue the discussion begun in the last section of Chapter 2, we will study how natural right doctrine was manifested in the activities of the local Liberal Party branches after the founding of its national headquarters in October 1881.

Period of Activism, 1881–1884

The Jiyūtō in Fukushima

The Aizu Jiyūtō branch was established in February 1882, four months after the establishment of the national party and two months after the Fukushima branch was formed in Fukushima Town, thus giving Fukushima prefecture two Jiyūtō branches. This came about

163. Takahashi, *Fukushima jiken*, p. 86.   164. Ibid., p. 37.   165. Ibid., p. 38.

in spite of earlier attempts by members of each area's political societies to form a unified party. The *Kyōaidōbōkai*, as we saw, was one such attempt. Symptomatic of its failure, as far as Aizu popular rights groups were concerned, was its building of the headquarters in distant Sendai, situated on the Pacific coast—as far away as it possibly could be from Aizu and yet still be situated in Tohoku.[166] The *Tōhoku Yūshikai*, to whose principles Hara and Endō were signatories, was referred to above as another such attempt; it experienced brief success for about one year, until the Aizu popular rights leaders broke from the group and formed their own Jiyūtō branch.

Although the various societies that composed the *Tōhoku Yūshikai* (*Sanshisha, Aishinsha, Sekiyōsha, Hokushinsha*, etc.) shared common principles as the basis of organization, in practice they could at best only unite into a loose confederation. The *shukuen* or the "old grudge" that had existed since the "Boshin War," when Aizu residents fought against Miharu Imperial troops, still served as an obstacle preventing organizational unity.[167] Also, the strong sense of regionalism characterizing Aizu, in part due to its geography and in part to its different patterns of landholding and agricultural production, had been manifested as recently as 1878, when, during the government's reorganization of the prefectures, the people there had sought to have the government create a separate Aizu prefecture.[168]

The strong sense of regionalism could also be seen in the explicit emphasis of the *Aishinsha* on "self-government" (in the earlier quoted "Statement of Aims") and the implicit emphasis on natural right while failing to mention its broader implications such as representative and constitutional government. That task had been left to a few individuals, such as Hara and Endō, but mainly to popular rights advocates of eastern Fukushima. For this reason, Takahashi could say about the *Aishinsha*, and hence about the Aizu Jiyūtō, that "its political coloring was duller than the other two societies [i.e., the *Sanshisha* and *Sekiyōsha*]."[169]

Of course, when the road project commenced under Governor Mishima's orders, the sense of regionalism and hence the Aizu Jiyūtō's desire for local self-government and, conversely, its dislike of central government intrusion into local affairs, were heightened. As pointed

166. Article II of its "Provisional Rules," appearing in Shōji, *Nihon seisha*, p. 162.
167. Kobayashi and Yamada, *Fukushima rekishi*, p. 188.
168. Takahashi, *Fukushima jiken*, p. 31.
169. Ibid., p. 18.

out in Chapter 1, it was a tension and conflict that has attended the politics of modernization in all places, i.e., the conflict between centralism and regionalism.[170] It was perhaps no accident, therefore, that the Aizu Jiyūtō was formed in the same month that Mishima was appointed to Fukushima. Certainly, it was no accident that the Aizu *Rengōkai*, "based on the aims and principles of the [local] Jiyūtō that principally sought to crush the road-building project" (as the Yama district head characterized it),[171] rose to defend the Aizu Jiyūtō's notions of self-government.

"The Provisional Rules Governing the Aizu Branch of the Jiyūtō" (*Jiyūtō Aizūbu kari no mōshiawase kisoku*) were not prefaced by a statement of principles—it probably was not necessary, since by its name alone it endorsed the principles of the national party—but from the articles themselves we can derive some notion of what ideas guided the Aizu branch.

> *Article I*: We will establish a regional branch of the Jiyūtō at Kitakata, Iwashiro *shū*, and call it the "Jiyūtō Aizu Branch." The party members of this branch will determine the nature of the organization in accordance with the conditions of this region.
>
> *Article II*: There will be one director (*buri*) and three officials for party affairs. All will serve a one-year term and will be elected by those in attendance at the regular party meeting.
>
> *Article III*: The Director will oversee (*sōtoku*) and supervise party affairs in the name of all branch members and shall supervise all decisions made at ordinary and extraordinary party meetings.
>
> *Article IV*: Party Affairs officials shall handle regular party matters of the branch under the supervision of the president.
>
> *Article V*: Officials will receive a wage to be determined by the president.
>
> *Article VI*: The expenses of the branch will be borne by the party membership.
>
> *Article VII*: All sub-branches will have one executive and, for convenience sake, all other functionaries shall be appointed by him.
>
> *Article VIII*: All those joining or leaving the party ought to be investigated by the leadership of the sub-branches.
>
> *Article IX*: In the various sub-branches, a list of the membership will be made at the end of every month and sent to headquarters at Kitakata.

170. See, for example, Samuel P. Huntington, *Political Order in Changing Societies* (New Haven, 1968), especially pp. 72–92.

171. *Fukushima kenshi* (FKS) XI:457. The report was dated 11 July 1882 and was submitted to the governor.

Article X: At the same time detailed reports about the situation and conditions of the region should be reported.

Article XI: In March and September of each year there will be a general meeting to which each sub-branch will send five delegates. The location of these meetings will be decided by a resolution at the immediately previous meeting.

Article XII: At the ordinary meetings the president will make a report on the budget, the finances, and the conditions of the party.[172]

The important ideas to be gleaned from this document are: (1) its realistic emphasis on a party that accurately reflects conditions of its immediate area, which, put into historical context, probably meant that some issues and principles espoused by the national party were considered more pertinent than others to the Aizu branch; (2) a strong executive, but one nonetheless checked by democratic elections by the party membership (estimated at about 300);[173] and (3) reasonably firm control by the center over its sub-branches; and within the sub-branches themselves, control over their own affairs by one figure who was appointed by central headquarters.

The manner in which the Aizu Jiyūtō branch organized its sub-branches clearly tells of its wish to reflect prevailing regional conditions. From evidence taken from later court testimony by party members and from the personal papers of Aizu Jiyūtō member Miura Shinroku, we can clearly discern the nature of its local organization.[174] The basic unit of local organization was the "cell" (*saibō*), as it was termed by the incident's participants during court interrogation; or the "organ" (*kumi*), as it was termed by Miura in his diary. Each "cell" consisted of anywhere from two to seven villages and had one "person responsible" (*sekininsha*) at its head. These "cell" leaders were appointed by the Aizu Jiyūtō headquarters, presumably by its four officials. Each "cell" took its name from the principal village included in it, and its leader usually came from this village.

Records leave us with examples of eleven "cells," consisting of thirty-nine villages in all. Here we provide only three examples: (1) The Komeoka "cell" was comprised of Komeoka itself, Kanno, and Miyakawa villages. It was headed by Miura Bunji, who was later tried for "treason" for his part in the Fukushima Incident, released, and

172. Shōji, *Nihon seisha*, pp. 55–56.
173. Takahashi, *Fukushima jiken*, p. 39.
174. Document No. 10 ("The Selection of Cell Leaders and Their Apportionment by Village"), in Shōji, *Nihon seisha*, pp. 62–63; it is discussed by Takahashi, *Fukushima jiken*, pp. 36–39.

then subsequently convicted for his role in the Kabasan Incident. (2) The Atsushio "cell," led by Endō Yūhachi, identified as one of the principal activists during the incident,[175] consisted of Atsushio, Sōta, Torimiyama, and Yamada villages. (3) The Yamato "cell," located ten kilometers west of Kitakata, included the village itself, Kofuneji, and Honhata; and the "person responsible" was Saitō Yamokichi, one of many individuals whose claim to fame stopped there, as far as historical records are concerned.

It is also important to note as a basis of temporal comparison how these same villages, before they became units or "cells," responded several years earlier to the Yama district petition to open a National Assembly (quoted earlier). Of the 271 signatories from the Yama district, the Komeoka "cell" accounted for 152, the Atsushio "cell" for only nine (Yamada village was not listed as having any petitioners), and the Yamato "cell" for ninety-six signatures; together these three cells contributed 94 percent of the signatures appearing on the petition. Hence considerable continuity existed from the second stage of popular rights development into the third stage.

The leadership of the "cells," and of the Aizu Jiyūtō in general, was a remarkably homogeneous group in terms of social, economic, and political status. Most were, as we have seen, village heads, and most came from villages situated in the northern half of the Aizu basin—Atsushio, Komeoka, Kanno, Shinai, etc. But superimposed on these commonalities, Takahashi tells us, were the "ties of blood and of marriage." Takahashi counts between thirty and forty village heads as *minken* leaders related by such ties.[176] Three brothers of Nakajima Yūhachi, for instance, were village heads of different Aizu villages and were later imprisoned after the incident. The headman of Kanno, Endō Naoyuki, and Toyama Teiji, headman of Iwatsuki village, were both brothers-in-law to Nakajima. In all, more than ten members of this family were later arrested. Another instance is that of Miura Bunji and Makabe Kitei, who were members of "branch families" (*bunke*) of Jiyūtō activist Miura Shinroku's "main family" (*honke*). The list goes on and on. Takahashi claims not only that "blood relations and marriage were at the core in the formation of the Aizu Jiyūtō leadership," but also that when government repression became severe these relationships held the movement together.[177]

When repression became more intense during the months leading up to the Kitakata Incident, the "cells" were employed in the tax

175. Takahashi, *Fukushima jiken*, p. 163.   176. Ibid., pp. 62–63.   177. Ibid.

boycott and mass litigation movements. It appears that in some villages—for example, Shinai village (part of the Kumagaya "cell"), where Akagi was a "hereditary" village head and, during village meetings, sat in the traditional seat of honor—the participation in these movements was large and very effective, no one having broken the boycott under government pressure.[178] Komeoka is another such example: In that village, headman Miura Bunji and *gōnō* Watanabe Shūya used the traditional moral force of their social positions to keep the members of their villages united during the tax boycott.

This point was suggested in the last chapter, that is, the close correlation between the village from which a leader came and the number of villagers mobilized from the same village. However, the reason for high rates of mobilization and village solidarity was not necessarily due only to bonds of traditional relationships between a village authority figure and its inhabitants, as suggested in the above two cases. It may also have been due to political reasons, e.g., political indoctrination of the village inhabitants by a political leader who, coincidentally, was also a headman. This seems to have been partially true of the influence of Akagi and Miura Bunji in the two cases just cited. In short, it seems that both traditional relationships and those defined by new political ideas served to bring villagers into the movement. Yet, although both were operative, the leaders of the movement were not appealing to tradition in their efforts to mobilize supporters, but instead were proclaiming the rights of man.

In addition to the "cells," the Aizu Jiyūtō also organized itself through, and lent its own organization to, the *Aizu Rengōkai*, which consisted of eighty-six towns and 493 villages located within the six districts comprising the Aizu region.[179] Among the executives of this organization were Nakajima Yūhachi ("head"), Uda Seiichi, Hara Heizō, and Miura Tokujirō, all of whom were identified in the last chapter as among those who were arrested for their part in the Fukushima Incident. Government reports at that time singled out Hara, Uda, and Maeda Kōsaku as the principal "troublemakers." One report claimed: "These three Jiyūtō members are representative of the malcontents; they call extraordinary meetings of the *Aizu Rengōkai* and make motions against the road-building."[180] Once the *Rengōkai* was suspended by Governor Mishima (see Chapter 1), these same Jiyūtō members plus several others—Yamaguchi, Akagi, Igarashi, etc.—

178. Kobayashi and Yamada, *Fukushima rekishi*, p. 204.   179. Ibid., p. 188.
180. *FKS* XI:457–58.

commenced organizing the tax boycott, mass litigation, and petition movements to reconvene the *Rengōkai*, taking all of these issues to the people of the region in the form of lecture meetings. At least fifty-two lecture meetings were held in April 1882, involving over 200 lecturers who traveled throughout the territory to speak about the various movements under foot.[181]

It was also during this same time that party activity, perhaps due to these lectures, spread to Aizu districts outside of Yama.[182]

Lecture meetings, rather than "academies" as in the case of the Eastern Fukushima Jiyūtō, served as the primary means to proselytize and recruit members to these various movements in Aizu. The topics of the lectures were as varied as the speakers. On one occasion, Hara, Uryū, Miura Shinroku, Endō Yūhachi, and Miura Tokujirō were the principal speakers.[183] Hara lectured about "The Battlefield of Reason" (*Dōri no senjō*), wherein he explained that "in a young society, only if reason is employed on the [political] battlefield can the ways of brute force be completely overcome," and he moved on to discuss how that thought related to the current political situation.[184] Uryū lectured on the natural rights of man and how their realization in positive law would bring society the rewards of heaven. Miura Shinroku gave a lecture entitled "The Incompatabilities of Society" (*Shakai no futekigō*), which anticipated by four years the radical liberal Ōi Kentarō's famous *Jiji yōron* (1886; "A Treatise on the Needs of These Times"), wherein Ōi called for a law to equalize landholdings.[185] In Miura's words, the lecture tried "to explain how in an enlightened society the inequalities of intelligence and wealth can be overcome" and argued that "now is the time to apply one's energies to the task of equalization (*yonarashi*) of wealth and education."[186] In another lecture, "*Chitose no ichigū*" ("One Chance in a Thousand Years"), he said that the Imperial Will calling for a national assembly and "giving people political rights to participate in government" would only have "one chance in a thousand" of being realized if it were postponed until 1890. For his part, Endō explicitly urged members of his audience "to join our political party in order to safeguard its principles."[187] All

181. Shōji, *Nihon seisha*, p. 174.
182. Takahashi, *Fukushima jiken*, p. 38.
183. Shōji, *Nihon seisha*, pp. 58–59.
184. Ibid., p. 59.
185. Hirano, *Ōi*, pp. 65–70. Also see Marius Jansen, "Ōi Kentarō: Radicalism and Chauvinism," *Far Eastern Quarterly* 2:3 (May 1952):305–16.
186. Shōji, *Nihon seisha*, p. 59.   187. Ibid.

of these addresses, incidentally, were given on 2 May 1882, at Kita-kata, and in "forced" attendance, taking notes, was a Kitakata police-man appointed by the local constabulary.

These speeches and ones like them were given throughout the Aizu region beginning in April 1882 and continuing until the Kitakata Incident in November. It is difficult to say exactly how many people heard them. It is known, however, that at one lecture broken up by the police at Wakamatsu, 300 people were in attendance.[188] At an-other, on 12 May 1882, at Wakamatsu, with Hara and Miura Shin-roku speaking, over 200 attended. Average attendance was less in smaller villages; for example, at a lecture in Aoki village on 26 May, broken up by the police, eighty villagers attended. Takahashi reports that the usual figure for a village lecture was "several tens," but he al-so notes that in one instance 1,200 people filled the lecture hall at an Aizu Jiyūtō meeting.[189] Whatever the figure, it is certain that the message of the Aizu Jiyūtō reached a good number of ears through its lecture meetings.

For this reason, and for the other reasons that have been men-tioned—"cells" relying on village leaders who were also Jiyūtō mem-bers, strong family ties among the leadership, and the use of the *Aizu Rengōkai*—Takahashi was correct in stating that its party organization was stronger than that of eastern Fukushima. The Eastern Fukushima Jiyūtō was diffuse and universalistic, looking more to the Tokyo cen-tral headquarters and to the Kōchi branch for ideological and organi-zational leadership than to itself. In a very real sense, its location, i.e., the fact that it was the Fukushima Jiyūtō, was incidental. It was Ji-yūtō, first and foremost, and the Fukushima Jiyūtō only secondarily. The writers of the history of the Liberal Party recognized this. In referring to the *Sanshisha* of Miharu (along with the *Kyūgasha* of Iwate), they said, "Suddenly they have become the leading advocates of liberalism (*jiyūshugi*)."[190]

In great part this universalism was undoubtedly due to Kōno Hiro-naka's leadership. Not only, as we have seen, was he the founder of local political societies in Fukushima, but he was also one of the early activists in the national popular rights movement and a founding member of the national Jiyūtō in October 1881. His goals for the na-

---

188. Ibid., p. 60.
189. Takahashi, *Fukushima jiken*, p. 98.
190. Itagaki Taisuke, *Jiyūtō shi*, 3 vols. (Tokyo, 1973; originally published in 1913 in 2 vols.), II:248.

tion were identical to his goals for Fukushima. These goals were best defined on 1 October 1881, in a platform policy of the Jiyūtō signed by himself and ninety-eight others:

> Our party seeks to expand freedom, defend rights, increase welfare and happiness, and map out social reform. . . . Our party seeks to establish a constitutional government in order to fulfill the above goals.[191]

Like most of the others who were national leaders of the Party, Kōno too was in favor of legal and nonviolent means to accomplish the above goals. Only once in his long and successful career as a politician of national reputation did he advocate violence (as we shall see). For the most part he strictly abided by the law. In fact, it was really only "accidental" that he became embroiled in the Fukushima Incident. Even after Governor Mishima had overturned the anti-road bill passed by the prefectural assembly, of which he was chairman, Kōno said, "This problem of road construction should definitely not be the main business of our party."[192] That he tried to ensure that this was the case is shown by the agenda of items discussed in the third regular meeting held at Fukushima Town on 20 May 1882 and attended by Kōno and twenty others. The four issues discussed were:

> 1. The submission of a written report to the Emperor asking for a shortening of the waiting period for convening the national assembly.
> 2. The warning to Governor Mishima about his arbitrary actions.
> 3. The recruitment of new party members and the establishment of party branches in other districts.
> 4. The decision whether to send party members to speak at various districts within the prefecture.[193]

Notice that nothing is said here about aiding the Aizu Jiyūtō; in fact, it was not until October that the struggle in Aizu became the most important item on the Fukushima Jiyūtō agenda.[194] But most importantly, throughout the entire episode, it appears that Kōno (and other easterners) was unable to extrapolate the important and more general question of self-government from the single issue of the Aizu road construction scheme.

It was only after repeated suppression of party activists by the Governor and the continued introduction of the Aizu affair as an im-

191. Quoted in Gotō Yasushi, *Jiyū minken: Meiji no kakumei to hankakumei* (Tokyo, 1972), p. 173.
192. Quoted in ibid., p. 178.
193. Takahashi, *Fukushima jiken*, p. 33.   194. Ibid.

portant topic into party meetings by others (such as Aizawa, Hanaka, Hirajima, etc.) that Kōno and several others committed the crime of sedition for which they were later prosecuted. The evidence for the crime of sedition ("treason") was a "written vow" (*seiyaku*) in the form of a "blood pledge" (*ketsumei*) that was literally sealed in blood by six young Jiyūtō members—Kōno Hironaka (thirty-three), Tamano Hideaki (thirty-four), Aizawa Yasukata (thirty-three), Hirajima Matsuo (twenty-eight), Hanaka Kyōjirō (twenty-six), and Sawada Kiyonosuke (twenty); it was dated 1 August 1882. Since this document bears considerable resemblance to manifestoes subsequently drawn up by the Kabasan and Chichibu rebels, we quote it here in full:

1. Our party will overthrow the oppressive government which is the public enemy of freedom and will endeavor to construct a political system that reflects the views of the public.

2. In order to achieve this goal of our party, we renounce personal life and property, we free ourselves from the ties of mutual kindness and affection, and will concern ourselves completely with the situation confronting us.

3. Our party honors and defends the constitution, as we resolved in our party conferences, and we endeavor to act as one mind and body in this matter.

4. In the event that realities crush the intentions of our party and we encounter all manners of disaster, even if time lapses over years and months, our party will never disband.

5. If a member transgresses his written vows and betrays the secrecy of our party and its members, then he should immediately kill himself.

These five articles of our vow should be carried out decisively, lest our party die.[195]

The vow was written by Hanaka and edited by Sawada,[196] and was found by the police on 1 December 1882, during an extensive search of the *Mumeikan* ("The Hall of No Name"), the Jiyūtō headquarters in Fukushima Town.[197]

The blood pact is interesting for its curious combination of natural right doctrine, as seen in its first article, and the self-sacrificing, "honor-above-everything" mentality that so strongly characterized the samurai of the Tokugawa period. It is no mere accident, then, that all six oath-takers were of the *shizoku* class (though Kōno and Tamano were déclassé).

195. Itagaki, *Jiyūtō-shi* II:254–55, or in Shōji, *Nihon seisha*, pp. 425–26.
196. Itagaki, *Jiyūtō-shi* II:255.
197. Maeda Renzan, *Jiyū minken jidai* (Tokyo, 1961), p. 265.

The *Mumeikan*, where the oath was found by the police, was the central headquarters of the eastern Jiyūtō branch. To a great extent, it took over the duties of the *Seidōkan* and the *Sekiyōsha* (and of other political societies) once the eastern Jiyūtō branch was founded. It was originally situated at the home of Okano Chisō in Fukushima Town; there, in late December 1881, twenty men from throughout all of Fukushima met to establish a Jiyūtō branch[198] (eight of them were later tried for treason). Prior to its first general meeting in March, it set up a schedule for regular party meetings, appointed representatives from each district to serve as liaison officers, made preparations to establish the *Fukushima Jiyū Shimbun*, and appointed editors for the paper; it established entrance and fee requirements, meeting times, and election procedures; it set up dormitories for visiting lecturers and popular rights advocates; and it established relations with the Tokyo headquarters and professed allegiance to the National Party.[199] In short, it was thoroughly organized as a Jiyūtō branch to serve all districts within Fukushima prefecture. However, since it made no mention of recruiting a local village membership, its organizational and ideological character more closely paralleled that of the national Party than it did the Aizu branch.

This is not to say that it was ineffective in spreading popular rights ideas. Although similar to the *Seidōkan* and *Sekiyōsha* in that it directed recruitment toward individual *meibōka* whom these organizations sought to mold into *minken shishi* ("warrior for popular rights"), the *Mumeikan* was also indirectly responsible for the growth of the popular rights movement among those living in the countryside. It had a "rippling effect" when an individual trained by these organizations would return to his village and organize a "political circle." Takahashi claims that many political circles sprang up throughout eastern Fukushima during the late seventies and early eighties;[200] here we will look at one named the *Dōshinkai* ("Society for Mutual Advancement"), which began operation in December 1881 at the village of Utsu, located about twenty kilometers north of Miharu (Tamura district).

During the interrogation of youthful Kamada Yūzō (eighteen), the name of his friend and fellow villager Ōkōchi Hidenori (twenty-five) came up, and the following exchange took place between Kamada and the prosecutor:

198. Shōji, *Nihon seisha*, p. 436.   199. Ibid., pp. 435–43.
200. Takahashi, *Fukushima jiken*, p. 27.

Q. From whom did you receive the rules of the Miharu Jiyūtō organization [the *Seidōkan*]?

A. They were distributed by Ōkōchi of the *Dōshinkai* of "Upper" Utsu village, Tamura district.

Q. When was this *Dōshinkai* established?

A. Around December, 1881.

Q. How many members does it have and who are its central figures?

A. There are fourteen or fifteen members and Ōkōchi is its leader.

Q. Who is this Ōkōchi?

A. He was a primary school teacher, but now he sells wine bottles.[201]

The questioning then changed topics to find out Kamada's relationship with Kōno and the *Mumeikan*:

Q. Around what month did you become acquainted with Kōno Hironaka?

A. On July 24, 1882, I first met him at the *Mumeikan*.

Q. When you came to the *Mumeikan*, whom did you speak about?

A. About Matsumoto Miyaji.

Q. Who is this Matsumoto Miyaji?

A. A primary school teacher in Miharu town who at the time was working for the Jiyūtō Party newspaper.

Q. For what purpose did you come to the *Mumeikan*, the "hangout of the Jiyūtō"?

A. In order to kill time with some friends . . . and to speak with Miyaji and Kōno about working for the newspaper. . . .[202]

Eventually the questioning moved on to Kamada's journey to Aizu on 13 October 1882, in order to see Uda Seiichi about a financial contribution to the party newspaper. He then recounts his reasons for deciding to stay and help in the fight there, mainly out of sympathy for friend Akagi Heiroku, who was losing his property to public auction for his refusal to pay taxes.

He was also asked:

Q. For what reason did you join the Jiyūtō?

A. To promote its principles of expanding the rights of liberty.[203]

Kamada, then a Jiyūtō member with close connection to the *Dōshinkai*, a "political circle," typifies the "rippling effect" that the *Seidōkan* (via Ōkōchi) had upon young *heimin* farmers of the rural areas. From contact with Ōkōchi, he became involved in *Mumeikan* affairs,

---

201. The complete interrogation is reproduced in Shōji, *Nihon seisha*, pp. 485–94. Both Kamada and Ōkōchi were tried for treason and therefore are listed in our sample (Appendix B).   202. Ibid.   203. Ibid.

which in turn led him to the Aizu road struggle, then to befriend Akagi, and finally to be tried as a "traitor" for a political crime.

Nor is this an isolated example. Sugamura Taiji, also tried for treason, and six other members of a political circle, the *Taishōkan* ("Great Righteousness Society") of a small village midway between Miharu and Utsu, were known to have marched into Aizu to assist the struggle in late October, announcing themselves as "Tamura *sōshi*" (political stalwarts of Tamura).[204] Their actions indicate the influence that the various "academies" of the Jiyūtō had upon individuals and the role that the *Mumeikan* could play in the transformation of abstract ideas into concrete action.

But the *Mumeikan*'s existence, like that of the Aizu Jiyūtō, was short-lived. Once the Kitakata Incident occurred in late November 1882, and the wholesale arrests began, both Jiyūtō branches and the various "academies" effectively folded. Although a few party stalwarts continued to fight for the principles of the Jiyūtō by litigation and local organizing, most members merely faded away. Not until the first Diet election in 1890 did any re-emerge, and then, as we shall see in the last chapter, some exchanged the clothes of the popular rights activists for the new suit of the nationalist.

The Jiyūtō and the Kabasan Rebels

Of all the principal characters involved in the three incidents under study, the Kabasan rebels distinguish themselves by placing ideology above organization. They were men of action who believed that acting according to the dictates of their ideals—quickly and without reservation—was more important than building an efficient organization that might implement their ideals. More than any of the other rebels of the *gekka jiken*, they were true revolutionaries, resolutely determined to overthrow the ruling authority of the Meiji state. In many ways their actions, if not their ideas as well, resemble those of nineteenth-century European and Russian populists whose "conceptions of 'obligations' towards the people, and 'sacrificing oneself for the people'"[205] prompted them to attempt suicidal attacks against the Russian state. The Kabasan rebels seemed to have believed with Herzen, "the true founder of Populism," that

---

204. Takahashi, *Fukushima jiken*, pp. 28–29.
205. Franco Venturi, *Roots of Revolution: A History of the Populist and Socialist Movements in Nineteenth-Century Russia*, trans. Francis Haskell, Introduction by Isaiah Berlin (New York, 1960), p.2.

the people suffer much, their life is burdensome, they harbour deep hatreds, and feel passionately that there will soon be a change. . . . They are waiting not for ready-made works but for the revelation of what is secretly stirring in their spirits. They are not waiting for books but for apostles—men who combine faith, will, conviction and energy; men who will never divorce themselves from them; men who do not necessarily spring from them, but who act within them and with them, with a dedicated and steady faith. The man who feels himself to be so near the people that he has been virtually freed by them from the atmosphere of artificial civilization; the man who has achieved the unity and intensity of which we are speaking—he will be able to speak to the people and must do so.[206]

And also like Herzen, as well as Bakunin, Chernyshevsky, Nechaev, and other Western Populists, the Kabasan rebels believed that if they acted faithfully *for* "the people," the people themselves would respond in revolution. They accepted the Bakuninist idea that "it was not the peasant masses who had to be prepared, but the small group of revolutionaries which would light the spark."[207]

In fact, as we saw in Chapter 1, the Kabasan rebels, much like their Western counterparts, did not really go to the people. In part this was due, again as in the case of the Russian populists, to "the need for secrecy," which "had prevented them from establishing even those personal and direct relations with the peasants" that were absolutely necessary in order to gain their support.[208] Conspiracy, intrigue, secrecy, and a self-imposed isolation from the very ones they intended to serve were conditions that the Kabasan rebels chose to endure because they had opted for the "small movement" strategy, but only after considerable debate within their ranks over the merits of the strategies of assassination versus raising a people's army. Not surprisingly, the Russian populists of the late nineteenth century had experienced a similar debate: between the forces of the *Zemlya I Volya* (Land and Liberty), who argued for "going to the people," and the *Narodnaya Volya* (The Will of the People), who favored employing small, conspiratorial groups armed with bombs to assassinate government officials.[209] In both the Russian and Japanese cases, the "assassination faction" emerged as the victor in the debate, but only after the fruitlessness of the methods of their opponents in the "debate" had been demonstrated.

206. Quoted in ibid., pp. 1, 35.   207. Ibid., p. 580.   208. Ibid.
209. Ibid., chaps. 20 and 21; Ienaga, *Kakumei shisō*, pp. 45–46, makes several interesting observations in comparing Japanese radicals with Russian populists; also see Wada, "Narodoniki," pp. 61–73.

What the adoption of the strategy of assassination does to organization has already been indicated in Chapter 1. What happens is that a small, conspiratorial organization comes to be the final outcome of recruitment, a process defined in terms of personalities, tactics, dates of events, chance, and other forces over which the men involved have very little control, rather than in terms of rules, guidelines, and programs—in short, anything that may impart viability to the group. Compared to the organizations of the Fukushima and Chichibu rebels, that of the Kabasan insurrectionists was ad hoc, dictated more by shared beliefs than by rational structures. In this section, we shall examine those "shared beliefs," the ideology of natural right which committed its believers to make revolution in its name.

Throughout much of the planning of the assassination, Koinuma Kuhachirō played the pivotal role in the conspiracy; or as one specialist has phrased it, "Koinuma was the principal axis of the plot from the beginning."[210] It was Koinuma who devised the plan of employing bombs, and who, along with Kōno Hiroshi, did much of the recruiting. But if Koinuma was able to attract members to the group because of his strong commitment to assassinationism, he was also capable of alienating them from the group. Ōhashi Genzaburō was one example. In the early stages of planning, Ōhashi's home had been used as a meeting place, and later as a place to make bombs. But disagreement with Koinuma over the "small movement" issue caused him to break with the rebels shortly before the rebellion. Ōhashi said: "In our talks Koinuma and I could not come to an understanding. He disregarded all that I said. Even though I frequently stated my position to our companions, I was worried since they disagreed with me."[211] Saeki Masakado was another example. He expressed doubts that political reform would necessarily follow once high-ranking officials were assassinated. He argued for more preparation and planning, especially among local residents whom he felt should be included. But "from the first my opinion was not acceptable as workable by the others, especially with regard to planning matters in local areas."[212] Consequently, Saeki quietly disappeared several days before the rebellion.

Koinuma's commitment to assassination was as strong as his commitment to the popular rights movement. His start in the movement may have had something to do with his failure as a businessman. We

210. *KJKS*, p. 772.   211. Ibid., p. 122.   212. Ibid., p. 798.

know that he suffered frequent financial losses during the mid-1870s, when he assisted in the family business of tea refining, milk production, and dyeing.[213] By 1879 or 1880, when he was in his late twenties, Koinuma began to get involved in the popular rights movement. His introduction to the movement probably came from his friends Arai Shōgo and Shioda Okuzō, two of the leading Jiyūtō activists in Shimotsuga district (Tochigi prefecture).[214] These three friends were among the hundred or so popular rights advocates of Tochigi who were originally involved in petitioning for the establishment of a national assembly in 1880.[215] In February of that year, Koinuma, Arai, and Shioda attended a large popular rights conference held in Tsukuba, Ibaraki prefecture, where members of political societies from across the country attended.[216] On 1 October 1882, these same three were among the leaders of the prefecture who established the Tochigi Jiyūtō; its membership eventually was the second highest in the nation (after Akita).[217] With the founding of the party, Koinuma immediately began serving as one of its many "traveling lecturers."[218]

In January 1883, after the Fukushima Incident, and after repeated setbacks in the push for self-government in the Tochigi prefectural assembly (of which Arai and Shioda were members),[219] Koinuma, Arai, Shioda, Fukao Shigeki (later discovered to be a police spy by Yokoyama Nobuyuki),[220] and others held a secret conference in a small inn located in Tochigi to discuss the significance of the Fukushima Incident and how it would affect the expansion of party strength. Several other such meetings were held during the same year, but the details are not known. It is known, however, that around this time Koinuma was becoming disenchanted with the ineffectiveness of peaceful politics. He said then:

> The carrying out of political intrigue by the clique government and its allegiance to a philosophy of conservatism, more than the remnants of feudalism, the authority they hold, and the arbitrary way they utilize the law to obstruct the advancement of popular sentiments, is responsible for the arrest in social

213. Nojima, *Kabasan jiken*, pp. 33–36; also Endō, *Kabasan*, pp. 31–32.
214. Endō, *Kabasan*, pp. 34–35.
215. Nojima, *Kabasan jiken*, pp. 44–45.
216. Ibid.; also *Ibaraki kenshi: shi, machi, mura hen* 1 (Mito, 1972):155.
217. Satō, "Jiyūtō-in meibo," p. 31.
218. Endō, *Kabasan*, p. 28.
219. Akagi Etsuko, "Tochigi ken no jiyū minken undō: chihō jichi no yōsō wo megutte," *Tochigi Shiron* II:1–15.
220. Nojima, *Kabasan jiken*, p. 58; and Endō, *Kabasan*, p. 36.

progress. Also, the citizenry behaves like a puppet, allowing the social order to become petrified. . . .[221]

Once having characterized this political and social malaise, he proffered his solution: "An extraordinary sickness demands an extraordinary remedy."[222]

The "remedy" that Koinuma chose, we of course know. It seems that he regarded the method of treatment as inseparable from the "remedy." He stated during interrogation: "I decided to use bombs for assassination as I recalled my earlier experience and imagined what a suitable device they would be for this purpose."[223] The "experience" to which he referred was the lessons he took in 1877 or 1878 from a certain Fukuda of Fukushima on how to make bombs.[224] Koinuma's story, however, differs from that of his disciple, Yokoyama Nobuyuki. Yokoyama testified:

Q. State the source of the invention.
A. In producing the bombs, there were many hardships we encountered: the the use of detonators, the [difficulty] of scientific books, etc.
Q. Yes, but weren't there other reasons for using bombs?
A. I got some facts from newspapers that told about their use by European and Russian nihilists (*kyomutō*), and felt they were better for assassinating people.[225]

It is strange that Koinuma's and Yokoyama's stories are not the same; since November 1880, Yokoyama had been Koinuma's near-constant companion, when at the age of sixteen he became Koinuma's permanent boarder.[226] An answer can only be conjectured: Although Yokoyama undoubtedly learned about bombs from Koinuma, he was attracted by reports on the nihilists and decided to imitate them.

The methods that Koinuma chose, however, were less important than the end he sought. During his trial he identified the nature of the problem and proposed the necessary solution:

Today's political system displays its oppression of liberty by high taxes and high prices for goods, by the difficulties of the poeple, and by their suffering. My hope is first, to aid the people in accordance with Jiyūtō ideas. My other hope, the highest one, is for like-minded men and myself to communicate and then to summon our energies for revolution or death (*kesshi kakumei*).[227]

221. Quoted in Endō, *Kabasan*, pp. 32–33.   222. Ibid.
223. *KJKS*, p. 103.   224. Ibid.   225. Ibid., p. 21.
226. Endō, *Kabasan*, p. 35.
227. *KJKS*, p. 103.

Like the Russian populists, Koinuma's first hope, then, was "to aid the people," but he realized that in order to do this it was first necessary to ally himself, not with "the people," but with "like-minded men." Nonetheless, he sought "from the beginning," in his own words, "to act on the hope that I might sacrifice myself for the nation."[228] A word of caution: that note of patriotism does not make Koinuma one of the ideological ancestors of the militaristic "Young Officers" of the 1930s, as one might suspect. The fascists of the thirties justified their violent activities by invoking the names of samurai who led the Restoration. Koinuma, however, drew upon an entirely different precedent: in his own words, "the overthrow of the English government that had obstructed the rights of liberty."[229]

No less committed "to aid the people" was the more cerebral Tomimatsu Masayasu, the head of a popular rights academy for Jiyūtō youth and the man to whom the leaderless Kabasan rebels turned in late September after Koinuma had been injured by one of his own bombs. Tomimatsu, unlike Koinuma, was a Jiyūtō leader of national renown and known in his native Ibaraki as "one of the great men of this region" (*sono chihō ni okeru ikkojin no ketsubutsu*). Along with such notables as Itagaki, Ueki Emori, Nakae Chōmin, Kōno Hironaka, Takano Shōzō, Miyabe Noboru, Naitō Roichi, and Ōi Kentarō, he was a signatory to the early *Aikokusha* petitions for a national assembly.[230] Because of his participation in the popular rights movement, and because of a new law proscribing the involvement of teachers and government officials in politics,[231] Tomimatsu lost his job as a primary school teacher in Shimodate around 1880.[232] This experience undoubtedly embittered him even more toward the government. He regarded this law and the loss of his job as an infringement upon the individual's right to establish relations with whatever and whomever he wished (the popular right movement and his friends in it). His feeling for the right of free association was reflected in the short poem he composed upon losing his job:

> If we search for the thing
> that makes a man what he is,
> isn't it one's true friends?[233]

228. Ibid., p. 102.   229. Ibid., p. 107.
230. Ibid., pp. 541–46.
231. Article VII of the *Shūkai jōrei*, made into law in April 1880.
232. Endō, *Kabasan*, pp. 57–58.
233. Quoted in ibid., p. 58.

Having lost his job, he devoted more time to politics. In October 1881, he was present at the establishment of the national Jiyūtō and from then on came to align himself with his good friend and radical Jiyūtō member, Ōi Kentarō. Within the Jiyūtō itself, Tomimatsu was regarded as a radical. A secret Jiyūtō report written in June 1884 (*Jiyūtō no seiryaku oyobi naijō*) about the internal conditions of the party said:

> Within the Liberal Party itself there are, of course, radicals [*kageki kyūshin no mono* (literally, "extreme and violent people")]. They have come to carry out radical activities, independent of the Party. They have come to be called the *Kesshi-ha* ["Revolution or Death Faction"]. There are several factions and they are dispersed among several areas, and take as their leaders Miyabe Noboru, Saitō Isao, and Ōi Kentarō.[234]

Following this there appeared the names of twenty-four individuals listed according to prefecture. Gumma had nine, Ibaraki eight, Chiba four, and several other prefectures one apiece. The report guessed that about 500 party members (between 20 to 25 percent of the total membership)[235] were active in this faction. Tomimatsu was named as one of its Ibaraki leaders and, moreover, according to Endō Shizuo, was one of the two pillars supporting the Ōi Kentarō faction within the *Kesshi-ha*. The other was supposedly Miyabe Noboru, one of the leaders of the Gumma Incident (May 1884).[236] It was perhaps in reference to the failure of the Gumma Incident to effect consequential change by employing the "large movement" strategy, thereby recommending consideration of the "small movement" strategy, that Tomimatsu said: "If the Gumma Incident had not occurred, then ours [the Kabasan Incident] would not have taken place."[237]

Yet, what "membership" in the "Revolution or Death Faction" meant, in the case of Tomimatsu at least, was a commitment to the "large movement" strategy of revolution. As we have seen, his particular scenario for revolution in Japan was somewhat different from the "assassinationism" advocated by most of his fellow Kabasan rebels. Tomimatsu's plan for revolution can be understood by looking at a pact that he, along with Oda Yoshinobu, who was later tied to the Chichibu Incident, and Saigō Kyokudō, a resident of Chichibu, wrote

234. Quoted in full in *KJKS*, pp. 549–51; also in Gotō Yasushi, "Jūshichinen gekka jiken ni tsuite," *Jiyū minkenki* II, ed. Horie Hideichi and Tōyama Shigeki, *Gekka to kaitai* I:246.
235. Satō, "Jiyūtō-in meibo," p. 31.
236. Endō, *Kabasan*, p. 128.
237. Gotō, "Jūshichinen," p. 259.

jointly in Hachiōji (Kanagawa) on 2 August 1884, but dated by them "Year One of the Era of Free Self Rule":

> We join forces to raise an army of revolution in Kantō, covering Kanagawa, Saitama, Tokyo, Gumma, Ibaraki and Tochigi. It will overthrow the oppressive government that makes itself the enemy of freedom, and we will build a new government that is completely free. Under heaven we join forces and make this great alliance that will bring good fortune to our country.[238]

In order to realize this ambitious plan, Tomimatsu understood that the organizing of a rebellion would mean involving the one organization that had the necessary resources and the connections—with the various popular rights organizations of the Kantō area—to allow it to superintend the rebellion and, subsequently, to form a new government. This central organization was, of course, the Jiyūtō headquarters in Tokyo. Accordingly, Tomimatsu dispatched one of his followers to Tokyo to speak to Ōi and Ueki about receiving party aid for this plan. Ōi, however, objected, arguing that the time was not yet ripe for a revolution; only Ueki Emori did not oppose the scheme.[239]

That failure did not stop Tomimatsu from trying on his own to organize a rebellion around the capital. In early August, Tomimatsu sent future Kabasan rebels Kobayashi, Isokawa, and Hirao to meet with some of his contacts in the Hachiōji Poor People's Party (*Komminto*). The goal of the emissaries was to try to persuade the Hachiōji Komminto to join the revolution. Upon returning, they reported to Tomimatsu: "They are unable to understand our reasons for revolution. They are lacking in principles, spirit and will, and they would not discuss the matter seriously."[240] Another attempt by Tomimatsu to recruit potential revolutionaries, this time the copper miners at Ashio, Tochigi prefecture, also met with failure. This series of failures to try to mobilize "the people" probably made Tomimatsu all the more receptive to the Kabasan rebels when they asked him to serve as leader. (See Chapter 1.)

Tomimatsu's commitment to revolution was not limited to attempts to raise armies. He also tried to educate those whom he regarded as

---

238. Quoted in full in Ebukuro Fumio, *Chichibu sōdō* (Chichibu City, 1950), p. 29; Gotō, "Jūshichinen," p. 262; Endō, *Kabasan*, p. 159; also see Oda's testimony concerning the pact, in *CJSR* I:131–32. Arendt's comments on the sense of the new which attended the French Revolution make for a fascinating comparison; see *On Revolution*, pp. 21–22.

239. Emura Eiichi and Nakamura Seisoku, eds., *Kokken to minken no sōkoku*, Vol. 6, *Nihon minshū no rekishi* series (Tokyo, 1974):164–65.

240. Nojima, *Kabasan*, p. 55.

potential revolutionaries. To this purpose, he established an "academy" for young popular rights advocates in his home at Shimodate, probably in August 1884, although it was likely operating informally before that time.[241] The name of the academy was the *Yūikan* ("Academy for Those with Purpose"). It appears that both its name and objectives were modeled after the central party's youth academy, the *Yūikkan* ("Academy of Unity"), as the following quote taken from the official party history indicates:

> The different *Yūikkan* that have been built in several areas seem to have members who are inclined toward the use of arms, stressing bravery among their young members, promoting sword competition, horse races [and so on]. . . . Among these small societies that study the literary and martial arts that are most popular are the *Yūikan* of Shimodate [i.e., Tomimatsu's] and those found in Kōchi prefecture.[242]

Helping Tomimatsu manage the *Yūikan* was fellow Kabasan rebel Tamamatsu; he served both as fencing instructor and as bodyguard to Tomimatsu.[243] They were described by one of their contemporaries in this way: "These two men nurtured political ideas and planned together in order to inspire activity among the young men of the area; they built this research academy that taught the literary and martial arts."[244] One of its members and later Kabasan rebel, Kobayashi, even left the presumably more prestigious central party's *Yūikkan* to study there: "I went for the opening of the *Yūikan* so I could study literary and martial arts. I decided to attend on the advice of [fellow Kabasan rebel] Hotta Komakichi. . . ."[245]

Hotta, however, did just the reverse of Kobayashi and left Ibaraki before the *Yūikan* was opened to become a student of the Tokyo *Yūikkan*. Hotta also tells us (in courtroom testimony) that there were "about thirty-seven or thirty-eight students at the *Yūikkan*."[246] We also know that at least thirteen of the Kabasan rebels met each other for the first time there, and later did much of their planning there as

241. Nojima, *Kabasan*, p. 219, says the founding date was 4 September; Taoka Reiun, another contemporary, says 10 August; see the latter's *Meiji hanshin den* (Tokyo, 1953; originally published in 1909), p. 68.

242. Nojima, *Kabasan*, p. 219; the pronunciation is almost the same. Each is a three-character word having the same first and last characters. But for the Tokyo *Yūikkan* the middle character means "one"; for Tomimatsu's *Yūikan* it means "to do" or "to perform" (see the Glossary).

243. *KJKS*, p. 467.

244. Nojima, *Kabasan*, p. 219.

245. *KJKS*, p. 453.   246. Ibid., p. 467.

well.[247] Kobayashi maintained, in fact, that the very decision to begin the rebellion was made at the Tokyo *Yūikkan*. Also, some of the Kabasan rebels who were living in the *Yūikkan* dormitory took advantage of their residency to purchase and hide bomb materials in their rooms.[248] One of its older students, Hirao Yasokichi, who also rebelled at Mount Kaba, wrote the manifesto which was copied and later distributed to Ibaraki peasants.[249]

It is not surprising that the Tokyo *Yūikkan* served as a hotbed of radical activity. In fact, it had been founded by the Jiyūtō headquarters in the hope that it would help to divert the radical tendencies of the party's more youthful members.[250] It had opened on 10 August 1884, after nearly a year of "concentrating its [the Jiyūtō's] energies on getting financial contributions."[251] Its first director was the old popular rights stalwart Kataoka Kenkichi, and at its opening ceremonies were other such Jiyūtō notables as President Itagaki, Hoshi Tōru, Ueki Emori, Ōi Kentarō, Miyabe Noboru, and Tomimatsu; in all, some 500 party members were in attendance.[252] Like the one in Ibaraki, the Tokyo *Yūikkan* was set up as "an institute for the study of the literary and martial arts."[253] Although it is not known precisely what kinds of subjects were studied, we can guess at what they were by examining some of the ideas of several of its students, albeit its more radical students—the ones who participated in the Kabasan Incident.

As stated earlier, Hotta was one who studied at the Tokyo *Yūikkan*. From the following exchange between him and the prosecutor, we clearly see that his reference to "the cabinet" (he probably meant the Council of State, or *Dajōkan*; the cabinet as such did not come into existence until 1885) indicates an awareness of its oligarchic powers:

Q. What was your purpose for attacking government officials?
A. To establish a political system having true liberties, not encumbered by existing organizations such as the cabinet; the present government interferes and oppresses; it needed to be overthrown.

247. See Kobayashi's testimony, ibid., pp. 455–56.
248. Ibid., p. 23; and Itagaki, *Jiyūtō-shi* III:49.
249. In Yokoyama's testimony, *KJKS*, p. 25, we read: "Q: Who wrote the manifesto? A: Hirao did." Even from contemporary sources—*Tōsui minken shi, Meiji hanshin den, Kabasan jiken* (Nojima), and *Jiyūtō-shi*—we learn little about Hirao. For a comparison of Hirao's manifesto and Ueki Emori's for the Iida Incident, see Endō, *Kabasan*, pp. 204–5. For a list of Hirao's personal effects found on his body, and for a physical description (postmortem), see *KJKS*, pp. 375 and 360.
250. Nojima, *Kabasan*, p. 137.
251. Endō, *Kabasan*, p. 144, quoting from the *Jiyūtō-shi*.
252. Nojima, *Kabasan*, p. 138.
253. Ibid., p. 137.

Q. What methods could you properly use other than brute force?

A.   Our party members have made speeches, pointing out the lack of government reform and its irrational operation, and have discussed the cruel way it treats its citizens. We seventeen [rebels] wanted to reform politics, to base it on free speech and discourse.[254]

The arguments for less concentration of power in the hands of the cabinet and for free speech as a way to reform the political system might very likely have come from a reading of Spencer or Rousseau, and Mill, respectively. Whatever the source, the emphasis is on the need to overthrow the government in order to create conditions which would allow political reform. The same thought is echoed in the words of Kobayashi, the Kabasan rebel who left the Tokyo *Yūikkan* in order to study at the Shimodate *Yūikan*:

I had always hoped for, and thought how to bring about, the prosperity and freedom that would advance the nation. Above all, I thought that the extremism (*kyūshinshugi*) of the radical party (*Kagekitō*) might bring about an atmosphere of liberty; it might reform politics by overthrowing the oppressive government of Japan.[255]

These ideas were not necessarily learned at either academy, for Kobayashi subsequently remarks that "I had held these ideas for several years and had mentioned them more than once to those I visited on my journey throughout our country."[256] As likely as not, his ideas merely received intellectual reinforcement from his studies. An equally important influence on his thinking were those people with whom he discussed these ideas. He names them as fellow Kabasan rebels Kōno Hiroshi, Sugiura, Isokawa, Yamaguchi, and Amano, "people like myself who were of the opinion that their goal should be to reform our wicked society (*ja-aku shakai*) by embracing liberalism (*jiyūshugi*)."[257] His appraisal of his friends was indeed correct. Kōno sought to effect his "greatest hope, revolution, in order to create a decent order."[258] Kotoda's "principal purpose was to use brute force (*wanryoku*) to reform the Meiji government."[259] Isokawa simply wanted to "reform politics."[260] Sugiura's goal was "to assassinate ministers of state in order to bring about the revolution (*kakumei*)."[261] In short, all seemed to agree with Kobayashi's definition of "wicked society": "an oppressive system of politics that crushes the common people."[262] But perhaps most telling with regard to the

254. *KJKS*, p. 468.   255. Ibid., p. 455.   256. Ibid.   257. Ibid., p. 462.
258. Ibid., p. 235.   259. Ibid., p. 42.   260. Ibid., p. 46.
261. Ibid., p. 191.   262. Ibid., p. 455.

humanistic and ideological motivations of the Kabasan rebels was a statement made by Kokugi Shigeo in a letter dated 1 August 1883, sent to Miura Bunji:

> My words seem inadequate to express how unbearable and strong my resentment is. I relentlessly plan reform for our society and commit myself to advancing the liberty and rights of the people whenever I look upon the wretched conditions existing today. My heart is nearly splitting, and you, my friend, I am sure, must feel the same. Our political system only treats unimportant, trivial details, and ignores the basic problems. Perhaps that is a job that you and our friends must take on.[263]

All these personal statements made by the different Kabasan rebels are important for the individual hopes, goals, plans, and frustrations that they express. Yet, very likely the most important statement made by any of the rebels is the one they made collectively, the manifesto written by the *Yūikkan* student Hirao, but signed by all sixteen men who climbed Mount Kaba. It is also important for the statement it makes about the nature of the ideology they shared, the doctrine of natural right. Because of its importance, we quote the entire document:

> Of first importance in creating a nation is to equalize the wealth and rights that heaven has bestowed on each individual, and to make clear the basis of equality. Secondly, the principle behind setting up government is to protect its citizens' happiness and natural liberties [*jimmin tempu no jiyū*]. Having done this, government should enact rigid laws, and should administer them impartially.
>
> Looking closely at the situation in our country, today we see that internally we do not yet have a national assembly, and externally we have not revised the foreign treaties. In order to achieve these objectives we embark on a course of political treason. It appears that our wise and virtuous Emperor is being neglectful, not realizing that this is not the time to make heavy exactions on the people who are walking the road of starvation. As individuals who regard themselves as humanitarians and as patriots, we regret this pitiful situation and cannot endure it. We cannot endure witnessing this breakdown, sitting idly by, and must, therefore, prop up our country as one would do for a large tree. Accordingly, we will assemble an army on Mt. Kaba, Makabe *gun*, Ibaraki *ken*, to fight for revolution, and to overthrow the despotic government that has made itself the enemy of freedom; and then to establish a completely free constitutional form of government.
>
> Fellow countrymen, all thirty-seven million of you, heed the call of our party. We who are here are not for the most part patriots of the *shizoku* type.

263. Quoted in Takahashi, *Fukushima jiken*, pp. 267–68.

Spread the word and announce it to your fellow countrymen. [Dated, 23 September 1884, and signed by sixteen men.] [264]

The philosophical basis of the Kabasan manifesto is straightforward natural right doctrine: All men possess the fundamental rights of liberty, property, and happiness; in some unexplained way, all men have contracted with one another "to protect" these rights by establishing a state; the legitimacy of the state rests upon this "contract"; at present, however, the manifesto maintains, neither the laws enacted by the state, nor the administration of them, are in accordance with the terms of the contract; neither foreign nor domestic policy is responsive to the rights of the citizenry; as "humanitarians and as patriots," the Kabasan rebels feel duty-bound to overthrow the government that has betrayed the trust of the people, and to erect in its stead a constitutional government which manifestly guarantees the natural rights of the people. Finally, in the last paragraph, the rebels make explicit that they are acting not as traditional style samurai who are intent merely to revenge some empty, valueless feudal code of honor, but rather as patriots concerned only for the rights of their fellow citizens.

This final point deserves some elaboration. It will be recalled from Chapter 1 that the recruitment process was guided not by the attempt to enlist "men of high repute," as was the case with, say, the young samurai who assassinated oligarch Ōkubo Toshimichi in 1878.[265] Instead, they sought like-minded men, setting aside the factor of social status. It was a classless affair, a point the government never quite understood, as the following exchange between Miura and his interrogator shows:

Q. Who was the leader?
A. No one.
Q. Was it Tomimatsu?
A. Only nominally; it was a *heimin-shizoku* [affair].[266]

It would be a mistake, nonetheless, to confuse the affair's classless nature with the fact that it was also "leaderless," and to combine the two facts to make the incident even more democratic than it really was. As the following testimony by Hotta indicates, the exigencies of

264. *KJKS*, p. 476.
265. Sidney R. Brown, "Political Assassination in Early Meiji Japan: The Plot Against Ōkubo Toshimichi," in *Meiji Japan's Centennial*, ed. David Wurfel, pp. 18–35.
266. *KJKS*, p. 32.

the situation did not lend themselves to the creation of a structured organization headed by a chosen or elected leader:

Q. Who were the ringleaders (*kyokai*) of the uprising?
A. There were no ringleaders.
Q. How could that have been?
A. We were never quite sure of the exact moment we would rise up, so we had no ringleaders or instigators.
Q. That being the case, then who among you acted as manager (*shukan*)?
A. If you use the term "manager" (*shuji*) in the sense of overseeing our finances, then it was the eldest (*nenchō*), Tomimatsu Masayasu, although he did not ever refer to himself as a manager, even at the *Yūikan*.[267]

To some extent, these remarks may have been made in an effort to save Tomimatsu from the death penalty (if so, it did not work), which is what leadership of the incident almost certainly meant, we can be sure, in the eyes of the rebels at the time of the trials. For we know from Chapter 1 that the rebels headed straight for Tomimatsu's *Yūikan* after the robbery failed and after Koinuma was injured. Tomimatsu's reputation, the name of the *Yūikan*, and its close location to Utsunomiya were all factors that drew the leaderless rebels there, and undoubtedly he gave the group the leadership that it would not have had otherwise. But the issue of leadership, while important, should not obscure the more important point of the classless nature of the incident. For it is this fact that points to the emergence of a new type of radical in Meiji politics: a type of radical who believed that shared ideas (rather than shared class status) were the most important factor in cooperating to bring about a democratic revolution.

And it was indeed revolution, and not mere rebellion, they intended to make. As this was apparently the first instance of attempted revolution during Meiji—after many rebellions that sought only to make the government responsive to certain limited demands—the authorities were anxious to discover whether it was in fact an attempt at revolution. Consider this:

Q. In one instance, you said your aim was "to change" (*henkaku*) the government in the sense of bringing in a new administration. In another you said your goal was "to overthrow" [*tempuku*] the "wicked Japanese government." Which is it?
A. Our goal was to overthrow completely the present government.[268]

267. Ibid., pp. 469–70.   268. Ibid., p. 461.

The term *tempuku* was used too often by other rebels as well to allow us to think that their aim was less than revolution. All seem to have digested enough natural right doctrine to be able to understand and act upon its revolutionary implications. Certain laws were regarded by the rebels as infringing upon, even violating, the basic natural rights of all men: the right to associate with whomever one wishes, as in the case of Tomimatsu; the right to take legal action without fear of arrest, as in the case of Monna; the right to have laws administered impartially; and the right to equal voice in government through a representative assembly, as declared by their manifesto. That all of this was not mere rhetoric was, of course, proven by their subsequent attempt at revolution, which sought to give concrete expression to their abstract ideas of natural right.

If the Kabasan rebels are to be faulted, it cannot be for not acting according to principles. Rather, it must be for what Tōyama Shigeki described in this way: "The mistakes they made during the pre-rebellion process, one could say, were silly."[269] "Naive," "unrealistic," "ill-planned," and "poorly organized" are all appropriate designations, in retrospect, for many of their actions and the rationale underlying them. They made no real or earnest attempt to establish relations with the people in the local area, nor did they take any positive action to mobilize local farmers, as did the leaders of the Fukushima Incident. They were "isolated men," as Endō put it, "caught in their own trap [*jijō-jibaku*], and like the Russian populists, purposely separated themselves from the people."[270] "Although the local people probably understood what the manifesto said, for them it was only an act of dangerous violence."[271] Only Tomimatsu, Monna, and Hirao believed throughout the entire affair that members of their party should endeavor to recruit local residents. But the few attempts that were made ended in failure. In contrast, the others appear not to have thought much beyond the original plan of assassination, which to their way of thinking precluded any thought of recruiting large numbers of people.[272] Instead, they believed blindly that this act itself would serve as an inspiration for "the masses" to rise in rebellion.

269. From his Introduction to *KJKS*, p. 1.
270. Endō's commentary in Appendix of *KJKS*, p. 797.
271. Ibid., p. 798.
272. Endō, *Kabasan*, pp. 104, 138–41. Endō believes that the self-imposed isolation was a function of the rebels' own sense of the lonely life of the "terrorist." Gotō, "Gekka," p. 217, also uses the term "terrorist" to describe the Kabasan rebels. Unfortunately, I believe both are guilty of reading twentieth-century "terrorism" into the nineteenth-century liberal movement.

A representative view of such blind trust was stated during the court interrogation of Yokoyama, Koinuma's right-hand man.

Q. How were the people able to trust in you?
A. They could clearly judge our purity [integrity: *keppaku*] by the manifesto we issued.
Q. What is the gist of the manifesto?
A. That it was necessary to raise an army [*gihei*, or literally "righteous army"], to make the government good, and to obtain and protect the freedom and natural rights of all men.[273]

The Kabasan rebels did indeed resemble the participants of the *Narodnaya Volya*. That movement's principal "theorist," Nechaev, promoted the "propaganda of the deed," which called for "liquidating the worst officials to give constant proof that it is possible to fight the government [and] to strengthen the revolutionary spirit of the people...."[274] Yokoyama's testimony, as we saw, attributed some influence to Russian nihilists and their use of bombs, probably referring to the 1881 assassination of Alexander II. Only the use of bombs was new, however, for assassination as "propaganda of the deed" had a long history in Japanese politics. After reciting a list of a number of high Tokugawa and Meiji government officials and politicians who had met their end by an assassin's sword, W. W. McLaren remarked: "There is something in the taking of the life of a fancied enemy of the country, no matter how highly placed, as a protest against or a criticism of his actions, that appeals to the Japanese mind, and the nation looks upon such conduct with a leniency [not in the case of the Kabasan rebels!] that is only to be explained by the defects of the military despotism under which they lived for centuries."[275]

For the Kabasan rebels, however, assassination was not a tool to be used merely to dramatize a cause. It was also for them a means to effect the type of political change that was dictated by their ideals. It was perhaps another of the ironies of history that the principal institution and instrument promoting much the same cause for which the

---

273. *KJKS*, p. 25.
274. David C. Rappoport, *Assassination and Terrorism* (Toronto, 1971), pp. 47, 49, 52.
275. W. W. McLaren, *A Political History of Japan During the Meiji Era, 1867–1912* (London, 1916), pp. 105–6. Also see Morikawa Tetsurō, *Meiji ansatsu shi* (Tokyo, 1967); and his *Bakumatsu ansatsu shi* (Tokyo, 1967). Also of interest is James Soukup, "Assassination in Japan," in *Assassination and Political Violence*, Vol. 8, Supp. D, ed. James Kirkham, Sheldon Levy, and William J. Crotty, A Staff Report to the National Commission on the Causes and Prevention of Violence (Washington, D.C., 1969), pp. 531–36.

Kabasan rebels fought, the Jiyūtō, was publicly embarrassed by this incident, and by others that had preceded it, and dissolved itself a month later, shortly before the outbreak of violence in Chichibu.

The Kommintō and the Jiyūtō

In both the Fukushima and the Kabasan incidents, many of the participants had a more or less direct relationship with the popular rights movement. The *Sekiyōkan*, *Seidōkan*, and the Aizu Jiyūtō branch, the Fukushima Jiyūtō branch, the *Mumeikan*, the Ibaraki and Tochigi Jiyūtō branches, the *Yūikan* and the *Yūikkan*, and relationships with well-known individuals of the central Jiyūtō had some influence on most of the Fukushima and Kabasan leaders, and even on some of the followers.

In the case of the participants in the Chichibu Incident, no such clear relationship existed.

By the time of the dissolution of the national Jiyūtō, on 29 October 1884, just two days before the Chichibu rebellion began, Saitama prefecture could only boast of a Jiyūtō membership of between 121 and 135 people; Chichibu district itself accounted for thirty of these.[276] And twenty of these thirty did not become members until late in the life of the party, between October 1883 and May 1884.[277] Among those listed in our sample, fourteen were either members, claimed to be members, or were locally regarded by fellow villagers as members, but two of the fourteen came from outside the prefecture. Consequently, on the surface at any rate, the relationship between the Jiyūtō and the Chichibu Incident participants is not a very strong one.

In order to investigate the ideological and organizational basis of the Chichibu Incident, therefore, it will be necessary to see whether a less direct relationship existed between the incident and the Jiyūtō specifically, or the popular rights movement generally. The key to approaching this question, it seems, is the nature of the organization that the Chichibu participants themselves built, the Kommintō. We should see whether this organization was *sui generis*, or whether it modeled itself in some way after the Jiyūtō or some other organization. We ought also to examine whether its members drew upon prin-

---

276. Satō, "Jiyūtō-in meibo," pp. 31–32. The figures 121 and 135 represent respectively the number of members recorded by the Jiyūtō party itself, and the number counted by Satō from the periodic membership lists published by the *Jiyū Shimbun*.
277. Ibid.

ciples espoused by the popular rights movement or whether, for instance, they drew upon the traditional peasant notion of "the right
to subsistence" as a rationale for revolt.[278]

Writers contemporary to the incident seem to have had no difficulty in categorizing the Chichibu revolt, although the categorizations
of each writer differed substantially. The author of the *Tōsui minken
shi* (1907) wrote: "Since the common people were motivated by the
desire to exterminate high interest creditors, and to petition for tax
reduction, it was a peasant uprising."[279] Thus by looking only at the
immediate aims and targets of the rebels, Sekido Kakuzō was able to
say that it differed little from a traditional Tokugawa-type peasant
uprising. Today's principal chronicler of Meiji disturbances, Aoki
Kōji, shares this view of seventy years earlier, modifying it only in
quantitative terms by referring to the incident as a "rebellion" (*hōki*)
because of the large numbers of people who participated.[280] Inoue
Kōji takes exception to this view, however, making what seems to be
an important distinction between the *hyakushō ikki* of Tokugawa
and the Chichibu Incident: "With a simple peasant uprising, at the
sound of gunfire the people scattered and their swords glistened in
flight, but in the case of the Chichibu Incident the farmers displayed
the attitude, 'Stop only upon death' (*taorete nochi yamen*)"; and for
this reason, he says, it was comparable to the famous Satsuma Rebellion (1877).[281]

In the official Jiyūtō party history, the *Jiyūtō-shi*, the incident
and its participants were characterized in this way:

> This group that gathered was composed of discontented farmers, gamblers
> and hunters, and having assembled in force mainly wrecked government
> property, threatened government officers, burnt land deed certificates, pun-
> ished high-interest creditors and landlords, stole and distributed money and
> goods, and generally expressed their discontent in a direct fashion. They took
> the name of *Shakkintō* (Debtors' Party) or *Kosakutō* (Tenants' Party) and in
> fact we probably ought to look upon them as *one vehicle for the extension of
> socialism* [emphasis added].[282]

278. See Rudé, *Crowd*, pp. 22–23, 30, 225, for the European notion of natural justice
used by the peasants, especially one manifestation of it, the "taxation populaire," as an example of peasants claiming the minimum right to subsistence.

279. Written by Sekido Kakuzō, Tokyo, 1903. This passage is quoted in Wagatsuma et
al., comps., *Seiji saiban* (Tokyo, 1969), II:68.

280. Aoki, *Meiji nōmin sōjō*, pp. 73, 83. Referring to the Chichibu Incident, Aoki said:
"It was an economic conflict between debtors and creditors."

281. Inoue, *Chichibu jiken*, pp. 183–84.

282. Itagaki, *Jiyūtō-shi* III:93.

This is interesting to note because even though it mentions, albeit more precisely, the same type of activities that characterized a traditional peasant uprising as outlined by Sekido, the *Jiyūtō-shi* writers arrive at a vastly different conclusion about the fundamental ideological character of the incident. Granted, this characterization may merely reflect an incomplete understanding of socialism at this time, or even a more general fear of socialism,[283] but it does nonetheless point to the existence of some ideological underpinnings to the political party formed by the Chichibu rebels.

That such was the case is further attested by yet another contemporary writer, the Shintō priest and Chichibu resident, Tanaka Senya. He did not see socialism as the driving ideological force of the rebels but rather saw "liberalism" (*jiyūshugi*) at its base. It was he who suggested the term *Jiyū Komminto* ("Liberal-Poor People's Party") to describe the Komminto's ideology in a term which has recently been popularized by the works of Inoue Kōji.[284] But while Tanaka credited the existence of an ideological relationship between the Jiyūtō and Komminto, he also noted that Komminto members had less than a complete understanding of Jiyūtō policy and principles, which in turn led to their failure to accurately reflect the ideas of the Jiyūtō: "The various types of wild language used by the poor people is connected to the Poor People's Party and falsifies the orders of Mr. Itagaki."[285] A clear instance of this can be seen in the testimony of "blind follower" Kobayashi Kenkichi (twenty-four), farmer and *heimin* from Gumma prefecture, arrested for violent activity:

Q. What do you think the ideology (*shugi*) of the Jiyūtō is?
A. Its ideology is to destroy those who control the money market, those banks and those usurers who greedily charge excessive interest; and it is to help the poor people.[286]

This seems to represent a clear instance of translating a political ideology with a goal orientation expressed at the level of the entire society into a justification for action which is oriented toward the

283. There is evidence that this was the case. Consider this short article in the *Japan Weekly Mail*, 7 June 1884: "A socialistic mass meeting was held in Osumi district, Sagami, Kanagawa prefecture on the 27th of last month." It was likely referring to a Komminto meeting.

284. Tanaka Senya, "Chichibu bōdō zatsuroku," 1884, from his diary; reprinted in its entirety in *Chichibu jiken shiryō* (*CJSR*), II:551–85. Also see Inoue, *Chichibu jiken*, pp. 74–79.

285. *CJSR* II:564.

286. Ibid., I:66.

achievement of limited goals at the level of local society. It also points to other things Tanaka said about the Chichibu rebellion. He noted four principal causes of rebellion. The influence of the Jiyūtō was only one; the other three were usury, antisocial gamblers, and an unresponsiveness on the part of the authorities toward the economic deprivations being suffered by the people.[287] Although Tanaka, like the vernacular press at the time, seems to place undue emphasis on the influence of "gamblers" (*bakuto*) in instigating the rebellion—we will examine this aspect later—he does seem to have been correct in the importance he placed on economic privation, and the authorities seeming unresponsiveness to it, as the main sources of the rebellion. This can be seen by examining, first, the demands that were made by the Kommintō and, secondly, the nature of the targets of the Kommintō.

The source of the Kommintō demands is seen most clearly in a poem written just before the rebellion by an unknown Chichibu resident, entitled "Making Tombstones":

> The wind blows,
> The rain falls,
> Young men die.
> The groans of poverty
> Flutter like flags in the wind.
>
> When life makes no sense,
> Even the old people quarrel.
>
> The words on our tombstones,
> Buried in the snowstorms of 1884,
> Are not visible by the authorities.
>
> In these times
> We must cry out loudly.[288]

Privation, despair, and rebelliousness are the themes of this poem, and the eradication of the source of these problems was the purpose behind the demands made by the Kommintō. These demands were: (1) a ten-year debt moratorium on repayment of all loans, and a repayment schedule based on annual installments over a forty-year period; (2) the closure of local schools (and hence no school tax) for three years; (3) consideration by the Home Ministry (*Naimushō*) of

287. Ibid., II:563.
288. Reproduced in Takamoto Gise, "Kommintō jiken," *Rekishi Hyōron*, Special ed. (November–December 1954), p. 57.

a reduction of miscellaneous taxes, and also the land tax; and (4) a reduction of local (village) taxes.[289]

Several things need to be mentioned about these demands. First, all are obviously economic demands, lacking in political content. The only apparent political facet of them is that they were directed at the government. Even the first demand, which sought debt relief from the financial burdens contracted privately between farmers and loan dealers, was directed at the government, as it was the only authority with power enough to resolve the problem. This demand could of course be construed as "traditional," inasmuch as there were instances during feudal times when, because of crop failure, a benevolent domain lord would respond to peasant demands and order all debts of farmers in his region to be canceled.[290] Yet in the Chichibu rebellion the four demands were being made of the government not by a village leader acting as a representative of the feudal community, but *rather by market-oriented individuals chosen from a political party whose membership transcended the village.* It is also important to recall that the political context in which these demands were made was also vastly different from that of even thirty years earlier.

Secondly, the occasion of the rebellion was not the first time the demands were made. In late August, Sakamoto Sōsaku had gone at the behest of other leaders to petition a loan dealer of Ogano for a four-year debt moratorium and a forty-year repayment scheme.[291] In early September, Tashiro Eisuke, Katō Orihei, and Kokashiwa Tsunejirō (Jiyūtō member from Gumma) met and decided: "From now on, no more meetings! We will assume responsibility to unite the poor people and go to and petition the Ōmiya authorities, state the situation, and take whatever court action is necessary."[292] They spoke to various village leaders, gained their support, and on 30 September, along with four others representing twenty-eight villages, they petitioned at the Ōmiya police headquarters, calling for the authorities to take action against usurers. The police chief, however, refused to meet with even one of their party. They tried the next day, this time sending Takagishi Zenkichi to Ogano and Ochiai Toraichi to Ōmiya, but again the authorities refused to see them.[293] At that point, a small peaceful demonstration of 500 to 600 people was organized

---

289. From the court interrogation of Tashiro Eisuke, Kommintō Army Commander; *CJSR* I:101.

290. For example, see Hugh Borton, *Peasant Uprisings*, pp. 99–106, 115–16, 146–54, for three instances of successful protests in this regard.

291. Inoue, *Chichibu jiken*, p. 42.   292. Ibid., pp. 43–45.   293. Ibid., p. 46.

at Ogano for the same purpose as that of the petitioners, but once again the authorities refused to meet with any of their representatives. Moreover, this second petition was even more modest than the first; it called for only a four-year moratorium on debt repayment and a ten-year repayment schedule.[294] Also, simultaneously, individual Kommintō members tried negotiating with individual creditors, but met with little success.

These attempts at using legal and peaceful means to make the authorities respond to their demands are emphasized here in order to show that the rebellion (and the demands made during it) was not spontaneous nor entirely unprovoked.

Nor was there a lack of precedent or motivation for abandoning the law and turning to violence. In early September, while these Chichibu individuals were busy using peaceful tactics, the Kommintō of Hachiōji had assembled 8,000 villagers, attacked the homes of loan dealers and government offices, and succeeded in having their village taxes reduced and in having the terms of loan repayment eased.[295]

These instances underscore Tanaka Senya's contention that one of the reasons for rebellion was the growing unresponsiveness of the authorities. Due in part to the flood of petitions coming since 1880 demanding a national assembly and to the tidal wave of petitions for financial aid since the Matsukata deflation policy began taking its toll, the central government reacted by writing an ordinance requiring the approval of local government officials before a petition would be accepted by the Tokyo government.[296] This action merely shifted responsibility to local governments which, as we have seen, were no more responsive than the central government. However, that did not stop a few "concerned individuals" from beginning a petition drive which sometimes developed into a larger movement. In this sense, the petitions themselves helped serve to recruit members to the poor people's movement.

The final point to be made about the Kommintō demands is the extent to which they had become slogans among the people of Chichibu by the time the rebellion began. On the morning of the first day of rebellion, 1 November 1884, at the Muku shrine in Yoshida village, a scene described in Chapter 1, the "Rebels' Agreement" (*Bōto yaku-*

294. Ibid.

295. Gakushūin Hojinkai Shigakubu, comp., *Chichibu jiken no ikkōsatsu* (Tokyo, 1968), p. 46; also see "Kanagawa jiken," *Nihon Rekishi Daijiten* III:69.

296. *Ikkōsatsu*, p. 45.

jōsho) was announced and all were asked to swear allegiance to the following purposes:

1. We will aid the poor people.

2. If negotiating with a money lender out of court, and he deserts the negotiations, we should take the specific remedy of property smashing and kill him.

3. We will take over the village government offices of the various villages and destroy or take the signed documents found there.

4. If one of our Party is apprehended or arrested during this incident, we will take specific action of rescuing him by attacking and destroying the police station or prison in question.

5. We will make a forcible appeal [*gōso*] to have various taxes and school expenses abolished, all taxes except the national land tax.[297]

Reading this agreement, it is easy to recall the earlier quoted testimony of Kobayashi Kenkichi, who recited the Jiyūtō "ideology" in much the same terms as the agreement. Also, in going through the court testimony of a number of those captured early in the incident, we see such comments as:

The reason [for joining] was to reduce school fees, defer loans, and to stamp out usury.

The reason was to destroy public documents concerned with loans and mortgages.

[The reason was] to besiege creditors and government offices and destroy all public documents concerned with debts.[298]

And so goes the testimony. Here we are not only seeing the Kommintō demands being expressed as reason for participating in violence, i.e., in order to have these demands realized, but we are also seeing what the targets of rebellion were.

What, then, were these targets? A police report dated 6 November 1884 stated:

With a common hatred they unite to coerce the authorities and money dealers, and the young rioters set fire to their buildings, destroying them completely. They also combine to menace rich farmers and in great numbers they plunder the goods and the money of the rich. After finishing there, they attack government offices. . . . They are led in this by gamblers and their spokesmen are members of the Jiyūtō; both these groups have authority.[299]

---

297. Tanaka Senya's papers in *CJSR* II:553. Also reproduced in *Seiji saiban shi* II:75. This latter work claims that Kikuchi Kanbei was the author.

298. *CJSR* II:14–46.   299. Ibid., I:621.

The invective aside, the facts support their report, at least concerning the targets of attack by the rebels. In a comprehensive report entitled "The Condition of the Towns and Villages Where the Rioters Raided,"[300] eighty-four villages and towns are listed as having been attacked. Within all of these towns, private homes were most affected, 556 in all having been damaged or destroyed. Village government offices were second with seven, followed by six police stations and four courthouses. Robbery was the most frequently committed crime—510 homes (497 in Chichibu district, thirteen in Kodama district) had either food, money, or weapons taken from them. At courthouses or police stations, over 500 official documents were either destroyed or damaged by fire—land registers, tax assessments, mortgage papers, house registers, etc. In terms of total property damage, the government estimated it at 43,783 yen. In terms of injuries sustained by the people involved, only sixteen people in all lost their lives (two policemen, fourteen rioters), and only twenty-two were *reported* injured (seven policemen, fifteen rioters). Of course, although all these figures are questionable as to accuracy, they nonetheless indicate how limited was the personal and property damage done, when contrasted to the great numbers of police and rebels involved.

The fact of this relatively minor damage also contrasts with what was reported in the newspapers at the time. Reports of widespread looting, plundering, rape, brutality, and violence in general dominated the newspapers. Even "the killing of women and children for the amusement of the rioters" was reported in a government pamphlet released to all the newspapers in mid-November, entitled *Saitama jiken dempō roku.*[301] The *Chōya Shimbun* referred to villages controlled by The Poor People's Army as "anarchist villages" (*musei no kyō*).[302] When it was reported on 5 November that the Tokyo garrison had been mobilized, the newspapers displayed even greater alarm concerning the extent of the violence.

Once members of the Kommintō were arrested and interrogated and something was learned about the nature of its organization, and once the government figures came out showing how mild the violence had been, government leaders and others expressed surprise.[303] Probably the principal reason for so little violence was (1) the specificity of the targets chosen by the Kommintō, as seen in the "Rebels'

300. Ibid., I:421–24, 446, 458, 487–502, 506–8.
301. Inoue, *Chichibu jiken*, p. 180.
302. Ibid., p. 185.   303. Ibid.

Agreement" (and indicated by the figures just shown); and (2) the strict organization guiding the Komminto.

On the same day that the "Rebels' Agreement" was announced, President Tashiro Eisuke had a subordinate read the Five Articles of the "Army Code":

> I personally will behead any and all persons who:
> 1. commit robbery;
> 2. violate women;
> 3. drink wine;
> 4. rob and burn without permission; or
> 5. violate orders given by leaders.[304]

It is of course impossible to say whether the threat of decapitation served to deter rebels from committing such crimes, especially since it is not known if the occasion ever arose. Regardless, most of the evidence points to a considerable measure of party discipline; certainly, no acts of rape or licentious drinking took place. That the Komminto was so disciplined and that its targets were so specific can be seen in the organizational character of the Komminto army itself, the process of organization and recruitment leading up to its establishment, and in the ideological cohesiveness of its leadership. Now to consider each of these in turn.

From our sample alone (Appendix C), where the "rank" or position of each rebel is listed, we can readily discern the tight manner in which the Komminto army was structured; we find a president (commander), a vice-president, division and vice-division commanders, squad commanders, secretaries, treasurers, supply officers, communication officers, and so on. With this kind of military ordering of the party we might expect a rigid chain of command to have existed that would have made Tashiro, at its apex, a supreme commander whose authority was inviolable. This, however, was not the case. What existed instead was a sharing of authority among a few individual leaders, not all of whom held the highest ranks. (Possibly some were given higher ranks but no real authority in order to induce them to exercise their local prestige to attract greater numbers of recruits.)

We can see how power was shared by relating what happened at a meeting of the principal leaders held at Anoyama on 26 October, five days before the outbreak of violence.[305] In attendance at Ano-

---

304. *CJSR* I:106–7.
305. Related in Inoue, *Chichibu jiken*, pp. 61–64; compare with those meeting on 12 October, at Shimo-yoshida, mentioned in Ide Magoroku, *Chichibu Komminto gunzo* (Tokyo, 1973), p. 21.

yama (see Chapter 1) were: Tashiro, Katō Orihei, Inoue Denzō, Koka-shiwa Tsunejirō (Gumma), Kikuchi Kanbei (Nagano), Ide Tamekichi (Nagano), Shibaoka Kumakichi, Sakamato Sōsaku, Kadodaira Sōhei, Takagishi Zenkichi, and Arai Shūzaburō.[306] Although they decided there to postpone the start of the rebellion to 1 November, before this decision was made Tashiro had proposed that they wait even longer, suggesting at least thirty days. His reasons, undoubtedly revealed at this meeting, come to us from a later police interrogation:

Q. Why did you wish a postponement?
A. Had we gotten a 30-day postponement, in addition to Saitama prefecture we could also have organized a simultaneous rebellion among the people in Gumma, Nagano, Kanagawa and Yamanashi prefectures. This would have created a situation where a forceful petition to the government to reduce taxes would have been accepted due to the violence. . . . Also the army we would have mobilized could have withstood an assault by the police and army. . . . Finally, this [extra mobilization] was necessary due to the proximity of our region to Tokyo.[307]

Tashiro, however, received support for his proposal only from Inoue Denzō. Whether a formal vote was taken or whether the numerical strength of each side was only intimated during discussion, it is not known. Regardless, those who favored commencing the rebellion immediately predominated.

It is claimed that Inoue's support of Tashiro's postponement argument stemmed from his visit to Ōi Kentarō in Tokyo on 20 September. Inoue told Ōi of the Komminto intention to rebel in late October, and Ōi supposedly expressed his strong disapproval, arguing, as he did with the Kabasan rebels, that it was a "rash undertaking" and that the time had not yet come for a Kantō-wide rebellion, especially since it appeared that the Komminto had not prepared sufficiently.[308] To ensure that his views would be well represented in Komminto councils, on 23 October he sent to Chichibu his own envoy, Ujiie Naokuni, in order to persuade the Komminto to abandon their plans for rebellion. Ujiie, however, as Ōi later testified, found himself in sympathy with the rebels and joined them.[309]

According to testimony later given by Kokashiwa, it was Katō Ori-hei, Vice-President of the Komminto army, who was the principal

306. Ebukuro, Sōdō, pp. 68–69.
307. CJSR I:102–3.
308. Inoue, Chichibu jiken, pp. 67–68.
309. Ibid., p. 68; also see Hirano, Ōi, pp. 114–15.

advocate of the "rebellion now" argument.[310] Reminiscent of the Kabasan rebels, Katō and the others of this "faction" (mentioned above) apparently assumed that once the Chichibu farmers rose in rebellion, those activists in surrounding areas would do the same. The logic of this dominant group was: "If the poor people of Saitama are planning [rebellion] independently, then so must those of the other prefectures as well."[311] Although this may have been faulty reasoning on their part, Tashiro was finally convinced by it. To the question put to him by the prosecutor, "Why did you limit yourself to the Chichibu region?" Tashiro replied:

> My Gumma friends, Kokashiwa Tsunejirō and Horiguchi Kōsuke, had been active there for three years, and Shimaki Tairokichi of Kanagawa prefecture whom we may regard as a person of Chichibu [was active there]. Katō Orihei, acting as a gambler, also mingled among the people there.[312]

Based, therefore, on the reports of his fellow rebels who had been canvasing in nearby regions, Tashiro allowed himself to believe in the possibility of adjoining regions rising in rebellion once the Chichibu rebellion began. Whether or not it was this self-deception that finally caused him to abandon the plan for a Kantō-wide rebellion and opt for the "rebellion now" argument is not known. Inoue Kōji does conjecture, however, that what may have convinced Tashiro ultimately was the sense of indomitability he felt upon seeing the large crowd of 3,000 that first day.[313]

In either case, the point is that despite the military structure of the Komminto army, decision-making power was not monopolized by its leader Tashiro. The second most important decision of all—when to rebel—was made collectively. The most important decision—whether to rebel—had already been made by most of these very same individuals on 13 October.[314] (See Chapter 1.)

In this regard, although Tashiro was first among equals in determining who would fill which positions in the party-army, the authority to do this was conferred upon him by these other leaders.[315] In fact, before he even began assigning duties, he first conferred with Inoue, Katō, Sakamoto, and Takagishi. Based on these talks, he said, "We will gather our comrades together and select people for roles and in-

310. Inoue, *Chichibu jiken*, p. 68.   311. Ibid., p. 69.
312. *CJSR* I:117.
313. Inoue, *Chichibu jiken*, p. 70.
314. See note 305, above.
315. *CJSR* I:103.

struct them on their duties."[316] He did that with the advice of the above-mentioned members on the eve of the revolt. "Thus, in this way," he said, "we together assigned roles and our course of action advanced."[317] Also, special authority was entrusted to battalion chiefs (*daitaichō*) Iizuka Morizō of Shimo-yoshida village and Arai Shūzaburō (Obusuma district), as well as to Kikuchi Kanbei. "We decided that this arrangement would last from October 31 to about noon on November 8. I tell you, during the process of deciding roles, there was no quarrelling."[318]

Tashiro's interrogator, probably reflecting widespread official surprise at this high degree of organization, questioned Tashiro repeatedly about the violent activities of Komminto members, whom the interrogator believed had contravened the oath they took on the first day of the rebellion.[319] During this questioning, Tashiro readily admitted that men under his command set fire to the houses of usurers, destroyed police stations, and extorted money, but insisted nonetheless, "We decided from the first that we would limit and restrict destruction to government places, police stations, and so on; *our intention was not only to destroy*" [emphasis added].[320] In speaking of burning the home of one usurer who had accumulated 50,000 yen "in ten years of cheating the poor," Tashiro said, "*We put our lives on the line in order to aid these poor people*" [emphasis added].[321] As Shibaoka, battalion commander and *kobun* to Tashiro, phrased it, "Extreme steps had to be taken to aid the poor people. The rich people aren't dying; it is the poor people in Chichibu who are starving to death."[322]

Neither did they confine themselves to destroying the homes of the rich; they also extorted money. Ide Tamekichi, collector of funds for the Komminto, was delegated the responsibility to visit the wealthy during the rebellion and convince them "to give money as a condolence gift [*kōden*] in order to redeem themselves, acquire the proper attitude, and attain innocence by providing for military expenses as a non-military way to aid the poor."[323] In this manner, almost 3,000 yen were collected, Tashiro informed the interrogators, adding that

---

316. Ibid.   317. Ibid.
318. Ibid., pp. 104–5. Ebukuro, *Sōdō*, p. 71, mistakenly claims that all ranks were assigned by Tashiro, Inoue, and Katō together.
319. For the entire (lengthy) exchange between Tashiro and his interrogator, see *CJSR* I:106–8.
320. Ibid., p. 107, emphasis added.   321. Ibid., pp. 109–10.
322. *CJSR* I:56.   323. Ibid., I:111.

for every "donation" a receipt was given.[324] (The Kabasan rebels had done the same for most of the money, food, and weapons they had appropriated.)[325]

Thus having structured itself along military lines, having established a pattern of decision-making among the leadership, and having found rather unconventional means of financing itself, the Komminto showed all the characteristics of an ongoing organization save one, that of recruitment. How did the Komminto go about getting new members? What means were employed in mobilizing the 3,000 people who assembled at Shimo-yoshida on 1 November 1884, and the other 7,000 or so who joined once the rebellion began?

About the 7,000, the authorities were probably correct in describing them as "blind followers" (*fuwa zuikōsha*), although little about them is really known. Most were probably not unlike young Kobayashi of Gumma, quoted earlier, who gave us the rather pedestrian view of what the Jiyūtō meant. He was also one of the many whom the authorities claimed were "coerced" into participating in the rebellion.[326] Paraphrased, the story he later gave the police went this way:

> I left home on October 31 to go to Saku district in Nagano to collect stones and charcoal with my brother. The first night we stayed at an inn in Minami-Kanra district (Gumma) and left the next morning early, and by night reached the Chichibu border, where we stopped for a drink. At about 10 P.M., "400 Jiyūtō people" arrived at this inn. We were asked to join the party and were told that if we did so, our financial troubles would soon end. They were all armed with guns, or knives, or bamboo spears. We decided to join.[327]

He went on to relate how during the next few days he was assigned the task (along with 100 others) of transporting ammunition to various army squads. He was then asked:

Q. While on the march did other people join the Jiyūtō?
A. Laborers (*ninsoku*) who were then working joined, but they did not know what they joined.[328]

We also see examples of traveling salesmen caught in the rebellion;[329] friends of friends who heard of a "gathering";[330] people whose relatives were ill and needed money for medicine;[331] people merely

---

324. Ibid.; also see Eric J. Hobsbawm, *Bandits* (London, 1969), p. 96, for a discussion of the same practice as it was carried out by the "expropriator" type of European bandit.
325. *KJKS*, pp. 138–41.
326. *CJSR* II:270–71; I:492.
327. *CJSR* I:65–66.   328. *CJSR* I:67.   329. *CJSR* II:14.
330. *CJSR* II:5.   331. *CJSR* II:11.

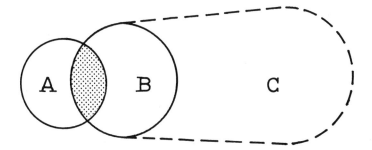

Figure 1.   Schema of Kommintō Organizational Structure
Source: Inoue Kōji, *Chichibu jiken: Jiyū minkenki no nōmin bōki*
(Tokyo, 1968), p. 84.

caught looting a place that the rebels had already attacked;[332] and so on. It was probably people similar to these who were among the group known as "blind followers." Whether, like our first example, they were "coerced" into joining is questionable. No doubt many claimed that they were coerced, once it was learned that the authorities would not prosecute in such instances.[333] This fact probably explains why such a large number, 3,238, surrendered themselves to the authorities. Moreover, "coercion" to participate should also be understood in the sense that Inoue interprets it: "It was a function of the strength of the cooperative relations of the village." He does concede, however, that there were instances where a demand for labor (*ninsoku saisoku*) resulted in *karidashi* ("those rounded-up") or the conscription of laborers by village organizers.[334]

To some extent this was also probably the case for a fair portion of the 3,000 original participants as well, although with this number "the strength of cooperative relations of the village" probably played a much larger role than did *karidashi*. Inoue provides us with a schema showing how this large number of people fit into Kommintō organization.[335] *C* represents the 3,000 people mobilized by the Kommintō; *B* represents the 100 to 130 people who were local organizers of the Kommintō; and *A* represents the thirty Jiyūtō members of Chichibu district. The grey area shows that about half of the thirty were Jiyūtō/Kommintō members, i.e., the fourteen individuals from our sample (mentioned at the outset of this section) who were either officially listed as members (e.g., Iizuka and Ochiai), claimed to be

332. *CJSR* II:6.
333. Inoue, *Chichibu jiken*, p. 194.   334. Ibid., p. 86.   335. Ibid., p. 84.

members (e.g., Tashiro and Katō), or were regarded locally as members (e.g., Ōno Naekichi and Arai Monzō). Inasmuch as those in *C* were the objects of mobilization for those included in *B*, we may treat them simultaneously. (Those in *B* may be considered the 127 people identified in Chapter 3 as "ringleaders and instigators"—for whom data was presented concerning age, residence, and occupation.)[336]

In many cases, the ties between those in *B* and *C* that bound them together during the rebellion were the cooperative ties of the village. Individual villages tended to be characterized by a population most of whom engaged in the same type of agricultural production, e.g., silk, mulberry, lacquer, etc. This required cooperation among the farmers in the harvesting and marketing of the same item. Village meetings became agricultural society meetings. The person or persons who dominated such meetings, the "men of renown," were usually the ones who were economically better off than the rest. At the time of the rebellion, however, many such individuals found themselves in as much financial difficulty as the rest of the village population. In such cases, they often served as local organizers for the Kommintō.

Consider the case of Arai Shigejirō of Isama village (which, as seen in Chapter 3, was ranked among the highest for contributing participants). He served as a "provisions officer" in the Kommintō.[337] He specialized in producing lacquer and cocoons, and, according to an 1873 survey, he owned .68 *chō* of dry land, enough to make him a middle-income farmer. In an 1884 survey he was classified as *shiryoku nashi*, or "without means." In late August, as "a new debtor," he began helping to organize the Kommintō and was known to have been in contact with Tashiro. A contemporary, Tanaka Senya, characterized him in this way: "There are many [Kommintō members] in Isama village. The lacquer tree farmer, Shigejirō, neglected his family business, trained his wife and daughter to use a sword, and frequently stopped farming upon hearing reports of freedom [movements]."[338] He had also recruited thirty households in Isama village for the Kommintō. By the time of the rebellion, he and four other Isama organizers (including Katō Orihei) led more than 180 people to the fight.

Ōno Naekichi, a heavily indebted farmer from Fuppu village and Vice-Commander of the First Battalion, is another example.[339] Like

---

336. Inoue uses the same figure; ibid.   337. Ibid., p. 85.
338. Reproduced in ibid., p. 86.   339. Ide, *Kommintō*, pp. 65–78.

Arai Shigejirō, he was known locally as a Jiyūtō member and had in the past served village members as a spokesman in meetings with creditors. Using three or four young men, he extended his recruitment drive outside his own village, even into Nagano prefecture; and by the time fighting commenced, he led 140 people in what he called the *Fuppu-gumi*, or "Fuppu organ." He is also known to have come under the political wing of Arai Shūzaburō, a former primary school teacher and "radical activist"[340] from Obusuma district. It is significant to note that Ōno has been credited with *lèse majesté*, the only known instance of this in all three of our studies: "Since we fight the Imperial Court itself, we will need reinforcements."[341] No mention is made whether reinforcements ever arrived, but it is known that Ōno's very tight-knit following remained that way until the very end of the rebellion.

Another means used by local Kommintō members to enlist support was to "induct" villagers into the Jiyūtō. One known instance of this method being used occurred just prior to the rebellion, between 27 and 30 October. On those days, Jiyūtō-Kommintō member Ōno Fukujirō, a 33-year-old farmer of Fuppu village, traveled to a dozen different nearby villages, called upon local leaders and indebted farmers, explained that a Jiyūtō-sponsored rebellion was about to take place, and invited them to join the party. Forty-nine farmers, according to Ōno's records, which were introduced as evidence during his trial, took the Jiyūtō oath, which was in fact the "Rebels' Agreement." Ōno in turn provided them with a membership certificate. It should be pointed out, however, that this action did not make them Jiyūtō members, nor were their names registered on any real party list. Although Ōno himself was in fact a member of the party, his sponsorship was insufficient, because for formal induction at least two party members must give their support. Ōno claimed at his trial that fellow member Inoue Denzō was co-sponsor in all cases, but Inoue's name does not appear on any of the membership cards which Ōno distributed.[342] It might also be recalled that at the very time that Ōno was inducting members, the Jiyūtō was in the process of dissolving itself

340. Inoue, *Chichibu jiken*, p. 82; also see Hirano, *Ōi*, p. 110, where he refers to Arai as one of the local "intelligentsia" (*interi*), along with seven other school teachers, two Shintō priests, and two school administrators, all of whom were members of the Kommintō.

341. Quoted in Tanaka Senya's diary; *CJSR* II:570.

342. *CJSR* II:123–39; and for Ōno's testimony, II:149–56. Neither does this seem to be an isolated case. Fukushima Keizō, a scribe in Sakamoto village, testified that he was similarly recruited by Arai Shūzaburō and several others. See *CJSR* II:92–6.

in Osaka. Nonetheless, it seems fair to assume that the reality of the position of the new inductees did not interfere with the illusion of membership. When one of Ōno's inductees was asked during interrogation, "For what reason did you respond to the instigation of Ōno Fukujirō . . . ?" the farmer answered, "To attend a Jiyūtō gathering at Hinozawa village in Chichibu district."[343]

Ōno's method of recruitment, based as it was on the Party's appeal and "platform," may or may not have been common practice. More likely, however, were the village and family relationships as well as the personal appeal and reputation of a particular leader. But whatever the case, there is little doubt that recruiters concentrated their efforts primarily at the village level, that as a result the basic organizational unit of the Kommintō was the village, and that in many cases the most completely mobilized villages were the same ones that produced the better-known Kommintō leaders. The best evidence for this is found in a comparison between those villages shown as contributing more than fifty "direct" participants (Table 6) and those villages from which the Kommintō leaders appearing in our sample came. Kami-hinozawa, for instance, the village organized by Muratake Shigeichi and Morikawa Sakuzō, contributed 52 percent of its population to the rebellion. Shimo-hinozawa, led by Iizuka Morizō, Arai Monzō and Kadodaira Sōhei, mobilized 36 percent of its population. The correlation between these high rates of mobilization and Kommintō organizers is not a spurious one. Other examples where this correlation holds include Inuki Jūsaku and Iida village; Imai Kōzaburō and San-yama village; and Miyakawa Tsumori and Inoue Denzō and Shimo-yoshida village. Of course, in themselves these correlations are not all that remarkable; in those times the interpersonal relationships of the village served as the principal means to tie followers to leaders. What is remarkable, and quite extraordinary, is that not only were the leaders outside the village authority structure for the most part, but that their authority seemed to have been derived from their serving as representatives of the Kommintō.

At this level of organization, i.e., the mobilizing of those in group C by those in group B, using the schema earlier borrowed from Inoue, the unifying ideological basis appears to have been expressed in terms of the four Kommintō demands quoted earlier. Relief from taxes and usurious loan rates was probably what ultimately convinced most

---

343. From the testimony of Motano Zaejirō; *CJSR* II:10. He is placed forty-seventh in Ōno's list of inductees.

people to organize in the one instance, and to be mobilized in the other. But superimposed upon this basically economic bond was one which originated with the group labeled *A* in Inoue's scheme, i.e., the "Jiyū-Kommintō" members, as Tanaka Senya called them. Most of these fourteen individuals were tied to one another since August, when they initiated the formation of the Kommintō. And although different kinds of relationships existed between different "Jiyū-Kommintō" individuals and their local Kommintō organizers, the relationship between these fourteen was essentially political, and specifically was based upon the common tie each had with the Jiyūtō. Recognizing this fact, and given the nature of the organizational relationship between Kommintō organizers and the villagers, we would expect a certain amount of Jiyūtō ideology to have filtered down directly to the Kommintō members, and indirectly to some of the 3,000 or so villagers.

Among the so-called Jiyū-Kommintō, those from Chichibu definitely listed in the Jiyūtō party membership list were Inoue Denzō, Iizuka Morizō, Ochiai Toraichi, Takagishi Zenkichi, Ogiwara Kanjirō, Kadodaira Sōhei, Ōno Fukujirō, and Sakamoto Sōsaku; from Nagano, Ide Tamekichi; and from Gumma, Kokashiwa Tsunejirō.[344] Although not usually credited with Jiyūtō membership, even though he claimed it, Kikuchi Kanbei's name appears in a 9 October 1884 listing of Nagano prefecture members.[345] All but a few of these eleven individuals appear to have been very active members as well. Takagishi was one of eight Saitama representatives at a Jiyūtō meeting in Tokyo in March 1884, also attended by Kabasan leader Tomimatsu Masayasu of Ibaraki and by Fukushima Incident participant from Gumma, Iga Wanato.[346] It is also known that Takagishi, along with Ochiai, Sakamoto, Inoue Zensaku (not a Jiyūtō member, but among our sample), and Arai Sadakichi (also in the sample), signed a "blood pact" in February 1883 that called for a national assembly, a decrease in taxes, and reform of the government.[347] Ochiai, Takagishi, and Sakamoto were, moreover, the initiators and original organizers of the Chichibu Kommintō in August 1884.[348] Ochiai re-emerged a year later, when he was arrested along with Ōi Kentarō in the abortive Osaka Incident.[349] He was also among those who joined the Party after Ōi lectured in

---

344. See sample, Appendix C.
345. This list is reproduced in Uehara Kuniichi, *Saku jiyū minken undō shi* (Tokyo, 1973), pp. 273–77.
346. Ide, *Kommintō*, p. 43.   347. *CJSR* II:612–13.
348. Inoue, *Chichibu jiken*, p. 38.   349. Hirano, *Ōi*, p. 112.

Chichibu in February 1884. After Ōi's tour, Jiyūtō membership in Chichibu rose from eight to fifteen in March, to twenty-six in early May, and to twenty-eight in late May. Besides Ochiai, two of the new March inductees were Takagishi and Sakamoto.[350]

Moreover, Inoue Denzō, as we have already seen, was in communication with Ōi in October 1884, and supposedly had spent some time at the Tokyo Jiyūtō headquarters in December 1883 with Iga Wanato, Kōno Hiroshi, and Murakami Taiji. Murakami, it is interesting to observe, was a Chichibu resident but a member of the radical Jiyūtō political society, the *Yūshinsha* of Takasaki in Gumma. It was headed by Miyabe Noboru, who was connected with the Kabasan conspirators and earlier had been arrested for allegedly taking part in the Gumma Incident of May 1884.[351]

An early twentieth-century historian writing on the Chichibu Incident claimed that Murakami was the important connecting link that tied the Tokyo and Chichibu Jiyūtō to the Gumma *Yūshinsha*.[352] Not only did Murakami apparently serve as a messenger between Takasaki, Tokyo, and Chichibu, but he is also credited (by Tashiro) with having recruited Tashiro into the Jiyūtō. Tashiro's interrogation went as follows:

Q. Are you affiliated with a political party?

A. In late January or early February of this year (1884), I joined the Jiyūtō. [Questioning the truth of Tashiro's answer, the interrogator asked:]

Q. Did you formally join the Jiyūtō at that time?

A. ... Murakami Taiji, who belonged to the Jiyūtō of our region, and who served as an intermediary between the Tokyo headquarters and our region, invited me to join the Jiyūtō in a conversation we had. I questioned him on its ideology (*shugi*). ... He answered by reciting twice in a loud voice, two poems.

Q. Do you remember these poems?

A. One I've forgotten. I can recall one or two lines of the other.

Q. State them.

A. One was, "Cut up wicked people, purify the public party; people who fish must seek them in valley rivers."

Q. Do you remember the other one now?

A. Now I recall very little. Something like, "Look upon your wife and children and do for civic affairs what a husband [does for his family]...."

Q. What then?

A. I continued thinking about what these poems meant.[353]

350. *Ikkōsatsu*, p. 44.   351. Ebukuro, *Sōdō*, p. 34.
352. Ibid., pp. 34–35.   353. *CJSR* I:114–15.

The questions and answers continued in this manner without Tashiro ever saying directly, or the interrogator ever believing, that he became a member of the Jiyūtō.

He was also asked about his relation to Inoue Denzō, Iizuka, Katō, and Takagishi, and whether they "were friends before the rebellion." Tashiro replied, "No, we only became friends in the course of the recent uprising."[354] He further identified them all as Jiyūtō members.[355]

Subsequently, Tashiro was asked a question to which the answer explains an important aspect of the relationship between the Jiyū-Kommintō members and Kommintō organizers.

> Q. Inoue and Murakami were both important people within the Jiyūtō, but you were made President over both of them. [Why] ?
> A. I will guess why this was so. By nature I like to help the weak and crush the strong. During these times when poor people suffer and many are affected, I have served as a middleman (nakama) in their difficulties and have served as a mediator for 18 years. The number of people I call kobun exceeds two hundred. I guess I was made president because I have demonstrated a belief in the necessity to aid the poor, as seen in my commitment to the four demands as outlined by Inoue Denzō [cited earlier].[356]

This "Robin Hood" attitude was formally recognized by the Court when it sentenced Tashiro to death on 19 February 1885, identifying him as "known in the rural party as a kyōkaku ['chivalrous man' or 'Robin Hood']."[357]

But besides this aspect of social concern shown by Tashiro towards the poor, there is the important point he made about his kobun. As we just saw, Tashiro claimed some 200 kobun to his credit as an oyabun-kyōkaku. Most were probably farmers who asked Tashiro, known locally as a "lawyer" (daigennin), to intercede on their behalf as a spokesman to creditors. In fact, when asked about occupation, Tashiro identified himself as a chūsaisha, one "who mediates for farmers in cases of lending, borrowing and other matters."[358]

Among those in the Chichibu sample, at least four were known to be kobun of Tashiro: Shibaoka, Ide, Horiguchi, and Ogiwara. From the court testimony of these four, it appears that this oyabun-kobun relationship was at least partly responsible for their involvement in the rebellion. The clearest evidence of this relationship is the case of

354. Ibid., I:115–16.   355. Ibid.   356. Ibid.
357. Ibid., I:362; also quoted in Ebukuro, Sōdō, p. 205. Also see s.v. "Kyōkaku," in the Nihon Rekishi Daijiten 3 (Tokyo, 1968):508–9.
358. CJSR I:100.

Shibaoka, the only other person in the sample, besides Tashiro, who was a resident of Ōmiya. In explaining how he became involved, he makes it clear that his personal relationship with Tashiro was among the principal factors:

> Q. Are you in debt?
> A. I took out a loan in August 1878, from Zawayama Yūno of about 24 or 25 yen.
> Q. And therefore you became a ringleader in this violence?
> A. It is not true that I hoped to have my debt canceled by joining the violence. . . . The poor people suffer high interest loans demanded by usurers. This makes them poorer; that, and the drop in prices of various goods. I decided that I would like to see those deplorable conditions ended and decided to devote all my energy, even my life, to aid the poor people. *My hopes rose gradually after talking with Tashiro* and I gradually became a ringleader of the rioters in this spirit. . . . It was not for my own gain that I joined the Komminto.
> Q. Tell us about the deliberations that led to your joining the Komminto.
> A. Around September 2 [1884], I spoke with Tashiro Eisuke. . . .
> Q. Was there a compact [*keiyaku*] that tied you [to the party]?
> A. No, . . . it was due to a debt of obligation [*ongi*] I owed to Tashiro [emphasis added].[359]

Ide's relationship to Tashiro, as well as Horiguchi's and Ogiwara's, was not clearly spelled out during interrogation. Although Ide characterized himself as "a simple follower of Tashiro Eisuke,"[360] his involvement in the rebellion did not stem from this alone. A Jiyūtō member since October 1882, he was an activist who, along with Kikuchi, went to Chichibu in late October in order to present a petition to shorten the waiting period for the convening of the National Assembly.[361] As Kikuchi stated their purpose:

> It should be obvious that the present-day government has rejected all virtue. It promises a national assembly by 1890. But now it is November 1, 1884. Today we will overthrow the present government by starting a rebellion that will spread throughout the entire nation. This will then become the revolution [*kakumei*] that will convene the national assembly.[362]

Ide was a serious revolutionary. In passing sentence on him, the court listed as one of his crimes the signifying of an Ōmiya government building occupied by the rebels as the "Headquarters of the Revolution" (*kakumei honbu*).[363] Ide, moreover, was not employing

---

359. *CJSR* II:55–56, emphasis added.   360. *CJSR* I:120.   361. *CJSR* II:214.
362. Quoted in *Ikkōsatsu*, p. 56.   363. *CJSR* II:215; Ide, *Komminto*, p. 119.

mere rhetoric, for in his capacity as the principal intellectual involved in the rebellion, he had considerable knowledge of notions like revolution. In the summer of 1970, one of his descendents discovered a number of Ide's books in an old family storehouse. Among them were Volumes 2 through 4 of *A History of the French Revolution* (*Fukkoku kakumeishi*); Herbert Spencer's *Social Statics*; a number of volumes on French laws, constitution, and contracts; Mosse's *Lectures on Self-Government* (*Jiji sei kōgi*); and so on.[364] That he read these is suggested by the fact that he was known to have spoken to lecture societies in Saku (a district in Nagano), where, among other things, he preached the need for self-government.[365]

When Ide and Kikuchi first arrived in Chichibu, they stayed at the home of another locally well-known *oyabun*, Katō Orihei.[366] Like Tashiro, Katō claimed Jiyūtō membership and a large *kobun* following of thirty or forty people, acquired mainly due to his renowned generosity as a "good pawnshop owner" (*shichiya ryōsuke*).[367] Among his *kobun* were Ochiai, Takagishi Zenkichi, and Sakamoto Sōsaku (the three initiators of the Kommintō, and all Jiyūtō members). The court's prosecutor characterized Katō as the "person of the strongest character among the leaders of the rioters."[368] He was also known to have served as a petitioner for fellow villagers plagued by unpaid loans and high interest creditors.[369]

Katō and Tashiro were also the ones to whom the press and the authorities referred when they spoke of the Chichibu rebels being led by "gamblers." Tashiro had, in fact, been arrested and fined on charges of gambling in mid-1884. But not only was this his only prior arrest; it should further be noted that gambling was not outlawed by the Meiji government until January of that same year.[370] Since mid-Tokugawa, gambling had flourished in rural areas, particularly in market towns like Ōmiya, where crops were sold for cash.[371] It was not unusual for successful gamblers to act as local *kyōkaku*, "god-

364. Ide, *Kommintō*, pp. 121–22.

365. Ibid., p. 127.

366. For example, see the testimony of Kido Isao, *CJSR*, II:15.

367. Inoue, *Chichibu jiken*, p. 37. Katō was even said to have renounced a debt of 150 yen. Kido, a Katō *kobun*, revealed much about his *oyakata*'s sterling personality during his interrogation. See *CJSR* II:15.

368. Inoue, *Chichibu jiken*, p. 37.

369. *CJSR* I:46 and 359.

370. Inoue, *Chichibu jiken*, p. 92. In his treatment of the Gumma Incident, Fukuda discusses the long history of gambling in sericulture regions, and stresses that the press was quick to label Gumma rebels as "gamblers" and to ignore the participation of local farmers. See his *Sanmin sōjō roku*, pp. 16–18.

371. *Nihon Rekishi Daijiten* III:509.

father-style," in order to build up a following large enough to make authorities think twice before interfering with their activities.[372] But the close association of these two roles of *kyōkaku* and "gambler" is not in itself reason enough to regard Tashiro as a mere gambler. He was also a "lawyer," a farmer, and one who did good deeds for those in his community. The same applied to Katō as well. As Inoue Kōji has said: "Katō was an *oyabun*, but this relationship of patronage did not necessarily mean that it was expressed through [relations between people frequenting] gambling halls. It was rather built upon the human relationships existing in the mountain villages."[373] But in any case, in those financially troubled times, it seems quite probable that good numbers of farmers sought to supplement their regular income by gambling (to which development the anti-gambling ordinance was probably a response).

Having seen the relationships among the Jiyū-Kommintō members were based on both shared (Jiyūtō) ideology and *oyabun-kobun* relations, we must now ask how these relations worked in organizing strictly Komminto members (having already seen how these Komminto members mobilized their own villagers), and we must also inquire whether the ideas of those at the top filtered down among organizers and followers.

We have already seen in Chapter 1 how the Komminto began, i.e., how on 10 August 1884, about a dozen men at the Ogano market happened to get into a discussion about how bad the times were, and decided then to meet two days later at Anoyama mountain to discuss whether they could do anything about it; how they decided to begin a petition campaign against creditors; and how the police continually broke up their meetings. The petition campaign was spearheaded by Jiyū-Komminto members and was apparently the original and central vehicle by which the 130 or so Komminto members organized themselves. They in turn organized the members of the villages from which they came. Some, such as Tashiro, were responsible for a number of villages. Tashiro spent ten days in mid-October traveling between eight villages for which he claimed mobilization responsibility. Undoubtedly, Tashiro relied on his *kobun* of these villages to assist his efforts.[374] But besides this type of personal relationship, there are also strong indications that the organizational activities of Komminto members employed the impersonal Jiyūtō ideology as a means to mobilize villagers.

372. Ibid.   373. Inoue, *Chichibu jiken*, p. 37.   374. Ibid., p. 71.

The *Jiyūtō fū*, or "Liberal Party current," had great influence on the local farmers, according to Arai Shūzaburō, Komminto organizer. One instance of this is the statement of a fifty-two-year-old illiterate farmer:

> As far as the terrible hardships being suffered by the general farming population during these times are concerned, we of the Jiyūtō and its President, Itagaki Taisuke, will carry out programs that will aid those people. . . . We will eradicate high interest loans and will work to have the various taxes reduced.[375]

This, according to Inoue Kōji, was an example of belief in the "myth [*shinwa*] of Itagaki" shared by many farmers. "The farmers," Inoue said, "probably felt proud of their relations with the Jiyūtō."[376] For many, of course, their ties with the Jiyūtō simply represented an instrumental alliance, a *mariage de raison* for the purpose of compelling the authorities to meet their demands, and further used to justify smashings or personal assaults against creditors and usurers. Yet some, as the testimony of Kido Isao indicates, equated their relationship with the Komminto with Jiyūtō membership:

> Q.   Are all the rioters Komminto members?
> A.   No, you are mistaken. They are called Jiyūtō members.[377]

And when asked to identify the ringleaders, Kido was easily able to cite Kikuchi, Murakami, Tashiro, and others as ones who were "fervent believers in liberalism" (*jiyūshugi*).[378] Likewise, another participant referred to local organizational meetings in Hinozawa as "Jiyūtō meetings."[379] In the reports filed by village heads to government officials about Komminto raids on their offices, they claimed the rebels announced themselves as "Jiyūtō members acting under the orders of the present President. We have come to aid the poor by stamping out usury, and have formed a union of several thousand for that purpose."[380] Or in the case where the rebels approached the village head of Yamada hamlet for assistance in recruitment: "[We are] members of the Jiyūtō seeking to add men to our force which is fighting against unfair political conditions brought about by the government."[381] Similarly, a pawnshop owner and dry-goods retailer from Ōmiya, from whom the rebels extorted a "donation," reported that the "request" for his money and goods was made in the name of the "Jiyūtō President." He also reported witnessing a speech made by Shiba-

375. Quoted in ibid.   376. Ibid., p. 81.   377. *CJSR* II:16.
378. Ibid., p. 15.   379. Ibid., p. 10.   380. *CJSR* I:353.   381. Ibid., p. 355.

oka to an Ōmiya crowd in which Shibaoka said he was acting on the orders of the Jiyūtō with the intent "to reform the government and effect a *yonaoshi* [world reform]."[382]

The Shintō priest Tanaka Senya, who observed the incident first-hand, provides additional evidence which suggests that the "Liberal Party current" had penetrated the consciousness of some farmer-rebels. He says that members of the Kommintō army called themselves "soldiers of the Jiyūtō" (*Jiyūtō no tsuwamono*) who were fighting "in order to equalize wealth and aid the poor people." Tanaka added, "When I listen to the words of the rebels . . . . I hear plans of going to Tokyo, joining Itagaki, driving out government officials, changing the oppressive government for a good one, and bringing in a period of peace and prosperity for the citizens by making them free."[383] In referring disparagingly to the rebels' "delusions of freedom" (*jiyū no bōsetsu*), Tanaka quotes a song he heard the rebels sing to the accompaniment of the *samisen*:

> Those without money,
> always suffering,
> now have gold:
> the Jiyūtō.[384]

Such evidence of villager awareness of the existence of the Jiyūtō, and its connection, however tenuous, with the Kommintō, does not of course prove, nor even suggest, that they involved themselves in the rebellion because of a belief in Jiyūtō principles learned from local Kommintō organizers. It only indicates a possible awareness of an extratraditional justification for revolt that they may have adopted from Kommintō organizers, who in turn had adopted them from the so-called Jiyū-Kommintō members.

Conclusion

Shōji Kichinosuke has written: "In this period of Absolutism, when the political parties were as yet undeveloped, political creeds centered around the problems of land and taxes."[385] Nakajima, one of the Aizu activists in the Fukushima Incident, made much the same point when he wrote: "The people who say give us back our rights and give us happiness are basically making one point about the road construction problem, namely, that by carrying out our goals for political re-

---

382. *CJSR* II:592.   383. *CJSR* II:556–57.   384. *CJSR* II:571–72.
385. Shōji, *Nihon seisha*, p. 236.

form, they can have their rights and their happiness."[386] Land, taxes, rights, and happiness—the people involved in the three incidents were protesting against an absolute government that denied them a measure of control over any of these. Their protest was a fight to gain control. To gain control they understood that first the government had to be reformed. And it had to be reformed in such a way as to allow the people continued control over their land, their taxes, their rights, and their happiness. Necessarily, a constitutional form of government that guaranteed the "inherent natural rights" (*tempu koyū no ken*) of all men was the best and only way to ensure continued popular control. To this end, a popularly elected national assembly had to be convened immediately, not in 1890 when it was convenient for the government, but in 1882 or 1884—Now! whatever the date—when the People needed it. But even granting that setting up an assembly was no easy task, that it was not to be entered into either quickly or lightly, at least in the meantime the government should permit free speech and association in order to enable the citizenry to arrive at enlightened decisions on important matters.

This was the reasoning the popular rights movement imparted to the people of the countryside; this, and what Ueki wrote in his song for the farmers: "If we call ourselves men, then each person must himself stand up and say, 'Man has rights!'" In each of our three cases, this is what happened. The farmers of Fukushima said they had the right to participate in decisions affecting their land, their roads, their labor, their taxes, and their lives; the Kabasan rebels said that all the people of Japan, and especially the poor who were victims of an oppressive government, had natural rights to share equally in the wealth of the nation; the Chichibu rebels said they had the right not to suffer impoverishment because of usury, speculation in the markets, excessively high taxes, and government policy that aided the entrepreneur and hindered the small independent producer.

In claiming these rights, the participants of the three rebellions were aided by natural right doctrine; it helped them to express in universal terms the way things *ought* to be, and to condemn in absolute terms the way things *were*. Natural right ideas were useful for these two complementary purposes because conditions had changed sufficiently to make obsolete the old political idiom derived from subsistence and Confucian ethics. The new language of natural rights did in

386. Ibid., pp. 310–11, from a document entitled "Tokubetsu Naisoku," referring to the internal rules of the *Aizu Rokugun Rengōkai.*

fact reflect the dramatic changes so recently experienced in politics, economy, and society. That the rebels could employ the language of natural rights as artfully as they did, moreover, bespeaks a type of rising political consciousness that could only be manifest in capitalist society, that is, a consciousness of the idea that political obligation to the State rested upon the State's recognition that property and freedom are the basic indivisible and inalienable rights of all men. The language of natural rights, in other words, could only be expressed in a capitalist society wherein logic demanded that all men have political freedoms equal to the economic freedoms intrinsic to a market economy. The truth of this is clearly seen in the political societies and parties created by commercial farmers: Their organizations derived legitimation from natural right doctrine, which was used to explain the very principles informing their groups and the aims their groups sought to effect. The economic interests of commercial farmers dictated the political language they could use with advantage, and their political language in turn defined their vision of what their relationship with the State should be in the future.

It seems clear that the thought, activities, and organization of the Fukushima and Kabasan rebels were imprinted in the language of natural rights; it is not clear in the case of the Chichibu rebels. They certainly represent our weakest case. For this reason we conclude this lengthy chapter with a short discussion of the relevance of natural right principles to the organization and activities of the Chichibu rebels.

Political organization in the Chichibu Incident, unlike the other two cases, sprang not from a pre-existing "political society," but instead from more traditional communal village relationships and practices. It would appear that the ideas of popular representation, responsible government, and constitutionalism were meaningful political goals mainly to the leadership of the Kommintō alone, and were only vaguely understood by the thousands of followers as slogans of Mr. Itagaki's Liberal Party. For these latter types, the rebellion derived its essential meaning from its goals to reduce taxes, to defer debts, and to smash the property of the wealthy and their apparent ally, the local government. These "soldiers of the Jiyūtō" no doubt understood the art of soldiery better than the art of politics and the language of political ideas. Why else would the rebellion's leaders phrase the objectives of the rebellion in terms such as "reform the government and effect a *yonaoshi*" or "equalize wealth and aid the poor people"?

The language was of an older type, closer to that of the later years of the Tokugawa period when peasants who lived their lives close to the subsistence level tried to compel rulers to honor an older norm of reciprocity, and farmers who produced marginal surpluses called for an end to government interference in the workings of the market. The language used by the Chichibu rebels tells of their as yet undeveloped political consciousness. Yet it was by no means atavistic or reactionary. The Chichibu rebels clearly understood that the necessity to protect their property was closely tied to the need to influence government; they comprehended the close relationship between political power and the distribution of wealth. The Chichibu farmers were indeed men of the market, as they had been for many years past; they saw with little difficulty that changes in the market affected their fortune. But because they were marginal producers of small surpluses, they were both more vulnerable to dramatic changes occurring in the condition of the market, and closer to the snares of indebtedness, bankruptcy, foreclosure, and even subsistence or hired-labor farming. Their economic position, hence their political position, hence the political language they used were all strikingly close to those of an earlier existence characterized by economic insecurity. It was easier for them to believe that poverty might just be inherent in the human condition, that economic freedom might just be a means of enslavement and not of liberation, that it might be easier to repair the world (*yo-naosu*) to an idealized former state of near equality and cooperative community relations than to remake the present world to accord with principles of economic justice in a market society, that is, to ensure a free competitive market unthreatened by profiteers, usurers, and monopolists. Their language was in any case not that of natural rights, the ideology that supported the unlimited appropriation of land, labor, and capital. Only their leaders, those of the so-called Jiyū-Kommintō, clearly saw that in order to prosper and even survive in the new political milieu of early Meiji a popular democracy or a representative government would be necessary. It remains problematical as to how many followers were actually able to comprehend this.

What is not problematical, however, was the new kind of organization devised by the farmers of Chichibu. Like the Fukushima farmers two years before, the Chichibu rebels made a complete break with the past in the way they organized themselves. In 1884, they rebelled as members or affiliates of a supravillage political party which had as its basic ideological position the idea that all men should have political rights *because* they were men. The call for "equalization of wealth" in this organizational context, and in the larger economic context of capitalist society, meant or had the potential to mean something radically different from the same call even twenty years earlier. We know only too well of the kind of result that has come in history when men believed that they possessed inherent rights and at the same time called for equality of wealth in the context of capitalist society. It was because they recognized this that the writers of the *Jiyūtō-shi* termed the Chichibu rebellion "socialistic." It would be going too far to assume that the Chichibu farmers saw this—what we see now or what the writers of the *Jiyūtō-shi* saw years after the rebellion—but it would be within the bounds of reason to suppose that although Chichibu provided less fertile soil for the growth of democracy than the ground in Fukushima and that which bore the Kabasan rebels, "rice-roots democracy" had nonetheless begun to take hold in the land of Chichibu.

5. Consequences and Conclusions

> If the Revolution is brought to an end in mid-passage, it will be judged by history as little more than a catalogue of bloody crimes.
>
> *Gracchus Babeuf at his trial, 1797*

The decade of the 1880s was not a propitious period for rebellions and rebels, particularly if they happened to be connected with the popular rights movement. In this last chapter, we will show what happened to the rebels after their capture by the authorities—to the individual rebels themselves and to the groups of which they were part. We will show in the first part of this chapter that to a considerable extent the rebels of all three incidents were victims of a pattern of political oppression that was well established by the time of the rebellions and indeed was itself in large measure a reaction to the advances made by the popular rights movement. We can say now that the repression which the rebels of each of the incidents suffered was excessive, and far beyond (at least) a modern Western conception of fairness or justice. The penalties imposed on the participants of the three incidents far outreached either the nature of their crime or any prior criminal records. Only four of the Fukushima participants, that we know of, had a prior record of crime; only two of the Chichibu leaders and eleven of the Kabasan rebels had criminal records. But even in the latter case, the crimes were of a political nature: Most stemmed from the rebels' part in the Fukushima Incident, and most were acquitted. It is necessary to realize this at the beginning of this chapter, for in the first section we seek to answer the question, "What happened to the rebels?"

The second section of this chapter will address itself to the issues raised in the Introduction, all of which revolve around the one central question, "Did the popular rights movement fail?" In approaching this question, we will draw upon many of the findings we reported earlier and briefly touch upon some not reported but which nonetheless help to provide us with an answer to the question. These findings concern the farmers' movement that occurred after the 1880s. Based on our own findings and those of others, we will challenge the dominant interpretations of North American scholarship which argue either that "the first attempt (at democracy) failed in Japan" or that it could not have failed because it was never tried. To anticipate somewhat, we will argue that democracy did not fail and that it was in fact "tried."

Consequences

What, then, of this so-called "pattern of political oppression?" It was based on two separate but interrelated facets of the immediate post-Restoration problems attending what some modernization theorists have termed "the crisis of consolidation." The first of these facets was the new government's demonstrated ability to effect one major type of sociopolitical reform after another *without* suffering any serious setbacks. The abolition of the old domains and the creation of a centralized administration; the land reform and land tax of 1872 and 1873; the *legal* dissolution of the feudal class system; the unification of the national market; conscription; and reforms in education, banking, communication, and industrialization—all were effected in quick succession with remarkable success by the Meiji oligarchs, who at the same time demonstrated a capability of dealing with unarmed and armed opposition to them. With such success at reform, the government leaders, like the proverbial miser who fears losing his wealth, grew more and more certain of their power and authority, but, at the same time, more and more anxious about their ability to maintain it. This certainty and anxiety were increasingly and steadily manifested in the number of repressive laws the government proclaimed to ensure continued and future success for its program of *fukoku kyōhei* ("rich country, strong military").

This point relates to the second facet dealing with the "crisis of consolidation." Domestic order was absolutely necessary in order to modernize, particularly in the midst of an international context rife with great-power imperialism. Without domestic order, Japan could not modernize; without modernization, she could not retain her political sovereignty. Indeed, the country had already been violated by embarrassing treaties of extraterritoriality and "most-favored nation" trading relationships. To Japan's modernizing leaders, these threats from without must have made the threats from within seem all the more dangerous. It must have seemed that no sooner had its new conscript army subdued the thousands of discontented samurai under Saigō Takamori in 1877 than an equally subversive body called the popular rights movement began to raise its ugly head. Yamagata Arimoto, chief architect of Japan's modern military forces and Home Minister at the time of the Kabasan and Chichibu rebellions, privately confided to allied oligarch Itō Hirobumi in a letter dated 4 July 1879:

> Itagaki's scheme is to call for the people's rights, slander the government, abuse officials with reckless and groundless attacks and thereby arouse disgruntled *shizoku* and spread unrest throughout the land. By prolonging this situation *he hopes to unite the people and overthrow the government at the opportune moment* [emphasis added].[1]

Four years later, when many thousands were organized into Jiyūtō branches, Yamagata was no less apprehensive. Complaining again to Itō about present laws not being harsh enough, he wrote:

> With this condition prevailing at present, I am apprehensive that unless we take drastic measures to deal with political parties, it will prove hopeless to attempt to achieve the goal of preserving the independence of our imperial nation.[2]

Yamagata, Japan's Bismarck, wanted yet more blood and more iron in order to preserve his nation's sovereignty. To do this he believed that yet stronger pieces of legislation had to be added to an already well-established pattern of political oppression.

What, then, was the nature of this political oppression?

It began in 1873 when newspaper codes and libel laws were enacted in order to curtail a press already showing signs of libelous liberal independence. In 1875, the press laws were made even more stringent, threatening fines, imprisonment, and suspension of publication for newspapers whose editors allowed intemperate criticism of the government and its policies. More than two hundred writers were punished during the next five years for violating the laws' provisions.[3] Shortly after the Jiyūtō and other parties were formed and had established their own organs, such as the *Jiyū Shimbun*, the government responded with an even tougher law in April 1883. For violating this

---

1. Quoted in Roger F. Hackett, *Yamagata Aritomo in the Rise of Modern Japan, 1838–1922* (Cambridge, Mass., 1971), p. 85.
2. Quoted in ibid., p. 101; the letter was dated 22 January 1883.
3. Scalapino, *Democracy*, p. 60, n. 49.

new newspaper and publishing code, 474 writers and editors were prosecuted during 1883 and 1884.[4]

Freedom of speech was limited in other areas as well. On 9 December 1880, the first of several laws restricting the right to petition was proclaimed.[5] A year before, in April 1879, less than a year after the government allowed prefectural assemblies to be elected to serve as advisory bodies to the governors, a law was invoked that threatened assemblymen with deprivation of all rights for a seven-year period if they "treasonably" overstepped their already much curtailed prerogative to debate legislation. In December 1882, the government went even further by proscribing communication and meetings between members of different prefectural assemblies.[6]

This last law was actually an amendment to the earlier Law of Public Meetings (shūkai jōrei) that had been enacted on 5 April 1880. This law forbade students, teachers, policemen, soldiers, and other government personnel to attend any political meeting or to join any political organization. It also placed restrictions on the scheduling and the content of political meetings, and it furthermore prohibited political societies from combining or communicating with one another. Violators could be prosecuted for treason. In January 1882, the effect of the Public Meetings law on political society members worsened when a new ordinance was issued, making offenders of this law and others subject to prosecution for a felony rather than a misdemeanor. Between 1883 and 1884, 309 individuals were prosecuted for breaking the meetings law, among whom were several of the leaders of the three incidents.[7] But perhaps more important than numbers arrested were the countless numbers of political meetings broken up by the police who were acting in accord with the provisions of this law. It is known, for instance, that in the first eight months of 1882, the Fukushima police reported observing 306 political meetings (Jiyūtō), broke up sixteen of them, and arrested two speakers.[8] Clearly,

---

4. Gotō, Jiyū minken, p. 146.

5. Ibid., p. 145. According to the 15 December 1882 issue of the Toyko Nichi Nichi Shimbun, petitioning had to be conducted in four steps: from the village head to the prefectural governor, to the relevant ministry, and then to the Dajōkan.

6. Gotō, Jiyū minken, pp. 145–46.

7. Ibid., those among our sample who were prosecuted were Saeki, Matsumoto, Yoshinaga, and Yoshida Kōichi. Details of a couple of dozen lecture meetings which were broken up by the police in eastern and western Fukushima can be found in Shōji, Nihon seisha, pp. 172–97; these documents show that two lecturers who suffered repeated police interference were Kotoda Iwamatsu and Kōno Hiroshi, both participants in the Kabasan Incident.

8. Shōji, Nihon seisha, p. 174.

the popular rights movement by this time was "considered a real and present danger by the Oligarchs."[9] But how, then, did this pattern of political oppression manifest itself in the three incidents?

We saw in Chapter 1 that after the Kitakata Incident of 28 November, wholesale arrests were made throughout the *entire* prefecture, not just in Yama district where the incident occurred or even in Tamura where the eastern Jiyūtō headquarters was located. Estimates vary, but anywhere between one and two thousand party members or supporters were arrested in late 1882, although more than half of these never set foot in Aizu during the entire summer of that year.[10] The reason for such wide-scale arrests seems to be clear. On 28 November, Governor Mishima wrote a secret message to his secretary Murakami:

> Concerning the wicked rioters at Kitakata, it is an opportune moment to arrest all those related people yet remaining [unarrested]. If you have an insufficient number of policemen, talk to the other police branches in the region, and mobilize and deputize the 150 men of the Miharu Fencing Club [*Gekkentō*]. Dispose of this problem firmly, omitting no one. Time is of the essence. You ought to call in the police from other districts if yours are insufficient. Send me a reply immediately.[11]

That night, the Aizu Jiyūtō headquarters was assaulted by forty policemen aided by special deputies, and forty-four Jiyūtō members were arrested. Within the next several weeks, 518 Aizu Jiyūtō supporters and members were initially charged with crimes ranging from being a "ringleader" and "inciting crowds to riot" to "instigation" and mere "rioting"; these were all felonies. About 325 of the 518 men were eventually charged with "blindly following and assembling to riot," a misdemeanor punishable by a fine of one to two yen.[12] Many of those Aizu men charged with the more serious crimes—and this applies to those from eastern Fukushima as well—found themselves thrown into veritable torture chambers without even being informed of the nature of their crimes. It is claimed that about 200 Jiyūtō members and supporters were tortured; and prison diaries, memor-

---

9. Hackett, *Yamagata*, p. 97. Also see Lay, "Brief Sketch," pp. 381–94, for a detailed account of the use to which repressive legislation was put by the Meiji government. Lay, too, says the legislation was prompted from fear of the popular rights movement; on pp. 393–94, he refers to the *gekka jiken*.

10. Shōji, *Nihon seisha*, p. 347; Takahashi, *Fukushima jiken*, p. 224.

11. Quoted in Takahashi, *Fukushima jiken*, p. 187.

12. Ibid., pp. 189, 224.

anda between officials, court records, and newspaper accounts seem to substantiate at least the fact, if not the number as well. Igarashi Takehide's court testimony, for instance, includes references to the marks on his body which he revealed to the court.[13] In April, the *Chōya Shimbun* published a report about a prisoner "frequently ordered to leave the jail and appear in the police station in muddy and snowy weather; that he was kept standing day and night without a morsel to eat; that he was refused food and that the police sergeants sometimes kicked his feet, causing blood to flow."[14] Jiyūtō member Haneda Kiyomizu from far-off Soma district was a victim of the arrest campaign; he was charged with "insulting an official" and forced to stand out in the cold; he contracted pneumonia as a result, and died in prison.[15] There are too many stories to discount them, stories of beatings, torture, and even suicide taking place in prison while these "traitors" were waiting to be tried.

Those who actually made it to court seem not to have fared much better. Most of the known Jiyūtō members were prosecuted at the Fukushima Felony Court or at the Wakamatsu Misdemeanor Court. Those found guilty at the former court were sentenced to six or seven years in prison; those found guilty at the latter, to between one and five years.[16] About thirty of those found guilty of felony charges later appealed the court's verdict, and in all cases the lower court's decision was overturned, testifying to the political nature of the charges brought against these men. Moreover, by the time these men were released, the judge who first sentenced them to prison, Akagi Kenichi, had been politically rewarded and promoted to succeed Mishima as Governor of Fukushima.[17]

If these are two indications of the political nature of the arrests, then the treason trials in Tokyo were another. The basis of the charge brought against all fifty-seven men was an alleged connection between the "blood pact" promising to overthrow the government, which was signed by Kōno Hironaka and five others (quoted earlier; see Chapter 4), and the Kitakata Incident that was supposedly led by the other fifty-one men charged with treason. The trial lasted nearly two months, from early February to early April 1883, and during that

13. Ibid., p. 206.
14. Quoted in the *Japan Weekly Mail*, 21 April 1883; also see Takahashi's version of the story, in *Fukushima jiken*, p. 208.
15. Takahashi, *Fukushima jiken*, p. 210.
16. Ibid., pp. 226–27.
17. Ibid., p. 225.

time it became apparent that there was no evidence to connect the Kitakata Incident to the "blood pact," so fifty-one of the men were acquitted. The "Blood Pact Six" did not do as well. Two of their lawyers, Hoshi Tōru and Ōi Kentarō, at times used the trial as a political platform to indict the government for its crimes; this certainly did not help the six.[18] Yet Ōi, who defended Tamano Hideaki, seems to have done his best to defend his client. Ōi's basic argument concerned the distinction between political and ordinary crimes, saying that it is unjust to prosecute anyone on the basis of his political ideas:

> As regards an attempt to plot the overthrow [of the government], if there was only intent, the mere thought of it, if there were no actual steps taken to effect it, then there was no crime committed. In the case before us, because there was no actual plan to overthrow the government, only a document [whose signers] agreed on [the idea of] overthrowing the government, definitely no law has been broken.[19]

Hoshi Tōru defended Kōno by arguing that when Kōno used the word *tempuku* ("overthrow"), he really meant *kairyō* ("reform").[20] Hanaka and Hirajima, however, said that the word *tempuku* meant for them what it did for everyone else, adding that "reform" could only occur if the government were overthrown. All six were found guilty of "conspiring to overthrow the government." Kōno was sentenced to seven years imprisonment, and the others to six years. Tamano died in prison the next January, and the others were released in February 1889, when they were pardoned on the occasion of the promulgation of the Meiji Constitution.

For both the eastern and western branches of the Jiyūtō, the aftermath of the Kitakata Incident was disastrous. Overt political oppression had cost the Jiyūtō its best leaders, a hundred or so at the upper levels of the party hierarchy, and hundreds at the lower levels. Among the many followers, a fear of being arrested kept many away from party-related lectures and meetings; attendance dropped. Some activists, such as Monna, Hara, and Saji who were acquitted of treason, tried taking Governor Mishima to court for abuses of power, but were threatened with arrest; many others who had escaped arrest earlier went into hiding, only to be caught two or three years later and sent to prison. Others, we know, turned to scheming and plotting the

18. Hirano, *Ōi*, p. 81.
19. Quoted in ibid., p. 42.
20. Shōji, *Nihon seisha*, p. 429; and Takahashi, *Fukushima jiken*, p. 244.

overthrow of the government; such was the case of the Fukushima men involved in the Kabasan Incident.

One would imagine that the Kabasan revolt was the perfect, clear-cut case for the government to prove treason. After all, sixteen men openly declared their intent to bring down the government by force, and actually tried to do so. Moreover, "since the government officials regarded the Kabasan Incident as extremely serious, they employed all their police and investigative powers to arrest all those concerned."[21] Obvious evidence, concerted investigation, and even an open admission of guilt by the rebels during pretrial interrogation pointed to treason. As Kōno Hiroshi stated their crime, "We who involved ourselves in this incident can only be understood as having committed treason." What could be clearer? Let Kōno himself explain what the government did. Continuing his above-quoted statement, Kōno said:

> But the policy of this administration is to pervert the law greatly. *We ought not to be prosecuted as ordinary criminals.* In other words, what the Justice Ministry has done is *to manipulate the law by debasing the charge*, but this cannot even for one day fool the Japanese people; it cannot protect the authority of the government; ultimately this act will come to be regarded as a great blot in the records of the Japanese judiciary [emphasis added].[22]

In other words, the government changed the charge against the Kabasan rebels from treason to "armed robbery," presumably in order to "depoliticize" the trial and to prevent the kind of negative publicity the government had received as a result of the Fukushima Incident treason trial. That trial had also served to catapult Kōno Hironaka into the ranks of the great patriots; the government did not want the same to happen to Hironaka's nephew Hiroshi and his fourteen compatriots.

The altering of the charge surprised the Kabasan rebels. All the pretrial questioning by police and government prosecutors—some of which was related in Chapter 4—concerned itself with the nature of their treasonable act, and in fact the rebels had been charged with treason on the basis of this early investigation. Not until 6 March 1885, after the preliminary hearings had been completed, was the charge changed to armed robbery resulting in murder.[23]

This alteration also made necessary changes in nearly 300 other charges, ones which had been laid against about 300 accomplices

21. Endō, *Kabasan jiken*, p. 243.
22. Quoted in Endō, *Kabasan jiken*, p. 244.
23. Taoka, *Hanshin den*, p. 78.

who came from Tochigi, Ibaraki, Fukushima, Yamanashi, Chiba, and Tokyo.[24] The list included such prominent popular rights advocates as prefectural assembly member Naitō Roichi of Aichi prefecture and Tanaka Shōzō of the Tochigi prefectural assembly—the government said about the latter: "Tanaka has long [behaved] like a crafty cancerous tumor; taking a hatchet to it was long overdue"[25]—and included such unknowns as Koinuma's entire family.

All but a handful of the 300 were released within a month to ten months after their arrest. Only such "principal offenders" (seihansha) as Ōhashi and Naitō were indicted for having given money or shelter to the rebels after the incident. Now, instead of being charged with aiding traitors, they were charged with aiding robbers.

Not until September 1885 did the trials begin. The fifteen rebels were tried in four different courts—Tokyo, Tochigi, Chōfu, and Chiba—nearest to the place where each was captured. In all four courtrooms sat policemen whose duty was to report on all Jiyūtō members and supporters attending the trials.[26] Once again, Ōi Kentarō was serving as defense attorney; but unlike the Fukushima trials, Ōi did not remain throughout the trial period, resigning in late September, probably in order to begin planning for his ill-fated expedition to liberate Korea.[27]

The trials began with protestations made by Kōno, Koinuma, Amano, and others against the change of the indictment. For example, Kōno reasoned, "If you examine the manifesto distributed by the defendants, then it ought to be readily apparent that the crimes of stealing money and raising an army were committed in order to carry out a crime against the State." Koinuma simply claimed, "Making the bombs was for one purpose only—to use them to overthrow the Meiji government." Yamaguchi advised, metaphorically, "If the court cannot judge our unworthy crime with the public eye of justice, then its incompetent eye ought to be closed forever." But it was Amano who pointed out to the authorities the real nature of the trial: "You fear

---

24. Ibid., p. 78; Endō, *Kabasan jiken*, pp. 240–41. The breakdown by prefecture was: Tochigi, 115; Ibaraki, 50; Fukushima, 47; and Yamanshi, Chiba, and Tokyo made up the remainder.

25. Quoted in Endō, *Kabasan jiken*, p. 241.

26. For example, at Kōno's trial on the day of 18 September, it was reported that twenty-eight or twenty-nine Jiyūtō members were among the 100 or so spectators. See Endō, *Kabasan jiken*, pp. 245, 252.

27. Wagatsuma et al., *Seiji saiban shi* II:54; Hirano, *Ōi*, p. 89; and Endō, *Kabasan jiken*, p. 251.

that by punishing us correctly you will make us into martyrs."[28] The government in fact disallowed the manifesto and the oral declarations of the rebels as evidence. One prosecutor argued, "Their plot to overthrow the government in order to effect social reform is merely an oral declaration; there is no evidence that makes them guilty of treason."[29] Yet one judge of the Tokyo trials believed their "mere oral declarations" and wished to try them for treason; he was dismissed.

In July 1886, the sentences were read. All were found guilty of armed robbery resulting in murder. After a circular letter had passed through the hands of each of the four trial judges, allowing them to agree on a proper sentence, Tomimatsu, Yokoyama, Miura, Kokugi, Kotoda, Sugiura, and Hotta were sentenced to death. Kusano, Isokawa, Kōno, Kobayashi, and Amano were given indefinite prison terms. Due to commiserative circumstances—it is not clear what this refers to—Tamamatsu and Hara received indefinite prisons terms, reduced from the death penalty. Koinuma was sentenced to fifteen years imprisonment, Monna to thirteen, Saeki to ten, and Ōhashi to nine; the accomplices escaped with light sentences. Of the principal rebels, only Yamaguchi was not sentenced; he died in prison while awaiting what most certainly would have been the death sentence.[30] Except for Tomimatsu, all those given the death sentence appealed, but on 12 August 1886 their appeals were denied. Yokoyama died in prison a month before he was to walk to the gallows; the others were hanged on 6 October 1886.

One year later, a memorial service was held in Tokyo for the seven dead Kabasan rebels. Hoshi Tōru, later a Diet member, Minister of Communications, and a victim of political assassination in June 1901, decried political extremism while at the same time intoning, "Those for whom we hold this memorial service did not lay down their lives in vain. Was not their purpose to put an end to bad laws?"[31] Just three months after that speech, a new law was passed—the Peace Preservation Law (hoan jōrei)—that gave the authorities the right to expel anyone "scheming something detrimental to public tranquility"[32]

28. All quotes are taken from Endō, Kabasan jiken, pp. 246–47.
29. Quoted in ibid., p. 248.
30. Taoka, Hanshin den, p. 79.
31. Quoted in Endō, Kabasan jiken, p. 260.
32. Quoted in Ike, Beginnings, pp. 185–86; also see Hackett, Yamagata, p. 105. Hackett says that this law had the goal of "permanently crippling the liberal movement with one blow." Aside from this, another new law, which was a direct result of the Kabasan Incident, was the Regulations Governing Explosives (Bakuhatsubutsu torishimari kisoku) of 27 December 1884. It forbade the making of explosives and threatened the death penalty for any-

from the capital for a fixed period of time; Hoshi Tōru was one of the 570 writers and political figures ordered out of the capital.

What of the Kabasan rebels not executed? Hara and Ōhashi died in prison of tuberculosis. The others were passed over in February 1889, when in celebration of the new Constitution most political prisoners were released from prison. Not until 1893 through 1894 were they freed, and then, even for the *shizoku* among them, their Constitutional rights were not restored until July 1897; but even then they were only given the rights accorded to *heimin*.[33]

Most of the Chichibu rebels were *heimin*; no vainglorious protests were uttered by them in an effort to convince the prosecutors of their treason. Yet, as we shall see, at least the newspapers were ready for a treason trial to be called a treason trial, and for the government to prosecute on the basis of hard evidence. And in this case, both the newspapers and the government were able to identify the real "traitors": They were the "agitators" and "instigators," not the "blind masses" who had been "led astray." In fact, the more than 3,000 farmers who surrendered themselves to the authorities for the most part escaped with an average fine of about one-and-a-half yen—although during the depression, when the average annual income was only twenty-eight yen, the fine must be regarded as heavy.[34] The lucky ones escaped altogether, retreating to distant hamlets where they easily found anonymity among their agrarian peers.[35] The authorities did not seek them out as they had done with those who escaped after the Kitakata Incident. Instead, they sought only those responsible for working the common people into such a frenzy that they revolted.

These types—"gamblers, Jiyūtō and Komminto members, and lawyers"[36]—were the targets of the law. And it was not the same kind of law that was practiced in the other two incidents. In those incidents, months and even a couple of years separated arrest, trial, and prosecu-

one using bombs for the purpose of injuring people, damaging property, or disturbing the public order. See Endō, *Kabasan jiken*, p. 265. It is interesting to note that this ordinance was used by the government just a year later in the prosecution of Ōi Kentarō and his confederates of the Osaka Incident. See Wagatsuma et al., *Seiji saiban shi* II:99.

33. *KJKS*, p. 503.

34. Based on Tanaka Senya's 1884 account; see *CJSR* II:553–54; also see *CJSR* II:271, for police statistics; and Inoue, *Chichibu jiken*, pp. 194–96.

35. See *CJSR* I:621, for information on the many rebels the government was unable to apprehend and the reasons why.

36. *Tokyo Nichi Nichi Shimbun*, 2 November 1884.

tion. In the Chichibu case, several days before the rebellion had ended, Home Minister Yamagata instructed his secretary to have a certain Judge Shimada and a prosecutor Okada sent to Ōmiya to help the local judiciary set up an Extraordinary Crimes Court (*Ringi Jūsai Saibanjo*) in order to deal with what he called the "bandits" (*hito*).[37] Yamagata also ordered a battalion of garrison troops to help round up the "bandits," as well as the "wandering outlaws" (*furō no kyōto*) who "prey on the sufferings of law-abiding citizens."[38]

Probably reflecting the government's views on the "bandits," the *Tokyo Nichi Nichi Shimbum* wrote:

> The immediate cause [of the rebellion] was mainly the agitation of villainous gamblers and radical wanderers. . . . Since they could not realize their European-type socialist party, they sought to create misery and death. . . . They agitated the unthinking poor people. . . . It was a terrible crime of treason. Treason was their objective, the greatest single danger in these times. This wide-scale rebellion gave rise to fears in everyone that *we were heading toward the point of revolution* [emphasis added].[39]

As if to emphasize the point even more, the *Tokyo Nichi Nichi Shimbun* was very specific in a 14 November (1884) editorial entitled "Destruction Is the Enemy of Society." After observing the tendency for "parties of destruction" (*hakaitō*) to emerge in other areas of the world—the anarchists in Russia, the Socialist Party in France, and the Fabian socialists in England—it said that in the Chichibu rebellion:

> Those responsible for the destruction in this uprising were the ones known as "Radical Party Members" [*kageki no seitō-in*]. They preached about the expansion of "unlimited freedom" [*museigen no jiyū*] to their followers. . . . Their radical talk about freedom is an empty and abstract theory. It is not possible to make all people equal, to do away with differences between the rich and the poor, between the high and the low. . . . Theirs is a politics of dissatisfaction; they call for the very destruction of the law.[40]

In subsequent articles and editorials, Jiyūtō party members came to be cited repeatedly as those "agitators who were appealing to the aspirations of society's lower classes."[41] Calls for the prosecution of

37. *Saitama-ken shi*, ed. Tayama Soka, Vol. 2, p. 585; and Chichibu Kyōikukai, comp., *Saitama-ken Chichibu-gun shi* (Tokyo, 1925), pp. 411–13.

38. Chichibu Kyōikudai, *Saitama-ken Chichibu-gun shi*, p. 409; and for the quote, *Tokyo Nichi Nichi Shimbun*, 6 November 1884, in an editorial entitled "Bōto ikki."

39. Editorial, "Bōto chintei," 13 November 1884.

40. *Tokyo Nichi Nichi Shimbun*, 14 November 1884.

41. Ibid., 24 November 1884.

the Jiyūtō, "not yet silent,"[42] though in fact already dissolved, grew more frequent, even in newspapers other than the *Tokyo Nichi Nichi Shimbun*, albeit in a less vindictive tone.[43] In the other papers, the "plight of the poor farmer" was stressed equally, and it was emphasized that in many cases "rioters reportedly compelled people to participate."[44] Whether it was because the newspapers called for leniency for the poor farmers, or because the sheer number of farmers (3,249 by 28 November)[45] would have made prosecution an impossible task, the government decided to prosecute only the thirty-seven men known as Tashiro's lieutenants (see Appendix C), the 115 who "instigated the masses," and the 103 men listed as "members of the Komminto."[46] Since all but fourteen were residents of Chichibu, we may seriously question the allegations of the government and the newspapers concerning the important role played by "outside agitators" and "wandering outlaws" in stirring up the "unthinking masses" to rebel. In any case, the specific charges laid against the nearly 250 rebel leaders were fomenting rebellion, robbery, and instigation of violence.[47]

Most of the Chichibu rebels received sentences of five to eight years imprisonment, although some, such as Tashiro's eighteen-year-old son, received as little as six months. Those receiving the longer sentences were for the most part released in February 1889 as part of the general amnesty. Tashiro himself and seven other "ringleaders" were sentenced to death in February 1885, less than three months after their arrest. Two months later, Tashiro, Katō, Arai Shūzaburō, Takagishi, and Sakamoto were unceremoniously hanged. The other

42. Ibid., 20 November 1884.

43. For example, the *Chōya Shimbun*, *Yūbin Hōchi Shimbun*, and *Yomiuri Shimbun*.

44. *Yomiuri Shimbun*, 6 November 1884; the Police also held this view; see *CJSR* II: 270–71, and *CJSR* I:487–501.

45. *CJSR* I:632–39; if indirect participants are counted, then the figure exceeds 6,000!

46. *CJSR* I:640–56. These figures are only for Chichibu. An equal number were prosecuted in Gumma, Kanagawa, and Nagano. See Ide, *Kommintō*, pp. 196–97. *CJSR* II:248 shows 201 people prosecuted in Gumma as of 8 December 1884.

47. *CJSR* II:249. The police chief of Ōmiya described these leaders as "party members and gamblers who disrupted the public peace and order." The facile notion of "outside agitators" or "professional revolutionaries" to explain the origins of conflict is a common one used by authorities to ignore or to obfuscate the actual conditions which gave rise to rebellion or revolution. Its use begs the question of what kind of conditions permitted outside agitators (if there were any) to have the disturbing effect they had. See, for example, Arendt's treatment of the "professional revolutionary" in *On Revolution*, pp. 262–64, where she says that revolutions occur despite, and not because of, agitation. The tendency of the authorities to disparage the character of "outside agitators" with epithets like "bandit" or "gambler" is a subject discussed by Rudé, *Crowd*, pp. 197–204, 211–12, and makes for an interesting comparison.

three had been sentenced to death in absentia. Inoue, as we know, had already escaped to Hokkaidō, where he lived the remaining thirty years of his life quietly as a farmer. Kikuchi had gone underground after the incident and was not apprehended until two years later. For some reason, his sentence was commuted from death to life imprisonment, but he was released in 1905 as part of an amnesty granted in celebration of Japan's victory over Russia. He returned to his village in Saku, where he lived the remainder of his life quietly with his son, the village doctor.[48] The third Chichibu rebel sentenced to death in absentia was Ochiai. Insofar as his later experiences parallel those of some of the post-incident experiences of rebels involved in all three incidents, we will give them more attention.

Ochiai did not resurface until the trials for the participants of the Osaka Incident in 1887, when it was discovered that he had been living the last several years under a false name. He related a story that included working in a mine for a while, brooding over the death sentence his fellow rebels received, and wondering how he could save them. He then went to Tokyo to seek the one man whom he believed might be able to assist him, Ōi Kentarō. He first visited Naitō Roichi, who had just recently been released from prison (Kabasan Incident), and together the two men went to the *Yūikkan* to speak with Ōi. Besides Ōi, also present were Arai Shōgo (also arrested for complicity in the Kabasan Incident), the brother of convicted Kabasan rebel Tamamatsu, and Kobayashi Kusuo. They explained their plot to effect a "liberal revolution" in Korea, and Ochiai agreed to join them. Ochiai was appointed to assist several others in robbing Tokyo merchants to raise money for the plot. He successfully completed the task and along with several others headed toward Nagasaki, where they were to meet the army of about 100 men that Ōi had assembled. But on the way there, Ochiai and his companions were arrested. Ochiai was subsequently sentenced to ten years imprisonment. Upon his release he returned to his Chichibu village, where he spent the remaining forty years of his life as a Christian convert working for the Salvation Army, and, according to another source, as an active supporter of nationalistic causes.[49]

48. Ebukuro, *Sōdō*, pp. 174–76; Nakazawa Ichirō, *Jiyū minken no minshūzō* (Tokyo, 1974), pp. 156–58; Inoue, *Chichibu jiken*, pp. 190–96; and *CJSR* I:640–56.

49. Ishikawa, *Tonegawa*, p. 212; Inoue, *Chichibu jiken*, pp. 37, 192–93. Also see *CJSR* II:611–20, for the letters Ochiai published after leaving prison. In them he described himself as a "loyalist advocate of imperial and constitutional rule" (*kinnō sonnō rikken shishi*), and although he does not apologize for his part in the Chichibu or Osaka incidents, he does rewrite history to the point of emphasizing his nationalistic motives for participating in them.

If the latter is true, then Ochiai was not alone in "switching" his liberal colors for nationalistic ones. His mentor in the Osaka Incident, Ōi Kentarō, is certainly one of the other, better-documented cases of this.[50] Less well known figures who were also participants of one or the other of our three incidents can also be cited. Shirai Enbei, for example, one of the young Tamura *minken* activists indicted (but acquitted) for treason in the Fukushima Incident, is another. First elected to the National Assembly in 1890, and again in the second Diet, he was an avid supporter of the Navy Expansion Bill (*Kaigun kakuchō-an*). When he subsequently lost his Diet seat to Kōno Hironaka, Shirai turned to banking by using his close contacts with the *zaibatsu* ("financial clique"). By 1915, he was again serving in the Diet as a Seiyūkai Party member, in large part due to the aid he received from the Party leader and later Prime Minister, Hara Kei.[51]

Two other examples of converts to nationalistic causes are Arai Shōgo (Osaka Incident) and Koinuma Kuhachirō, leader of the Kabasan Incident. After his release from prison in 1889, Arai was elected to serve as a member of the Tochigi prefectural assembly in 1890; several years later, he served in the Colonial Ministry. Koinuma, "father of the assassination faction," also spent his later years as an assemblyman in the Tochigi legislature, where he oftentimes had to suffer the opposition's jeers of "Kabasan General" (*Kabasan Shōgun*). Koinuma's biggest disappointment during this period stemmed from the failure of Kōno Hironaka, then Minister of Agriculture and Commerce, to get him a post in a central government ministry.[52]

These examples raise doubts as to the seriousness of the early *minken* leaders' commitment to the principles of natural right and to the movement that incorporated those principles. Such cases as these seem to lend support to the argument that says the liberal movement was never very liberal, that Itagaki's chameleonlike qualities were not unique to the upper echelons of the popular rights movement, but in fact characterized all levels of participation. Yet, at the same time, is it fair to assume that men like Koinuma did in fact abandon their principles? Would this not be an act of assigning guilt by association? To ascertain whether they did in fact abandon their earlier held principles would require an in-depth examination of their later acts and speeches in the prefectural assembly and elsewhere. To do this would take us well beyond our immediate concerns. However, we may sug-

50. See for example, Jansen, "Ōi Kentarō, pp. 315–16.
51. See Appendix B.
52. Endō, *Kabasan jiken*, p. 272.

gest that a commitment to democracy as well as to nationalism is not necessarily a contradiction in values, particularly if sufficient attention is accorded to the international context in which Japan, the Japanese in general, and the democrats within Japan found themselves in the 1880s and 1890s. It should be remembered that this was a time of international violence, of big-power diplomacy and imperialism, which taught the weaker nations that armed might best served as the basis of a nation's sovereignty. Japanese conservatives and liberals alike understood this lesson. However, the liberals, unlike the conservatives, believed that the necessity of Japan being militarily strong should not interfere with the development of social justice at home. But again, to treat the entire question of the compatibility of a belief in democracy with nationalistic sentiments would require much more attention than it is possible to give here. Having said this, it seems necessary to treat one other result of the *gekka jiken* for which we have sufficient evidence: the dissolution of the institution to which these incidents were so closely tied, the Jiyūtō.

It would be a mistake to say that the Jiyūtō dissolved itself on 29 October 1884, a month after the Kabasan Incident and two days before the Chichibu Incident, *because* of these and other incidents like them.[53] There is little doubt, however, that the various *gekka jiken* that occurred prior to dissolution were an important contributing factor.[54] Despite the party's claims, each time a rebellion broke out, that the party had nothing to do with it, the fact that the leadership in each rebellion were members of the party (or claimed to be), and their following adopted Jiyūtō principles as slogans of rebellion, was impossible for the authorities to ignore and impossible for the Party to disprove.[55] The official party history, the *Jiyūtō-shi*, makes the further point that these incidents served to provoke ever stronger government oppression: "Beginning with the Fukushima and Takada 'hells,' and continuing with the Gumma and Kabasan violent uprisings,

53. Note: Scalapino, *Democracy*, p. 107, says that the Jiyūtō dissolved *after* the Chichibu *jiken*; Norman, *Emergence*, p. 183, says that the Kabasan Incident occurred in *1885*; both are wrong.

54. Besides the Fukushima and Kabasan incidents, they are the Takada *jiken* (March 1883), the Gumma *jiken* (May 1884), the Kamo *jiken* (July 1884), and the Akita *jiken* (June 1881). For the Akita and Takada incidents, see Aoki Keiichirō, *Nōmin undō* II:324–37, and 349–53; for the Kamo *jiken*, see Hasegawa Noboru, "Kamo jiken," in *Jiyū minkenki no kenkyū*, Part II, ed. Horie and Tōyama, *Minken undō no gekka to kaitai* I:121–204.

55. For example, a *Jiyū Shimbun* editorial of 28 September, several days after the Kabasan Incident, denied any Party involvement. Yet the party history says that it was unable "to control innumerable fervent patriots" and cites this as one reason for dissolution. See Endō, *Kabasan jiken*, pp. 267–68.

the government effectively prohibited the freedoms of speech, publication, and assembly. As a result, it became impossible for the Jiyūtō to carry out its movement with unity and moderation."[56] Of course, since we know that these "freedoms" had been severely restricted well before the occasion of the incidents, we must conclude that the authors were speaking in relative rather than absolute terms. In any case, the party historians point especially to that section of the Public Meetings Law that forbade communication between the central headquarters and its "branches" (in fact, the law also forbade combinations, so the branches were separate entities) as responsible for party disunity, because it prevented central control over the activities of the members on the periphery.

Not only the deleterious effects of repressive legislation contributed to the dissolution of the Jiyūtō. Since its inception, the party had been plagued by factionalism between the radicals and the gradualists at the highest levels of the party hierarchy. The split between these two party factions had been very pronounced at the time of Itagaki's trip abroad in 1882, but was even more evident in March 1884, when at the party convention the two members most critical of President Itagaki's policies and furthest removed from him ideologically, Ōi Kentarō and Hoshi Tōru, were elected as advisors to the President, contrary, needless to say, to Itagaki's wishes.[57] Against this backdrop of repressive laws and party factionalism, the Kabasan Incident occurred, guaranteeing dissolution. As the party history says, "After that our party decided to dissolve."[58]

Dissolution, however, was effected only at the center. It certainly did not affect the decision of the Chichibu Komminto to rebel. Neither did it have any impact on the popular rights societies of Iida and Nagoya in December 1884, when they tried their hand at revolution. Briefly, the Iida-based *Aikoku Seigensha* (Nagano prefecture) and the Nagoya-based *Aikoku Kōdō Kyōkai* (Aichi prefecture) together con-

56. Itagaki, *Jiyūtō-shi* III:74. Also see Masumi, *Nihon seitō shi* I:349–61.

57. Gotō, *Jiyū minken*, p. 186.

58. Itagaki, *Jiyūtō-shi*, p. 75. An interesting historical comparison on the effects that rebellion can have on the cause of democracy would be between Shay's Rebellion in western Massachusetts in 1786 and the *gekka jiken*. Shay's Rebellion, Parrington says, "provided the object lesson in democratic anarchy which the 'friends of law and order' greatly needed" (*Colonial Mind*, pp. 28–82). In terms of targets and demands, Shay's Rebellion resembles the Chichibu Incident. An excellent article on the subject of popular rebellion in eighteenth-century America which shows the effect of rebellion on democratic movements is Pauline Maier, "Popular Uprisings and Civil Authority in Eighteenth-Century America," *William and Mary Quarterly*, 3rd sers., 27:1 (January 1970):1–35.

spired to overthrow the Meiji government. Their plan involved the use of counterfeit money to raise funds for arms, the infiltration of the Nagoya army barracks by *minken* advocates for purposes of recruiting soldiers to mutiny, and the mobilizing of farmers in Aichi, Nagano, and Kanagawa. Planning lasted over a year, and, as was mentioned, the leaders of the incident recruited no less a personage than Ueki Emori as author of their revolutionary manifesto. The plot, however, was discovered in the early stages of its execution and quickly suppressed.[59] But even this was not the last of the *gekka jiken*. In June 1886, the Shizuoka Incident occurred; it was a plot by ex-Jiyūtō members to assassinate certain leaders of the government who were due to meet at a resort in Shizuoka. Not even planned as well as the Kabasan Incident, this last of the "incidents of intensified violence" ended not with a bang, but with a whimper.[60]

After this succession of failures on the part of Jiyūtō members to alter the Meiji government by employing violence, the popular rights movement changed considerably. By 1886, the depression that had so oppressed farmers earlier in the eighties had begun to subside, and signs of prosperity were beginning to manifest themselves. The new political movement that sprang up in 1887, the Daidō Danketsu Undō (The Movement of a Union of Like Thinkers), seemed politically atavistic, resembling more the *minken* movement as it was in its earlier stages than as it was in its developed stage: It was largely led by and composed of ex-samurai and landlords, and sprang up from the issue of Japan's independence (or lack of it) from foreign control, especially the treaties imposing extraterritorality. But as this movement took shape, it included a number of liberals like Ueki Emori whose concerns for the nation went beyond that of treaty revision, also emphasizing the need for reduction of the land tax and for freedom of speech and assembly. But in part because it did not seek support on a wide scale from the millions of farmers in the countryside, in part because its leaders were co-opted by the government, in part because of new repressive legislation (e.g., the Peace Preservation Law), and in part because splinter groups were forming in preparation for the altered political situation that would attend the constitutional phase of Japan's political development, the Daidō Danketsu move-

---

59. Details of this incident can be found in Gotō Yasushi, "Iida jiken," in *Jiyū minken undō*, comp. Meiji Shiryō Kenkyū Renraku Kai III:102–47.

60. See Haraguchi Kiyoshi, "Shizuoka jiken no shakaiteki haikei," in *Minken undō no tenkai*, comp. Meiji Shiryō Kenkyū Renraku Kai, 9 (Tokyo, 1958):30–123.

ment collapsed.[61] Several new political parties emerged to take its place, but, unlike the old Jiyūtō before its demise, the new parties did not seek mass support; they did not have to, for under the new constitution property qualifications determined that only 460,000 citizens out of Japan's population of fifty million would determine by their votes which of the elitist parties would control the parliament.

Conclusions

Japan entered its constitutional era with seven "national" political parties. None were popularly based, and all were very nationalistic. A mere 1½ percent of the population could vote in Diet elections. The government was controlled by oligarchs and "transcendental cabinets" which permitted little power to the parties and no power to the people, whom they regarded as children to be led.[62] New laws restructuring local government in 1888 were implemented in order to isolate the villages, foster patriotism, and prevent "the spread of ideological movements and . . . party strife into the realm of local government"—in short, to keep "the countryside peaceful and stable."[63] Forty percent of Japan's farming population were tenants. Only an estimated 5 percent of the population could vote in local elections, i.e., 5 percent were regarded officially as citizens (kōmin). And finally, if the Fukushima case is at all representative, rural political societies in 1890 were dominated by shizoku and wealthy heimin, mainly the gōnō stratum of the farming class.[64]

In the face of all this evidence, not to mention the later developments of the 1930s, how can we argue that the first attempt at democracy succeeded in Japan? And can we really say that it was even attempted?

The findings presented thus far strongly suggest that democracy was attempted, especially at the lower levels of society and politics.

---

61. See Shōji, Nihon seisha, pp. 566–69; Scalapino, Democracy, pp. 112–13; Ike, Beginnings, pp. 181–87; and Gotō, Jiyū minken, pp. 193–213. Lay, "Brief Sketch," p. 402, also comments upon the movement, with particular attention given to its disorganized approach to politics.

62. Steiner, Local Government, p. 36.

63. Steiner, "Political Participation," pp. 233, 235. Also see Kano, Kindaika no shisō, pp. 129–31, where he succinctly analyzes the disastrous effects of the 1888 local government reform on the popular rights movement at the local level. He notes three effects in particular: (1) greater central government control over local affairs; (2) less access of local government to higher levels of administration; and (3) increasing control over local affairs by local "small emperors" (shō-tennō). Also harmful to the local democratic movement were the Constitution and the 1890 Imperial Rescript on Education.

64. Shōji, Nihon seisha, pp. 571–72.

Now, to summarize briefly what those findings were: In the first chapter, it was shown how the rebels of each incident invoked Jiyūtō symbols, slogans, and organizational precepts as a means to give to their anti-government activities a measure of legitimacy and coherence. In all three incidents, a recurrent demand of the rebels was a constitutional and representative form of government; this they regarded as necessary for the implementation of a system of local self-government, of a political system based on the natural rights of man, and of an economic system responsive to the financial plight of small independent producers of agricultural commodities. In the second chapter, we outlined those historical, social, economic, and political elements that together combined to create the necessary objective conditions for the emergence of a liberal-democratic movement. They were: a tradition of rebellion in the areas where the *gekka jiken* of the 1880s occurred, a tradition that included an important economic "leveling" component; a constantly changing agrarian social structure that witnessed the political ascendency of the middle-level farmers, whose vulnerability to the changing market situation was accompanied by increased participation in, and leadership of, peasant uprisings against local and domain authorities; the attempts by the new Meiji government to exploit the agrarian community in order to create a solid industrial base for the modernizing economy; and the rise of the popular rights movement, which changed dramatically from a movement led and composed by the old feudal elite of southwest Japan to a Kantō-centered and commoner-led and composed liberal party that derived its strength from the scores of members and affiliated political societies spread throughout Japan.

The types of people who were members of the local popular rights societies and parties and, more precisely, those whose membership in such groups was recorded by their participation in one of the three rebellions (a fact in itself an indication of how deep was their commitment to the movement) were the topic of the third chapter. There we saw that the leadership in each incident was largely drawn from the local elite and was a fairly homogeneous group in terms of the different characteristics for which information was given, but that differences existed between the leadership of each incident. One important difference was that the leadership in the Fukushima Incident came mainly from the small *gōnō* stratum of agrarian society, but in the Chichibu Incident from the middle-level farmer stratum. However, despite this difference, it appeared that, relative to landholding patterns in each region, the leadership was neither very wealthy nor very poor, but rather fell somewhere in between. Also in this respect, it appeared that the followers closely resembled the leadership, although to a much greater extent in Chichibu than in Fukushima; yet, there too, according to the figures on land tax payment, it appears that many of the followers in the Fukushima Incident were also middle-level farmers. Finally, it was suggested that this fact of middle-level farmers involving themselves in rebellion finds considerable support in the comparative history of rebellion and revolution.

Chapter 4 sought to place the people examined in the previous chapter into an ideological and organizational context. We saw that the different organizations employed by the rebels were governed by a liberal-democratic ideology that made the rights of the individual, as opposed to the rights of the State, into the central principle governing socioeconomic and political existence. Although the political creed they followed, natural right, was oftentimes centered around problems of land, labor, and taxes, and their organizations around traditional types of social relationships, nonetheless their democratic organizations and ideology differed from and transcended local economic concerns and traditional social relationships. Evidence was also offered to show the existence of extensive "rice roots" participation in popular rights organizations and a consciousness of and enthusiasm for democratic ideas, though it must be conceded that local elites seem to have been more involved and to have had a deeper understanding than their followers.

This brief review of the evidence marshaled thus far, I believe, should remind us that democracy was in fact "tried." Those who say it was not appear to be guilty of deducing antecedent political developments from the nature of succeeding political circumstances. In other words, those who say democracy was not tried look mainly at the list of undemocratic socioeconomic and political features characterizing Japan in its constitutional era and infer from that set of circumstances that earlier movements could not have been democratic. Or in other terms, they look at the political institutions of the Japanese state as of 1890, conclude that they are oligarchic or Confucian, and then further conclude that the processes leading up to that situation must have been consistent with that outcome. In part their mistake stems from the level of politics at which they focus their study and perform their analysis, namely, the elite level, staffed by national government and party figures and the institutions through which they expressed themselves. A study, for example, of Itagaki and the other early popular rights advocates will show that they were not interested in, nor did they promote, universal franchise free of property qualifications; but a study of Ueki Emori's writings and activities or of the *Sanshisha* and the *Seidōkan* and one of its leaders, Sakuma Shōgen, will show that *minken* advocates at the local level were interested in, and did promote, these ideas. There is also little indication that the early leaders of the popular rights movement sought to educate all men, irrespective of social status, about their inherent natural rights; but the political societies of Fukushima did, and the Kabasan rebels sought to create just such a society where natural rights would be the legal rights of all men. A study focused at the national elite level of politics would also fail to show that both the Fukushima and Chichibu rebels sought to effect a type of national government that would be more sensitive to the needs of the people as they were expressed at the local level of government. Even the less articulate Chichibu rebels realized that this could only come about by democratic reform at the highest levels of government; nowhere is there any indication that the early national *minken* leaders or the national government were responsive to this notion of local self-government, perhaps the very foundation of a democratic system.

Hence, it is quickly and unreservedly conceded that at the upper levels of party politics and government, democracy was not attempted. But to say that it was not attempted at all because "none of the Meiji leaders advocated the establishment of a democratic form of government"[65] is not only to ignore the proclaimed purposes of thousands of commoners who came to believe in and fight for their rights as men, but it is also to neglect that vast majority of the population who lived their social, political, and economic lives not in the capital but in the small hamlets spread throughout Japan. Though many of these people may not have been "relevant political actors" in the sense that they were without substantive political rights and in the sense that they were unable to realize a democratic system of government, their fight for rights made them nonetheless political actors.

This argument receives reinforcement from the comparative material on rebellion and revolution which was introduced in Chapter 4. One need not be a Marxist in order to see lower-class rebellion as political in character, although it does seem necessary, as Barrington

---

65. George Akita, *Foundations of Constitutional Government in Modern Japan, 1868–1890* (Cambridge, Mass., 1967), p. 161.

Moore has suggested, to eschew a liberal reading of history in order to sympathize with "the victims of historical processes" and to question "the victors' claims."[66] But in any case, the point remains that rebels do not have to explicitly raise questions about the structure and control of government (although many of our rebels did) in order to qualify as political actors. The very fact of rebellion indicates a challenge to authority, a serious and even lethal questioning of the grounds of obedience, and reflects a mistrust in, or disapproval of, government as it presently exists. When rebels settle upon local merchants or wealthy farmers, not to mention local government officials, as their targets of rebellion, they are "saying" that they understand *who* benefits from the existing power structure and *who* is serving it. They are "saying" that they know who has power, the power which oppresses them in one form or another. This much at least can be said even for the peasants who revolted during the Tokugawa period. But for the Meiji *farmers*, even more can be said. Their rebellions coincided with, nay, stemmed from the development of new economic and political relations brought into being by the liberal market society. They understood that a simple appeal to "natural justice" or a "subsistence ethic" would only be met with the unanswered echoes of their own voices. Justice in market society, they understood, was (or should be) responsive to demands made by the constituents of the market, those whose investments of land, labor, and capital produce the wealth which the government relies upon for its very existence. To maintain its authority and accordingly the support of its constituents, the government had merely to provide those elemental services that were needed for the market to operate smoothly, but most of all to remain beneficially noninterventionist. The Meiji government did in fact assume such a posture in the late seventies, and as a result commercial farmers throughout Japan enjoyed unprecedented prosperity. But the Matsukata deflationary policies coupled with government policy to develop a modern infrastructure necessary to rapid economic growth, along with the authoritarian methods the government used to effect new policies, shocked many farmers into realizing what popular rights activists had been saying for several years: the freedoms to appropriate land, labor, and capital in market society are meaningless without political guarantees to support them. Among commoners, the *gōnō* strata were the first to understand this, having already tasted the fruits of liberal market society. Middle-income farmers

66. Moore, *Social Origins*, p. 523.

who had only recently taken the step forward from subsistence to surplus followed only when it seemed likely that in "Mother-May-I" fashion they would be compelled to take the long step backward. Faced with this prospect, they could easily discern the consequences of arbitrary political authority exerting itself in liberal market society. The political theory of liberalism, natural right doctrine, which many believed in before there was any compelling reason stemming from the growth of capitalism, emerged in this context as a defender of the rights of the individual and the community against the arbitrary Meiji government. It gave direction and definition to the popular battle to secure political muscle sufficient to defend the rights of property against government interference. There were Winstanleys who sought to deny the rights of property and secure equal freedoms for all, but they were years ahead of most. For most, the fight for freedom was in fact a fight for property. The original point remains: the rebels of the 1880s sought a democratic system of government, a thoroughly liberal one; they were relevant political actors.

This brings us to the second and more difficult question: "Did this early attempt fail or succeed?" Having already admitted that it failed in terms of not being able to effect a constitutional democratic form of government, and conversely, to prevent the establishment of the imperial absolutist form of government (as embodied in the Meiji Constitution), we must at the same time emphasize that "failure" can only be understood as having occurred at one level, again at the level of national politics, or in Robert Scalapino's terms, at the level of "the landed and capitalist elites," those whom he identifies as early popular rights leaders.[67] It was these types of early "liberal leaders" who failed, because, again in Scalapino's terms, "neither of these groups could truly represent the cause of liberalism or the principles of a liberal party movement."[68] The landed groups, he says, "were interested primarily in refighting the battle of feudalism and in stemming the tide of urban industrialization. They had an interest in liberalism mainly to the extent that it could be used as a tool in battle." The capitalist elites, as he expresses it, "rather than concen-

67. Scalapino, *Democracy*, p. 114. Norman, *Emergence*, p. 172, blames failure on the fact that bourgeois activists were rural-based rather than urban-based. A case might be made to the effect that Norman's customary and penetrating insight into political developments was blurred because of Marxist strictures regarding the necessary mode of political development, preventing him therefore from fully recognizing the democratic gains made in the countryside.

68. Scalapino, *Democracy*, p. 115.

trating upon broadening individual and corporate rights beyond the sphere of government ... were quite naturally seeking to exploit the full potentialities of governmental paternalism."[69]

On this point I stand in complete agreement. At the national elite level, the democratic movement did fail. Almost all of Scalapino's analysis of the *minken* movement was performed at this level, and on these terms it is much too incisive to argue against. Yet because Scalapino concerns himself almost entirely with the national elites of the movement, he necessarily ignores the local elites and non-elites, those who have served as the focus of our study. He says of them: "The lower economic classes could scarcely play a vital role in a sustained political movement, particularly a liberal movement, occurring in this period." He concedes that "the peasant class, whose activities, as we have seen, took the form of scattered violence under the impetus of economic misery" could serve "as a subsidiary force in some respects." But he adds that "the rigorous logic of Japanese political evolution dictated that the role of the masses in this period would be one essentially negative in character."[70]

On the contrary, our study indicates that the "lower economic classes" were coming to play a more "vital role" in the movement all the time, first through the organizing of political societies, political study circles, lectures, petitions, and so on, and then later through the increasing extent to which they were organizing themselves in the Jiyūtō itself and in related parties such as the Kommintō. Moreover, who is to say whether they could have "sustained" the movement? The authorities and the national party leaders hardly gave them a chance. Furthermore, when Scalapino says "particularly a liberal movement," we must interpret this to mean that the undifferentiated "masses" were unable to understand liberal principles. Yet we have seen instances where admittedly illiterate farmers claimed they were rebelling for a constitution and for Jiyūtō principles. While this might be regarded as mere "mouthing borrowed slogans, though even these were of some importance in mustering popular support for a radical cause,"[71] there is no reason not to believe that, like the Parisian crowds mouthing *Vive le Tiers État!*, the Kommintō rebels, for instance, had assimilated these ideas and given them a content more in line with their own particular economic interests. Certainly, even the

69. Ibid.   70. Ibid., p. 114.
71. Rudé, *Crowd*, p. 221.

more illiterate of the "peasants" could understand that element of natural right doctrine which says all men are equal. It was not altogether different, after all, from the "leveling" aspects of the *yonaoshi ikki* that their fathers or perhaps even they themselves joined in the late 1860s. Moreover, we have seen how such slogans as "Itagaki's World Reform" and "Aid the Poor, Equally Distribute the Wealth" were employed by the Kommintō rebels.

Scalapino is right, however, when he cites "economic misery" as an impetus behind "peasant" violence, but he is wrong if he believes it to have been the only factor. Ideas, as just indicated, were another impetus; party organizers and petitions that communicated these ideas to the farmers were certainly another; and a third was the *type* or source of economic misery, i.e., whether it stemmed from excessive taxation, or from the knowledge that prices were high because of commodity speculation, or from food shortages in the countryside due to the need to feed urban consumers, or from loan dealers who fed upon those farmers forced to mortgage their land (and hence, fall into tenancy), or from producing a surplus of cash crops only to discover that the market had no need for them. The point to be made is that many factors contributed to violence, not simply undifferentiated "economic misery."

Finally, it is questionable whether one can refer to the "role of the masses" as essentially negative in character. Aside from the value judgment implied with regard to the use of violence (particularly since the farmers were also victims of violence), their role was negative only in the eyes of the authorities. And after all, the authorities had a very narrow conception of what the "positive role" of the farmers should be: In the earlier-quoted words of Thomas Smith, it was "to be relentlessly exploited for the modernization of the non-agricultural sector of the economy."[72] Naturally, any attempt to avoid exploitation, or conversely, to demand the political and social rights that should be accorded to men *qua* man, would be regarded as "negative" by the authorities. But for the farmers who rebelled, rebellion was a positive action that circumstances and principles required them to take. It was a positive expression of solidarity, made in the midst of a political situation that would not allow them to employ peaceful means with any hope of success. It is this situation to which Scalapino *should* refer, I believe, when he uses the expression "the rigorous logic of Japanese political evolution."

72. See Chapter 2, n. 118.

If, then, it can be granted that the democratic movement failed at the top but succeeded, if only for a short time, at the bottom, what about the rest of the "failure thesis"? Was this first attempt in the 1880s a prophecy if not a prediction of the bankrupted attempt to establish a democratic form of government in the Taishō period, the so-called "Taishō Democracy"? Is it true that "the history of Japan after 1931 represented the logical culmination of previous trends—an era in which ultra-nationalism and militarism took a dominant position, easily breaking through such negligible obstacles as were placed in their path"?[73] Did the "logic" of Japanese history dictate that authoritarianism, ultra-nationalism, and militarism were to be the norm of Japanese politics? In other words, is it democracy, not fascism, that is aberrant?

The implications of this theory are vast and beyond our scope or ability to deal with here in the concluding pages. But a few words are necessary, not only because we must finish answering the question concerning success or failure of democracy in the long run, but also because of the relevance which this entire proposition has for democracy in Japan today. For if the "failure thesis" is a sound one, then we must prepare ourselves for a resurgence of ultra-nationalism in the Japanese body politic in the years ahead.

Even if we accept Scalapino's fairly elaborate definition of democracy as an essentially correct one—briefly, recognition of the innate dignity of man, and of his right to make choices in an "open society"[74]—we must still regard it as incomplete. These principles by themselves, or even when they are incorporated in political institutions as guiding maxims and reinforced by the guarantee of positive, common, or constitutional law, are meaningless *unless* there exists within the citizenry such a firm commitment to these principles that they are willing to fight to defend them. A tradition of rebellion against political oppression is needed, one that, whether it is called democratic or not, manifests itself over long periods of time as fights to preserve the innate dignity of man and his right to make choices. This is not to say that all rebellion is inherently democratic, for certain conditions have to prevail before liberal democracy is possible; it is only to say that a tradition of rebellion can impart to those living in a postfeudal, capitalist market society—one where choice in the marketplace is inherent in the order—the impetus to demand and

73. Scalapino, *Democracy*, p. 346.
74. Scalapino, *Democracy*, p. xi.

fight for the same rights in the political sphere as they have in the economic. A free market permitting the freedom to own and lose property and to enter into contracts—where justice comes to be defined in terms of the keeping of contracts and injustice in terms of the breaking of contracts—logically expresses itself politically by the freedoms to choose governors and to enter into political associations that serve to defend these economic rights. Also, needless to say, the right to enter into such economic and political contracts must be paralleled by political freedom of expression.

In the constitutional era, this logic manifested itself in many ways. The farmers of the 1880s had learned that imperial absolutism was absolute and that they were not going to change the political system by armed rebellion. But that does not mean they ceased rebelling. They continued, but their post-*gekka jiken* rebellions reflected, as they had in the past, the changing socioeconomic and political context. Hence, their rebellions after 1890 were not against the authorities—a trend we already observed in Chapter 2—but instead against landlords, village officials, and merchants: Rights could be demanded from these less-than-absolute personages. Between 1888 and 1897, virtually all of the recorded 579 "disturbances" (inclusive of many forms of rebellion) were aimed against these types of local power figures; less than 4 percent were aimed against the central government. Tenant-landlord conflicts and struggles against village officials accounted for 55 percent of all the disturbances of this period.[75] Suffice it to say that this trend continued, both in terms of quantity and type, through the remainder of the Meiji period, through the Taishō period, and even into the Shōwa period, after the militarists were well into the process of assuming power. There were, for example, more tenant disputes in 1937—the year Japan invaded China—6,170 of them, than there were during any year of Meiji or Taishō.[76] Moreover, many of these tenant disputes against landlords were aided by tenant unions, a relatively new feature in the ever-developing tradition of rural rebellion in Japan.

Of course, these figures remain only a numerical intimation that the vast majority of Japan's population, the farmers, were continuing to fight for their rights. Further studies are needed to determine whether these struggles had strong anti-government undertones, or whether they reflected more generalized beliefs in the principles of

75. Aoki, *Meiji nōmin sōjō*, pp. 90–91, 122–23, 144–45.
76. Inaoka, *Nihon nōmin undō*, pp. 104–5.

equality, freedom, and the rights of man. But if I may do what I have accused others of doing, and make two deductions, then I would say, first, that the warm reception the people of Japan gave to Taishō Democracy, and second, the equally warm one they gave to the democratic reforms effected by the Occupation after the Second World War, lead us to infer that the effects of the democratic experiment begun by the farmers of the 1880s were not lost to subsequent generations.

Appendix A

DECLARATION OF RESTORATION OF RIGHTS

1. [Our purpose is to] restore our rights and guarantee happiness.
2. We will carry out these resolutions with unbending will.
3. The rights we want to be restored:
   a. Improper elections of [Rengōkai] council members.
   b. Implementation of the road project is contrary to [Rengōkai] resolutions.
   c. The course (route) of the road was arbitrarily decided.
   d. A request for an extraordinary meeting [of the Rengōkai] was rejected.
4. Upon restoration of the above rights, the Rengōkai should be reconvened and carry out the following objectives:
   a. The route of the road should be in accord with population density in the Aizu region.
   b. The route of the road should be responsive to the interests of the people of the area.
   c. A committee [of local representatives] should be established in order to inspect and decide upon how the road construction will be carried out.
   d. Unless the people in the neighboring district agree to carry out their part of the road construction, no work will be done.
5. If these purposes just cited are not attended to, then we will not do construction work.

This document, of which the above is an excerpt, appears in Shōji Kichinosuke, ed., *Nihon seisha seitō hattatsu shi* (Tokyo, 1959), pp. 312-13.

Author's Note to Appendices B, C, and D

Appendices B, C, and D consist of biographical data on the participants of the Fukushima, Chichibu, and Kabasan incidents respectively. The reasoning behind the selection of the individuals who appear in each of these three appendices can be found in the opening pages of Chapter 3. The code used in each of the appendices to indicate biographical data is as follows:

1. Prefecture (*ken*)
2. District (*gun*)
3. Village (*mura*) or town (*machi*)
4. Age at the time of the incident
5. Status (*heimin* or *shizoku*)
6. Occupation
7. Financial status/landholdings (in *chō*)
8. Literacy
9. Political party and/or political society affiliation
   (In the Chichibu case only, rank in the Kommintō Army is substituted.)
10. Prior arrest
11. Other
12. Principal sources of information

Appendix B
FUKUSHIMA ACTIVISTS

Kōno Hironaka　河野広中
1. Fukushima
2. Tamura
3. Miharu
4. 33
5. *Heimin* (déclassé samurai)
6. "None" (court testimony);
   merchant, politician
7. Wealthy
8. Yes
9. Jiyūtō; *Sanshisha* (head)
   Sekiyōsha (head)
10. No
11. Leader of national Jiyūtō;
    later, government official
12. Takahashi, *Fukushima minken*,
    pp. 181–85; *FKS*, pp. 755–65

Kawaguchi Genkai　川口元海
1. Fukushima
2. Ishikawa
3. Yotsugura
4. 27
5. *Shizoku*
6. Doctor
7. ?
8. Yes
9. Jiyūtō
10. ?
11. ?
12. *FKS*, pp. 774–75

Uda Seiichi　宇田成一
1. Fukushima
2. Yama

3. Shibage
4. 32
5. *Heimin*
6. Farmer/village head
7. 3 to 8 *chō*
8. Yes
9. Jiyūtō; *Aishinsha* (head)
10. ?
11. Prefectural Assembly member,
    1879, 1881, 1892, 1896
12. Takahashi, *Fukushima minken*,
    pp. 229–34; *FKS*, pp. 725–32

Hirajima Matsuo　平島松尾
1. Fukushima
2. Atachi
3. Nihonmatsu
4. 28
5. *Shizoku*
6. Teacher
7. ?
8. Yes
9. Jiyūtō
10. ?
11. Friend of Ueki; elected to Diet
    seven times
12. Takahashi, *Fukushima minken*,
    pp. 185–88; *FKS*, pp. 897–909

Miura Bunji　三浦文治
1. Fukushima
2. Yama
3. Komeoka
4. 26
5. *Heimin*

6. Farmer, village head
7. 18.2 *chō*
8. Yes
9. Jiyūtō; *Aishinsha*
10. Yes (*Kitakata jiken*)
11. Kabasan participant
12. Takahashi, *Fukushima minken*,
    pp. 251–53

Yoshida Kōichi   吉田光一

1. Fukushima
2. Ishikawa
3. Ishikawa
4. 37
5. *Heimin*
6. Shintō priest; village head
7. .5 *chō* (1907)
8. Yes
9. Jiyūtō; *Sekiyōsha*
10. February 1882
11. Village head, 1881, 1886, 1892
12. Takahashi, *Fukushima minken*,
    pp. 208–13; *FKS*, pp. 766–70

Tamano Hideaki   田母野秀顕

1. Fukushima
2. Tamura
3. Miharu
4. 34
5. *Heimin*
6. Shintō priest
7. ?
8. Yes
9. Jiyūtō; *Sanshisha* (founder)
10. ?
11. Friend of Ōi Kentarō
12. Takahashi, *Fukushima minken*,
    pp. 188–95; *FKS*, pp. 911–21

Akagi Koichi   赤城小一

1. Fukushima
2. Yama
3. Kumagaya

4. 19
5. *Heimin*
6–11. ?
12. *FKS*, pp. 732–33

Matsumoto Yoshinaga   松本芳長

1. Fukushima
2. Tamura
3. Miharu
4. 40
5. *Heimin*
6. Farmer/village head
7. Bankrupt (landless)
8. Probably
9. Jiyūtō; *Seidōkan* head
10. March 1882
11. Friend of Kōno Hironaka
12. Takahashi, *Fukushima minken*,
    pp. 200–203; Shōji, *Nihon Seisha*,
    pp. 334–35

Aizawa Yasukata   愛沢寧堅

1. Fukushima
2. Sōma
3. Koze
4. 33
5. *Shizoku*
6. Farmer; teacher
7. 4.6 *chō*
8. Yes (Confucian studies)
9. Jiyūtō; *Hokushinsha* (head)
10. ?
11. Prefectural Assembly, 1879–81;
    Newspaper editor, 1890s
12. *FKS*, pp. 765–66; Takahashi,
    Fukushima minken, pp. 267–69

Igarashi Takehiko   五十嵐武彦

1. Fukushima
2. Yama
3. Iwagetsu
4. 32
5. *Heimin*

6. Farming; village head
7. *7 chō*; later bankrupted
8. Yes
9. *Aishinsha*
10. Kitakata Incident
11. *Rengōkai* leader; District Council head, 1896, 1905
12. *FKS*, pp. 733–37; Takahashi, *Fukushima minken*, pp. 265–66

Kageyama Masahiro　景山正博

1. Fukushima
2. Tamura
3. Miharu
4. 36
5. *Shizoku* (court testimony, *heimin*)
6. Druggist/merchant
7. *7 chō*
8. Yes
9. Jiyūtō; *Sanshisha*
10. ?
11. Prefectural Assembly, 1881; Friend of Kōno Hironaka
12. Takahashi, *Fukushima minken*, pp. 196–99

Hanaka Kyōjirō　花香恭次郎

1. Fukushima
2. Shinobu
3. ?
4. 26
5. *Shizoku*
6. None
7. (None?)
8. Yes
9. Jiyūtō; *Iwashiro kyōkai*
10. ?
11. One-time newspaper reporter
12. Shōji, *Nihon seisha*, pp. 527–28; *FKS*, pp. 910–11, 928–29; Takahashi, *Fukushima minken*, pp. 20, 33

Akagi Heiroku　赤城平六

1. Fukushima
2. Yama
3. Shinai
4. 47
5. *Heimin*
6. Farmer
7. *1.6 chō*
8. Yes
9. Aizu Jiyūtō; *Aishinsha*
10. ?
11. Home, headquarters for local Jiyūtō
12. *FKS*, pp. 851–54; Takahashi, *Fukushima minken*, pp. 174, 247–49

Suzuki Shun'an　鈴木俊安

1. Fukushima
2. Ishikawa
3. Iwase
4. 50
5. *Heimin*
6. Doctor
7. ?
8. Yes
9. Jiyūtō
10. ?
11. Studied under Gotō Shimpei
12. Takahashi, *Fukushima minken*, pp. 48

Sawada Kiyonosuke　沢田清之助

1. Fukushima
2. Atachi
3. Nihonmatsu
4. 20
5. *Shizoku*
6. Teacher
7. Little
8. Yes
9. Jiyūtō (*Mumeikan*)
10. ?

11. Hirajima was mentor
12. Takahashi, *Fukushima minken*, pp. 224–25

Satō Kiyoshi   佐藤清
1. Fukushima
2. Date
3. Okura
4. 30
5. *Shizoku*
6. None
7–8. ?
9. Jiyūtō
10. ?
11. Former prefectural assembly member of Miyagi; helped Kōno build *Kyōaidōbōkai*
12. *FKS*, pp. 776–80; Takahashi, *Fukushima minken*, pp. 20, 172

Matsumoto Miyaji   松本宮治
1. Yamagata (born)
2. Yama (relocated)
3. Yonezawa
4. 33
5. *Shizoku*
6. Teacher
7. ?
8. Yes
9. Jiyūtō
10. No
11. ?
12. Shōji, *Nihon seisha*, pp. 340–41

Teruyama Shūgen   照山秀元
1. Fukushima
2. Tamura
3. Miharu
4. 36
5. *Heimin*
6. Buddhist priest/farmer
7. ?
8. Yes
9. Jiyūtō

10. Yes
11. ?
12. Shōji, *Nihon seisha*, pp. 335–36

Yanaginuma Kamekichi   柳沼亀吉
1. Fukushima
2. Tamura
3. Miharu
4. 22
5. *Heimin*
6. Teacher
7. ?
8. Yes
9. *Seidōkan*
10. ?
11. ?
12. Shōji, *Nihon seisha*, pp. 171–72; Takahashi, *Fukushima minken*, p. 85

Shirai Enbei   白井遠平
1. Fukushima
2. Tamura
3. Sugeya
4. 36
5. *Heimin*
6. Sake manufacturer/farmer/village head
7. 6.7 *chō*; wealthy
8. Yes
9. Jiyūtō; *Kōfūsha*
10. ?
11. Prefectural Assembly, 1880; District head, 1890; Diet, 1890, 1892, 1915 (Seiyūkai); Established bank; friend of Hara Kei
12. Takahashi, *Fukushima minken*, pp. 286–90

Sugamura Taiji   菅村太事
1. Fukushima
2. Tamura
3. Kitachi

4. 18
5. *Heimin*
6. Shintō priest
7. ?
8. Yes
9. *Taishōkan* (political circle)
10. ?
11. Later a Diet representative
12. Takahashi, *Fukushima jiken*, p. 85; Takahashi, *Fukushima minken*, p. 56

Yamaguchi Chiyosaku　山口千代作
1. Fukushima
2. Kawanuma
3. Onomoto
4. 34
5. *Heimin*
6. Farmer/village head
7. 16 *chō* (landlord)
8. Yes (Chinese and English studies)
9. Jiyūtō; *Aishinsha*
10. ?
11. Prefectural Assembly, 1879, 1880, 1881; Diet, 1890, 1892; knew Ueki Emori; later, pro-government
12. *FKS*, pp. 878–85; Takahashi, *Fukushima minken*, pp. 236–40; Shōji, *Nihon seisha*, p. 221

Satō Sōmatsu　佐藤惣松
1. Fukushima
2. Tamura
3. Ogura
4. ?
5. *Heimin*
6–11. ?
12. Shōji, *Nihon seisha*, p. 561

Matsumoto Shigeru　松本茂
1. Fukushima
2. Tamura
3. Miharu

4. 40
5. *Shizoku*
6–7. ?
8. Probably
9. *Sanshisha/Seidōkan*
10. ?
11. ?
12. Shōji, *Nihon seisha*, p. 561

Kōno Hiroshi　河野広体
1. Fukushima
2. Tamura
3. Miharu
4. 17
5. *Heimin*
6. None
7. (Father wealthy)
8. Yes
9. *Seidōkan*
10. No
11. Kabasan participant
12. *FKS*, pp. 867–75 (See Appendix D)

Katō Sōhichi　加藤宗七
1. Fukushima
2. Tamura
3. Okura
4. (young)
5. *Heimin*
6. Aide to village head
7–10. ?
11. ?
12. *FKS*, pp. 865–67

Kariyado Nakae　苅宿仲衛
1. Fukushima
2. Futaba
3. Karino
4. 28
5. *Shizoku*
6. Shintō priest/farmer/teacher
7. 6 *chō*
8. Yes

9. Jiyūtō; *Hokushinsha*
10. ?
11. Ran for Diet seat, 1890, 1892; arrested for Kabasan and Osaka incidents; *Seiyūkai* party

Asaka Saburō　安積三郎

1. Fukushima
2. Tamura
3. Miharu
4. 29
5. *Heimin*
6. Merchant/druggist
7. ?
8. Probably
9. Jiyūtō
10. ?
11. ?
12. Shōji, *Nihon seisha*, pp. 175-76; *FKS*, pp. 875-78

Yamada Shingai　山田深海

1. Fukushima
2. Atachi
3. Nihonmatsu
4. ?
5. *Shizoku*
6-11. ?
12. Shōji, *Nihon seisha*, p. 561

Sekine Tsunekichi　関根常吉

1. Fukushima
2. Ishikawa
3. Tadake
4. 17
5. *Heimin*
6. Farmer
7. ?
8. Yes (former student)
9. Connected with *Mumeikan*
10. ?
11. ?
12. *FKS*, pp. 854-64; Shōji, *Nihon seisha*, p. 171

Nakajima Yūhachi　中島友八

1. Fukushima
2. Yama
3. Sangawa
4. 30
5. *Heimin*
6. Farmer/weaver
7. 2.4 *chō*
8. Yes
9. Jiyūtō; *Aishinsha*
10. ?
11. Prefectural Assembly, 1881, 1886, 1890, 1892; *Rengōkai* leader
12. Takahashi, *Fukushima minken*, pp. 225-29; *FKS*, pp. 737-46

Sonobe Yoshiyuki　園部好幸

1. Fukushima
2. Tamura
3. Miharu
4. 27
5. *Shizoku*
6. Village head
7. ?
8. Yes
9. *Seidōkan*
10. ?
11. ?
12. Shōji, *Nihon seisha*, pp. 332-33; Takahashi, *Fukushima minken*, p. 85

Miwa Shinzaemon　三輪信左衛門

1. Fukushima
2. Tamura
3. Okura
4. 35
5. *Heimin*
6. Farmer/village head
7. ?
8. Yes
9. *Sanshisha*
10. ?

11. ?
12. *FKS*, p. 770; Shōji, *Nihon seisha*, pp. 333-34

Satō Katsuzō 佐藤勝造
1. Fukushima
2. Tamura
3. Miharu
4. ?
5. *Heimin*
6-11. ?
12. *FKS*, p. 770

Matsuzaki Gihachi 松崎儀八
1. Fukushima
2. Tamura
3. Yokodo
4. ?
5. *Heimin*
6-11. ?
12. *FKS*, p. 770

Sakuma Shōgen 佐久間昌熾
1. Fukushima
2. Tamura
3. Miharu
4. 34
5. *Shizoku*
6. Village head
7. ?
8. Yes
9. *Sanshisha*
10. No
11. Head of *Seidōkan*
12. Shōji, *Nihon seisha*, pp. 329-30; Takahashi, *Fukushima minken*, p. 24

Ōkōchi Hidenori 大河内英象
1. Fukushima
2. Tamura
3. Utsu
4. 25

5. ?
6. Teacher/peddler
7. ?
8. Yes
9. *Seidōkan*; *Dōshinkai*
10-11. ?
12. Takahashi, *Fukushima jiken*, p. 85

Kurihara Sōgorō 栗原足五郎
1. Fukushima
2. Tamura
3. Miharu
4. 17
5. *Shizoku*
6-7. ?
8. Yes
9. *Seidōkan* (student)
10. ?
11. ?
12. *FKS*, p. 865

Satō Mankichi 佐藤万吉
1. Fukushima
2. Tamura
3. Kanya
4. ?
5. *Heimin*
6-11. ?
12. Shōji, *Nihon seisha*, pp. 560-62

Suzuki Shigeru 鈴木栄
1. Fukushima
2-11. ?
12. *FKS*, p. 884

Kamada Yūzan 鎌田猶三
1. Fukushima
2. Tamura
3. Utsu
4. 18
5. *Heimin*
6. Farmer
7. ?

8. Probably
9. *Dōshinkai*; *Seidōkan*; Jiyūtō
10. ?
11. ?
12. *FKS*, pp. 885–91

Uryū Naoshi   瓜生直七
1. Fukushima
2. Yama
3. Atsushio
4. 23
5. *Heimin*
6. Farmer/village head (father)
7. 2.7 *chō*; bankrupt 1882
8. Yes
9. *Aishinsha*
10. Yes (April 1882)
11. ?
12. Takahashi, *Fukushima minken*,
    pp. 245–47

Miura Tokujirō   三浦篤次郎
1. Fukushima
2. Tamura
3. Miharu (?)
4. 26
5. *Heimin*
6. Lawyer's aide
7–11. ?
12. Takahashi, *Fukushima jiken*,
    p. 34

Ishii Teizō   石井定造
1. Fukushima
2. Tamura
3. Utsu
4. 20
5. *Heimin*
6. Farmer
7. (Son of landlord)
8. "Minimal"
9. Jiyūtō

10. ?
11. Formed own political circle
12. Shōji, *Nihon seisha*, pp. 330–32

Yasuda Keitarō   安田慶太郎
1. Fukushima
2. Tamura
3. Utsu
4. 17
5. *Heimin*
6. Son of farmer
7–8. ?
9. *Dōshinkai*
10. ?
11. ?
12. Shōji, *Nihon seisha*, pp. 330–32

Nagasaka Hachirō   長坂八郎
1. Gumma
2. Nishi-Gumma
3. Takasaki
4. 37
5. *Shizoku*
6. None
7. ?
8. Yes
9. *Yūshinsha*
10. No
11. Friend of Kōno Hironaka
12. *FKS*, pp. 783–89; Shōji, *Nihon
    seisha*, pp. 336–40

Yamaguchi Jūyū   山口重脩
1. Gumma
2. Yutano
3. Imori
4. ?
5. *Shizoku*
6–8. ?
9. *Yūshinsha*
10–11. ?
12. Endō, *Kabasan jiken*, p. 53

Iga Wanato 伊賀我何人

1. Gumma
2. Nishi-Gumma
3. Takasaki
4. 30
5. *Shizoku*
6-8. ?
9. Jiyūtō; *Yūshinsha*
10-11. ?
12. *FKS*, p. 775

Takahashi Sōta 高橋壮太

1. Gumma
2. Nishi-Gumma
3. Heika
4. ?
5. *Heimin*
6-8. ?
9. *Yūshinsha*
10-11. ?
12. *FKS*, p. 775

Ōki Kenbei 大木権平

1. Gumma
2. Nishi-Gumma
3. Takasaki
4. ?
5. *Heimin*
6-8. ?
9. *Yūshinsha*
10-11. ?
12. *FKS*, p. 775

Matsui Tasuhito 松井助一

1. Gumma
2. Nishi-Gumma
3. Takasaki
4. ?
5. *Shizoku*
6-8. ?
9. *Yūshinsha*
10-11. ?
12. *FKS*, p. 775

Arao Kakuzō 荒尾覚蔵

1. Kōchi
2. Tosa
3. Kotakasaka
4. 27
5. *Shizoku*
6. None
7-8. ?
9. Connected with *Mumeikan*
10. ?
11. Arrived in Fukushima, 15 November 1882
12. *FKS*, pp. 781-83

Kawaguchi Seichū 川口清忠

1. Kōchi
2. Tosa
3. Kotakasaka
4. ?
5. *Shizoku*
6-11. ?
12. *FKS*, p. 780

Ogawa Matao 小川又雄

1. Kōchi
2. Tosa
3. Karairu
4. ?
5. *Heimin*
6-11. ?
12. *FKS*, p. 780

Okamoto Masae 岡本正栄

1. Kōchi
2. Tosa
3. Choe
4. ?
5. *Heimin*
6-11. ?
12. *FKS*, p. 781

Sugiyama Shigeyoshi 杉山重義

1. Ehime

2. Onsen
3. Sugiyama
4. ?
5. *Shizoku*
6-10. ?
11. Leader of Kitakata incident; later, professor at Waseda University
12. Takahashi, *Fukushima minken*, p. 246

Appendix C
CHICHIBU ACTIVISTS

Tashiro Eisuke　　田代栄助

1. Saitama
2. Chichibu
3. Ōmiya
4. 51
5. *Heimin* (ex-samurai)
6. Farmer; "mediator"
7. Indebted 80 yen; mortgage on .6 *chō*
8. Yes
9. President/Supreme Commander
10. Early 1884
11. Claimed Jiyūtō membership; local notable
12. *CJSR* I:100–118; Inoue, *Chichibu*, pp. 27, 50–52

Katō Orihei　　加藤織平

1. Saitama
2. Chichibu
3. Isama
4. 34
5. *Heimin*
6. Pawnshop owner
7. 1.6 *chō* (mortgaged)
8. ?
9. Vice-President; Vice-Commander
10. No
11. Claimed Jiyūtō membership;

local notable
12. *CJSR* I:45–47, 359–61, 382, 631; Inoue, *Chichibu*, pp. 37–38; Ide, *Kommintō*, pp. 17, 33–34

Miyakawa Tsūmori　　宮川津盛

1. Saitama
2. Chichibu
3. Shimo-yoshida
4. 56
5. *Heimin*
6. Shintō priest
7. ?
8. Yes
9. Treasurer
10. ?
11. ?
12. *CJSR* I:384, 640; II:191–94

Shibaoka Kumakichi　　柴岡熊吉

1. Saitama
2. Chichibu
3. Ōmiya
4. 46
5. *Heimin*
6. Farmer
7. Indebted 25 yen
8. "Barely"
9. Treasurer/Battalion Commander

Note that in this appendix there appear nine men who bear the surname "Arai." All nine have been checked against three different lists, Tashiro Eisuke's (*CJSR* I:103–4) and two lists compiled by the government (*CJSR* I:378–83 and pp. 640–56). Not all nine "Arai's" appear in any one listing, but the first six in our list appear on all three; about the last three we cannot be certain about the biographical information. We can only assert that the last three were *real* people who quite possibly went by other first names at some time or another.

10. No
11. *Kobun* of Tashiro
12. *CJSR* I:382; II:50–66, 218–20

Kikuchi Kanbei   菊地管平

1. Nagano
2. Minami-Saku
3. Aiki
4. 40
5. Probably *heimin*
6. "Lawyer"
7. ?
8. Yes
9. Chief of Staff
10. ?
11. Wrote Army Code; Jiyūtō member
12. *CJSR* I:380, 631, 640; II:431; Ide, *Kommintō*, pp. 104–33; Inoue, *Chichibu* pp. 56–57

Arai Shūzaburō   新井周三郎

1. Saitama
2. Obusuma
3. Nishinoiri
4. 22
5. *Heimin*
6. Teacher (primary school)
7. From a "propertied family"
8. Yes
9. Battalion Commander
10. No
11. *Kobun* of Katō Orihei; active in petition movement; brother also arrested
12. *CJSR* I:81–87, 325–26, 368–70, 382, 640; Inoue, *Chichibu*, pp. 82–83; Ide, *Kommintō*, pp. 136–58; *CJSR* II:195–96

Tomita Seitarō   富田政太郎

1. Saitama
2. Chichibu
3. Ota

4. 19
5. *Heimin*
6. Farmer
7–8. ?
9. Platoon Commander
10. ?
11. Early Kommintō organizer
12. *CJSR* II:188–89; I:380

Inoue Denzō   井上伝三

1. Saitama
2. Chichibu
3. Shimo-yoshida
4. 31
5. *Heimin*
6. Silk broker
7. "Fairly wealthy"
8. Yes (village copyist)
9. Treasurer
10. Yes (no conviction)
11. Jiyūtō member; friend of Ōi Kentarō; escaped arrest (November 1884)
12. Inoue, *Chichibu*, pp. 32–33, 191–92; Ishikawa, *Tonegawa*, pp. 215–18; Ide, *Kommintō*, pp. 236–57; *CJSR* I:640

Asami Ihachi   浅見伊八

1. Saitama
2. Chichibu
3. Yokose
4. 26
5. *Heimin*
6. Farmer
7–8. ?
9. Platoon Commander
10. ?
11. ?
12. *CJSR* II:156–57, 226–28

Arai Torakichi   新井寅吉

1. Gumma
2. Tago

3. Kamihino
4. 43
5. *Heimin*
6. Farmer/charcoal maker
7. "Poor farmer"
8. No
9. Platoon Commander (for Isama village)
10. No
11. Married; children
12. *CJSR* I:62–65; Ide, *Komminto*, pp. 193–209; Inoue, *Chichibu*, pp. 77–78

Arai (Tōnakichi?)　新井(十七吉)

1. Saitama
2. Chichibu
3. Fuppu
4. ?
5. *Heimin*
6–8. ?
9. Vice-Commander, 1st Battalion
10–11. ?
12. *CJSR* I:640

Iizuka Morizō　飯塚守三

1. Saitama
2. Chichibu
3. Shimo-yoshida
4. ?
5. *Heimin*
6. Farmer
7–8. ?
9. Commander, 2nd Battalion
10. ?
11. Jiyūtō member; escaped arrest
12. *CJSR* I:640

Ochiai Toraichi　落合寅一

1. Saitama
2. Chichibu
3. Shimo-yoshida
4. 35
5. *Heimin*

6. Part-time farmer
7. .7 or .8 *chō*
8. Learned reading and writing in prison
9. Vice-Battalion Commander
10. ?
11. Jiyūtō member; *kobun* of Katō Orihei; escaped arrest; arrested for Osaka *jiken*
12. *CJSR* II:611–21; Ide, *Komminto*, pp. 34–53; Inoue, *Chichibu*, pp. 36–37; Ishikawa, *Tonegawa*, pp. 212–15

Takagishi Zenkichi　高岸善吉

1. Saitama
2. Chichibu
3. Kami-yoshida
4. 35
5. *Heimin*
6. Farmer/dyer
7. Indebted 20 yen; near bankrupt
8. Yes
9. Platoon Commander
10. No
11. Jiyūtō member; early Komminto organizer; *kobun* to Katō Orihei; petitioner for debt relief
12. *CJSR* I:47–48, 376–77, 382; Ide, *Komminto*, pp. 34–53; Inoue, *Chichibu*, pp. 37, 83; Nakazawa, *Bungei*, p. 15

Inuki Jūsaku　犬木寿作

1. Saitama
2. Chichibu
3. Iida
4. 32
5. *Heimin*
6. Farmer
7–8. ?
9. Platoon Commander
10. ?

11. Early petitioner for debt relief
12. *CJSR* II:234–35; I:382, 640

Muratake Shigeichi   村竹茂市
1. Saitama
2. Chichibu
3. Kami-hinozawa
4. 45
5. *Heimin*
6. Farmer
7–8. ?
9. Platoon Commander
10. ?
11. Prison sentence: 7 years, 6 months
12. *CJSR* II:179–80; Inoue, *Chichibu*, p. 99

Sakamoto Isaburō   坂本伊三郎
1. Saitama
2. Chichibu
3. Shiroku
4. 34
5. *Heimin*
6. Bamboo craftsman
7–8. ?
9. Platoon Commander
10. ?
11. *Kobun* of Katō Orihei
12. *CJSR* I:381, 640; II:201

Shioya Nagakichi   塩谷長吉
1. Saitama
2. Chichibu
3. Shiroku
4. ?
5. *Heimin*
6. "Gambler"
7–8. ?
9. Platoon Commander
10–11. ?
12. *CJSR* II:239–40

Henmi Yaichi   逸見弥一
1. Saitama

2. Chichibu
3. Makinichi
4. 47
5. *Heimin*
6. Farmer
7–8. ?
9. Platoon Commander
10–11. ?
12. *CJSR* I:379, 641

Arai Monizō   新井紋蔵
1. Saitama
2. Chichibu
3. Shimo-hinozawa
4. 31
5. *Heimin*
6. Farmer
7–8. ?
9. Platoon Commander
10. ?
11. Known locally as Jiyūtō member; died while serving 6-year prison term
12. *CJSR* I:641; Inoue, *Chichibu*, p. 87; *CJSR* II:184–85

Ogiwara Kanjirō   萩原勘二郎
1. Saitama
2. Chichibu
3. Misawa
4. 23
5. *Heimin*
6. Farmer/fencing instructor
7. Indebted 50 yen
8. ?
9. Platoon Commander
10. ?
11. Jiyūtō member; *kobun* of Katō
12. *CJSR* II:185–86; Inoue, *Chichibu*, p. 57

Inoue Zensaku   井上善作
1. Saitama
2. Chichibu

3. Shimo-yoshida
4. ?
5. *Heimin*
6-8. ?
9. Provisions Officer
10. ?
11. Died serving prison term
12. *CJSR* I:641

Arai Shigejirō 新井繁次郎
1. Saitama
2. Chichibu
3. Isama
4. 44
5. *Heimin*
6. Farmer (silk and lacquer)
7. .68 *chō*; bankrupt (1884 village survey)
8. No
9. Provisions Officer
10. ?
11. Possibly Jiyūtō member; advisor to Tashiro; sentenced to prison term of 6 years, 6 months
12. *CJSR* I:381, 641; Inoue, *Chichibu*, p. 86; Ide, *Kommintō*, p. 17

Izumida Shitomi 泉田蔀
1. Saitama
2. Chichibu
3. Shimo-ogano
4. ?
5. *Heimin*
6-11. ?
12. *CJSR* I:641

Ide Tamekichi 井出為吉
1. Nagano
2. Minami-Saku
3. Kita-aiki
4. 25
5. *Heimin*
6. Farmer/ex-village head

7. Father a landlord, land worth 725 yen
8. Yes
9. Collector of funds
10. No
11. Jiyūtō member; petitioned for national assembly, 1884; 8-year prison term
12. *CJSR* I:118-21, 382, 641; II:214-15; Inoue, *Chichibu*, pp. 55-56; *Tokyo Nichi Nichi Shimbun*, 17 November 1884

Miyakawa Toragorō 宮川寅五郎
1. Shizuoka
2. ?
3. Hamamatsu?
4. 40
5. *Heimin*
6. Day laborer
7-11. ?
12. *CJSR* II:230-32, 236-37

Genkubo Jirōshi 彦久保次郎吉
1. Saitama
2. Chichibu
3. Akuma
4. ?
5. *Heimin*
6-8. ?
9. Ammunitions officer
10. ?
11. Died in prison
12. Ishikawa, *Tonegawa*; *CJSR* I:104

Kadomatsu Shōemon 門松庄右衛門
1. Saitama
2. Obusuma
3. Nishinoiri
4. 53
5. *Heimin*
6. Farmer
7-8. ?
9. Ammunitions officer

10. ?
11. Died during 6-year prison term
12. *CJSR* II:161-62, 193-94, 225-26;
    I:378, 641; Ishikawa, *Tonegawa*,
    p. 233

Arai Komakichi   新井駒吉

1. Saitama
2. Chichibu
3. Akuma
4. 49
5. *Heimin*
6. Farmer
7-8. ?
9. Firearms platoon commander
10. ?
11. Komminto organizer
12. *CJSR* II:220-21; Ishikawa,
    Tonegawa

Arai Sadakichi   新井(貞次郎)
    (or Sadajiro)

1. Gumma
2. Tago
3. Kamihino
4. 24
5. *Heimin*
6. Farmer
7. ?
8. Yes
9. Firearms platoon commander
10. ?
11. Sentenced to death
12. Ide, *Komminto*, pp. 194-209;
    CJSR I:641

Shimazaki Sosaku   嶋崎宗(由)作

1. Saitama
2. Chichibu
3. Nakino
4-8. ?
9. In charge of pack horses
10. ?

11. Died in prison
12. *CJSR* I:641; Ishikawa, *Tonegawa*,
    p. 233

Kokashiwa Tsunejiro   小柏常次郎

1. Gumma
2. Tago
3. Shimohino
4. 42
5. *Heimin*
6. Carpenter
7. 10 *cho*
8. Yes
9. In charge of pack horses
10. ?
11. Jiyuto member (wife also);
    friend of Miyabe Noboru
12. *CJSR* I:122-30, 622, 641; Inoue,
    Chichibu, pp. 43-44; Ide, *Kom-
    minto*, pp. 160-82

Ōno Naekichi   大野苗(又)吉

1. Saitama
2. Chichibu
3. Fuppu
4. ?
5. *Heimin*
6. Farmer
7. Indebted 225 yen; 1.1 *cho* land
    mortgaged
8. ?
9. Battalion vice-commander
10. ?
11. Known locally as Jiyuto; died in
    prison
12. *CJSR* II:253-54; Inoue, *Chichibu*,
    pp. 40, 83, 87-88; Ide, *Komminto*,
    pp. 65-78

Ishida Mikihachi   石田造酒八

1. Saitama
2. Chichibu
3. Fuppu

4. 27
5. *Heimin*
6. Farmer
7. Indebted 50 yen
8. ?
9. Platoon Commander
10. No
11. Sentence: 6 years
12. *CJSR* I:379; Ide, *Kommintō*, pp. 61–78; *CJSR* II:167–68

Ōno Yūkichi　大野由吉

1. Saitama
2. Hanzawa
3. Oka
4. 43
5. *Heimin*
6. Farmer
7–8. ?
9. Platoon Commander
10. ?
11. Brother of Ōno Naekichi
12. *CJSR* I:381; II:208; Inoue, *Chichibu*, p. 40

Imai Kōzaburō　今井幸三郎

1. Saitama
2. Chichibu
3. Sanyama
4. 36
5. *Heimin*
6. Farmer
7–8. ?
9. Platoon Commander
10. ?
11. Sentence: 7 years
12. *CJSR* I:378; II:229–30, 237–38

Arai Makijirō　新井(牧次郎)

1. Saitama
2. Chichibu
3. Isama
4. 44

5. *Heimin*
6. Farmer
7–8. ?
9. Rifle platoon chief
10–11. ?
12. *CJSR* I:381; II:366–67

Kobayashi Torizō　小林酉蔵

1. Saitama
2. Chichibu
3. Ikoda
4. 22
5. *Heimin*
6. Farmer
7–8. ?
9. Platoon Commander
10. Twice for gambling
11. ?
12. Ide, *Kommintō*, pp. 199, 204–7

Morikawa Sakuzō　森川作蔵

1. Saitama
2. Chichibu
3. Kami-hinozawa
4. 35
5. *Heimin*
6. Farmer
7–8. ?
9. Platoon Commander
10. ?
11. Prison sentence of 15 years; died in prison
12. *CJSR* I:382, 366–67; Ishikawa, *Tonegawa*, p. 233

Kadodaira Sōhei　門平総平

1. Saitama
2. Chichibu
3. Shimo-hinozawa
4. 31
5. *Heimin*
6. Farmer
7–8. ?

9. Messenger
10. ?
11. Jiyūtō member; the one who first recruited Tashiro
12. *CJSR* I:382; II:232–34

Sakamoto Sōsaku   坂本宗作
1. Saitama
2. Chichibu
3. Fuppu
4. 27
5. *Heimin*
6. Blacksmith
7. Near bankrupt
8. ?
9. Messenger
10. ?
11. Jiyūtō member; *kobun* of Katō Orihei; early Kommintō organizer; death sentence
12. *CJSR* I:373–76; II:9–10, 135; Inoue, *Chichibu*, p. 37; Ide, *Kommintō*, pp. 34–53

Shimada Seizaburō   嶋田清三郎
1. Saitama
2. Chichibu
3. Honnogami
4. 27
5. *Heimin*
6. Farmer/rice-polisher
7–8. ?
9. Messenger
10. ?
11. Prison term: 3 years, 6 months
12. *CJSR* I:378, 642; II:168–69

Komai Teisaku   駒井貞作
1. Saitama
2. Chichibu
3. Shimo-hinozawa
4. ?
5. *Heimin*

6–8. ?
9. Messenger
10–11. ?
12. *CJSR* I:642

Takagishi Kenzō   高岸駅蔵
1. Saitama
2. Chichibu
3. Isama
4. 45
5. *Heimin*
6. Farmer
7–8. ?
9. Messenger
10. No
11. Member of Isama village Health Association; died in prison
12. *CJSR* I:292–97, 379, 642; II:100–106, 166–67

Arai Morizō   新井森蔵
1. Saitama
2. Chichibu
3. Onohara
4. ?
5. *Heimin*
6–11. ?
12. *CJSR* I:642

Horiguchi Kōsuke   堀口幸助
1. Gumma
2. Nishi-Gumma
3. Shibugawa
4. ?
5. *Heimin*
6. Manager of Law Office
7–8. ?
9. Messenger
10. ?
11. Persuaded Tashiro Eisuke to join Kommintō; *kobun* of Tashiro
12. *CJSR* I:642; Ide, *Kommintō*, p. 16; Inoue, *Chichibu*, p. 50; Sakai, "Chichibu Sōdō," p. 6

Appendix D
KABASAN ACTIVISTS

Koinuma Kuhachirō　鯉沼九八郎

1. Tochigi
2. Shimotsuga
3. Inaba (Mibu machi)
4. 32
5. *Heimin*
6. Landlord farmer/merchant
7. 60 *chō*
8. Yes
9. Jiyūtō
10. No
11. Early popular rights activist; married, children
12. Endō, *Kabasan*, pp. 29–33; Nojima, *Kabasan*, p. 150; *KJKS*, pp. 102–16, 572

Tomimatsu Masayasu　富松正安

1. Ibaraki
2. Makabe
3. Shimodate
4. 36
5. *Shizoku*
6. Ex-school teacher
7. ?
8. Yes
9. Jiyūtō; *Yūikan* head
10. No
11. Friend of Ōi Kentarō; early popular rights activist; founding member of Jiyūtō
12. *KJKS*, pp. 44–48, 477–80, 484, 514–17, 519; Nojima, *Kabasan*, pp. 219–23; Endō, *Kabasan*, pp. 57–59

Tamamatsu Kaichi 玉永嘉一（玉松嘉一）

1. Ibaraki
2. Makabe
3. Shimodate
4. 26
5. *Shizoku*
6. Farmer/fencing instructor
7. ?
8. Yes
9. Jiyūtō; *Yūikan*
10. ?
11. Bodyguard of Tomimatsu
12. *KJKS*, pp. 50–52, 497–503; Nojima, *Kabasan*, pp. 219–23

Hotta Komakichi　保田(多)駒吉

1. Ibaraki (born in Tokyo)
2. Makabe
3. Shimodate
4. 24
5. *Shizoku*
6. "None"
7. Lived off others
8. Probably
9. Jiyūtō (November 1882); *Yūikkan*
10. No
11. ?
12. *KJKS*, pp. 465–74; Nojima, *Kabasan*, pp. 207–8

Sugiura Kippuku　杉浦吉副

1. Fukushima
2. Yama
3. Okawada

4. 37
5. *Shizoku*
6. Farmer
7. ?
8. Yes
9. *Hokushinsha*
10. ?
11. Friend of Kōno Hironaka
12. *KJKS*, pp. 189–204, 313–14, 809; Takahashi, *Fukushima*, p. 263

Miura Bunji   三浦文治

1. Fukushima
2. Yama
3. Komeoka
4. 28
5. *Heimin*
6. Farmer/village head
7. 18.2 *chō*
8. Yes
9. Jiyūtō
10. Fukushima Incident, December 1882
11. Executed 1886
12. *KJKS*, pp. 28–32; Nojima, *Kabasan*, pp. 146–47; Takahashi, *Fukushima*, pp. 60, 251–53, 271–75

Isokawa Motoyoshi   五十川元吉
(Motokichi)

1. Fukushima
2. Tamura
3. Miharu
4. 24
5. *Shizoku*
6. Farmer
7. Impoverished
8. Yes
9. *Seidōkan*
10. Fukushima Incident (released)
11. Friend of Kōno, Kotoda, Kusano; moved to Korea, 1904

12. *KJKS*, pp. 46–50; Nojima, *Kabasan*, pp. 113–18; Endō, *Kabasan*, p. 89

Yamaguchi Moritarō   山口守太郎

1. Fukushima
2. Tamura
3. Miharu
4. 18
5. *Shizoku*
6. None
7. ?
8. Yes
9. *Risshisha*; *Seidōkan*
10. No
11. Died in prison
12. *KJKS*, pp. 422–33, 809; Nojima, *Kabasan*, p. 104; Endō, *Kabasan*, pp. 59–60; Takahashi, *Fukushima*, pp. 261–62

Amano Ichitarō   天野市太郎

1. Fukushima
2. Tamura
3. Miharu
4. 19
5. *Shizoku*
6. None
7. Poor
8. Yes
9. *Seidōkan*
10. ?
11. Father friend of Kōno Hironaka; killed in Boshin War
12. *KJKS*, pp. 216–26, 230–31; Nojima, *Kabasan*, pp. 103–4; Takahashi, *Fukushima*, pp. 261–62; Endō, *Kabasan*, pp. 59–60

Kotoda Iwamatsu   琴田岩松

1. Fukushima
2. Tamura
3. Miharu

4. 23
5. *Shizoku*
6. Journalist/unemployed
7. Father: sake manufacturer
8. Yes
9. Jiyūtō
10. Fukushima Incident
11. Ties with Tochigi Jiyūtō
12. *KJKS*, pp. 42–44, 602, 609; *FKS*, p. 790; Nojima, *Kabasan*, pp. 97–98; Taoka, *Hanshin*, pp. 59–60; Endō, *Kabasan*, pp. 54–55, 68–69

Kusano Sakuma 草野左久馬
1. Fukushima
2–3. No fixed residence
4. 19
5. *Shizoku*
6. None
7. ?
8. Yes
9. Jiyūtō
10. ?
11. Early activist in popular rights
12. *KJKS*, pp. 44–46; Endō, *Kabasan*, pp. 87–88; Nojima, *Kabasan*, pp. 118–20

Hara Rihachi 原利八
1. Fukushima
2. Yama
3. Shimoshiba
4. 35
5. *Heimin*
6. Farmer
7. "Middle-income" farmer
8. Yes
9. Jiyūtō (Aizu branch)
10. Escaped Fukushima arrest round-up
11. Friend of Uda Seiichi; died in prison
12. *KJKS*, pp. 32–40; Endō, *Kabasan*, pp. 142–48

Kōno Hiroshi 河野広体
1. Fukushima
2. Tamura
3. Miharu
4. 19
5. *Heimin*
6. None
7. (Father: wealthy merchant)
8. Yes
9. *Risshisha*; *Seidōkan*
10. Fukushima Incident
11. Nephew of Kōno Hironaka; active in popular rights since 16 years old
12. *KJKS*, pp. 274–55, 565, 809; Taoka, *Hanshin*, pp. 59–61; Nojima, *Kabasan*, pp. 107–112; Endō, *Kabasan*, pp. 65–70

Yokoyama Nobuyuki 横山信六 (Shinroku)
1. Fukushima
2. Yama
3. Atsugawa
4. 21
5. *Shizoku*
6. Ex-policeman
7. Unemployed; impoverished
8. Yes (Meiji Hōritsu gakkō)
9. Jiyūtō
10. Fukushima Incident
11. Boarder of Koinuma; died in prison, 1885
12. *KJKS*, pp. 20–28; Endō, *Kabasan*, p. 36; Takahashi, *Fukushima*, pp. 266–71

Kokugi Shigeo 小針重雄 （小釘重雄）
1. Fukushima
2. Nishi-Shirakawa
3. Shinda
4. 21
5. *Heimin*
6. Railroad repairman

7. Father: headman, sake manufacturer
8. Yes (Medical school)
9. Jiyūtō, *Seinenkan* (Tokyo)
10. ?
11. Friend of Miura, Hara, and Kōno;
executed 1886
12. *KJKS*, pp. 40–42, 580; Takahashi,
Fukushima jiken, pp. 266–71

Hirao Yasokichi   平尾八十吉

1. Tochigi
2–3. ?
4. 30?
5–7. ?
8. Yes
9. *Yūikkan*
10. ?
11. Killed during Incident
12. *KJKS*, pp. 25–26, 38–39, 360,
375; Nojima, *Kabasan*, p. 137;
Endō, *Kabasan*, pp. 202–5, 219

Kobayashi Tokutarō   小林篤太郎

1. Aichi (born in Fukushima)
2. Hekiumi
3. Noda
4. 18
5. *Shizoku*
6. Farmer
7. ?
8. Yes
9. *Yūikan*
10. No
11. Friend of Naitō Roichi
12. *KJKS*, pp. 453–64; Endō, *Kabasan*,
pp. 88–89, 91–93; Nojima,
Kabasan, p. 112

Arai Shōgo   新井章吾

1. Tochigi
2. Shimotsuga
3. Sugami
4. ?

5. *Heimin*
6. Farmer/village head
7. Wealthy farmer
8. Yes
9. Jiyūtō
10. March 1884
11. Joined Osaka Incident; wife,
daughter of Etō Shimpei; later
government figure
12. Endō, *Kabasan*, pp. 33–34

Shioda Okuzō   塩田奥造

1. Tochigi
2. Shimotsuga
3. Sugami
4. 35
5. *Heimin*
6. Farmer/merchant
7. Wealthy farmer
8. Yes
9. Jiyūtō
10. March 1883 for insulting official
11. Prefectural assemblyman till 1882
12. *KJKS*, pp. 95–101; Nojima,
Kabasan, pp. 72–73

Sakagihara Keibu   榊原経武

1. Tochigi
2. ?
3. Tochigi City?
4. ?
5. *Shizoku*
6. Lawyer
7. ?
8. Yes
9. *Yūikkan*
10. ?
11. Prefectural assemblyman, 1887;
Mayor, 1937; married to sister of
Monna
12. Endō, *Kabasan*, p. 35

Fukao Shigeki   深尾重城

1. Tochigi

2-10. ?
11. Suspected police spy
12. Endō, *Kabasan*, pp. 36–37

Monna Shigejirō (Mojirō)　門奈茂次郎

1. Fukushima
2. Kita-Aizu
3. Wakamatsu (no fixed address)
4. 23
5. *Shizoku*
6. Ex-policeman
7. ?
8. Yes
9. *Mumeikan*
10. Fukushima Incident (acquitted)
11. Admirer of Baba Tatsui
12. *KJKS*, pp. 14–20, 28; Nojima, *Kabasan*, pp. 191–92; Ishikawa, *Tonegawa*, pp. 170–78, 234–46

Ōhashi Genzaburō　大橋源三郎

1. Tochigi
2. Shimotsuga
3. Tocho
4. 32
5. *Heimin*
6. Farmer
7. Wealthy
8. "Barely"
9. *Jiyūtō*; *Yūikan*
10. No
11. Friend of Koinuma; one of original planners of incident
12. *KJKS*, pp. 116–31, 348–50; Nojima, *Kabasan*, pp. 121–22; Endō, *Kabasan*, pp. 134–37

Saeki Masakado　佐伯正門

1. Ishikawa
2. Kanezawa
3. Shimoatara
4. 24
5. *Shizoku*
6. Teacher/reporter

7. Unemployed
8. Yes
9. *Jiyūtō*
10. Four times, 1881–83
11. Friend of Koinuma
12. *KJKS*, pp. 133, 315, 256–66; Nojima, *Kabasan*, pp. 122–25; Endō, *Kabasan*, pp. 82–85

Iwanuma Saichi　岩沼佐一

1. Tochigi
2. Shimotsuga
3. Tochigi
4. 31
5. *Heimin*
6. Attorney
7. ?
8. Yes
9. *Jiyūtō*
10–11. ?
12. *KJKS*, pp. 67–70

Iwamoto Shinkichi　岩本新吉

1. Tochigi
2. Shimotsuga
3. Inaba
4. 20
5. *Heimin*
6. Teacher
7. ?
8. Yes
9. ?
10. No
11. Friend of Koinuma
12. *KJKS*, pp. 70–76

Tateno Yoshinosuke　館野芳之助

1. Ibaraki
2. Tsuzurakaza
3. Kotsutsumi
4. 27
5. *Heimin*
6. Farmer
7. ?

8. Yes
9. Jiyūtō (Spring 1883)
10. No
11. Friend of Tomimatsu; later implicated in Osaka Incident
12. *KJKS*, pp. 128–34

Tanaka Shōzō　田中正造
1. Tochigi
2. Shimotsuga
3. Yanaka
4. 43
5. *Heimin*
6. Farmer/prefectural assemblyman
7. Wealthy farmer
8. Yes
9. Kaishintō
10. ?
11. Diet member, 1890; after 1891,
antipollution campaigner
12. *KJKS*, pp. 803–4; Nojima, *Kabasan*, p. 101; Strong, "Pioneer"

Kurihara Sōgorō　粟原足五郎
1. Fukushima
2. Tamura
3. Miharu
4. 18
5. *Shizoku*
6. Merchant (kitchenware)
7. ?
8. Yes
9. *Seidōkan*
10. December 1882
11. Fukushima Incident participant
12. *KJKS*, pp. 55, 512–13, 570

Yamada Yūji　山田勇治
1. Iwate
2. Minami-Iwate
3. Yamagiwa
4. 19
5. *Heimin*

6-10. ?
11. Hid Kobayashi after Incident
12. *KJKS*, pp. 55, 511–12

Naitō Roichi　内藤魯一
1. Aichi
2. Hekiumi
3. Kami-jubara
4. 37
5. *Shizoku*
6. Politician/writer
7. Could vote in local elections
8. Yes
9. Jiyūtō; *Yūikkan*
10. No
11. Prefectural assemblyman, 4 times;
Diet, 1906, 1908 as Seiyūkai
party member
12. *KJKS*, pp. 512–13; *Nihon Rekishi
Daijiten* VII:315

Yazu Tetsunosuke　谷津鐵之助
1. Tokyo
2. Nihonbashi
3. Nihonbashi
4. 22
5. *Heimin*
6. Son of inn owner
7-10. ?
11. Hid Tamamatsu after Incident
12. *KJKS*, p. 55

Kōyama Hachiya　神山八弥
1. Fukushima
2. Ōnuma
3. Matsuya
4. 26
5. *Heimin*
6-10. ?
11. Hid Yokoyama, Hotta, and Kobayashi after Incident
12. *KJKS*, pp. 55, 512–13

Glossary

Aikoku kōdō kyōkai　愛国公道協会　A Nagoya-based popular rights society
Aikokukōtō　愛国公党　Public Party of Patriots
Aikoku seigensha　愛国正現社　A Nagano-based popular rights society
Aikokusha　愛国社　Society of Patriots
Aishinsha　愛身社　An Aizu-based popular rights society
Aizu　会津　A region in Fukushima prefecture
Aizu rokugun rengōkai　会津六郡連合会　Six Aizu Districts' Joint Committee
ansatsushugi　暗殺主義　"Assassinationism"; see *shō-undō*
Baba Tatsui　馬場辰猪　A popular rights thinker
battōtai　抜刀隊　"Drawn-sword unit"
bōdō　暴動　Violent action; uprising
Boshin sensō　戊辰戦争　The Boshin War
Chiba Takusaburō　千葉卓三郎　Drafter of a populist constitution; Itsukaichi village, Kanawawa prefecture
Chichibu jiken　秩父事件　The Chichibu Incident
chō　町　2.45 acres or .992 hectares
chōsan　逃散　"Running away"; desertion of a village by its inhabitants as a means of protest
chūnōsō　中農層　Strata of middle-income farmers
Daidō danketsu undō　大同団結運動　Movement of a Union of Like Thinkers
daigennin　代言人　An unlicensed lawyer (early Meiji)
daihyō osso　代表越訴　Appeal made by village representatives over the heads of local officials
daimyōjin　大明神　"Divine Rectifier"
dai-undō　大運動　"Large movement" strategy; see *kyoheishugi*
Danjōgahara　弾正ケ原　An open field near Kitakata, Fukushima
dōshi　同志　Comrade; like-minded fellow
Dōshinkai　同進会　A splinter popular rights society from the Mumeikan
dōshinsha　同心社　Like-thinking society; society of kindred spirits
fuon　不穏　Unrest, discontent, disturbance
fukoku kyōhei　富国強兵　"Rich country, strong military"
Fukushima jiken　福島事件　The Fukushima Incident

Fukuzawa Yukichi 福沢諭吉 A onetime liberal thinker

funō 富農 Rich farmer

furō no kyōto 浮浪の兇徒 Wandering outlaw

fuwa zuikōsha 付和随行者 Blind follower

gekka jiken 激化事件 Incident of intensified (violence)

genōsō 下農層 Strata of "lower" (small-income) farmers

getsu shibari 月縛り "Bound by the month": refers to a debt repayment scheme

gian shingi ken 議案審議権 Right to deliberate on legislation

gimin 義民 Martyr

gōhō tōsō 合法闘争 Lawful struggle

gōnō 豪農 Wealthy farmer

gōshi 郷士 Low-ranking samurai-farmer

gōso 強訴 Forceful appeal

gunchō 郡長 District ("county") head

gunshū 群集 Popular demonstration

gunyōkin boshūkata 軍用金募集方 "Collector of Army funds"

hakaitō 破壊党 Party of destruction

han 藩 Fief or domain (Tokugawa period)

hangyaku seishin 反逆精神 Spirit of rebellion

hanten 半纏 Short coat

heimin 平民 Commoner

hito 匪徒 Bandit

hōki 蜂起 Armed rebellion

Hoshi Tōru 星亨 A national leader of the Jiyūtō, and a lawyer

hyakushōdai 百姓代 Farmers' representative

ikki 一揆 Uprising

ippan jimmin 一般人民 Ordinary people

Itagaki Taisuke 板垣退助 President of the Jiyūtō

jichi kenri 自治権利 Right of self-government

jiken 事件 "Incident"; refers to various kinds of disturbances, ranging from popular demonstrations to armed rebellions

jinzai 人材 Capable or talented man

jiyū minken undō 自由民権運動 The freedom and people's rights movement (popular rights movement)

Jiyūtō 自由党 The Liberal (or Freedom) Party

jōnōsō 上農層 Strata of "upper" (high-income) farmers

Kabasan jiken 加波山事件 The Kabasan Incident

kafuchō dorosei 家父長奴隷制 System of patriarchical slavery

Kageyama Hideko   景山英子   Female popular rights activist; participant in the Osaka Incident

kairyō   改良   Reform

kakumei dōmei   革命同盟   Revolutionary alliance

kakumei honbu   革命本部   "Headquarters of the Revolution"

Kanno Hachirō   菅野八郎   Nineteenth-century (Tokugawa) rebel

kanri bujoku zai   官吏侮辱罪   Slandering (insulting) an official

Kantō   関東   Districts surrounding Tokyo

karidashi   駆出し   Roundup (of forced labor)

Kawanuma gun   河沼郡   Aizu region district

Kawazumi Tokuji   川澄徳次   Popular rights activist, and leader of Iida Incident

kazoku   華族   Peer or noble

kesshi kakumei   決死革命   "Revolution or Death!"

kimoiri   肝煎り   Village head

kirikanegashi   切金貸   "Limited loan"; a usurious loan scheme

Kitakata jiken   喜多方事件   Popular demonstration occurring in the town of Kitakata, November 1882

Kobayashi Kusuo   小林樟雄   Okayama prefecture popular rights activist, involved in the Osaka Incident

kobun   子分   "Client" or follower in parent-child relationship (*oyabun-kobun*)

kochō   戸長   Village administrator in the early Meiji period, in some regions equivalent to village headman

kōden   香奠   Condolence gift

kōdō mokuhyō   行動目標   Goals for action

Kōjunsha   交詢社   Early popular rights society

Kokkai kisei dōmeikai   国会期成同盟会   Association for the Establishment of a National Assembly

koku   石   A unit of dry measure equivalent to 4.96 bushels

kokujihan   国事犯   A crime against the State

kome sōdō   米騒動   Rice riot

Kommintō   困民党   Poor People's Party

kōrigashi setsuyu seigan   高利貸説諭請願   Petition admonishing usurers

kōtō   公党   Public party

kuchō   区長   Subdistrict head

kumigashira   組頭   Group headman

kuni   国   Province (pre-Meiji)

Kyōaidōbōkai   共愛同謀会   Early popular rights society in Fukushima

kyoheishugi   挙兵主義   "Raise-an-army-ism" (see *dai-undō*)

kyokai   巨魁   Ringleader

kyōkaku　侠客　"Robin Hood" figure

kyomutō　虚無党　Nihilist party

kyōto shūshūkyōsa　兇徒聚衆教唆　To assemble crowds for the purpose of rioting

Kyūshintō　急進党　Radical Party

Makabe gun　真壁郡　A district in Ibaraki prefecture

meibōka　名望家　Man of repute

minkenka　民権家　Advocate of popular rights

Mishima Michitsune　三島通庸　Governor of Fukushima prefecture at time of Fukushima Incident

Miyabe Noboru　宮部襄　Leader of the Gumma Jiyūtō, and leader of the Gumma Incident

Mumeikan　無名館　"Hall of No Name"; Jiyūtō headquarters, Fukushima

murahachibu　村八分　Ostracism from the village

Murakami Taiji　村上泰治　Young organizer of Chichibu liberals

murakata sōdō　村方騒動　Intravillage dispute

Muramatsu Aizō　村松愛蔵　Popular rights activist and leader of the Iida Incident

Murano Tsuneemon　村野常右衛門　Popular rights activist from Kanagawa and later a Seiyūkai politician

Nakai Chōmin　中江兆民　Popular rights thinker

nanushi　名主　Village headman

nengu　年貢　Annual land tax (Tokugawa)

Nihon kokka kokken-an　日本国家国憲案　Draft Constitution of the Japanese Nation; written by Ueki Emori, 1881

ninsoku saisoku　人足催促　Forced labor (literally, "demand for labor")

Nisshinkan　日新館　Hall of Daily Renewal for ex-samurai in Wakamatsu, Fukushima prefecture

nōhanki　農繁期　Farmers' busy season

nōheitai　農兵隊　Peasant army

Ōi Kentarō　大井憲太郎　Leader of the radical wing of the Jiyūtō

Okunomiya Kenshi　奥宮健之　Popular rights advocate who helped establish the Rickshamen's Party

Ōmeisha　嚶鳴社　Popular rights society

Ōnuma gun　大沼郡　District in the Aizu region

osso　越訴　"Bypass" appeal, made directly to a higher authority

Ōya Masao　大矢正夫　Kanagawa prefecture popular rights activist; participant in the Osaka Incident

rekihō　歴訪　Round of calls

Risshisha　立志社　Early popular rights society of Tosa

rōnin　浪人　Masterless samurai

saibō　細胞　Cell (political)

Sakū　佐久　Region in Nagano prefecture bordering on Chichibu

Sakura Sōgorō　佐倉惣五郎　Seventeenth-century peasant martyr

sambōchō　参謀長　Chief-of-Staff

sampō dōro　三方道路　Three roads (project) in Aizu, Fukushima

Sanshisha　三師社　Popular rights society located in Miharu, Fukushima prefecture

Seidōkan　正道館　Popular rights academy for youth, established by the Sanshisha

seihansha　正犯者　Principal offender

seisha　政社　Political society

Sekiyōkan　石陽館　Popular rights academy for youth, established by the Sekiyōsha

Sekiyōsha　石陽社　Popular rights society located in Ishikawa, Fukushima prefecture

sen　銭　One hundredth of a yen

Shakaitō　車会党　Rickshamen's Party

Shakkintō　借金党　Debtors' Party

Shakuchitō　借地党　Leaseholders' Party

shichichiken　質地券　Certificates of pawned land

shinbokukai　親睦会　Friendship association

shiro-hachimaki　白鉢巻　White headband worn by farmers

shishi　志士　Patriot or man of spirit

shizoku　士族　Ex-samurai

shōshū　嘯集　Popular assembly, sometimes leading to a demonstration

shō-undō　小運動　"Small movement" strategy; see *ansatsushugi*

shōya　庄屋　Village headman

shukai　首魁　Ringleader

shūkai jōrei　集会条例　Law regulating public meetings

shūso　愁訴　Collective and legal appeal

shutsugeki　出撃　Sortie

sōshireikan　総司令官　Supreme Commander

Sugita Teiichi　杉田定一　Popular rights thinker and activist

sukegō　助郷　A village providing transport for relay stations (Tokugawa period) and the commuted tax thereof

takeyari　竹槍　Bamboo spear

Teiseitō　帝政党　Imperial (government) Party

tempu jinken　天賦人権　Natural rights

tempu koyū no ken　天賦固有の権　Inherent natural rights

tempuku　顚覆　Overthrow

tenma　伝馬　Post stations

terakoya　寺子屋　Temple school

tochi heibun hō　土地平分法　Land equalization law

Tōhoku　東北　Northeastern region of Honshu

tomurai gassen　弔い合戦　Vendetta; battle of revenge

tonshū　屯集　Popular gathering

toshiyori　年寄　Elder (of a village or other jurisdiction)

ton'ya　問屋　Wholesale house

Tsukuba-san　筑波山　Mountain in Ibaraki prefecture

uchikowashi　打毀し　Literally, "to smash and destroy," usually a house

Ueki Emori　植木枝盛　Popular rights thinker and activist

Ujiie Naokuni　氏家直国　Popular rights activist and assistant to Ōi Kentarō

Utsunomiya　宇都宮　Town in Tochigi prefecture

Wakamatsu　若松　Town in the Aizu region

waraji　草鞋　Straw sandals

Yagi Shigeharu　八木重治　Popular rights activist and leader of the Iida incident

Yama gun　耶麻郡　District of the Aizu region

Yano Fumio　矢野文雄　Popular rights thinker

yonaoshi ikki　世直し一揆　World reform rebellion

yonarashi ikki　世均し一揆　Equalize (level) the World rebellion

Yūikan　有為館　Popular rights club in Shimodate, headed by Tomimatsu Masayasu

Yūikkan　有一館　Popular rights club in Tokyo, probably the model for the *Yūikan*

Yūshinsha　有信社　Popular rights society in Gumma prefecture

yūshō reppai　優勝劣敗　"Survival of the fittest"

zaguri　座繰り　Hand-reeling

zenpan sōdō　全藩騒動　All-domain uprising (Tokugawa)

Works Cited

Japanese Sources

Akagi Etsuko. "Tochigi ken no jiyū minken undō: chihō jichi no yōsō wo me-gutte" [The Freedom and Popular Rights Movement of Tochigi Prefecture: Its Elements of Local Political Autonomy]. *Tochigi Shiron* 2 (1970):1–15.

Aoki Keiichirō. *Nagano ken shakai undō shi* [A History of the Socialist Movement in Nagano Prefecture]. Tokyo: Gannandō Shoten, 1965.

———. *Nihon nōmin undō shi* [A History of the Farmer Movement in Japan]. Vol. 2. Tokyo: Hyōron Shinsha, 1958.

Aoki Kōji. *Hyakushō ikki no nenjiteki kenkyū* [A Chronological Study of Peasant Uprisings]. Tokyo: Shinseisha, 1966.

———. *Hyakushō ikki sōgō nempyō* [A Comprehensive Chronology of Peasant Uprisings in the Tokugawa Period]. San'ichi Shobō, 1971.

———. *Meiji nōmin sōjō no nenjiteki kenkyū* [A Chronological Study of Farmers' Disturbances in the Meiji Period]. Tokyo: Shinseisha, 1967.

Bushū yonaoshi ikki shiryō [Historical Materials on the World-Reform Uprisings of the Bushū Area]. Compiled by Kinsei Sonrakushi Kenkyū Kai. Tokyo: Keiyūsha, 1972.

Chichibu jiken shiryō [Historical Materials on the Chichibu Incident]. 2 vols. Compiled by Saitama Shimbun Sha. Urawa: Saitama Shimbun Sha Shup-pan-bu, 1970.

Chichibu Kyōikukai, comp. *Saitama-ken Chichibu-gun shi* [A History of Chichibu District of Saitama Prefecture]. Tokyo, 1925.

Chōya Shimbun. September to December 1884.

Ebukuro Fumio. *Chichibu sōdō* [Violence in Chichibu]. Chichibu City; Chichibu Shimbun Shuppan-bu, 1950.

Emura Eiichi. "Kokujihan Takada jiken" [Treason and the Takada Incident]. *Shien* 84–85 (November 1963):60–79.

Emura Eiichi and Nakamura Seisoku, eds. *Kokken to minken no sōkoku* [Rivalry Between People's Rights and State's Rights]. Vol. 6 of *Nihon minshū no rekishi series*, Tokyo: Sanseidō, 1974.

Endō Shizuo. *Kabasan jiken* [The Kabasan Incident]. Tokyo: San'ichi Shobō, 1971.

Fukuda Kaoru. *Sanmin sōjō roku: Meiji jūshichinen Gumma jiken* [A Record of Sericulturalists' Rebellion: The Gumma Incident of 1884]. Tokyo: Seiun Shobō, 1974.

Fukushima-ken shi [A History of Fukushima Prefecture]. Vol. 11. *Kindai shiryō* [Historical Materials of the Modern Era], Part I. Fukushima: Kenchō Bunsho Kōhōka, 1964.

Gakushūin Hojinkai Shigakubu, comp. *Chichibu jiken no ikkōsatsu* [Considerations on the Chichibu Incident]. Tokyo, 1968.

Gotō Yasushi. "Iida jiken" [The Iida Incident]. In *Jiyū minken undō* [Freedom and Popular Rights Movement], Vol. 3, pp. 102–47. Compiled by Meiji Shiryō Kenkyū Renraku Kai. Tokyo: Ochanomizu Shobō, 1956.

———. *Jiyū minken: Meiji no kakumei to hankakumei* [Revolution and Counterrevolution in Meiji: Freedom and Popular Rights]. Tokyo: Chūō Kōronsha, 1972.

———. "Meiji jūshichinen no gekka shojiken" [The Various Violent Incidents of 1884]. In *Jiyū minkenki no kenkyū* [A Study of the Freedom and Popular Rights Period], Part 2: *Minken undō no gekka to kaitai* [Violence and the Dissolution of the Popular Rights Movement], Vol. 1, pp. 205–69. Edited by Horie Hideichi and Tōyama Shigeki. Tokyo: Yūhikaku, 1959.

Hagibara Susumu. *Sōdō—Gumma-ken nōmin undō shi nōto* [Rebellion—Notes on the History of the Farmers' Movement of Gumma Prefecture]. Maebashi: Gumma Jōhōsha, 1957.

Haraguchi Kiyoshi. *Boshin sensō* [The Boshin War]. Tokyo: Kakusensho, 1963.

———. "Shizuoka jiken no shakaiteki haikei" [The Social Background of the Shizuoka Incident]. In *Minken undō no tenkai* [Development of the Popular Rights Movement], Vol. 9, pp. 30–123. Compiled by Meiji Shiryō Kenkyū Renraku Kai. Tokyo: Ochanomizu Shobō, 1958.

Hasegawa Noboru. "Kamo jiken" [Kamo Incident]. In *Jiyū minkenki no kenkyū* [A Study of the Freedom and Popular Rights Period], Part 2: *Minken undō no gekka to kaitai* [Violence and the Dissolution of the Popular Rights Movement], Vol. 1, pp. 121–204. Edited by Horie Hideichi and Tōyama Shigeki. Tokyo: Yūhikaku, 1959.

———. "Meiji jūshichinen no Jiyūtō" [The Liberal Party in 1884]. *Rekishi Hyōron*, special edition (November–December 1954):1–16.

Hashimoto Yoshio. "Kommintō jiken" [Poor People's Party Incident]. *Rekishi Hyōron*, special edition (November–December 1954):17–32.

Hayashi Motoi. "Kabasan jiken nanajū shūnen" [The Seventieth Anniversary of the Kabasan Incident]. *Rekishi Hyōron* 59 (January 1955):54–70.

———. *Zoku hyakushō ikki no dentō* [A Second Series of the Tradition of Peasant Uprisings]. Tokyo: Shinhyōronsha, 1971.

Hirano Yoshitarō. *Minken undō no hatten* [Development of the Popular Rights Movement]. Tokyo: Ondorisha, 1948.

———. *Nihon shihonshugi shakai no kikō* [The Social Structure of Japanese Capitalism]. Tokyo: Iwanami Shoten, 1974. (Originally published in 1936.)

———. Ōi Kentarō. Tokyo: Yoshikawa Kōbunkan, 1960.

Ibaraki-ken shi: shi, machi, mura hen [History of Ibaraki Prefecture: Cities, Towns, and Villages]. Vol. 1. Mito, 1972.

Ibaraki-ken shiryō: Kindai seiji shakai hen [Historical Materials on Ibaraki Prefecture: Modern Politics and Soceity]. Vol. 1. Ibaraki: Ibaraki-ken shi hensan kindai shi daiichi bu-kai, 1974.

Ide Magoroku. *Chichibu Kommintō gunzō* [The Chichibu Poor People's Party Group]. Tokyo: Shinjimbutsu Ōraisha, 1973.

Ienaga Saburō. *Ueki Emori kenkyū* [A Study of Ueki Emori]. Tokyo: Iwanami Shoten, 1960.

———, ed. *Ueki Emori senshū* [Collected Works of Ueki Emori]. Tokyo: Iwanami Shoten, 1974.

———. *Kakumei shisō no senkusha: Ueki Emori no hito to shisō* [Pioneer of Revolutionary Thought: Ueki Emori, the Man and His Ideas]. Tokyo: Iwanami Shoten, 1976. (Originally published in 1955.)

Inaoka Susumu. *Nihon nōmin undō shi* [A History of the Farmers' Movement in Japan]. Tokyo: Aoki Shoten, 1974. (Originally published in 1954.)

Inoue Kiyoshi. *Nihon no rekishi* [A History of Japan]. Vol. 2. Tokyo: Iwanami Shoten, 1976. (Originally published in 1965.)

Inoue Kōji. *Chichibu jiken: Jiyū minkenki no nōmin hōki* [The Chichibu Incident: Farmers' Rebellion in the Period of Freedom and Popular Rights]. Tokyo: Chūō Kōronsha, 1968.

———. "Chichibu jiken: Sono shakaiteki kiban" [The Chichibu Incident: Its Social Bases]. In *Jiyū minken undō* [Freedom and Popular Rights Movement], Vol. 3, pp. 65–99. Compiled by Meiji Shiryō Kenkyū Renraku Kai. Tokyo: Ochanomizu Shobō, 1956.

Irokawa Daikichi. "Kommintō to Jiyūtō" [The Poor People's Party and the Liberal Party]. *Rekishigaku Kenkyū* 247:8 (August 1961):1–30.

———. *Shimpen Meiji seishin shi* [A Revised Edition of the History of the Meiji Spirit]. Tokyo: Chūō Kōronsha, 1973.

———, ed. *Tama no gosennen: Shimin no rekishi hakkutsu* [Five Thousand Years in Tama: Unearthing the History of Its Citizens]. Tokyo: Heibonsha, 1970.

Irokawa Daikichi, Ei Hideo, and Arai Katsuhiro. *Minshū kempō no sōzō: Uzumoreta kusa no ne no ninmyaku* [The Creation of Popular Constitutions: Buried in the Human Pulse of Grass Roots]. Tokyo: Hyōronsha, 1970.

Ishikawa Naoki. *Tonegawa minken kikō* [An Account of Popular Rights Along the Tone River]. Tokyo: Shinjinbutsu Ōraisha, 1972.

Itagaki Taisuke. *Jiyūtō shi* [A History of the Liberal Party]. Vols. 1 and 3. Tokyo: Iwanami Shoten, 1973. (Originally published in 1913.)

Kabasan jiken kankei shiryō shū [A Collection of Historical Documents Concerning the Kabasan Incident]. Compiled by Inaba Seitarō. Introduction by Tōyama Shigeki. Afterword by Endō Shizuo. Tokyo: San'ichi Shobō, 1970.

Kano Masanao. *Nihon kindaika no shisō* [Ideas in Japan's Modernization]. To-kyo: Kenkyūsha, 1972.

Kawashima Yukinobu. *Kōtō hōin kohan roku* [A Record of the Public Trials at the High Crimes Court]. Tokyo: Kindai Nihon Shiryō Kenkyū Kai, 1955.

Kobayashi Kōjin. *Shinano nōmin shi* [History of the Farmers of Nagano Prefec-ture]. Nagano: Shinano Mainichi Shimbun-sha, 1946.

Kobayashi Seiji and Yamada Akira. *Fukushima-ken no rekishi* [A History of Fukushima Prefecture]. Tokyo: Yamagawa Shuppansha, 1973.

Koike Yoshitaka. *Chichibu oroshi—Chichibu jiken to Inoue Denzō* [Strong Wind in Chichibu—Inoue Denzō and the Chichibu Incident]. Tokyo: Gendai Shi Shuppansha, 1974.

Kokusho Iwao. *Hyakushō ikki no kenkyū zokuhen* [A Supplementary Study of Peasant Uprisings]. Tokyo: Minerva Shobō, 1959.

———. "Meiji shonen no hyakushō ikki" [Peasant Uprisings in Early Meiji]. In *Meiji isshin keizai shi kenkyū* [A Study of the Economic History of the Meiji Restoration]. Edited by Honjō Eijirō. Tokyo: Kaizōsha, 1930, pp. 703-25.

Maeda Renzan. *Jiyū minken jidai* [Era of Freedom and Popular Rights]. Tokyo: Jiji Tsūshinsha, 1961.

Masumi Junnosuke. *Nihon seitō shiron* [An Historical Treatise on Japanese Polit-ical Parties]. Vol. 1. Tokyo: Tokyo Daigaku Shuppan Kai, 1965.

Mita Munesuke, ed. *Jiyū to minken* [Freedom and Popular Rights]. Vol. 5 of *Meiji no gunzō*, 10 vols. Tokyo: San'ichi Shobō, 1968.

Morikawa Tetsurō. *Bakumatsu ansatsu shi* [A History of Assassination During the Bakumatsu Period]. Tokyo: San'ichi Shobō, 1967.

———. *Meiji ansatsu shi* [A History of Assassination During the Meiji Period]. To-kyo: San'ichi Shobō, 1967.

Murano Ren'ichi and Irokawa Daikichi. *Murano Tsuneemon: Minkenka jidai* [A Biography of Murano Tsuneemon: His Period as Popular Rights Advo-cate]. Tokyo: Chūō Kōron Jigyō Shuppan, 1969.

Nagatani Yasuo. "Gumma jiken no shakaiteki kiban ni kansuru kenkyū nōto" [Research Notes on the Social Bases of the Gumma Incident]. *Shien* 32:1 (February 1971):81-90.

Nakazawa Ichirō. "Chichibu jiken hachijūkyu shūnen ni yosete" [On the Eighty-ninth Anniversary of the Chichibu Incident]. *Bungei Chichibu* 6 (1974): 4-28.

———. *Jiyū minken no minshūzō: Chichibu Kommintō to nōmintachi* [The Dem-ocratic Crowd of Freedom and Popular Rights: The Chichibu Poor People's Party and the Farmers]. Tokyo: Shin Nihon Shuppansha, 1974.

———. "Ochiai Toraichi no ikō wo megutte" [Concerning the Posthumous Letters of Ochiai Toraichi]. *Rekishi Hyōron*, special edition (November–December 1954):26-49.

Namatame Yasushi. *Kabasan jiken no ikkōsatsu* [An Overview of the Kabasan

Incident] . Takahagi, 1962.

Nihon Rekishi Daijiten [Encyclopedia of Japanese History] , 1968 edition, III: 508–9. S.v. "Kyōkaku" [Robin Hood] , by Tamura Eitarō.

Nojima Kitarō. *Kabasan jiken* [The Kabasan Incident] . Edited by Hayashi Motoi and Endō Shizuo. Tokyo: Heibonsha, 1966. (Originally published in 1900.)

Ōe Shinobu. "Minken undō seiritsuki no gōnō to nōmin" [Farmers and Wealthy Farmers in the Period of Development of the Popular Rights Movement] . *Rekishigaku Kenkyū* 186 and 189 (August and November 1955):14–23; 23–34.

–––. *Nihon no sangyō kakumei* [Japan's Industrial Revolution] . Tokyo: Iwanami Shoten, 1968.

Ōishi Kaichirō. "Fukushima jiken no shakai keizaiteki kiban" [The Socioeconomic Bases of the Fukushima Incident] . In *Jiyū minkenki no kenkyū* [A Study of the Freedom and Popular Rights Period] , Part 2: *Minken undō no gekka to kaitai* [Violence and the Dissolution of the Popular Rights Movement], Vol. I, pp. 1–120. Edited by Horie Hideichi and Tōyama Shigeki. Tokyo: Yūhikaku, 1959.

Ōmachi Masami and Hasegawa Shinzō, eds. *Bakumatsu no nōmin ikki* [Peasant Uprisings of the Bakumatsu Period] . Tokyo: Yuzankaku, 1974.

Ōno Fumio. *Saitama-ken no rekishi* [A History of Saitama Prefecture] . Tokyo: Yamagawa Shuppansha, 1971.

Saitama-ken shi [A History of Saitama Prefecture] . Vol. 2. Edited by Tayama Soka. Tokyo, 1921. (Originally published in 1912.)

Sakai Toshihiko. "Chichibu Sōdō" [The Chichibu Rebellion] . *Kaizō* 10 (October 1928):1–19.

Sasaki Junnosuke, ed. *Murakata sōdō to yonaoshi* [Village Conflicts and World Reformation] . 2 vols. Tokyo: Aoki Shoten, 1972.

–––, ed. *Yonaoshi* [World Reform] . Vol. 5 of *Nihon minshū no rekishi* series. Tokyo: Sanseidō, 1974.

Satō Seirō. "Meiji jūshichinen gogatsu no Jiyūtō-in meibo ni tsuite" [Concerning the List of Liberal Party Members of May 1884] . *Rekishigaku Kenkyū* 178 (December 1954):31–38.

Sekido Kakuzō. *Tōsui minken shi* [A History of Popular Rights in the East] . Ibaraki, Shimodate: Yōyūkan, 1907.

Shimoyama Saburō. "Fukushima jiken oboegaki" [A Note on the Fukushima Incident] . In *Jiyū minken undō* [The Freedom and Popular Rights Movement] , Vol. 3, pp. 148–86. Compiled by Meiji Shiryō Kenkyū Renraku Kai. Tokyo: Ochanomizu Shobō, 1956.

–––. "Fukushima jiken shōron" [A Short Treatise on the Fukushima Incident]. In *Jiyū minken* [Freedom and Popular Rights] , pp. 161–200. Vol. 10 of *Nihon rekishi* series. Edited by Sakane Yoshihisa. Tokyo: Yūseidō Shuppan Kabushiki Kaisha, 1973.

–––. "Jiyū minken undō—sono chiikiteki bunseki" [The Freedom and Popular

Rights Movement—A Geographical Analysis]. *Tōkei Daikai Shi* 37 (February 1962):199–224.

———. "Meiji jūshichinen ni okeru Jiyūtū no dōkō to nōmin sōjō no keikyō" [The Direction of the Liberal Party in 1884 and the Background of Farmer Rebellions]. In *Jiyū minkenki no kenkyū* [A Study of the Freedom and Popular Rights Period], Part 3: *Minken undō no gekka to kaitai* [Violence and the Dissolution of the Popular Rights Movement], Vol. 2, pp. 1–116. Edited by Horie Hideichi and Tōyama Shigeki. Tokyo: Yūhikaku, 1959.

———. "Minken undō nōto" [Notes on the Popular Rights Movement]. In *Jiyū minken* [Freedom and Popular Rights], pp. 289–309. Vol. 10 of *Nihon rekishi* series. Edited by Sakane Yoshihisa. Tokyo: Yūseidō Shuppan Kabushiki Kaisha, 1973.

———, ed. *Jiyū minken shisō* [The Thought of Freedom and Popular Rights]. Vol. 2, with commentary by the editor. Tokyo: Aoki Shoten, 1961.

Shinobu Seisaburō. *Jiyū minken to zettaishugi* [Freedom and Popular Rights and Absolutism]. Tokyo: Nihon Hyōronsha, 1950.

Shōji Kichinosuke. "Jiyū minken undō no keizaiteki haikei" [The Economic Background of the Freedom and Popular Rights Movement]. In *Jiyū minken undō* [The Freedom and Popular Rights Movement], Vol. 3, pp. 188–236. Compiled by Meiji Shiryō Kenkyū Renraku Kai. Tokyo: Ochanomizu Shobō, 1956.

———. "Yonaoshi: Nōmin hanran" [World Reformation: Farmer Rebellions]. In *Nōmin tōsō shi* [History of Farmers' Struggles], Vol. 2, pp. 161–85. Tokyo: Kokura Shobō, 1974.

———. *Yonaoshi ikki no kenkyū* [A Study of World Reformation Uprisings]. Tokyo: Sanseidō, 1974.

———, ed. *Nihon seisha seitō hattatsu shi* [A History of the Development of Political Societies in Japan]. Tokyo: Ochanomizu Shobō, 1959.

———, Hayashi Motoi, and Yasumaru Yoshio. *Minshū undō no shisō* [The Thought of Mass Movements]. Tokyo: Iwanami Shoten, 1970.

Takahashi Tetsuo. *Fukushima jiken* [The Fukushima Incident]. Tokyo: San'ichi Shobō, 1970.

———. *Fukushima jiyū minken undō shi* [A History of the Freedom and Popular Rights Movement in Fukushima]. Tokyo: Rironsha, 1954.

Tamura Eitarō. *Kindai Nihon nōmin undō shiron* [An Historical Treatise on the Japanese Farmer Movement]. Tokyo: Getsuyō Shobō, 1948.

Tanaka Senya. "Chichibu bōdō zatsuroku" [Miscellaneous Notes on the Chichibu Incident]. In *Chichibu jiken shiryō* [Historical Materials on the Chichibu Incident]. Vol. 2 (1884), pp. 551–85. Compiled by Saitama Shimbun Sha. Urawa: Saitama Shimbun Sha Shuppan-bu, 1970.

Tanaka Sōgorō. *Nihon no jiyū minken* [Freedom and Popular Rights in Japan]. Tokyo: Yuzankaku, 1947.

Taoka Reiun (pseud.). *Meiji hanshin den* [A Commentary on Rebellious Retainers of the Meiji Period]. Tokyo: Aoki Shoten, 1953. (Originally published in 1909.)

Tokyo Nichi Nichi Shimbun. November 1882 to January 1885.

Tsuchiya Takao and Ono Michio, eds. *Meiji shonen nōmin sōjō roku* [A Record of Farmer Rebellions in Early Meiji]. Tokyo: Keisō Shobō, 1969. (Originally published in 1931.)

Uehara Kuniichi. *Saku jiyū minken undō shi* [A History of the Saku District Freedom and Popular Rights Movement]. Tokyo: San'ichi Shobō, 1973.

Wada Harumi. "Jiyū minken undō to Narodoniki" [The Popular Rights Movement and the Narodnaya (Volya)]. *Rekishi Kōron* 2:1 (January 1976): 61-73.

Wagatsuma Sakae et al., comps. *Nihon seiji saiban shi roku: Meiji go* [An Historical Record of Political Trials in Japan: Late Meiji]. Vol. 2. Tokyo: Daiichi Hōki Shuppan Kabushiki Kaisha, 1969.

Wakasa Kuranosuke. "Chichibu jiken ni okeru Jiyūtō Kommintō no soshiki katei—Chōfu mura o chūshin toshite" [The Organizational Process of the Jiyūtō and Kommintō in the Chichibu Incident—The Case of Chōfu Village]. *Rekishi Hyōron* 260:3 (March 1972):30-50.

Yamada Minoru and Nakaune Shōichi. "Murakami Taiji no saiban" [The Trial of Murakami Taiji]. *Rekishigaku Kenkyū* 186 (August 1955):24-30.

Yokoyama Toshio. *Gimin: Hyakushō ikki no shidōshatachi* [Martyrs: Leaders of Peasant Rebellions]. Tokyo: Sanseidō Shobō, 1973.

Yomiuri Shimbun. September to December 1884.

Yoshino Sakuzō, comp. *Meiji bunka zenshū* [Collected Works of Meiji Culture]. 24 vols. Tokyo, 1928-30. Vol. 5: *Jiyū minken hen* [Volume on Freedom and Popular Rights]. 1928.

Yūbin Hōchi Shimbun. September to December 1884.

English Sources

Akita, George. *Foundations of Constitutional Government in Modern Japan, 1868-1890*. Cambridge, Mass.: Harvard University Press, 1967.

Arendt, Hannah. *On Revolution*. New York: Viking Press, 1963.

Ashley, Maurice. *Oliver Cromwell and the Puritan Revolution*. New York: Collier Books, 1958.

Bailyn, Bernard. *The Ideological Origins of the American Revolution*. Cambridge, Mass.: Harvard University Press, 1967.

Beasley, W.G. *The Meiji Restoration*. Stanford, Calif.: Stanford University Press, 1972.

———. "Political Groups in Tosa, 1856-68." *Bulletin of the School of Oriental and African Studies* 30:2 (1967):382-90.

Becker, Carl L. *The Declaration of Independence: A Study in the History of Political Ideas*. New York: Vintage Books, 1942. (Originally published in 1922.)

Befu, Harumi. "Duty, Reward, Sanction, and Power: Four-cornered Office of the Tokugawa Headman." In *Modern Japanese Leadership: Transition and Change*. Edited by Bernard Silberman and H. D. Harootunian. Tucson, Arizona: University of Arizona Press, 1966, pp. 25–50.

Bellah, Robert. *Tokugawa Religion: The Values of Pre-Industrial Japan*. Glencoe, Ill.: Free Press, 1957.

Borton, Hugh. *Peasant Uprisings in Japan of the Tokugawa Period*. In *Transactions of the Asiatic Society of Japan*. Vol. 16. Tokyo, 1938; New York: Paragon Book Reprint Corp., 1968.

Bowen, Roger W. "The Politicization of Japanese Social Bandits." In *Asian Bandits and Radical Politics*. Edited by Paul C. Winther. Forthcoming.

Brinton, Crane. *The Anatomy of Revolution*. New York: Vintage Books, 1956.

Brown, Sidney Revere. "Kido Takayoshi: Meiji Japan's Cautious Revolutionary." *Pacific Historical Review* 16 (May 1956):152–62.

———. "Political Assassination in Early Meiji Japan: The Plot Against Ōkubo Toshimichi." In *Meiji Japan's Centennial: Aspects of Political Thought and Action*. Edited by David Wurfel. Lawrence, Kansas: University of Kansas Press, 1971, pp. 18–35.

Burton, W. Donald. "Peasant Struggle in Japan, 1590–1760." *Journal of Peasant Studies* 5:2 (January 1978):135–71.

Chambliss, William Jones. *Chiaraijima Village: Land Tenure, Taxation, and Local Trade, 1818–1884*. Tucson, Arizona: University of Arizona Press, 1965.

Chesneux, Jean. *Peasant Revolts in China, 1840–1949*. London: Thames and Hudson, 1973.

Choi, Kee-il. "Tokugawa Feudalism and the Emergence of the New Leaders of Early Modern Japan." *Explorations in Entrepreneurial History* 9:1 (1956): 72–84.

Craig, Albert. *Chōsū in the Meiji Restoration*. Cambridge, Mass.: Harvard University Press, 1961.

Crocker, W. R. *The Japanese Population Problem: The Coming Crisis*. London: Allen and Unwin, 1931.

Dore, Ronald P. "Education: Japan." In *Political Modernization in Japan and Turkey*. Edited by Robert E. Ward and Dankwart A. Rustow. Princeton, N.J.: Princeton University Press, 1964, pp. 176–204.

———. "The Legacy of Tokugawa Education." In *Changing Japanese Attitudes Toward Modernization*. Edited by Marius B. Jansen. Princeton, N.J.: Princeton University Press, 1965, pp. 99–131.

———. "The Meiji Landlord: Good or Bad?" *Journal of Asian Studies* 18:3 (May 1959):343–55.

Duus, Peter. "Whig History, Japanese Style: The Minyūsha Historians and the Meiji Restoration." *Journal of Asian Studies* 33:3 (May 1974):415–36.

Eckstein, Harry. "On the Etiology of Internal Wars." *History and Theory* 4 (1965):433–63.

Eisenstadt, S. N. *Modernization: Protest and Change*. Englewood Cliffs, N.J.: Prentice-Hall, 1966.

d'Entrevès, A. P. *Natural Law: An Introduction to Legal Philosophy*. London and New York: Hutchinson's University Library, 1951.

Foner, Eric. *Tom Paine and Revolutionary America*. London, Oxford, and New York: Oxford University Press, 1976.

Gooch, G. P. *English Democratic Ideas in the Seventeenth Century*. Second Edition with Supplementary Notes and Appendices by H. J. Laski. New York: Harper & Row, 1959. (Originally published in 1927.)

———. *Political Thought in England, Bacon to Halifax*. London: Oxford University Press, 1960. (Originally published in 1915.)

Gough, Kathleen, "Peasant Resistance and Revolt in South India." *Pacific Affairs* 41:4 (Winter 1968–69):526–44.

Gregg, Pauline. *Free-born John: A Biography of John Lilburne*. London: George G. Harrap, 1961.

Hackett, Roger F. *Yamagata Aritomo in the Rise of Modern Japan, 1838–1922*. Cambridge, Mass.: Harvard University Press, 1971.

Hall, John C. *Rousseau: An Introduction to His Political Philosophy*. Cambridge, Mass.: Schenkman, 1973.

Hill, Christopher. *The World Turned Upside Down: Radical Ideas During the English Revolution*. New York: Viking Press, 1972.

———, ed. *Winstanley: The Law of Freedom and Other Writings*. Middlesex, England: Penguin Books, 1973.

Hobsbawm, Eric J. *Bandits*. London: Weidenfeld and Nicolson, 1969.

———. "Peasants and Politics." *Journal of Peasant Studies* 1:1 (October 1973): 3–22.

———. *Primitive Rebels: Studies in Archaic Forms of Social Movement in the 19th and 20th Centuries*. New York: W. W. Norton, 1959.

Honjō Eijirō. *The Social and Economic History of Japan*. Kyoto: Institute for Research in Economic History of Japan, 1935.

Huntington, Samuel P. *Political Order in Changing Societies*. New Haven and London: Yale University Press, 1968.

Ike, Nobutaka. *The Beginnings of Political Democracy in Japan*. Baltimore: Johns Hopkins Press, 1950; New York: Greenwood Press, 1969.

Irokawa Daikichi. "Freedom and the Concept of People's Rights." *Japan Quarterly* 14:2 (April–June 1967): 175–83.

———. "The Survival Struggle of the Japanese Community." *Japan Interpreter* 9:4 (Spring 1975):466–94.

Jansen, Marius B. "The Meiji State, 1868–1912." In *Modern East Asia: Essays in Interpretation*. Edited by James B. Crowley, New York: Harcourt, Brace and World, 1970, pp. 102–8.

———. "Ōi Kentarō: Radicalism and Chauvinism." *The Far Eastern Quarterly* 2:3 (May 1952):305–16.

Japan Weekly Mail. January 1883 to January 1885.

Kawabe Kisaburō. *The Press and Politics in Japan.* Chicago: University of Chicago Press, 1921.

Koch, Adrienne, ed. *Jefferson.* Englewood Cliffs, N.J.: Prentice-Hall, 1971.

Laski, Harold J. *The Rise of European Liberalism: An Essay in Interpretation.* London: Unwin Books, 1962. (Originally published in 1936.)

Lay, A. H. "A Brief Sketch of the History of Political Parties in Japan." *Transactions of the Asiatic Society of Japan.* Part III, vol. 30 (1902):363–462.

Leiden, Carl, and Schmitt, Karl M. *The Politics of Violence: Revolution in the Modern World.* Englewood Cliffs, N.J.: Prentice-Hall, 1968.

Lockwood, William W. *The Economic Development of Japan: Growth and Structural Change, 1868-1938.* Princeton, N.J.: Princeton University Press, 1954.

———, ed. *The State and Economic Enterprise in Japan: Essays in the Political Economy of Growth.* Princeton, N.J.: Princeton University Press, 1965.

Mabbott, J. D. *The State and the Citizen: An Introduction to Political Philosophy.* London: Hutchinson University Library, 1965.

MacCormack, John R. *Revolutionary Politics in the Long Parliament.* Cambridge, Mass.: Harvard University Press, 1973.

McLaren, W. W. *A Political History of Japan During the Meiji Era, 1867-1912.* London: Allen and Unwin, 1916; New York: Russel and Russel, 1965.

———, ed. "Japanese Government Documents, 1867-1889." *Transactions of the Asiatic Society of Japan.* Part I, vol. 42 (1914).

Macpherson, C. B. *The Political Theory of Possessive Individualism.* London: Oxford University Press, 1962.

———. *The Real World of Democracy.* Toronto: Canadian Broadcasting Company, 1965.

———. "The Social Bearing of Locke's Political Theory." In *Life, Liberty and Property: Essays on Locke's Political Ideas.* Edited by Gordon J. Schochet. Belmont, Calif.: Wadsworth, 1971, pp. 60–85.

McWilliams, Wayne C. "Etō Shimpei and the Saga Rebellion, 1874." Paper delivered at the Association for Asian Studies Conference, Toronto, 21 March 1976.

Maier, Pauline. "Popular Uprisings and Civil Authority in Eighteenth-Century America." *William and Mary Quarterly,* 3rd sers., 27:1 (January 1970)1–35.

Martin, Kingsley. *French Liberal Thought in the Eighteenth Century: A Study of Political Ideas from Bayle to Condorcet.* Edited by J. P. Mayer. New York: Harper & Row, 1962; Harper Torchbooks, 1963. (Originally published in 1927.)

Marx, Karl. "The Eighteenth Brumaire of Louis Napoleon." In *Selected Works* Vol. I. Moscow: Progress Publishers, 1969, pp. 394–487.

Mayet, Paul. *Agricultural Insurance in Organic Connection with Savings Banks, Land Credit, and the Commutation of Debts.* Translated and revised by Reverend Arthur Lloyd. London, 1893.

Moore, Barrington, Jr. *Social Origins of Dictatorship and Democracy: Lord and Peasant in the Making of the Modern World*. Boston: Beacon Press, 1966.

Morris, Morris D. "The Problem of the Peasant Agriculturalist in Meiji Japan." *Far Eastern Quarterly* 15:5 (May 1956):357–70.

Niwa Kunio. "The Reform of the Land Tax and the Government Programme for the Encouragement of Industry." *The Developing Economies* 4:4 (December 1966):465–71.

Norman, E. Herbert. "Feudal Background of Japanese Politics." Ninth Conference of the Institute of Pacific Relations. Hot Springs, Virginia. January 1945. Secretariat Paper No. 9, International Secretariat, Institute of Pacific Relations, New York.

———. *Japan's Emergence as a Modern State: Political and Economic Problems of the Meiji Period*. New York: Institute of Pacific Relations, 1940.

———. *Soldier and Peasant in Japan: The Origins of Conscription*. New York: Institute of Pacific Relations, 1943; Vancouver: Publications Centre, University of British Columbia, 1965.

Parrington, Vernon L. *Main Currents in American Thought: the Colonial Mind, 1620–1800*. Vol 1. New York: Harcourt, Brace, and World, 1954. (Originally published in 1927.)

Passin, Herbert. "Japan." In *Education and Political Development*. Edited by James S. Coleman. Princeton, N.J.: Princeton University Press, 1965, pp. 272–312.

Pittau, Joseph, S. J. *Political Thought in Early Meiji Japan, 1868–1889*. Cambridge, Mass.: Harvard University Press, 1967.

Plumb, J. H. *The Growth of Political Stability in England, 1675–1725*. Middlesex, England: Penguin Books, 1969.

Polin, Raymond, "John Locke's Conception of Freedom." In *John Locke: Problems and Perspectives*. Edited by J. W. Yolton. Cambridge, England: Oxford University Press, 1969, pp. 1–18.

Pollak, Louis H., ed. *The Constitution and the Supreme Court: A Documentary History*. Vol. 1. Cleveland and New York: World, 1966.

Rappoport, David C. *Assassination and Terrorism*. Toronto: Canadian Broadcasting Company, 1971.

Rudé, George. *The Crowd in History: A Study of Popular Disturbances in France and England, 1730–1848*. New York: John Wiley, 1964.

Sakata Yoshio, and Hall, John W. "The Motivation of Political Leadership in the Meiji Restoration." *Journal of Asian Studies* 16 (November 1956):31–50.

Sansom, Sir George B. *A History of Japan, 1615–1867*. Stanford, Calif.: Stanford University Press, 1963.

Scalapino, Robert A. *Democracy and the Party Movement in Prewar Japan: The Failure of the First Attempt*. Berkeley and Los Angeles: University of California Press, 1967. (Originally published in 1953.)

Scheiner, Irwin. "The Mindful Peasant: Sketches for a Study of Rebellion." *Jour-

nal of Asian Studies 32:4 (August 1974):579–91.

Schurmann, Franz. *Ideology and Organization in Communist China.* 2nd ed. Berkeley and Los Angeles: University of California Press, 1968.

Scott, James C. *The Moral Economy of the Peasant: Rebellion and Subsistence in Southeast Asia.* New Haven and London: Yale University Press, 1976.

Scott, John Anthony, ed. and trans. *The Defense of Gracchus Babeuf Before the High Court of Vendome.* Boston: University of Massachusetts Press, 1967.

Smith, Thomas C. *The Agrarian Origins of Modern Japan.* New York: Atheneum, 1966. (Originally published in 1959.)

―――. "Landlords and Rural Capitalists in the Modernization of Japan." *Journal of Economic History* 16:2 (June 1956):165–81.

―――. *Political Change and Industrial Development in Japan: Government Enterprise, 1868–1880.* Stanford, Calif.: Stanford University Press, 1968. (Originally published in 1955.)

―――. "Pre-Modern Economic Growth: Japan and the West." *Past and Present,* No. 60 (August 1973):127–60.

Social Contract: Essays by Locke, Hume, and Rousseau. With an Introduction by Sir Ernest Barker. London: Oxford University Press, 1974. (Originally published in 1960.)

Soukup, James. "Assassination in Japan." In *Assassination and Political Violence.* Vol. 8, Supplement D. Edited by James Kirkham, Sheldon Levy, and William J. Crotty. A Staff Report to the National Commission on the Causes and Prevention of Violence. Washington, D.C., 1969, pp. 531–36.

Soviak, Eugene. "The Case of Baba Tatsui: Western Enlightenment, Social Change, and the Early Meiji Intellectual." *Monumenta Nipponica* 18:1–4 (1963): 191–235.

Stanlis, Peter J. *Edmund Burke and the Natural Law.* Ann Arbor: University of Michigan Press, 1965.

Steiner, Kurt. *Local Government in Japan.* Stanford, Calif.: Stanford University Press, 1965.

―――. "Popular Political Participation and Political Development in Japan: The Rural Level." In *Political Development in Modern Japan.* Edited by Robert E. Ward. Princeton, N.J.: Princeton University Press, 1968, pp. 213–47.

Strong, Kenneth. "Tanaka Shōzō: Meiji Hero and Pioneer Against Pollution." *Japan Society of London Bulletin* 2:14 (June 1972):6–11.

Takizawa Matsuyo. *The Penetration of the Money Economy in Japan and Its Effects upon Social and Political Institutions.* New York: Columbia University Press, 1927.

Thompson, E. P. "The Moral Economy of the English Crowd in the Eighteenth Century." *Past and Present,* No. 50 (February 1971):76–136.

Thompson, F. M. L. "Landownership and Economic Growth in England in the 18th Century." In *Agrarian Change and Economic Development.* Edited by E. L. Jones and S. J. Woolf. London: Methuen, 1969, pp. 41–60.

Tilly, Charles. "Collective Violence in European Perspective." In *Violence in America: Historical and Comparative Perspectives*. Edited by Hugh Davis Graham and Ted Robert Gurr. New York: Bantam Books, 1969, pp. 4–45.

———. "Town and Country in Revolution." In *Peasant Rebellion and Communist Revolution in Asia*. Edited by John Wilson Lewis. Stanford, Calif.: Stanford University Press, 1974, pp. 271–302.

———. *The Vendée*. New York: John Wiley, 1967.

Tilly, Charles; Tilly, Louise; and Tilly, Richard. *The Rebellious Century, 1830–1930*. Cambridge, Mass.: Harvard University Press, 1975.

de Tocqueville, Alexis. *The Old Regime and the French Revolution*. Garden City, N.Y.: Doubleday, 1955.

Varley, Paul H. *The Ōnin War: History of Its Origins and Background with a Selective Translation of "The Chronicle of Ōnin."* New York and London: Columbia University Press, 1967.

Venturi, Franco. *Roots of Revolution: A History of the Populist and Socialist Movements in Nineteenth-Century Russia*. Translated by Francis Haskell. Introduction by Isaiah Berlin. New York: Grosset and Dunlap, 1960. (Originally published in Italy in 1952.)

Wolf, Eric R. "On Peasant Rebellions." *International Social Science Journal* 21:2 (1969):286–93.

———. *Peasant Wars of the Twentieth Century*. New York, Evanston, and London: Harper & Row, 1969.

Index

Adams, Samuel, 184, 189
Aikokukōtō (Public Party of Patriots), 108, 109
Aikokusha (Society of Patriots): in "formative period," 108, 109, 110; in period of "organization and promotion," 112, 113, 114, 115; relationship with *Kyōaidōbōkai*, 227; mentioned, 245
Aishinsha (Society of Mutual Regard): principles and membership of, 223–28; mentioned, 25, 216, 219, 226*n*, 229
Aizu Jiyūtō: confrontation with Mishima, 9–16; local organizing, 20–25; alliance with Fukushima Jiyūtō, 25–28; arrest of members, 31; as party of village heads, 227; formation of, 228, 229, 230, 231; provisional rules of, 230–31; leadership of, 232; meetings of, 234–35; mentioned, 149, 226, 236, 256, 289
Aizu region: maps showing, 7, 9; districts of, 11; Tokugawa uprisings in, 78, 79; economic development of, 99–102; as center of political activity, 223–40 *passim. See also* Aizu Jiyūtō; *Aishinsha*; *Rengōkai*
Aizu rokugun rengōkai (Six Aizu Districts' Joint Committee). See *Rengōkai*
Akagi Heiroku, 21, 134, 143, 226, 227, 233, 239, 240, 319
Algeria, 71
Allied Occupation, 3, 4, 7, 313
Amano Ichitarō, 40, 41, 42, 45, 221, 250, 293, 294, 336
American Revolution, 188, 189; revolutionaries in, 180, 182, 184, 185, 186
Aoki Kōji, 82, 85, 104, 257
Arai Shigejirō, 53, 270, 271, 331
Arai, Shōgo, 39, 39*n*, 196, 243, 299, 338
Arai Shūzaburō, 51, 57, 58, 60, 63, 64, 145, 265, 267, 271, 279, 297, 328
Arendt, Hannah, 5, 186, 197
Articles of War (Army Code): in Chichibu Incident, 51, 264
Asaka Land Reclamation Project, 15, 157–58
Assassinationism (*ansatsushugi*), 38–43 *passim*; 49, 241, 242, 246, 250, 255–56.

See also *Shō-undō*
Assisting Village (*sukegō*), 85, 86. *See also* Tenma Sōdō
Association for the Establishment of a National Assembly (*Kokkai Kisei Domeikai*), 113, 114
Atsushio, 15, 24; cell of, 232

Baba Tatsui, 191, 192
Babeuf, Gracchus, 188, 200, 200*n*, 285
Bailyn, Bernard, 184, 189
Bakufu (Tokugawa), 80, 84, 85
Bakumatsu, 79, 214
Bakunin, 241
Bentham, Jeremy, 200
Berlin, Sir Isaiah, 6
Blood Pact, in Fukushima Incident, 237, 290–91
Bōdō (violent movement), 81, 91, 117
Borton, Hugh, 80
Boshin War, 15, 223, 229
Brecht, Bertolt, 122

Cash crops. *See* Market Economy
Cells (*saibō*), 178, 231, 232, 235
Chernyshevsky, 241
Chichibu: silk industry, 54, 102, 103, 104, 151*n*; effects of Matsukata deflation policy on, 104–7 *passim*; rebellions in, 74, 75, 78, 79, 85, 87, 89; economic conditions of, 94, 95; Jiyūtō membership in, 115. *See also* Chichibu Incident
Chichibu Incident: 49–69, 70, 74, 89, 177, 178, 256, 257, 284; participants in, 128, 129, 137–41, 143–46 *passim*, 150–51, 159–64, 171, 172, 213–14, 295–97; organization in, 177, 178, 282–84; ideology in, 181, 258, 283; causes of, 70, 259–62, 281; violence during, 262–63. *See also* Kommintō
China, 71
Chōsan ("running away"), 80, 81, 83, 118
Chūnōsō (middle-level farmers). *See* Farmers
Chūzenji Temple, 29
Civil disobedience. *See* Tax boycott; Fukushima Incident

Designer:	Laurie Anderson
Compositor:	Marin Typesetters
Printer:	Braun-Brumfield
Binder:	Braun-Brumfield
Text:	11/13 IBM Journal Roman
Display:	18/20 Perpetua
Cloth:	Holliston Roxite B 53665
Paper:	50 lb. P & S Offset Vellum